Customer Service Excellence

CUSTOMER SERVICE EXCELLENCE

Trends and Strategies

Dr. S.B. Nageswara Rao
Dr. C. Madhavi

KANISHKA PUBLISHERS, DISTRIBUTORS
NEW DELHI-110 002

KANISHKA PUBLISHERS, DISTRIBUTORS
4697/5-21A, Ansari Road, Daryaganj
New Delhi -110 002
Phones : 2327 0497, 2328 8285
Fax : 011-2328 8285
E-mail : kanishka_publishing@yahoo.co.in
kanishkabooks@gmail.com

Customer Service Excellence: Trends and Strategies
First Published-2004
Edition-2022

ISBN: 978-81-7391-697-7

PRINTED IN INDIA

Published by Madan Sachdeva for Kanishka Publishers, Distributors, 4697/5-21A, Ansari Road, Daryaganj, New Delhi-110002, Typeset by Sunshine Graphics, Delhi, and Printed at G.S. Printers, Delhi.

Foreword

The book entitled *"Customer Service Excellence—Trends and Strategies"*, is an apt book which clearly picturises that in today's regime of Liberalisation, Privatisation and Globalization survival of any business is possible only by providing excellent customer service. The book is compilation of research papers of wide coverage relating to multiple dimensions of customer related areas. It is edited in simple and lucid style. The book consists of four parts viz., Customer Acquisition and Retention, Customer Service Quality, Customer Relationship Management and Emerging Trends in Customer Service.

Customer acquisition and retention is feasible only through service. Many articles have demonstrated how customization helped in acquiring and retaining customers. It is also emphatically stated that retention of customers is easier and much more important than going in for new customers. Articles on customer service quality have virtually recognized that service is critical factor and service alone can retain customers. Providing service is not only for service industry but also manufacturing companies. Providing the best service is the sustainable competitive advantage.

Papers on customer relationship focused on the rationale, benefits and strategies for developing customer relationship. This phase of the book highlights and provides measures to improve the relationship with current customers. Many papers have specified strategies such as effective segmentation to identify the customers with whom the organization wants to maintain relationship, improved services to meet the needs of the relationship, updating customer database and to follow-up. On-going global changes in the field of IT has revolutionized almost all operations of marketing in transmitting product related information, building relationships, selling real time marketing and servicing customers. These developments add values to the customer service.

India has to go a long way for reaching global service standards in many industries and to turn the approach from customer satisfaction to customer delight. This book is highly useful for teachers and research scholars to gain research knowledge in these areas and also helps the practising managers to know the trends in marketing scenario for better decisions. I congratulate Dr. S.B. Nageswara Rao and Dr. C. Madhavi for the efforts taken in compiling this book.

Dr. L.B.VENKATRANGAN
Vice-Chancellor
Annamalai University
Annamalainagar

Preface

In recent years customer service has gained importance and dramatic growth is observed in this field. One of the major ways of survival of a firm is by delivering consistent higher quality service which will not only help to acquire and retention of customer but also in building the corporate image. Service is an intensive value creating source. This value addition is possible by service activities inside and outside the company. Nowadays, service are becoming vital for manufacturers. According to service quality literature, the service provider should offer more than what the consumer want instead of what they would like to offer. Manufacturing success today depends on rapid feedback from the market place, better customized products, accurate delivery and reasonable price. "Zero Customer Defect" is the goal of service providers. Customer delight is possible by extending service more than his expectation in different dimensions to eliminate the line between a product and service.

This book attempts to identify and indicate the areas of customer service to excel in the market. It has wide coverage of customer acquisition and retention, quality service, service dimensions, legal aspects relating to service and service industries.

There is always a gap between service expectation and the experience level of service. Historically, service was not of much importance and it was a separate discipline from product. Presently, service is part and parcel of a product.

This change is accelerating and the task of marketing manager is critical. The materials in this book were brought under one cover from the academicians of this country to serve the need of the managers and the students of marketing in the current era of tremendous changes.

The materials in this book are collected from academicians from all over India. After screening, correcting and editing the materials are arranged. The materials are organized around the following heads:

I. Customer Acquisition and Retention Strategies
II. Customer Service Quality
III. Customer Relationship Management
IV. Recent Trends in Customer Service

We appreciate the opportunity given by University Grants Commission for sponsoring a National Seminar on "Customer Service Excellence."

We are greatly indebted to Annamalai University for permitting us to organize the seminar and for the fullest support.

We place on record, our deep sense of gratitude to all those contributors, who had shown keen interest and sincerity in preparing papers.

We thank the faculty members of the Department of Business Administration, Annamalai University, and the Faculty members in the Management Wing, Directorate of Distance Education for all their cooperation and support.

Dr. Bhardwaj, Professor of English, Directorate of Distance Education deserves special recognition for his expert language assistance.

Our special thanks to Kanishka Publishers and Distributors, New Delhi for the effort put in for publishing the work.

Dr. S.B. Nageswara Rao
Dr. C. Madhavi

Contents

Part II: Customer Service Quality

Part III: Customer Relationship Management

Part IV: Emerging Trends in Customer Service

PART I

Customer Acquisition and Retention Strategies

1

Customer Acquisition and Retention Strategies in Commercial Banks

S. SUJATHA*

Introduction

Banking has played a great role in developing the savings habit amongst the people and lending to needy sectors of the economy. We are now on the threshold of the 21st century. Banks are now moving on from local to the global arena. Banking being a service oriented industry, customer satisfaction is an integral part of the business. With the liberalisation sweeping across the country and the financial sector in particular, the Indian Banking scene is in for a brilliant transformation. Banks have started realising that business goes to those who seek clients, serve them satisfactorily and strive hard to retain them. When the market bristles with larger number of players viz., foreign banks with superior technology and new generation private banks with their lean management, the customer has become increasingly aware of the wider choice of institutions. So the customer of today may not come back to the bank tomorrow and the potential customer may not turn up at all if the service available is not as per his/her desire.

Importance of Customer Acquisition and Retention

The current banking scenario, being in the throes of rapid changes, is marked by fierce competition, high level of customer expectation and most prominently a technology driven culture. Therefore, customer service in banks is a perennial issue for discussion. In a deregulated environment, customer expectations will rise as they

* Dept. of Bank Management, Alagappa University, Karaikudi.

look for more convenient and flexible options available to them at competitive rates from many players operating in the field. This has made customer patronage a formidable task. Customer is now a new watchword in Indian banking scene. Banks will have to come closer to the customers, proactively anticipate their emerging needs/expectations and evolve effective means to meet those expectations. In an environment where customer is the king, the new mantra for the organisation will be to upgrade itself from merely a "Service Provider" to "Value Provider". This new approach is required to design a system by which service is delivered after identifying the customer needs to satisfy them.

Broadly speaking, every bank should make longer customer relationship goals. Because customer retention is a tangible and actionable strategy which keeps the bank to face competition in a comfortable manner. Hence retaining a customer is often cheaper than to find a new customer. Therefore, retention and acquisition strategy calls for systematic efforts whereby the bank employees keep constant touch with their customers. It may be in the form of personal visits, phone calls, writing letters or mailing publicity pamphlets etc. It takes time, energy and efforts to retain customers and establish solid relationship with them. Nevertheless, banks are finding these efforts worthwhile and profitable. Irrespective of their size, an effective strategy would be aimed at retaining all the customers. This is bound to be profitable in the long run.

Research Survey on Customer Retention

Of late, a study carried out on behalf of the Indian Banks Association (IBA) on "Customer Relationship Management" has found that customer retention is an issue that is being faced in foreign and new generation private banks. The study covered customers and employees of various banks during the year 2002. The study found that customer retention was strong among nationalised and old private banks placed at 76 per cent and 72 per cent respectively. In the case of SBI the percentage was 72. But what is surprising is that in case of new generation private banks it was placed at a low of 60 per cent while in the case of foreign banks it was 64 per cent. In terms of product knowledge and easier access of customer service like ATMs, undertake branch computerisation and issue plastic cards, the response was lowest in the case of SBI, but for new generation private banks and foreign banks, it was robust. Not surprisingly, the level of customer satisfaction was placed at a high 92 per cent in the case of foreign banks, and at 50 per cent in the case of nationalised and old generation private banks.

Customer Acquisition and Retention Strategies

Banking business requires to retain the existing customers and win new loyalties through the following ways.

- Bankers have to interact with the customer who comes to the branch to open an account. The branch employees should help the customer in opening the account. During the process of opening of an account, if customer is given utmost attention, he remembers the first day forever. His entry and exit for service should consume as minimum time as possible. Opening of an account becomes a cycle of customer orientation internally. Any bank would have three types of customers; future, present and past. The potential customer has not done business with the bank to date. Past customers have done business with the bank but have moved to the competitor bank. In other words, he has not lost faith in the bank so is recoverable with special efforts. Therefore, banks should strive to convert future customer to present customer, and regain past customer.
- Banks should necessarily have to know the customer and understand his requirement. The next step is to inform about various services and facilities available with the bank. Merely describing the product features and expecting the customer to make the right choice may not always be the right strategy. If the customer selects a scheme, which he subsequently finds out not meeting his requirements fully, he gets dissatisfied. In order to ensure satisfaction, bank employees may also have to guide the customer in making the right choice from among the available range of services and facilities.
- Banks plan their products and services on the basis of the customer needs and wants. Every type of customer has his own locust standing and expectation. Rural area customer steps in for deposits and small loan for

agricultural and allied activities, urban and metro dwellers have different expectations from banks, it is quite natural and their environment is different. So, creation and delivery of service in time with customer needs and expectation is the best business strategy to be adopted by the banks so as to retain the customers.

- Customer feed back should form the basis for bringing about improvement in the quality of service and novelty of product designs, this may help the banks to get a good idea about changing customers needs as also initiate corrective measures to render customer service in a better way. In order to retain customers the marketing departments in banks needs to evaluate bank service in terms of customer perspectives. For this banks will have to formulate a suitable mechanism that provides the required feedback from the customers at periodic intervals.
- Successful organization has realised that prompt attention to customer complaints is an essential ingredient of an effective retention and acquisition strategy. Banking business has always been depending on word of mouth publicity by satisfied customers. On an average satisfied customers talk about the service of five others, an unhappy customer narrates his experience to ten others. So whenever a customer approaches the banker with grievance or complaint, the banker should act swiftly to redress the complaint received.
- The customer always looks for easy and flexible and does not accept cumbersome procedures any longer. He wants immediate service. So, the banker has to build internal relationship chains to augument the services positively and effectively in the shortest time span. Customer has no time to wait for banker, as the bankers are no longer a monopoly. He is just bent upon crushing all monopolies and he need service in time and he does not want to wait; and expects everything. So, training and development department should suitably rehearse their employees alike in the activities and prompt effectiveness.
- Customer friendliness is very important strategy in

banking. Here customer is not an enemy, but a very important force to reckon with. Without his blessings, any business will disappear sooner or later. In this situation bankers should clearly know that customers are not intruders but they are the very meaning and purpose for the service. Whenever a customer interacts through telephone call or a letter or a standing instruction or a complaint, the banker should handle the situation with due attention and care.

- Banks cope with technological developments taking place in different sectors of economy. Branch level computerization, installation of ATMs, SWIFT, anywhere banking etc., will not help in retaining customers. But the bank management should give adequate training to the operating staff in computer application, systems and procedures.
- Banks have also developed standards for customer service. The IBA has evolved and communicated to banks a set of 'time norms' for completing some of the common services offered by the banks. Implementation of these standard norms ensures the banker to provide better service and retain the customer for long run.
- Banks provide personalized services to their customers. In the growing recognition of the fact that a customer is not a faceless entity or a mere statistic, customers are not just token numbers and account numbers. They are persons with feelings. In order to sustain this every efforts should be made by bank employees to identify them by name. This is a hallmark of personalized service.
- Banks needs to develop a comprehensive customer information system at branches so as to know the customer better and understand his needs more accurately. Database on various aspects of customers like age, qualification, income level, taste and preference etc., should be created which will help in providing continuous feedback for anticipating customer needs.
- Bankers should undertake constant effort to upgrade the quality of customer service so as to and retain the customer on the basis of service factor, not the price factor.

In addition to this, the banker should develop the element of trust in the minds of depositors as well as borrowers. Next, he has to balance the power of communication and conceivability to test whether the customer misunderstands. The banker should sound polite and firm, a tight rope walk indeed, but for the sake of customer relations.

Conclusion

The future of banking is fast changing for Indian banks. Customer service is the life-blood of a banker's business. Therefore, bankers will have to satisfy business. They will have to satisfy customers by giving them what they want rather than what banks have. By doing so, they establish a stable and everlasting relationship with clients/customers.

2

Customer Satisfaction

The Base for Customer Acquisition and Retention

C. MADHAVI*, C. SAMUDHRA RAJAKUMAR*, M. ARUL*
& JOHN WILLIAM FELIX**

A product is a bundle of values. The values may be comfort, safety, pride, economy etc. Each product may offer a combination of some values. The values priority may vary from individual to individual. Even for an individual the values priority may vary from product to product. Further, priority of values varies based on the situation.

Application

It is necessary to satisfy the expectation levels of different values and identify whether there is any gap between expectation and experience of such values. If needed action plan to fill the gap is to be taken to satisfy the customers. Satisfaction of a customer is the base of retaining the customers and helps to acquire new customers.

Expectation (E_1) and Experience (E_2) of value

To retain the customers, it is highly important to verify how far these perceived values are satisfied. By nature, consumers tend to compare the actual experience with their expectation based on the benefits they derive, while using the product. If the expectation is higher than the experience ($E_1 > E_2$) it is said to be negative

* Faculty Members, Dept. of Business Administration, Annamalai University.

** Faculty Member, Dept. of Community Medicine, Annamalai University.

disconfirmation, if the expectation is equal to the experience it is confirmation ($E_1 = E_2$); and if the expectation is less than the experience, it is said to be positive disconfirmation ($E_1 < E_2$). Negative disconfirmation leads the dissatisfaction and the other two confirmation and positive disconfirmation to satisfaction. It is explained by an arrow diagram and given below:

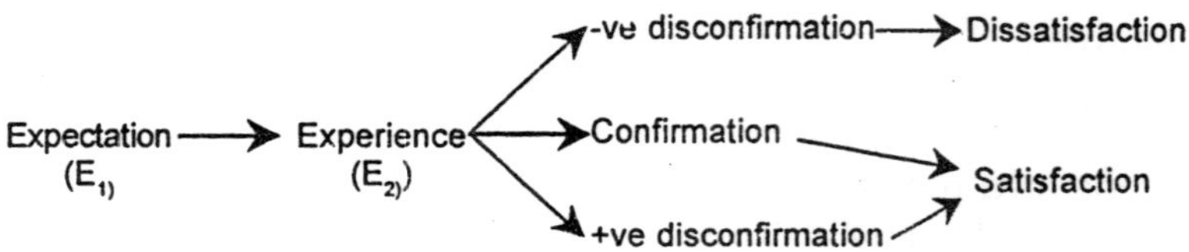

Objectives

The main objectives of the study are:

- To measure the level of expectations of values
- To measure the experience level of the values
- To identify whether there is any significant difference between the values expected and experienced.

Methodology

To study the above specified objectives, first attempt was made to identify the values attached to the product television.

Pre-test two was conducted with a sample size of thirty to standardize the questionnaire. First part of the questionnaire contains a list of 28 attributes relating to the product, television. The respondents were asked to indicate the level of importance attached to each attribute.

The second part of the questionnaire was intended to measure the expectation level of values identified by the pre-test I and the third part relating to the experience level of these values.

Corn-bach alpha was used to measure the reliability of the questionnaire.

Table 1: Reliability Coefficient

Section	*Q. Nos.*	*Alpha Value*
Part I	1 to 28	0.79
Part II	1 to 11	0.84
Part III	1 to 11	0.81

The alpha value reflected the high degree of internal consistency. With certain deletion of listed values the questionnaire was finalized for further study.

Sampling Design

The sample for the study was drawn from Annamalainagar by taking a random sample of 100 respondents. Among the 100 respondents, 79 were found to be fit for further analysis.

Tools for Analysis

The generated data had been duly analysed using the statistical tools viz., factor analysis, rank correlation test for agreement, ANOVA and 't'-test.

Analysis

To identify the value dimensions of television, factor analysis was carried out. The eight factors having Eigen values greater than 1.0 were extracted. These eight factors represented by 65.8 per cent of the variance of the attributes considered for the study.

The factors identified were 'technology, aesthetic value, durability, service, physical characteristics, status, economic value and functional value.

The priority of values identified by the respondents were studied using Friedman's two-way ANOVA. The test confirmed the existence of significant differences among their perception levels of values at 1 per cent level. Further, non-parametric multiple comparison test was also done to identify the order of priority among the perceived values. The order of priority found is listed below:

Table 2: Priority of Values

S. No.	*Values*	*Order of Priority*
1.	Quality	I
2.	Durability, Technology, Status and Physical characteristics	II
3.	Economy, service and availability	III
4.	Guarantee	IV
5.	Resale value	V

Expectation and experience levels of values derived by reducing the attribute using factor analysis were measured using 10 point scale. Using paired t-test association between the expectation and experience for each value was studied and the result is indicated below:

Table 3: Expectation and Experience of Values

Values	*'t'-value*	*d.f.*	*Sig.*
Technology	-0.04	78	0.984
Aesthetic value	+4.62	78	0.001*
Durability	-4.60	78	0.001*
Service	-3.01	78	0.003*
Physical characteristics	1.30	78	0.195
Status	0.04	78	0.965
Economic value	4.30	78	0.001*
Functional value	1.53	78	0.105

From the paired 't' test economic and aesthetic values, durability, and service were found to be significantly distributed. Further, aesthetic and economic values were found to be positive. It implied that the experience levels for these values were distributed in the higher side than the expectation. But, in the case of durability and service the t-values were found to be negative which implied that experience of these values were negative but significant. Negative sign indicates that the experience of these values were found to be less than the expected level and the differences were also significant.

Recommendation

Expectation and experience were positively and significantly distributed for economic and aesthetic values. In the case of economy, this might be due to the fact that the consumers mentally accepted the price of the product, while buying itself. Aesthetic value was also similarly observed during the purchase.

Service and durability were the values for which the difference between expectation and experience were found to be negative and this state might lead to an overall dissatisfaction. These areas, thus, must be given immediate attention by the manufacturers and attempts must be made to convert the negative disconfirmation state to positive disconfirmation to have satisfaction.

Managerial Implication

This study helps to identify the gap. By taking appropriate action, customers can be satisfied. Customer satisfaction alone can retain the customers and ultimately, this acts as the base for new customers.

3

Managing Customer Acquisition and Retention Strategies

K. CHANDRASEKAR*

The importance for Customer service is due to the focusing of companies on customer's problems, for mutual value creation and sharing through interdependence. Customer Relationship Management (CRM) is a: *"Management process of Acquiring Customers by understanding their requirement, Retaining customers by fulfilling their requirements more than their expectations and attracting new customers, through customer specific strategic marketing approaches"*.

Customer Acquisition

Customer acquisition is the major objective of all the organizations. Different organizations provide services in order to increase their customer database. Customer Acquisition strategies focus on making the buyers prospective customers. The sources of input for acquisition include suspects, enquiries, former customers, competitor's customer referrals, existing buyers, competitor's former customer, etc.

Acquisition Sources

Every organization concentrates on getting more and more customers for their products and services by utilizing different strategies. Some of the major sources on which organizations focus their attention are:

Suspects, enquiries, lapsed customers, former customers, competitor customers, competitor's enquiries, competitors lapsed customers, referrals, existing buyers, etc.

* Vysya Institute of Management Studies, Salem (TN).

The suspects are the most important segment who has the real potential to become prospective customers. Proper responses to the enquiries, following a focused approach will result in customer acquisition. Identifying and rectifying the reason for lapses will help to recover the lapsed customers.

Approaches to Acquisition

Every Organization tries to attract as much customers as they can for their products or services Organizations follow acquisition strategies such as Focused approach, Win-win strategy, integrated communication, Customer Interaction Management (CIM), and Consumer Behavior application strategies.

Focused Approach

Organizations are more focused towards people who can be categorized as knowers and preferers, to convert them into prospective customers. The former is that group which knows only about the existence of product without any preference, while the latter has some preference, but not acted on it.

Win-win Strategy

The organization should provide a win-win platform applicable to the prospective customers and for itself. Both the customer and organization should aim at achieving the target with reduced cost of service.

Integrated Communication

Organization should have open and interactive communication with the prospective customers. It brings confidence in the minds of customers and helps to move them into acquisition.

Customer Interaction Management (CIM)

Interaction plays a lead role in building customer relationships. Customer Interaction Management (CIM) constitutes the customer relationship technologies with additions of technology-based interactive solutions. The CIM stands for intensive interaction between customers and the organization, which is supported by technology enabled mechanisms such as

1. Online Interaction Tools: Interactive websites, e-mails, web communities, chat rooms, etc.
2. Off line Interaction Tools: Telephones, Fax, Face-to-Face interaction, interactive television network and so on.

Customer interaction management requires customer database, profiling of the customer database and internal system of audit. Electronic data interchange helps to establish CIM for transmitting information in an B2B environment and B2C environment.

Consumer Behaviour Approach

Companies also undertake research on consumer behaviour to identify the behavioural patterns of the customers. The likes and dislikes of the customers are identified and the organizations can focus their attention on providing more value added service to attract customers and influence their behaviour to convert them into loyal customers of the organization.

Extended Problem Solving Approach

Customers are got in the mist of 'Fear, Uncertainty, Doubts' during their buying. They are in the stage of extended problem solving in which fear, uncertainty, doubts are very great. The FUD has to be minimized to make customer more and more loyal.

Decision Process

Buyer's purchase decision process has more influence over the acquisition. The factors governing decision process should be analyzed and studied to tune up acquisition.

Acquisition of Non-customers

Marketers have realized that there is more value for their money by focusing on the non-customer segment. Planning to tackle non-customers is a crucial deal where a number of questions are to be answered. Depending on the composition of the market segment, the sensitivity of the customers can be tactfully dealt.

AIWA Music systems tackled its stiff competitors like BPL, Sony, Philips and many others, by spotting their product feature and its advantages over the competitors, through media planning.

Himalayan Drugs, 'Ayurvedic Concepts' succeeded in tackling customers, who are less exposed to Ayurvedic products.

Factors in Acquisition

Existing customers are the real media of advertising who bring in new customers. Their views are highly rated by the prospective customers. It is essential to manage the existing customers, by giving rewards and incentives.

In Customer Acquisition, the prospective buyer begins with his enquiry about services and interacts with the organization for gathering information, which is exchanged for adoption of the customer, as permanent customer.

The process of acquisition runs through various stages of enquiry, interaction, exchange, co-ordination and adoption, wherein, in the enquiry stage, the prospective customer collects all information regarding the product and organization, and then interacts with the organization, to see if the above information are correct, after which, he passes to the next stage of exchange to settle the terms of exchange, mode of delivery and other things related to exchange. Coordinated efforts lead the customer to adoption of the product or service.

Acquisition of customers is not an independent process. It is influenced by many factors such as type of product, buying patterns, types of customers and environmental forces. Products may be convenience goods, shopping or speciality goods, which affects each stage of acquisition process. Convenience products may be bought in the enquiry stage itself, while speciality products like refrigerator, computer, etc., involves all the stages of acquisition.

Even the buying patterns of the customers decide the customer acquisition. Buying may be rational or emotional. A rational buyer is more systematic than an emotional buyer. The acquisition of an organizational buyer is more complex depending on the organization's policy, while an individual customer can be attracted more easily.

Environmental forces focus its attention on the market conditions, operations of competing forces, supply and demand conditions, purchasing power, etc. Attracting a customer also has to deal with the behaviour and life style of the customer.

Customer Retention

Customer Retention is the process of keeping customers in the customer inventory for an unending period by meeting the needs and exceeding the expectations of those customers. Retaining customers is very important than to attract new customers, because the cost of servicing existing customers is less than the cost of providing services to new customers. Customer retention enables a long-term relationship of mutual benefit, both to the organization and to the customer concerned.

Customer Retention speaks about customer Loyalty where he focuses on an emotional and committed relationship with the organization. Customer retention is the approach of converting casual customers into committed loyal customers.

Loyal Customers Remain Longer

Customer retention is closely interlinked with Customer loyalty. Loyalty is usually measured in terms of longevity of the patronage of customers. Customer retention tries to convert a 'customer by chance' into a 'customer with loyalty'. A loyal customer who is retained turns up his focus of relationship from an ordinary transactional relationship to an emotionally built and committed relationship with the organization, which benefits the organization in the long run. Customer loyalty plays a significant role in retention, since loyalty may also arise from a reluctant customer or even a non-customer, which shall be a spurious or artificial or shared loyalty. So loyalty based on retention is welcomer.

How to Retain

Retained customers are the real assets of an organization who help in spreading the goodwill of organization. This helps in acquiring new customers to increase customer inventory. Hence today, all organizations are concentrating on retaining the existing customers.

Customer Retention allows to minimize customer acquisition cost. Organizations, now-a-days are concentrating more on customer retention than acquisition. These Retention strategies include Corporate Performance Evaluation, Employee Retention strategies, Competitive Benchmarking, Preventive strategies, Customer Complaints Handling, customer Satisfaction strategy and Relationship Marketing.

Internal Marketing Plan

It is a means of bringing the activities of the organizational employees and its impact on the eventual customer to the front and focus attention on those actions required to improve the performance of internal customer chain. The delivery of customer satisfaction encourages and improves cross-functional working to sustain heightened service quality for internal as well as external customers.

Employee Retention

It is more obvious that companies, in order to retain loyal customers, focus on employee retention. It is believed that employee with high morale, integrity and job satisfaction will produce quality products, which will in turn contribute in retaining the loyal customers.

Competitive Benchmarking

Retention is targeted at the customers. Hence, it would be appropriate to ask the customers to rate the services provided by the company and based on the components identified, the relative importance of the company with that of the competitors is measured. This helps to identify the services from customer's point of view.

Complaints Management

Complaints are a good source of improvement for an organization. Complaints are viewed as opportunities given by customers for the organization towards value-added performance. Organization must have the tendency to act upon complaints as soon as it is received and offer corrective measures. Careful handling is required to deal with unexpressed or unregistered complaints, since it leads the customers to attrition. Companies have come up with online complaint management systems such as automatic response system, call centers, answer centers, etc.

Continuous Delivery Systems

A strategy used by some companies is to create relationships by turning discrete service delivery into continuous delivery. Bus and Train services offer season tickets valid for a particular period to help customers to get rid of making day-to-day choices.

Retention through Satisfaction

A satisfied customer tends to remain longer with the organization. Satisfaction is the state of mind that occurs when the customer feels that his expected requirement is fulfilled by what is offered by the organization. Organizations have to keep on building up their ability to continuously satisfy their target customers so as to maintain customer retention, because customers cannot be continuously retained by rendering expected level of satisfaction. Customers may change their level of satisfaction from expected to desired and further desired to exciting level. Customer care programmes, which exceed customer expectation, will lead to higher rate of retention.

Organizational Performance

Retention strategies require an organization to be in continuous learning, learning from customer's preference, competitor's strategies, technology advantages, social, cultural changes, life style, spending and buying patterns, and so on. Organization having the characteristics of continuous learning can easily adapt itself to meet the customer's need and thereby increase customer retention.

Relationship Marketing

Relationship marketing approach considers customers as insiders to business and aims to build long term and never ending relationship with them. Organization finds it very difficult and challenging to retain customers. Intensive competition has led to frequent brand switching. Relationship marketing has emerged as a new approach enabling marketers with brand new tools and techniques to reach, acquire, retain and expand customer base.

Companies also often use strategies of Continuous Delivery and offering Incentives to maintain the customer relationship. They offer more personalized services with total responsibility for maintaining the customers.

Data Mining

Some companies like the Telecom majors such as Hutchinson Max Telecom, BPL Mobile and Modi Telstra have deployed tools to sift data for insights into customer behaviour. Companies collect information from customers and use this information to seek better understanding of their needs.

Data mining refers to the analysis of data to generate useful and meaningful information. This information can then be used for initiating marketing actions like special promotions and loyalty programme. Data mining helps to execute customer strategy in an organization with ultimate goal of lower costs, higher revenues and profits. Primary objectives of data mining are to attract new customers and retain existing ones. Banks, credit card companies, telecom companies and retail chains, among others are major believers in data mining.

By means of advertising the product along with a response feature, like contest form, we can attract new customers and a database is created from the responses. Data mining helps to identify the prospective customers from the database and to make contacts.

In retaining customers also data mining is of much useful. Not only are existing customers retained, but also better customers are developed, declining or lost customers are won back. Problems are identified and customer defections are analyzed. For example, 3M company uses suggestion forms, toll-free numbers and e-mails to get in touch with customers who provide ideas for their product improvement.

In general, segmenting of markets becomes easy with data mining. Basically only 20 per cent of the customers account for the bulk of sales. Hence, the marketing efforts have to be focused on them. The next level of buyers, i.e., medium buyers need to be communicated with good offers to convert them into heavy buyers. The low users are to be serviced in innovative ways to increase their usage.

Conclusion

Customer Acquisition and Retention are the most sophisticated process in a business. It helps to develop and maintain the customer data inventory in an organization. Companies are following various strategies to acquire and retain customers with them. But an integrated approach with the organizational goals will help to minimize the cost and time in acquiring and retaining. Today's competitive marketing world opens the door for those Companies who satisfy the customer with Quality and Value, without any defections. Companies succeed only with the help of healthy Customer Acquisition and Retention practices.

4

Catch and Care

A Game Winning Strategy

P.N. KALIYAPERUMAL*

Introduction

The life span of a firm is determined by how it has rightly defined its business. The business definition must be expressed in a manner that the firm can have a fairly long life responding well to all future environmental changes that are featured by customer needs. The definition must be revealing the firm's capabilities to answer such questions as: a) Who is going to be satisfied?, b) What is going to be satisfied?, and c) How are customer needs being satisfied? The miserable ends that many of the international corporations have witnessed today are the result of their failures to define their businesses rightly so that they were unable to meet the customer needs under the changed situations caused by new technologies. Thus, the focus of the business definition is customer satisfaction.

IBM, originally a typewriter manufacturing company, has sustained the threats by the computer industry as it has readily adapted to the new environment. The company has extended so naturally its business to computers, word processors and office equipment. It still remains in business with a new vigor because it has defined its business rightly so that it is in fine tune with the changes that are likely to occur in information technology. Thus, it is learnt that the business definition must be relevant all time so that it can answer the question "What should be our business?"

---

* Professor & Head, MBA Department, Priyadarshini Institute of Management Studies, Priyadarshini Engineering College, Vaniyambadi (TN).

The present study is a general description of the problems related to customer loyalty. The discussion is split into two parts: (i) Issues and (ii) Case studies.

I. ISSUES

Relationship Marketing

Relationship marketing starts with the customer.[1] The single most element assuring a success to the firm is the customer.[2] Managing customer relationship is known as relationship marketing. Excellence in relationship marketing means the largest that the firm has added to the customer value chain. Customers having got the highest satisfaction with the quality of the firm's product/ service turn to be active and vocal advocates for the firm. They play an important role as a referral source.[3]

Thus, the modern business strategy is relationship strategies focused on "Customer Pull" rather on 'Product Push'. In the present competitive world, the customer has become more powerful as much as a king. The key to success is producing world class goods that satisfy the customer expectations. World-Class goods meet international standards so that globalization is never a problem to the firm. The customers, today, are getting more value-conscious rather than price-conscious. Essentially, the customers are shrewd evaluators of VFM, even shrewder judges of MFV goods and services.[4] This means that the firm needs to make the customers happy. The customers are considered as assets. More importantly the company is established by the customers. The realization that making the customer happy and loyal is the sole requirement for the firm to exist and grow has become a world-wide phenomenon, giving thrust to relationship marketing.

Trade-off between Customer Satisfaction and Shareholder's Welfare

The firm exists and grows with reference to its capabilities to catch and care the customer. 'No Customer' means 'No business'. The beginning of a business means identifying the customers. That is, the firm must decide where it has to focus (who are its customers?). The firm's decision in this regard is based on its capabilities to satisfy the customer needs that are brought into focus.

Customer Segmentation (Market Segmentation)

The traditional approach to segmenting customers is based on customer profiles constructed from geographic, demographic, psychographic and buyer behaviour within a firm. It is the responsibility of the marketing manager to identify the right group of customers as the target group. This cannot be done in a vacuum because the firm's capabilities in selection of the target customers involve costs and hence the involvement of the cost accounting manager cannot be dispened with. Thus, identifying customers is a cross-functional activity. Here, the point to be noticed is that the firm takes care of the customer satisfaction in providing quality products or services with a built-in conscience about its own existence, which is determined by its profitability. The firm's stake-holders include not only its buyer customers but also its share-holders. At any cost, the interests of the share-holders should not be staked. This means that the operations manager has to strike a better trade-off between customer satisfaction and share-holder welfare in his production management function.

In this context, the organizational goals aiming at revenue maximization (shareholder's wealth) must be customer based.[5] The balancing of customer satisfaction with profit goals of the company is a complex but extremely is an important part of the operation's managers role. The customer can reduce the business world to shambles, if their interests are ignored. He is in-charge in the new world disorder.[6]

Customer Acquisition

After identifying the customers, the next task is understanding the customer's needs. The operation manager holds the responsibility of understanding the customer needs. That is, he collects the data about the attributes that the customer wants from the products that are to be produced. The products are designed as per the customer's requirements—that is, the products are so designed that they meet the customers' expectations. Understanding the customer needs and producing the products accordingly is less a big problem in the case of customized production; but it is a difficult task with respect to mass production. In the job-shop manufacturing, customer contact is obtained and so the products can be seen to be made according to the customer requirements. The products can be tested whether they satisfy the customer expectations. Once a customer is acquired, it may not be a big problem for a firm to retain him if it is engaged in customized production. The only harder task is acquiring the customer in the product introduction stage.

The problem is how to catch the customer and what is the best strategy to adopt for that. The traditional approach to this problem is conducting market research. This is found to be expensive, time consuming when the company has the customer base to be very large and world-wide. The modern strategy is offering attractive gifts and better services.

Customer Retention

The firm must be ever alert in keeping the customer with it-that is, keeping them loyal. For this, the best types of customer care programmes are to be thought and practised. Today, customers have become more sophisticated, more demanding, less loyal and less willing to forgive companies whose products and services do not meet their high standards. The customers are restless and brainy, updating their knowledge about the availability of options. They are demanding, faster, better and cheaper alternatives.[7] For retaining the customer, the company must understand their expectations. The first issue in revenue maximization is to understand what they are buying as opposed to what the company is offering.[8] Their expectations relate to the product being offered by the company and also encompass the process of shopping, buying, after sales service, use and disposal. This concerns with Total Quality Management (TQM).

We need a three dimensional approach to understand the customer expectations: (a) to study the changing needs and wants, (b) to evaluate whether the company's promise is fulfilled and superior value is created, and (c) to understand how the competitors' promises that their products can offer higher value are met. Customer value is found in the combination of the three, which include quality, price, and speed. Quality to the customer often means that the product performs well; that it is priced competitively (efficiency); and that it is provided quickly and it is adapted when needed (responsiveness).

The firm's response time is also an important factor to be examined in the study of customer retention. A successful firm responds quickly to the customer needs, when changed. The higher the speed the firm responds to the new environment, the greater the competitive advantage it gains. That is, the customer defection rate is put under control.

In general, reducing response time requires (i) a marketing function that it can quickly transmit customer requests to manufacturing, (ii) manufacturing and materials management functions that can quickly revise the production schedules in response to unanticipated changes in customer demands, and (iii) information systems that can help manufacturing and marketing in this function. Thus, retaining customers requires a variety of actions by the company, which can be made possible only when each of the functional areas has ensured its total involvement in it.

"Know thy customers" is one of the keys is to achieving superior customer responsiveness. Knowing the customer means that the employees think themselves as the customers-that is, they listen to what the customers have to say. In short, this means bringing the customers into the company—that is, bringing customer's opinion by soliciting feedback from customers on the company's goods and services. Customers feed back helps the company to fine-tune the merchandise it sells.

Customer retention is produced by customer satisfaction. A satisfied customer does more propagation of products (the referral function) and services free of cost. It is estimated that it typically costs five to six times more to get the new customer than to retain the existing customer.

Some estimate that it takes a second to lose a customer and months to acquire one. This shows that the firm must take care of the existing customers giving no room for their leaving because of dissatisfaction with the products and services that it has offered.

The feed back shows the customer's unmet needs. By satisfying their unmet needs, the customers are made delighted.

Economics of Customer Defection and Loyalty

Customer dissatisfaction means loss of business (market share). The firm, for controlling the production cost, must try to reduce the customer defection rate. The average cost rises with increase in the customer defection rate. This is shown in Figure 1.

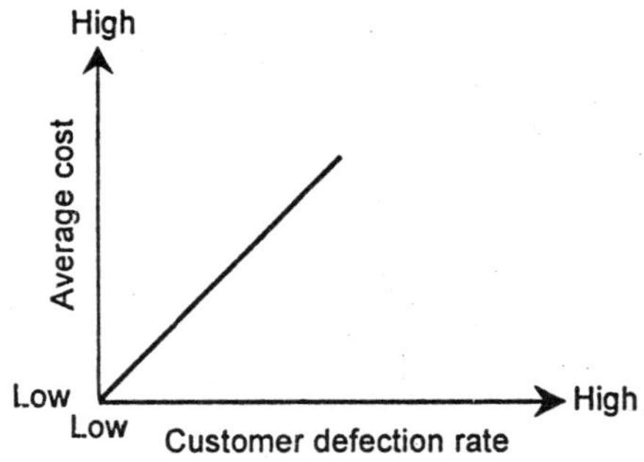

Fig. 1: Relationship between Average Cost and Customer Defection Rate.

There is a positive relationship between profit and customer loyalty. Customer loyalty increases the firm's total profit. But the average profit increases, after a stage, at a decreasing rate and then flatters over time. This is explained in Figure 2: The slope declines because the customer retention costs run faster than the profit per customer earned.

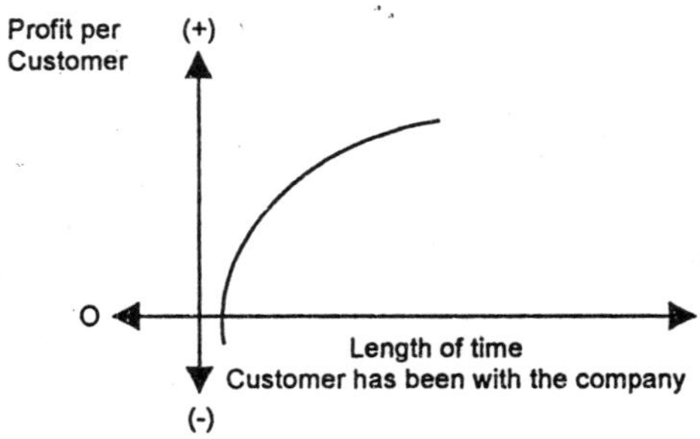

Fig. 2: Relationship between Customer Loyalty and Profit Per Customer's.

The Product Life Cycle *Inter-Alia* the Customer Life Cycle

The product life cycle is the customer's reaction to the product that has been floated in the market. The introduction stage represents customer catching. The length of time that is required for catching customers enough to work to the firm's capacity points to the introduction phase in the product life cycle. If the number of customers acquired is very small compared to the number needed for stepping up the production to the optimum level and if takes a longer period to attract the customers so that excessive production does not occur, the introduction stage extends to a longer time. This signals the firm to take active steps to promote the sales. For this, what is to be done is effective advertising and wider publicity. Added to this are attractive gift schemes. In this context, we need to lay emphasize on retailing. The retailers have an important part to play in marketing the product. For encouraging them, the company must offer attractive discounts/ margins. Empirically speaking, retailers take interest in selling those products which give him higher margins. Some estimate that a reasonal return of 30 to 40 per cent is essential for keeping the customers[distributors/retailers] loyal to trade[Ibid].

Once the product has set in the customer's mind, if it is a high quality one, the sales rise. The product enter's the next stage (Growth Stage). The demand for the product or the customer adoption rate is very high. The profitability per customer retained is also very high.

In the open economy, where the free play of market forces determines the customer requirements, knowing that the firm earns enormous profits, new firms enter the market. That is, competitive products are put into the stream. In this stage, customer acquisition rate is insignificant-that is, it has almost reached the ceiling. In contrast, customer defection will take place. The firm's continuance in business is put under stresses. Now, the problem is how to overcome this stage that is, how to make the customer loyal and remain with the firm. If the firm is successful retaining the customers or keeping the customers inventory undepleted, its position in the business gets stabilized. The product life cycle tappers off, meaning the maturity stage. On the other hand, the firm is trapped into the decline stage, when the customer defection begins and rises unmatched by the customer acquisition. That is, the competitors outperform the firm by providing better products and services. Their products offer superior value when compared to the firm's product.

A firm can lengthen the maturity stage in many ways. If it has reached a stage beyond which price reduction, in order to retain the customers is impossible, it can retain the customers by offering better services/higher values. A dissatisfied customer leaves the firm. To retain the *status quo,* the firm needs to acquire as many customers as needed to offset the depletion. But this is hardly possible in the case of a larger customer base. What is less impossible is to identify the reasons for the defection and correct the deficiencies. However, it is impossible to keep the retention level in constancy. After a stage, the customer wants to use an alternative product. This tendency is not uncommon and is a basic human behaviour in all cases. This attrition leads to defection. However, the firm can regain the lost business by recatching the lost customer. In this stage, the defection may have been due to the competitor's competitive prices. But, if the firm could offer higher values/services by improving the product features attuned with the new customer needs, reacquisition is possible. As long as the customer care is put-in the front line and the customers are quite satisfied with the firm's performance. The customer defection rate can be stopped to emerge. If the firm finds any quality gap to exist with respect to its product or service, that must be corrected in order to keep the customer in its fold. The quality gap may be in any form-deficiency in service, delay in supplies, non-availability of spares, etc. The firm can deal with this problem so effectively that customer loyalty has become unvulnerable.

The best way to retain the existing customer and recatch the exiled customers is to attend to their complaints so quickly that they are felt happy. The company can know about the reasons for the customers leaving through customer survey. This is important to be dealt with in relationship marketing.

Thus, the product life cycle is another form of customer life cycle describing the market reaction to the product. This is shown in the following Figure 3.

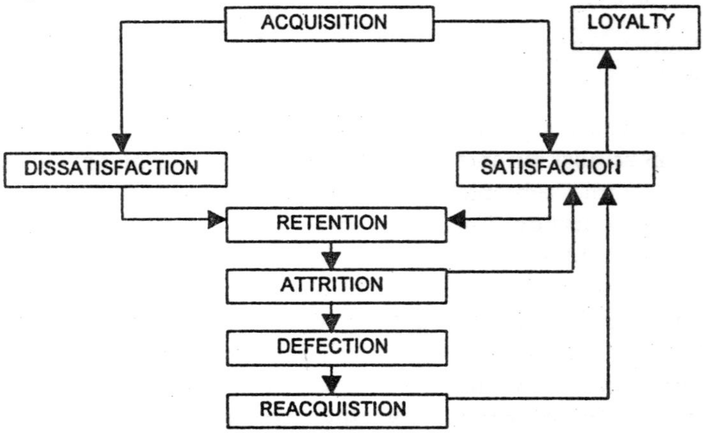

Fig 3: Customer Life Cycle.

From the above points, it may be learnt that the product life cycle can take a turn to rise both at the maturity stage and even after entering the decline stage but after a time gap. The customer life cycle reflects mostly the product life cycle but also the service life cycle.

Customer Life Cycle and Customized Products and Services

The concept, the customer life cycle may well be understood by life cycle cost. The life cycle cost can be defined as the total cost to the user of purchasing, and maintaining a product over its life.[9] The concept, the customer life cycle with respect to customized production and service exhibits either continuity overtime or discontinuity at snap shots. Customer acquisition in this sector is mostly through the referrals. The firm enjoys repeat orders and repeat visits when the customers are satisfied. As long as the firm can keep the customer in good spirit., it grows in leaps. The problem of customer retention has many dimensions to deal within the custom focused areas, which are in brief customer centric and hyper-sensitive. In these areas, even a small fall in customer satisfaction will cause defection. However, it will not be much difficult in customized production to recover the lost customer in contrast with mass production (fast moving consumer goods).

The probability that the firm has zero defection in very high only in customized production. In the opposite, business will become liquidated very fast when the customer dissatisfaction mounts heavily or exceeds the tolerance limits.

Customer Acquisition and Retention in Upper Class Life-Style Market

Enjoying life is the general characteristic of the upper-class people. Customer acquisition and retention have certain uniqueness in this segment. In this segment, brand image is the major determinant of customer acquisition. Car manufacturing is the best example for discussion in this context. Customers in the A and B segments are attracted through the brand image, on one hand, and the price on the other hand. In C and D segments, where the car price ranges from 15 to 30 lakhs, customers are acquired through the brand image only. Product features like look, convenience, safety (least about fuel consumption), etc are the chief variables determining the demand. The question of customer retention may be said unrising in cases like passenger cars manufacturing. But, when discussing the aspect in a broader perspective, it can be understood that customer retention is in a different form, unlike in others. To illustrate, one, when becoming a particular company's customer by buying its product first hand, remains as its customer even when he sells the product after use by buying again the company's product. This time, the purchase may be of some other brand. To illustrate, customer, X, purchased Maruti 800 two years ago. After using it for two years, he has now sold it and has bought Maruti Zen. People prefer a particular brand because of its excellent performance and after sales service facilities. Similar is the case of motor-bikes. Further, the firm can get the new customers as the second hand buyers of its product. Their addition helps the firm to promote the sales of its spares.

Acquiring and then retaining the customer is a difficult task in hospitality industry like star hotels and restaurants. Acquiring the customer is as much important as retaining the customer and vice-versa. Service quality is considered the bottom line for their continuance in business with fair returns. More importantly, customer retention has an pronounced effect on these enterprises, because repeat visits are badly required for their financial base to be made stronger.

In the life style market, certain products are purchased only one time. Their life cycle is determined mostly by the new customers. For example, certain building materials like mosaic tiles, marbles etc. are bought only once and there will be no repeat purchases. In such cases, the customer acquiring process is a continuous one. The growth phase in the product life cycle with respect to these products can be lengthened to a considerable extent by changing their designs and other features attuned with the new environment. In this context, the customer is simply a buyer.

Customer Acquisition and Retention through Innovation

The firm can use the internet to catch the customer cutting across the spatial barriers. The customer requirements/specifications can be had on line and accordingly the product be made. The technological revolution has been ushered in automobile assembling recently. Cars are assembled with special features as required by the customer. Toyota is the leader in this segment.

Training

Customer excellence can be created without much difficulty in such areas as hotels, restaurants, clubs, etc. To escalate the customer satisfaction or to produce the customer delight what is required basically is personalized service. The employees in this segment must be educated well so that they have pleasing manners aimed at receiving the customer repeat visits. One important thing to be noted is that the employees must be trained so that they know what is to be talked to and what is not to be talked to the customer. A market is customer oriented by convincing every employee that customer satisfaction in his or her responsibility.[10] A right environment is most needed for acquiring and then retaining the customer.

II. CASE STUDIES

A. Cellular Industry, the Attentions now on Attrition

Price is paramount in customer acquisition and retention (Hosangady).

SAS India devised analytic CRM applications for orange in the Mumbai circle and for Air Tel in New Delhi.

The process involved identifying customers who are likely to churn because of reasons as varied as dropped calls, tariff plans, network quality, billing, customer service, additional services, and special promotions, and helping service provides take appropriate measures like devise specialised packages to prevent them from leaving.

"Typically developing economies like India are dominated by the prepaid segment, which is price-sensitive and tickle to that extent", says Hosangady. Affordable tariff packages have indeed propelled the prepaid segment, which contributes an estimated 60 per cent of the total subscriber base (53 lakh subscriber) in India. What is more, ever about half of the prepaid customers pay less than Rs 500 per month, according to COAI calculation. "For that reason price will play a major role in acquiring and retaining customers", he says—"In particular the prices relating to monthly rentals, security fees, and activation charges. As the market matures, added-value services will gain in importance". Experts indicate the inflexion normally happens when teledensity touches 10 per cent work.

Since that still in some distance away, the competition will continue to manifest itself in the painful price was based on customer segmentation and tariff bundling. Mohit Boetra, Chief marketing officer for Air Tel, says: "faced with varying customer demands and their low switching costs owing to stiff competition, one needs to know the customer well and effectively satisfy his needs so that cost-effective incentives can be devised to increase customer loyalty and retention".

Bharit's game plan is clearly inspired by the fact that in any mobile market prepaid is used as a device to penetrate the market and hence the accent is on the affordability and ease of purchase; bundled added—value services enhance the attractiveness of the product. But to move towards and sustain market share, the focus shifts to the valuable post-paid segment.

Courtesy: Business India
Nov 11-24, 2002

B. Age of Customer Control

Sound of Thunder (SOT)—A Multi-cuisine restaurant.

Case target segment: Young urban professionals[yupies].

Its vision is to convert customers into advocate (those who will tell others about SOT) and ambassadors (those who will work to promote SOT) through its interactive service.

Problem: The interactive customer service programme has run into trouble on account of its yuppie customer's varying expectations of what constitutes good service.

Anecdote: A pair of young girls are chatting at their table in SOT. The waiter blows his (music) pipe with thunder sound as a gesture of warm reception to these visitors.

Executives comment were solicited to judge whether the type of service can satisfy the customer. Now the comments follow:

[Comments by Pankaj Batra, Director Marketing, Indian Subcontinent, Pizza Hut.]

SOT should accept the fact that there is a gap between its vision of customer service and the ground-level execution by its staff, and focus on this areas to bridge the gap.

- Understand customer needs. The more we know about our customers, the better we can serve them now and the more likely we are to retain them in the future.

This can be done in a variety of ways, the simplest of which is by talking to them about their needs, expectation and experience.

- Training employees on customer service. There is a gap between trendliness and intrusiveness. SOT needs to develop detailed training modules on recognition of customer types, sensitisation its staff to customer behaviour in each type. The training programme must be modified to include restaurant situation, simulations, role-plays and so on.
- Measure customer satisfaction. The feedback is shared with the team on a periodic basis in a systematic manner. It should set an example by recognizing and rewarding food service, *"what gets measured, gets done and what gets rewarded, gets repeated."*

Comments by Vilas Pawar, President and CEO, Bistro Hospitality, India

There is little doubt that with an abundance of products innumerable categories. Customer satisfaction is fast becoming a key differentiator. In post-liberalisation India, it is clear that if a company does not succeed in keeping that smile on the customer's face, it will spell doom. That is what happened at Sound of Thunder.

What should the Restaurant's Management's do?

First of all, look at the service from the customer's perspective. And a typical customer of any restaurant or service of this sort, would usually evaluate the quality of service by the following ways:

Tangibles: The appearance of the facilities, personnel and communicate material, which is this case would be the menu, signs and so on.

Empathy: The case and concern shown by the business personnel towards the customer. what matters critically, is the company's activity to understand the customer's point of view.

Assurance: The knowledge and courtesy of employees and their ability to inspire trust and confidence.

While the first point is directly related to the product, the other two involve the human factor as well, which will always be inconsistent and this is where training should play a vital part.

Data suggests that 68 per cent of customers who quit, do so because of poor service.

A satisfied customer does more propagation of products and services free of cost. Also, it typically costs five-to-six times more to get a new customer than to retain an existing customer.

The waiter should have realized that the two ladies had come to the restaurant not to spend time with him, but together.

The Case of Officious Service

Mantra for guest service SWAT—S-Smile, W-Wait, A-Attend, T-Thank.

Conclusion

Customer satisfaction is the basis for all management decisions aimed at increasing profitability/maximizing revenue. The marketing manager plays a key role in identifying and acquiring the customer. Customer satisfaction is measured by comparing what customers expectations are and what the product has offered to the value chain. The gap between them is the unmet part of the customer satisfaction, which leads to the customer defection. The customer is delighted when the customer satisfaction derived is more than expected. A successful firm retains the customer by improving the quality of its product or service in comparison with the competitors. The customer is loyal to the company, when the cost life cycle is very short.

REFERENCES

1. David W. Cravens, *Strategic Marketing*, The McGraw Hill, 1997, p. 225.
2. Rober Cross, *Revenue Management*, University Press, 1999, p. 13.
3. Martin Christopher & Others, *Relationship Marketing*, Butterworth Heinemann, Oxford, p. 22.
4. Tara Sinha, *Advertising and Marketing*, 31 March 2001, p. 63.
5. Rober Cross, *Ibid*.
6. Diefer Huekeoteim, President, Hilton Hotels Corporation, quoted by Roba Cross, *Ibid*.
7. Rober Cross, *Ibid*.
8. *Ibid*.
9. Martin Christopher, *Ibid*.
10. J.M. Juran & Others, *Quality Planning and Analysis*, Tata McGraw Hill, 1997, p. 90.

5

Earning Customer Loyalty

Customer Acquisition and Retention Strategies

R. AMUDHA* & V. SELVAM**

Introduction

In the present scenario, more and more companies are realising that their most precious asset in this competitive world is their existing customer base and have started allocating funds to customer loyalty and retention programmes. The newly emerging economy shows that growth rates in most of the product sectors are strongly positive. There is still a lot of the population waiting to be tapped by aggressive marketers. In spite of this, market in India have remained fragmented and insular and it is customer relationships which have helped in building up a strong customer base. Very often, when offerings from various competitors are nearly at par in terms of quality and performance, it is the personal touch or an equation between a buyer and a seller which will tilt the scale in favour of the seller.

Today's economy which is customer driven, is indispensable to ensure that the company does not lose him. It is inherent to keep our equity for which, we need to build relationships in fair weather.

Basic Steps to Acquire New Customers

The basic marketing approach signifies the process of Identifying, Segmenting, Developing and Retaining customers by

* Lecturer, College of Management Sciences, VIT, Deemed University, Vellore.

** Lecturer, College of Science and Humanities, VIT, Deemed University, Vellore.

communicating and rewarding desired behaviour. In this process the following steps enable to acquire and retain more and better customers.

1. *Situation Analysis*: Evaluate your existing approach to customer acquisition and retention, and make recommendations for finding profitable new customers and increasing the value of your current customers.
2. *Market Segmentation*: Analyze your market opportunity and identify the most promising segments.
3. *Campaign Development*: Create a robust marketing plan, ready for execution.
4. *Retention Marketing Plan*: A dynamic ongoing customer retention strategy, using personalized communications to increase the lifetime value of your customer base.
5. *Loyalty Programs*: Analyze your customer segments and recommend ROI based programs to reward your best customers, keep them buying and stimulate referrals.

Trends to Earn Customer Loyalty

The pioneers of this model include Patricia Seybold, Don Peppers and Martha Rogers. These trends are based on a certain analysis called 'Customer Scenario mapping' developed by Patricia Seybold.

Consumers are Smarter and Expect More

The consumers today are better educated and their purchase decisions are taken with greater scrutiny as they have access to adequate data for comparison shopping. The advertisement and publicity media provide the customers with ample product information. This leads to stronger expectations and demand for product quality and customer service. To meet these demands the companies, need to emphasize differentiation, value addition and launch loyalty-based marketing programmes

The 'Net' as a Facilitator

The Internet Channel has changed the buying habits of customers. As a customer on the Internet is clogged with various options, with both branded products or services and other cheaper options, the customer can have a very economical deal enabling to save nearly 40 per cent on normal rates.

High Labour Costs Affecting Customer Service

The increasing cost of quality labour, erodes the customer service level particularly in fast food and mass merchandising. The critical decline in customer service quality, damages and severs relationships of former loyal and profitable customers.

Price or Cash Based Offers

The consumers are attracted to the best offers and readily switch over to the other best offer programmes of the competitors, particularly in cellular industry. BSNL Cellone service, Reliance Cellular services, introduce customer loyalty programmes by establishing value and creating barriers to exit.

New Competitors in the Global Market

The global economy have paved the way to increased competition. To compete with them, the domestic marketers have to establish stronger value propositions, in the hope of blocking foreign threats to obtain market share. The Hero Motors implementing their unique 'Passport' programme has expanded in a big way bringing back lakhs of its old customers.

Customer Focused Marketing Technology

The data warehousing system developed by the technical giants Microsoft and Oracle, collect and mine, valuable customer information in real time. Incorporating these systems with software innovations (such as Epiphany's E5 to use the data for smart) and ROI based loyalty marketing programmes is becoming an innovative issue.

Mergers and Acquisitions Impact on Customer Loyalty

Mergers and Acquisitions have a significant impact on brand or product loyalty and may cause customers to look for alternatives. For instance, the merger of ANZ Grindlays Bank with Standard Chartered Bank has reportedly seen many loyal customers of the former switching to 'desi' banks, such as ICICI Bank.

Scenario Mapping

This involves envisioning alternative versions of the future and strategic responses, adapting to one or more scenario to occur in the market. Scenario planning allows the companies to more rapidly modify its strategic decisions as actual events unfold. The company shall put themselves in their competitors' position and predict the possible outcomes and generate strategies.

Contingency Planning

Contingency planning is an extremely important component and it means taking a different path than originally planned. The next step is to track for any indicators, if those scenarios are starting to emerge and develop contingency plans for events likely to evolve in a new environment.

Speculate the Change in Consumer Behaviour

The key issue to create an edge for the marketers of the future, is the ability to predict change. The dynamism of the consumer mind need to be in the hands of the marketer well before the consumer has actually morphed. This speculation of change in Consumer Behaviour shall help to take a strategic move in customer retention.

The Value of Customer Retention

All corporate profits are ultimately earned from conducting successful relationships with customers. Among the source of all the profits, customer relationships should be valued and protected. Every customer relationship is an asset and has an economic value or Lifetime Market Value (LMV). A customer's LMV is determined by taking average customer transaction amount and multiplying it by the number of transactions he or she will conduct with organisation over time. For example, if average customers buys Rs. 1,000 worth of product every quarter, for roughly three years then your average customer's LMV is: Rs. 1,000 x 4 x 3 = Rs.12,000. Companies who devote the majority of their energies and resources to getting new customers usually do so, at the expense of their existing customers. The resulting neglect can erode the trust and "equity" found in repeat customer relationships.

Market Share, as Represented by the Water Level in a Bucket

If customers begin to feel ignored or neglected, they ultimately take their business elsewhere. The study reveals that 4 per cent of the customers move or die; acquiring other company friendships –5 per cent; leave the company due to competitors –9 per cent; product dissatisfaction –15 per cent; Lack of customer contact strategy –67 per cent. The influence on Profits is the retention of current customers. Think of a firm's customer base as a water in a bucket, as in Figure 1.

Fig. 1

Customer erosions correspond to leaks in the bucket, causing the level of sales to drop. To replace them the firm must attract new customers. These may be newcomers to the market of customers of the competitors. To make the level rise, the inflow at the top must be greater than the outflow at the bottom. There are two ways to achieve this goal: the firm can turn up the tap by seeking new customers more aggressively, or it can take steps to plug leaks by keeping its current customers from leaving.

A commonly quoted rule of thumb based on a series of frequently quoted studies is that the cost of winning a new customer is on an average about five times greater than the cost of retaining a current customer.

Customer Relationship Marketing—Significance

Customer vs. Employee Satisfaction

Most of the researches which suggest a comprehensive retention strategy, is composed of quality strategy and tactical programmes. Researches have suggested a strong link between employee satisfaction and customer retention. They have opined that high customer retention will lead to higher employee satisfaction rather than dissatisfied customers. As a result employees will tend to stay longer with the company. "Higher retention of the right calibre of employees create a stable and experienced labour force that delivers higher service quality and lower this leads to higher customer retention and of course increased profitability".

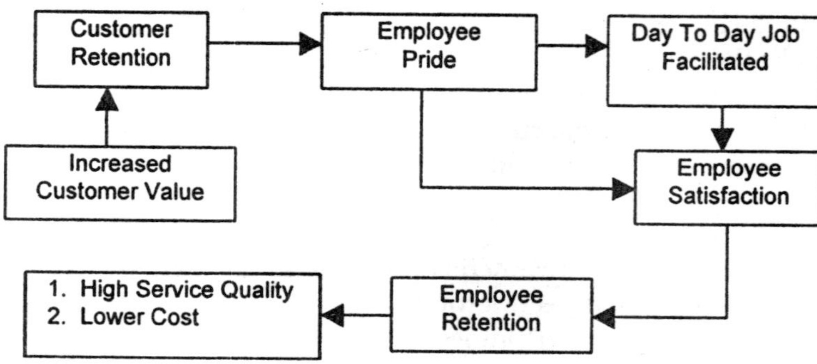

Customer vs. Firm/Company

Companies have woken up to the reality that, to be competitive, they have to be more and more customer focused. They have to respond to a demanding, choosy and unforgiving customer whose priority is not to buy products but to find the most cost-effective way of fulfilling their needs. Firms do not have much choice with the advent of cut-throat competition, the patronage of the customers can no longer be taken for granted and this new choice empowered customer is naturally in a position to dictate terms. So companies are forced to respond and attend to their customers—understand their overt needs, do psycho analysis to unveil their innermost desires and wants, intuiting their slightest whims and then use all the available resources to meet those needs and even try to surpass them.

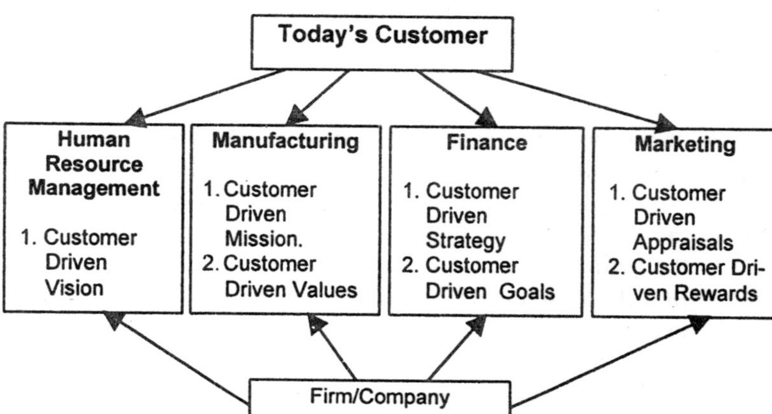

In the buyers market today, the marketer is making all efforts to make the customer his lodestar. By focusing every aspects of its processes on the customer, the company will be able to serve unmatched value to the customer and also generate greater long term profits than its competitors.

Customer vs. Suppliers

Customers can be retained and new ones can be more easily attracted. Good customers grow and refer others, resulting in expanded business opportunities with the help of suppliers teams.

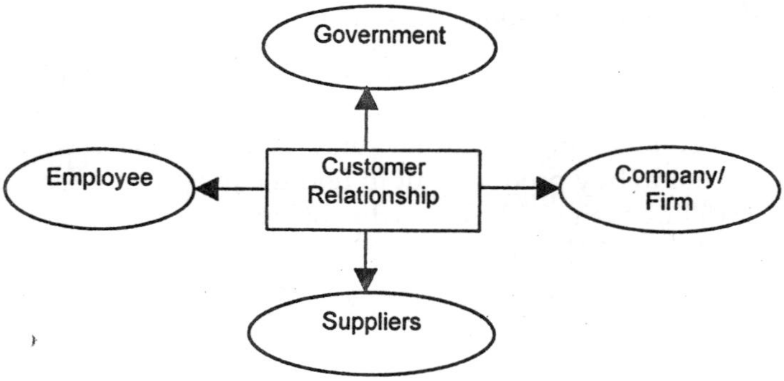

Three Levels of Retention of Customers

Level 1: The customer is tied to the firm primarily through financial incentives—Lower prices for greater volume purchases or lower prices for customers, who have been with the firm a long time.

Level 2: Strategies bind customers to the firm through more than pricing incentives. While price is still assumed to be important, in this level retention marketers build long term relationships through social as well as financial bonds. Customers are viewed as "clients" not nameless faces, and become individuals whose needs and wants, the firm seeks to understand services are customized to fit individual needs, and marketers find ways of staying in touch with their customers, thereby developing social bonds with them.

Level 3: Strategies are the most difficult to imitate and involve structural as well as functional and social bonds between

> the customer and the firm. Structural bonds are created by providing services to the client that are highly customized and frequently designed right into the service delivery system for the client. Structural bonds are often created by providing customized services to the client that are technology based and serve to make the customer more productive.

Thus Customer retention isn't high science. It is a long term, disciplined, methodical programme that succeeds with consistent implementation, unflagging follow-through, and genuine commitment. Wondering how to achieve some of those all-important incremental sales gains? The answers are right in front of you... it's the customer! The one you already have.

Conclusion

A successful customer retention marketing implementation strategy starts with understanding the needs of the customers. Unfortunately, customers' needs are often the last element to be considered in many company's CRM strategies. The key to success in customer relationships is to deliver a great 'quality of customer experience'. Thus the primary building block of the marketing process—'the consumer', needs to be made aware of the offer, create interest in the proposition, stoked into a position of desire and pushed to the precipice of the purchase decision.

In order to achieve the goal of creating superior customer value, business firms are trying to build relationship chains throughout the organisation. This requires integration of elements widely dispersed across different functions of the business. These elements include research and development, value engineering, in bound logistics, order fulfilment and customer service (including after sales service). It may also be borne in mind that it is through continuous delivery of superior customer value that enduring customer relationships are built. It is built on the basic proposition that the purpose of all business processes is to create and sustain mutually, advantageous relationship throughout the chain, culminating in enhanced customer value. This means that just as it is felt necessary to have strong supplier relationships, it is equally necessary to have strong relationships with customers.

REFERENCES

1. Bansal Shuchi, *"The Market Goes to the Customer"*, Business World, Aug. Issue, p. 7, 1998.
2. Tandon Anshu, *"Are You adding Value by Building Relationships"*, Business Today, Jan. Issue, p. 21, 1997.
3. Frederick F. Reichheld and W. Earl Sasser, *"Zero Defections: Quality Comes to Service"*, Harvard Business Review (Sep./Oct. 1996), pp. 105-111.
4. Frederick F. Reichheld, *"The Truth of Consumer Retention"*, Journal of Retail Banking, 13(4), pp. 21-24.
5. Frederick F. Reichheld and David W. Kenny (1990), *"The Hidden Advantages of Customer Retention"*, Journal of Retail Banking, XII, Winter pp. 19-23.
6. Charles B. Weinberg and Christopher H. Lovelock, *"Pricing and Profits in Subscription Service Marketing: An Analytical Approach to Customer Valuation"*.
7. Roland T. Rust and Anthony J. Zahorik,*"Service Marketing"*, Addison, Wesley Longman Incorporation, Singapore, 1st Edition, 1999.
8. Valerie A. Zeithaml and Mary Jo Bitner, *"Service Marketing"*, McGrawHill Co. Intl., Edition, 1996.
9. Suja R. Nair, *"Consumer Behaviour in Indian Perspective"*, Himalaya Pub. House, 1st edition, 2001.
10. M. Muhamed, CEO, Innovative Media,*"Earning Customer Loyalty"*, Praxis, Business Line Journal on Management, Jan. 2003, p. 52.

6

Customer Retention

An Integrated Strategy of 4 C's

JAYASREE KRISHNAN*

During the past two decades, customer satisfaction management has emerged as a strategic imperative for most of the firms. In the 1980's achieving higher satisfaction ratings became a goal in itself. Only during the 1990's was there a wide spread realization that customer satisfaction ratings were only means to strategic ends, i.e. customer retention. Today the emphasis is shifting. Beyond designing strategies to *attract* new customer and create *transaction* with them, companies are going out to *retain* current customers and build lasting relationship with them.

Why Customer Retention

Customer retention helps a firm to increase its profitability and understand consumer preferences and needs. An organization cannot work in an ivory tower. It should gin customer's support to continue operating and this support is gained from loyal customers. The changing demographics, the slow growth of economy more sophisticated competition, overcapacity in many industries mean fewer customers to go around. Attracting new customers has turned to be very difficult. Hence, marketers have to change the tendency of finding new customers at the cost of the old ones, but also have to realize that cutting down of defections in halves would double the average company's growth rate,

The present paper describes the special features and elements of an effective customer retention strategy that a firm requires to

* Assistant Professor, Department of Management Studies St. Joseph's College of Engineering, Chennai.

achieve success, it focuses on the fact that to keep customers delighted, the marketers in future have to replace the traditional marketing by a differentiated marketing formed by integrating the four C's namely Co-operation, Customization, Customer service, and Customer Value.

Co-operative Spirit

To retain customer a co-operative spirit between the marketer and the customer is essential. The traditional marketing system has failed to develop a meaningful and workable relationship between them which is an essential prerequisite for customer retention. Customer relation goes through beyond the traditional exchange and enables the marketer to estimate the customer's sentiments and buying intentions so that the customer can be provided with product or services before he starts demanding. This approach provided with product or services before he starts demanding. This approach would not only create a favourable impression in the mind of the customer, but also provides an opportunity to a marketer to come closer to the customer—a prerequisite to best cooperation.

Relationships have proved to be the central element in the success of business since time immemorial. They are the invisible threads which bind all business associates. To remain competitive and to carve a niche in a global market, it has become imperative that a spirit of cooperation exists between both the customers and the marketer.

Customization

As the customer becomes conscious of his position in the market, his preferences and needs become more complicated. Virtually all executives today recognize the need to provide outstanding service to the customers. Focusing on the customer, however, is both an imperative and a potential curse. In their desire to become customer driven, many companies have resorted to inventing new programmes and procedures to meet every customer's request. But as customers need grow increasingly diverse, such an approach has become a surefire way to add unnecessary cost and complexity to operations.

Companies throughout the world have embraced mass customization in an attempt to avoid those very pitfalls and provide unique value to their customers in an efficient manner. Readily available information, technology and flexible work processes permit them to customize goods or services for individual customers in high volume and relatively low cost. Blend of standardization and customization called mass customization would help a firm to achieve dual goals of cost reduction and differentiation.

Customer Service

Customer service is one of the key factors that keep customers delighted. Delighted customers are gauging their progress not just by the return on assets but also by happy returns of customers. It adds value to the basic product and therefore, can be used as a main weapon against competitors. To compete on service today—one has to be really good. There is a clear relation between level of service and customer loyalty. The higher the level of service delivered, the more the customers would want to continue business and the higher the profits.

Customer Value

Customers in future are expected to be more rational in their buying decisions and therefore strongly value oriented. This has driven many marketers towards customer centric organizations. As long as the perceived worth of the market offering is higher than the customer's investment in terms of prices and efforts to realize the offering, he would consider the offering valuable. One of the popular techniques used to ensure delivered value is the Value Chain—a systematic means of analyzing and categorizing activities. It provides a systematic means of analyzing the contribution of individual activities in a business to the overall level of customer value the firm produces. Such an assessment enables a firm to enhance the value of its market offering by reviewing the activities which has little value to the offering and identifying the possibilities to add more value at each stage. The role of individual activities within a value chain to improve the firm's overall ability to create value cannot be underestimated, this role becomes even more significant when played in combination. This is because the value chain is not a collection of independent activities but a system of interdependent activities. Overall value for the customers is created not by individual activities but by group of activities that come to form what is known as core process and systems. Hence, in the process of value creation the marketer should view the entire process as a whole system despite the varying importance of individual activities.

Conclusion

In this changed era of marketing where the focus is on the retention of customer by customer delight, the present paper recommends a strategy of 4 C's to help organizations in achieving their goals. The organization should understand the critical dimensions of each of the components of the strategy and the relationship that exists between them in order to ensure their integration. Therefore, a marketer has to ensure closer alignment of crucial elements of the strategy where each element should be focused on towards meeting customer requirement.

7

Customer Retention in Service Sector

With Specific Reference to Banks Operating in India

V.J. SIVAKUMAR* & H. PEERU MOHAMED**

One goal of managing supply and demand and enhancing productivity is to provide customers with a more consistent and higher level of service quality. While saying so, it is absolutely important for a bank to go in for more and more newer channels to serve the customers effectively and offer them convenience at their doorsteps by way of online banking, door services, phone banking and more number of ATMs. Even though the cost of introducing these innovative services in the initial stages is high, the benefits accruing out of these will offset the expenses in a period of two years time. More than that today when almost all the banks are fighting with one another to lure the customers, it is becoming a necessity that the bank goes in for these measure at the earliest rather than becoming a me too player after everybody else offers them. These newer channels will definitely offer the customer convenience, increases productivity thereby forcing the customer to stay with the bank thereafter.

This increase in the consistency and level of service quality by going in for newer channels should also produce a higher level of customer satisfaction. With increased customer satisfaction should come future repeat purchase behavior. However, satisfied customers do not always remain loyal or purchase from the same

* Faculty of Marketing, Loyola Institute of Business Administration (LIBA), Loyola College, Chennai.

** Co-ordinator, School of Management, Anna University, Chennai.

company. They may purchase from a competitor because of a lower price, superior service, or for some other reason. They may switch simply because they are bored with the current firm and want some variety or new sensory stimulation which could only be done by studying the consumer behavior of the customers over a period of time. Therefore, services must go beyond satisfying customers. We must understand the psychology of the consumers while devising the strategies for customer satisfaction. They must be oriented towards building relationships that will result in customer retention and repeat purchase behavior.

Customers range from individuals who are extremely brand loyal at one end of a continuum to individuals who demonstrate repeat purchase behaviour at the other end. Customers who are brand loyal will buy only from their preferred bank. They will not substitute another bank. The reasons for this kind of loyalty may be due to the actions of service personnel at services which affect the level of satisfaction experienced by customers and, or may be due the judicious management of the value delivered to the customer. This can be done by providing training to the employees in the bank. A bank may have gone in for very high level of customer relationship management programs but if the watchman at the bank is rude in his encounters with the customer then all the money spent on the high end CRM packages is likely to go down the drain. So, it is absolutely important that training is given to all the staff starting from the office boy to the Managing Director on Customer Relationship Management.

In the case of a Loyal customer otherwise referred to as the true customer the bank has got to identify them and ensure that they are given preferential treatment. A new software has come in banking industry by which the employee or the manager will be intimated as soon as a loyal customer enters either the ATM or the online channel or the phone banking by way of a flash on the computer screen giving all the information about the customer and the purpose of his visit so that the employee concerned can serve the customer even before the customer puts in his query. For doing this the bank should educate its employees on the 20:80:30 rule. Which says that 80 per cent of the profits comes from 20 per cent of the customers and the 80 per cent profit which comes from 20 per cent customers, is spent on 30 per cent of unprofitable customers. If the bank is to make increased profits then it should give priority to its 20 per cent profitable customers and stop spending money on the 30 per cent unprofitable customers. This can be done by properly studying the customers financial and family background, their purchase patterns over a period of time and estimating their future potential.

The customer value is the perceived combination of factors that in the customer's mind creates a superior value for them. The four factors that make up the customer value package are price, technical service quality, functional service quality and company image. All these factors are totally in the hands of the bank to administer. While talking about price, the bank has to ensure that the pricing mechanism is as per the expectations of the customers. Pricing should neither be too high nor too low. If the pricing is too high, customers expectation level may go up and satisfying them will become a problem. When the price charged is too low, customers will start to perceive the services to be of a low quality and thereby may not come to the bank at all. Therefore, the pricing should be realistic. But, today we find that the foreign banks provide better service at a higher cost to the customer. On the other hand, we find the nationalized banks provide lesser quality services at a lower cost. There is a big vacuum in-between the two extremes. It is only here that the newly formed private sector banks like the ICICI and HDFC can pitch in and try to position themselves. But the reality is that these new generation private banks offer services more or less like the foreign banks and there by leaving a huge segment of customers who want better service levels at a lower cost whose needs remain unmet. I do not dispute the fact that better quality service costs more and, that may be the reason why the foreign banks demand a price for it. If we examine the functioning of a foreign bank there are many unnecessary services offered like sending the monthly statements by courier mailing to all customers, offering a Debit card to all customers irrespective of whether they want it or not and a host of similar services which costs a lot to administer. With regard to the technical service quality there remains a large difference between the foreign banks and the nationalized banks where the foreign banks have gone in for total computerization of all their transactions whereas the nationalized banks are still trying with the brick and mortar way of doing business. The functional service quality is largely dependent on the automation that is prevalent in the banks where again the foreign banks being highly automated leads the way. With regard to the image of the bank the foreign banks have cultivated an image of a lean and dynamic place to bank with, whereas, the nationalized banks have developed a fat, flabby and inefficient white elephant image. However, there is a large difference between the State Bank of India and the other nationalized banks. The State Bank of India practices the art of mass banking in the true sense where even pensioners prefer to bank with. Such being the case the bank being a part of the Government cannot refuse to transact with segments which are not profitable to it. Like in the case of pensioners where they draw the entire money on the first of every month from their account with no residue left. There are still other services left like the Public Provident Fund (PPF) and similar services, which are in no way profitable for the bank and still cannot be avoided. Another aspect of the nationalized banks is with regard to the advantage they have in the size of their distribution being spread to almost every nook and corner of the country with innumerable branches. Whereas in the case of the foreign banks the number of branches are limited and hence, it is possible to offer highly specialized services to specific profitable segments of customers.

Business buyers and consumers experience various states of satisfaction with a service. These customer satisfaction states are angry, dissatisfied, irritated, OK, pleased and excited. The state of satisfaction is determined by how consumers perceive the service they received compared to what they had expected prior to the service. In doing so, the bank should manage the expectations of the customers so that they can exceed their expectations and offer delight to them. In order to do that the promises which are made by the banks should be properly communicated to the customers. The explicit promises like the advertisements and the promises made by the field sales staff and the counter staff should be well tuned that they promise only what is possible to deliver rather than promising the stars and finally disappointing them while providing the service. In this case again the customers expectations are also different for the foreign banks and the nationalized banks. In the case of foreign banks customers are expecting better technical and functional quality services along with personalization, customization and special attention. Whereas in the case of nationalized banks customers expect standard and routine services without any fringe benefits and lower charges. If the service is performed at the level that is expected or predicted, the satisfaction level is considered to be just "OK".

Understanding the various states of satisfaction will help banks understand why they must go beyond customer satisfaction. Merely satisfying customers will not be enough to remain competitive in today's global market. This can be done by understanding what the customers expect and by effectively meeting their expectations. One method of effectively meeting the customer expectations is by compatibility management. To illustrate, think about the following statements made by customers of a bank. One male customer said, "It's a nice place, but it's always so crowded. I don't like going." Another female patron made the statement "I never go after 12.00 anymore because there is this one woman there who is so rude. I can't stand her." From an elderly customer came the remark, "The young people act like we should be sitting around in a nursing home. They think we are in their way and don't like us being there."

The above statements clearly indicate the important role other customers play in customer retention. In all cases, customers were satisfied with the service. However, they were dissatisfied with the way they were being treated by other customers. The bank cannot ignore this since it is the responsibility of the bank to manage customer compatibility which is an important aspect of delivering satisfaction to customers. In order to manage customer compatibility the bank must first decide on the target group of customers to serve and must give priority to that segment and attract it. In case the bank decides to serve more than one segment of customers the employees must see to it that there is more and more exchanges and interactions within that segment of customers and prevent cross segment interactions. This activity should be so done without offending the customers. This can be done by arranging the tables and sofas in such a way that interaction between intragroups is discouraged and intergroup interaction is encouraged. Banks can also prohibit behaviors that other customers may find offensive or distasteful. For example, advising the customers not to bring their children to the bank and if all they bring allotting a separate place where children can play in one end without disturbing the other customers.

It is also the responsibility of the bank to ensure the behavior of certain customers which may jeopardize the health or safety is prohibited for the benefit of other customers. Customers should be served by the order-of-arrival and prohibit behaviors that infringe upon the rights of other customers. This strategy works well when there are multiple service employees and the length of time for individual transactions varies. Most consumers become irritated if they get on a line that takes longer than another line, or a customer in front of them takes longer than they believe is appropriate.

Employees in the bank can also assume the role of a matchmaker by putting homogenous groups together and to separate the heterogeneous groups so that conflict can be minimized. Separating families with children from other customers and separating smokers from nonsmokers are examples which may minimize conflict.

Employees should be trained to spot good acts that could be rewarded. Service employees must also be able to perform the job of controllers of unacceptable behaviour from the customers end by advising them and cheering them up when the moods are otherwise like, dressing themselves to be a point of attraction in the premises. For example, dressing themselves like clowns or angels or as Santa Claus so that the customer is not made to meet the same old face day in and day out and thereby enlivening the entire atmosphere for retention in the long run. Banks have to address these issues and adopt similar strategies in future depending on the preferences of customers to ensure that customers are retained with the bank at all times.

8

Customer Retention

Core of Marketing Success in the 21st Century

G. ANJANEYA SWAMY* & DEEPAK RAAJAN**

Marketing is in transition now. All along the history of modern marketing, many marketing gurus have ceaselessly hammered into the business managers' logic market acquisition and customer base as the obvious paths to marketing excellence. But in today's new economy, marketers find that traditional marketing concepts do not work as effectively as they did before. Promotional expenses have skyrocketed like never before. The high cost of acquiring new customers today is truly phenomenal. The digital revolution has democratised information. Bargaining power of the customer is enhanced by the information power. Customers literally can access any kind of information be it technical or otherwise from various sources from industry specific journals to the internet and make simple cost–benefit analysis before a purchase decision. Increase in buyer bargaining power is also attributed to the intense competition in nearly all sectors. Today we can clearly visualise a condition where there is a plethora of products available and too little buyers for them. It is clearly a buyers market—a very well informed buyers market at that. Busy juggling the 4 elements of marketing mix, to widen their market base, the marketers quite often tend to overlook the potentials of their existing customers. After the initial euphoria with the new customer dies down, all the effort in acquiring is quickly forgotten and focus moves towards acquiring new customers. In the context of this tough

* Professor, School of Management, Pondicherry University.

** Research Scholar, School of Management, Pondicherry University.

market, the industry increasingly realising the value of the existing customer, this paper asserts an argument to put Customer Retention in the core of any marketing strategy. Taking into account the diverse business environments, this paper also attempts to provide guidelines on various aspects for evolving a Dynamic Customers Retention Programme.

Traditional Retention Activities

All organisations do their share of customer retention activities. But largely they are conducted by the gut feeling of the manager rather than in a systematic and structured manner. They are nothing more than knee jerk win back efforts. Such efforts look extremely awkward and desperate in the eyes of the customer especially after the competitor has made inroads into the customer's purchase domain. Effective customer retention is possible only with a concerted effort of all the related functions of the organisation. It follows a definite pattern in identifying the valued customer for a long term, making retention programmes in relation with the existing valued customers, creating a corporate core value system to focus on the customer, train employees to their task, and strategically realign the functions in the organisation where necessary. With regard to the customer cycle in terms of the transaction levels between the organisation and the customer, Richard Shapiro, CEO, MJ Rich Associates enumerates 4 stages[1]

- *Excitement*: Sales crew is excited on landing on the new customer. The customer in turn is happy with all the initial attention he receives.
- *Marketing focus shift*: Customer satisfied with the initial responses is happy with the purchase and the sales team with reduced commission on that existing account lose interest in the customer. Simultaneously, service function is handed from the initial team to new account management.
- *Reduction of customer attention*: Competitor build up starts with the customer slightly disillusioned about the service levels of the organisation. With current profitability of the existing customer high, marketing force concentrates on new customers.
- *Reselling to existing customer*: Customers demand stronger relationships and review competitors that offer them

better deals. The organisation realises the defection or a possible defection and is forced to start reselling to the same customer.

Reasons for Defections

Why do the customers defect towards competitors or even substitutes when the organisation perceives a seemingly perfect marketing system in place? Marketers all along pondered over this question. Mostly the reason behind defections may be a complex mix of various marketing oversights. Yet extensive researches have broadly classified the important causes for customer defection as:

- price of the product,
- quality of the product,
- lure of the substitute market,
- organisational or extra-organisational politics, and
- quality of customer service.

These areas may not account for in isolation with each other.

Looking at the various factors leading to defection, price of the product is largely a financial decision and quality of the product is generally a technical decision. The effect of the substitute market outside the industry is an environmental variable that largely is out of scope of the organisation to influence. Organisational effectiveness will control the defections due to internal politics, like for instance, the goodwill of Reliance Industries rests on the Ambani family and any internal power shifts towards a non family member in the organisation might negatively impact customer loyalty. Under ideal conditions, external politics is outside the scope of the organisation. Like the new cola drink Mecca Cola introduced in the Islamic States to counter Coca Cola that is seen largely as an American icon. Coca Cola can do very little to change the situation. So that brings us to our relevant realm of analysis—the quality of service bringing about customer retention.

In saturated markets where product and price differentiations are largely very difficult to achieve, what stands apart is the customer service. The psychological issue here as Lynda R. Paulson says is, "Shoppers may forget what they purchase, but they do remember how they are treated, how they are made to feel."[2] What really stands out on behalf of the organisation in the eyes of the customers is the quality of service provided.

Benefits of Customer Retention

The greatest of benefits that an organisation reaps from customer retention are gaining customer's unhindered goodwill, collaboration and loyalty. Organisations also earn the mundane tangible benefits. Customer retention enhances the profitability of the organisation by cutting down on the *replacement costs.* Organisations harping only on market acquisition are just like leaky buckets; customers are lost as quickly as they are earned and more effort and resource has to be pooled in to fill up the customer base. So, effective customer retention benefits the organisation on lower acquisition costs.

Moreover, the happy existing customers are more likely to spend for *further re-buys* during their minimum spend period. Every *new customer* if motivated enough is likely to spend on further business transactions with the organisation.

There is lesser strain on the financial management of the organisation. The allocation of finances can avoid shoe lace budgets to acquire newer customers, since marketing and business with existing customers are comparatively lower. Thus *operating costs are reduced* considerably.

Existing customers usually do not wait for discounts offered. Instead, the organisation makes sales mostly at *premium price.* Striking a rapport with the organisation, they go about future transactions as a routine affair. Organisations feel the necessity to throw in freebies for loyal customers to please them. But it must be remembered that it is the feeling created because of the freebies that pleases the existing customers rather than the freebie itself. "Freebies don't get customers for life, but creating good feeling will."[3]

Effective strategies retaining the customer through one's minimum spend time are a *powerful source of referrals.* This is a service that the customer does voluntarily. To top it all, is a completely free advertisement and by far the most effective.

Elements of a Successful Retention Programme

Tactical Checks to Prevent Customer Defection and Retain

Bundling together of products and services is a tactical move by organisations to offer combinations of their products and services as a single composite product. This is especially true and has proved to be very effective in the service industry. For instance, if Red Hat offers the Linux operating system, it bundles along with the OS, numerous useful third party softwares like Netscape Navigator and GIMP. A consumer, thus, will be discouraged to defect to a competitor like Mandrake who might offer a different set of bundle.

Usage analysis of its existing customer is followed by organisations that have effective customer retention strategies. The usage levels of customers is categorised as heavy, medium and light. The heavy users form the most profitable segment of customers. Their usages are considered usually as more emotive than logical. They are also the most susceptible to competitors' campaign. Organisations almost always prey upon the heavy users because the profitability of the marketing activity is the highest with this level. The medium users are the ones that are deliberate in their actions with the logic of quality of service reflecting on their usage. They constantly compare and benchmark to get the best value for their money. The occasional users are classified as light users. It might be just curiosity or the need to experiment that guides their usage. While organisations need to be always on guard related to their heavy users, it would do excellent in retaining their customers when they strive to satisfy the normal or medium users who are more rational in their decisions. In this way the organisation would be automatically satisfying their other segments and strategically elevating the stature of the company in the market.

Complaint analysis could prove to be a true gold mine for the organisation. The rule number one for any retaining activity is that no complaint is trivial enough to be ignored, because, "with people, the little things are the big things;"[4] instead, positive complaints can be encouraged. Complaints can be turned around to boost the performance of the organisation. They offer valuable insights into the minds of the customers. Apart from attending to the immediate concerns of the customers, if the complaints are thoroughly analysed with a holistic outlook, it might throw up a multitude of opportunities to serve the customer better. Used along with an efficient segmentation of customers on the basis of their usage, organisations can map clearly not only what it takes to retain its valuable existing customers but also how to go about acquiring new customers.

Segmentation and Value of a Customer

Key to any effective customer retention programmes is a good segmentation system and fixing up representational customer values to the segments. Traditionally, the value of customer was determined by the returns on investment made. While this is alright when it comes within the scope of single purchase transactions, it does not incorporate the value addition the existing customer provides the organisation over a longer period of time. As an alternative the Lifetime Value (LV) concept of the customer is being propounded by marketing gurus of the day. In simple terms, Robert C. Blattberg[5] says that, Lifetime Value of a customer is the sum of all future customer revenue streams minus the product and servicing costs, acquisition costs and remarketing costs. It implies that a pleased customer's value reduces the cost of all future transactions to that customer. The lifetime could vary from situation to situation according to the nature of product or service, business environment, etc. The Lifetime can be age, working life, product life cycle, and the like. The process of fixing the Lifetime Value on individual customers being very strenuous and time consuming, the organisation stands to gain by going for Lifetime Value fixation on aggregate of segmented groups. Customer loyalty promotes increased Lifetime Value raising the profitability of the organisation.

Loyalty Profiling

Studies have revealed that a loyal customer provides twice or thrice more business and that it costs about six times more to acquire a new customer than to retain an existing one. In addition, free referrals of the customers help enhance the customer base of the organisation. Management of customer loyalty starts with charting the loyalty profiles of the customers. There are various factors involved in the profiling to be considered as, frequency of purchase, service calls frequency, emotional and financial importance of transaction, product differentiation degree, and ease of switching towards competitors. These factors help in classifying the loyalty profiles and arrive at the reasons for the loyalty. Basically customers are loyal either due to emotional reasons or purely pragmatic ones. It could also be a combination of the two in various degrees. Attempting to satisfy the pragmatic section of the customer segment would raise the performance of the organisation and hence would largely satisfy all other segments.

Organisational Change

Eventually, the issue is not just on prevention of defection—but increasing the spending of the existing customers that truly justifies customer retention. Strategic mindset shift towards customer retention propelled by management through the company culture is crucial. Employees are the determinative stake holders here. The philosophy of customer retention once internalised in the organisational culture by employees, it results a subtle competitive difference. Its importance is vivid in Walt Disney's lecture to his employees of the theme park Disney World, "do what you do so well that they [customers/visitors] will want to see it again and show their friends."[6] Clearly the emphasis is not just to prevent defection but encourage multiple re-buys—in this case revisits to the park. For instance, in Disney World, not just the technicalities of the ride and adrenalin pumping thrills are important, but also the thoughtfulness of giving candy to a scared kid matters equally. That is relationship management at its best

Structural changes in the organisation like empowering employees for effective Customer Retention activities, involvement of the quality control department in the retention programme, good incentives for retention activities comparable to the customer acquisition activities are a few tactical moves that can be done to foster self responsibility culture and effectuate a strategic shift in the organisational change towards customer retention.

Conclusion

The preceding analysis makes it amply clear the importance of making customer retention as the core of marketing strategy. The elements of an effective customer retention strategy emphasise the need for not just a few stop gap retention programmes, but a strategic shift in the marketing thought towards proactive retention activities. This holds the key to marketing excellence.

REFERENCES

1. Richard R. Shapiro, President, Rich Associates '*Retaining Your Most Profitable Customer*' in Best of Class. Pub. Executive Excellence Publishing, pp. 229-33.

2. Lynda R. Paulson, President, Success Strategies Inc., *'Customers for Life'* in Best of Class. Pub. Executive Excellence Publishing, pp. 239-40.
3. *Ibid.*
4. Stephen Covey, Co-Chairman—Franklin Covey Co., *'Serving the One'* in Best in Class Pub. Executive Excellence Publishing, p. 10.
5. Robert C. Blattberg, *'Managing the Firm'* in Chain Store Age Executive, Jan. 1998.
6. Walt Disney's advice to his workforce at the opening of Disneyland quoted by Ed. Yager, *'More Than Satisfaction: Building Customer Loyalty'* in Best in Class Pub. Executive Excellence Publishing, p. 101.

9

Customer Value

Key for Customer Acquisition and Retention

A.S. MOHANRAM*, C. MADHAVI** & A. MARAN***

Not so long ago, companies and brands had any other option but to advertise heavily in above the Line media to promote their services and products. That was the only option, to be heard above every one else. Technological advances and techniques of data base marketing have made it possible to do the unimaginable in these markets: getting to know their customers on a one-to-one basis. As a result, awareness of individual customer's specific needs and dislikes has become increasingly important to succeed in these markets. While media becoming more and more expensive fragmented, cost of advertising and promotion has become prohibitive.

It was established that building closer relationship with customer's resultant in better returns to companies through the following means

- Increase use of company services
- Charging price premiums for customized services
- Referrals by satisfied customers that brought new customers

While these can help to increase the bottom line, the marketer has to understand the customer life cycle management, which is the key to customer retention and customer acquisition.

* Prof., St. Joseph's College of Engineering.
** Reader, Annamalai University.
*** Asst. Prof., Sri Ram Institute of Management Studies.

What is Customer Life Cycle?

Customer Life Cycle has four important components. They are:

- Customer Need Assessment and Acquisition
- Customer Development through personalization and customization
- Customer Equity leverage through Cross-selling and Up-selling
- Customer Retention and Referrals to new customers

Customer Relations Management revolves around the management of customer Life Cycle. We start with customer acquisition either through the traditional advertising or through referrals. Then we move on to customer development through personalization of communication and customization of products and services through a mutual-learning process. Then we go on to leverage the customer equity through cross selling and up selling. We work for the retention of Existing customers and benefit by the new customers that they get through their personal Referrals.

Customer Acquisition

Many companies (including dotcom companies) continue to use the traditional mass media advertising to get new customers. We need a critical mass of customers before referrals can bring further customers (or do we?).

Personalization and Customization

Though this has been extensively studied, the question remains, whether customization is needed in all product categories.

Cross-Selling, Up-Selling and Referrals

Theoretically, cross-selling and up-selling can meet the customer requirements. However, the idea seems to predominantly meet with the seller's need to maximize his revenues by exploiting his relationship with the customers.

Customer Migration

Whatever be the CRM programmers used by companies, there will be a certain amount of Customer migration at different stages of the customer life-cycle due to various reasons. Studies need to be conducted to assess customer attrition at various stages to arrive at recommendations for managers to minimize the same.

Arthur Anderson, a global consultancy firm made a study of best practices and developed a frame work for identifying, developing, and retaining customers as global best practices. They are:

1. Understanding Markets and Consumers
2. Involving Customers in the design of products and services
3. Marketing and Selling the products and services
4. Involving customers in the delivery of products and services
5. Providing Customer service
6. Managing Customer Information.

A company can view the above process in a value-chain framework and analyze how value is added at each link. Expectedly, the processes that play an important role in the value chain are those that involve the customer. The essence of best practices is what companies can learn from customers and how the two can work together in a mutually beneficial.

Understanding Markets and Consumers

This process requires companies to try and map the markets in which they operate, and the customers at whom their products or services are targeted. Companies should realize that the term market is not just their customer, but their suppliers, competitors, and the government. Any mapping, then, should represent how the company fits into the total market environment. The totality of a company's comprehension of its customers, though, is dependent on its willingness and ability to survey them. This knowledge can help a company segment its market, and customize value-propositions to segment.

Involving Customers in the Design of Products and Services

Customer surveys are of no use to companies if the information distilled from them does not reach the people involved in product or service-design. The ideal approach is to forge a partnership with the customer. Intermediary manufacturers can try and maintain a presence on the supplier's shop floor. The benefits: prototypes can be tested in controlled atmospheres with the assistance of partner customers and customer feedback becomes a continuous input not a discrete, one-time affair.

Marketing and Selling the Products and Services

The best approach to the marketing process takes a leaf out of Joseph McCarthy's 4Ps theory.

Three of the Ps—Price (competitive-pricing), Place (effective channel-management), and Promotion (communicating with the customers)—are common to both. The significant difference is that the best-practice-mode calls for identifying loyal customers, rewarding them, retaining them, and at the logistics level, developing a system for processing orders that suits their needs best.

Involving Customers in the Delivery of Products and Services

- A company can use delivery, the time it takes a company to reach its product to the customer,
- And the way in which the customer receives the product to acquire an edge over its rivals. This might involve offering a range of delivery options to become the customer's suppliers of choice, customizing delivery systems to retain core customers, understanding the customer's delivery needs by looking at the consumer's business and, most importantly, developing the distribution capability to meet customer-requirements.

Providing Customer Service

The focus of this process is the front-line employee who actually deals with customer's problems. Improving the quality of this interface by empowering the employee or, still better, defining her role as be of managing the customer, not the customer's problems—can improve a customer's perception of service quality. Companies also need to work on increasing the interaction between the man behind the grievances-counter and the managers in the backroom responsible for the company's policy on customer service.

Managing Customer Information

Technology makes it possible for a company to record information about where, how, and how much customers buy. Database mining and inputs from front-line employees can help a company collect insights on consumer preferences. These preferences can then be communicated throughout the company.

Companies that manage to adhere to these best practices in most of their key processes are different from other companies in three basic ways. They believe that they can improve along all dimensions of their performance even if they are already the best in class.

They build strong relationships with their suppliers at one end of the value chain, and their customers at the other end. Moreover, they view their business not from a product or a functional-perspective, but as a collection processes. Customers-focus is at the core of most key processes, not all. It does, however, have a role to play in all other dimensions of a company's operations, from recruiting the right kind of employees to choosing the right info Tech strategy.

- A company can also view its processes in a value-chain framework and analyze how much value is added at each link.
- Expectedly, the processes that play an important role in the value chain are those that involve the customer. The essence of best practices, the AA approach posits, is what companies can learn from customers and how the two can work together in a mutually beneficial relationship. If you are a CEO, worried about where all your benchmarking initiatives are headed, how does enhanced customer-focus sound? Here is where customer value comes in. What is customer value?

Customer Value

Today's highly competitive marketplace, where mere satisfaction does not ensure loyalty, decrees this. To take potential defectors by surprise, you have to move beyond customer expectations—by anticipating the needs and then surpassing them with constantly superior products or service. Alternatively, delighting the customer. Nor must delight be a one-off offering, which can be bartered for a lifetime of purchases. You must be prepared to do it again and again, increasing the level of satisfaction at each encounter with the customer.

How does customer delight transcend customer satisfaction? The product is essentially created by a bundle of benefits that comprises the core—key elements in a product or service; the ring of expectation—what customers expect; and the ring of enhancement or augmentation—what companies add to a product or service to surpass customer expectations.

Creating Customer Delight

The Psychological Appeal of Delight

ITS people touch—is its most visible face, compelling customers to look at products outside in. When the billion American Express (Amax) opens a makeshift travel office in the middle of a road—as it did in quake-hit Mexico City—or when a publisher ensures that maverick *management guru Tom Peters* get his morning newspaper at 5.05 a.m., just when he needs it, it is forever etched in customer memory. Only companies that understand market perceived quality—what quality means to the customer and what the competition can deliver—can manage delight so successfully. For, it means promising the best that competition can offer and doing even better. When the *Wipro Corporation* (Wipro) handled a project for its client, Sequent Computers based in the US, to upgrade its computer hardware, the promised time of delivery was 365 days. But Wipro managed to deliver it a whole 30 days earlier, generating unexpected benefits for the customer.

In customer-focused companies that treat customers as strategic assets, exceeding expectations has become almost a passion. When the Delhi office of its customer, *Hindustan Liver Limited* caught fire, *Tata Information Systems* Ltd. (TISL) flew down 14 of its engineers from different parts of the country by noon the following day to retrieve data from a half-burnt server. When the engineers took the disc out it was still burning. TISL not only provided its office for the use, but also had the system running within 72 hours.

Measuring Delight

Just How Do You Find Out Whether Your Custmer is Delighted?

The classic proxy: measure his satisfaction. A high score will not guarantee delight—since delight connotes complete satisfaction plus surprise—but a low score will warn you of your failure.

'Customer satisfaction measurement may not be a predictor of customer behaviors. However, it can tell you are what are going wrong". Most important, it can identify the areas that are ripe for the kind of value-addition that leads to customer delight. Blue Dart express, started using customer satisfaction measurement systems

Preparing to Deliver Delight

Delight Today is Expectation Tomorrow

And expectation today is the basic need tomorrow. Self-directed teams and empowered employees bring the customer closer to the organization. If the employee is able to resolve the customer's problem instantly, the smile of delight is clearly distinguishable. For instance, when an *American Express* employee pays the airfare of a customer caught in an emergency from his own pocket, it reflects the commitment of the company to internal customer satisfaction. Amax employees have clearly-defined job goals, which indicate what the employee must do to add value to the customer.

10

Customer Acquisition and Retention Strategies

SELVALAKSHMI*

Introduction

"Customer is the king" and modern day businesses fully endorse the view. Customers will come to us and remain with us if they think they will receive, and do receive what they want, not what we assume they want but rather what they say that they want. With the onset of globalization, customers expectations on quality, service and customization have become high. The scenario has changed from a seller's market to that of a buyer's market.

In a Seller's Market, Seller to Customer

Take as is or leave it, Pay the maximum price
Expect mediocre or low quality, No complaints entertained
Availability or delivery dates uncertain
Pay cash in advance.

In a Buyer's Market, Customer to Seller

I remember the treatment you gave me;
Let me chose the best value for my money
What are your guarantees, your service
I want it, when I want it, as I want it.

The marketing concept has, therefore, shifted the company's attention from the factory to customers and to their varying needs.

* Lecturer, Thiagarajar School of Management, Thirupparankundram, Madurai (TN).

According to Fredrick F. Reichheld, "the first step in managing a loyalty-based business system is finding and acquiring the right customers." This forces the firms to expend a co-ordinated marketing effort with a total customer orientation. Integrated marketing is much more than simply "speaking with one voice". It is the integration of all marketing efforts around achieving business goals—more profitable revenue through effective customer acquisition and retention.

Search for Value and not for Numbers

The term mass marketing is used less and less these days. Instead, today marketers are concerned with focus or targeting. Many firms are trying to decide which types of customers they can serve well rather than trying to be all things to all people. The firms are also particular in spending their energy and efforts only on customers who can make a significant contribution. To understand the right customers who would give more value in terms of profits a focused approach of customer acquisition becomes indispensable. The first step towards acquiring valuable customers is through an effective segmentation and targeting strategy.

Customer Profiling

To achieve this, it is not enough to rely only on demographic information. While demographic profile has a place in helping us determine market size, location, product usage and segment growth, it does not provide an insight into the reason behind the choice of the customers. Demographics do not touch motivation, perceived needs, actual needs, fears and the like. So while we have done well with demographic data and should not abandon it, we must add use of information about behaviour and wishes—i.e. psychographics—so we know why people behave as they do so and can appeal to them on that basis.

Segmenting according to Behaviour and Wishes

Few markets are homogenous but consist, rather of identifiable segments. The psychographic tools based on which the markets can be segmented can be the following:

(*a*) The first is according to the stages in the family life cycle. The stages range from unmarried to newly married to various stages of full nest to empty nests to widowed.

Importantly each comes with a set of behaviours and desires or needs and therefore with a set of marketing opportunities. For example, couples in the last of the full nest stage are interested in expensive durables for their children as well as their education, along with planning for their retirement. The insurance company or bank that recognized this and portray such people in their advertisements will be well awarded.

(*b*) The second method is according to today's many different lifestyles, which include one based on family values, another based on economic simplicity, the "me" generation and those best characterized by a scarcity of time. This would help identify the potential segments. For example, the fast food industry, which has been smart enough to see that time is often today's most precious commodity for many, used "quick and easy preparation" as their core offering which helped them to attract new customers.

It has been understood that firms frequently focus on attracting customers (the "first act") but then pay little attention to what they should do to keep them (the "second act"). James L. Schorr, then executive vice president of Holidays Inns illustrated the importance of the "second act" through the Bucket Theory.

The Bucket Theory of Marketing

The Bucket Theory of Marketing is an illustration used to explain the importance of the defecting customers. Growth in revenue, or profits over a specific period acts very much like a bucket being filled with water. Adding new customers and increasing the revenue form existing customers fill the "bucket". Sales, advertising and promotion programs help in pouring business to the top of the bucket. But the bucket also has several "leaks" from customers who stop purchasing or decrease purchases from a prior period. The theory gives a fair idea about the ineffectiveness of our marketing efforts as long as there is a hole in the bottom, which gives way for some customers to leave our organizations for reasons known only to them. The bucket theory also explains why a relationship strategy that focuses on plugging the holes in the bucket makes so much sense.

The equation for this leaky bucket is:

> New customer revenue + Existing customer growth – Defected customer revenue – Declining customer revenue = Overall revenue growth (decline)

It is more often easy and practical to identify the new customer revenue and the existing customer growth from the accounting database. The information at the individual customer level will give a fairly good idea about the customer migration.

Customer Migration

The measurement of customer migration is identifying what happens to individual customers during a specific period of time. The individual customer may either totally defect from our product or may come down in their contribution of revenue to the firm (purchase decliners)

Customer Defection

A study indicates that it costs a company four times as much to acquire a new customer as it does to retain an existing one. This is due to the fact that most customers defect at a high value point in their life cycle.

For example, a company can spend Rs. 10, 00,000 on a campaign to acquire new customers who may really be valuable only during 2005 or spend Rs. 5,00,000 to retain customers who are profitable now.

Why Customers Defect?

It has been found that an average company loses 10 per cent of its customers per year. The Life Insurance Corporation of India, which has a base of over 4950 agents for selling its policies, has only 319 agents who are actively in the business now.

Customers may leave our company due to the following reasons:

1. They die, or no longer buy products of our category
2. They are unhappy with the price
3. They are unhappy with the product
4. They are unhappy with the way they are treated.

Cellular companies lose 25 per cent of their customers every year and following are the primary reasons why customers defect from such subscription based service providers.

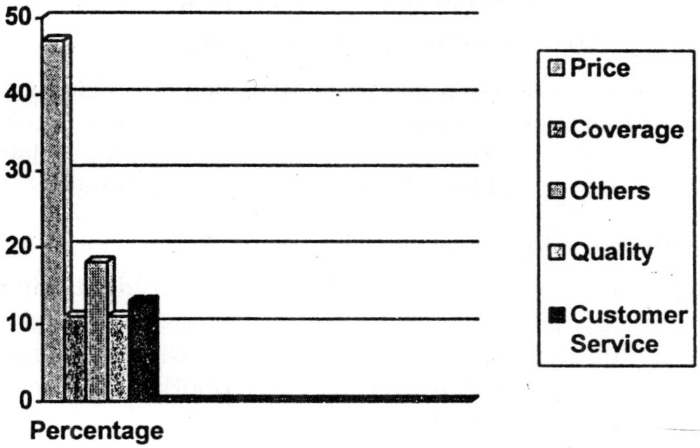

Fig. 1

Source: "Curbing Wireless Customer Churn Off", Wireless Week (5 December 2000).

From the chart, it is evident that while competitive pricing is a major reason for churn, factors such as customer service, service quality and regional coverage also drive customer defection decisions. On the whole 53 per cent of wireless subscribers churn for reasons other than pricing. Research shows that, 96 per cent of subscriber churn in service providers is lost with no feedback to the provider.

Purchase Decliners

The decline in the customer revenue, before defection is often very predictive from the behaviour of the customers. To effectively identify the decliners in the mix it is critical to look beyond the revenue and include product penetration in the equation. Product penetration is a key indicator of customer loyalty and customer churn. A customer who is decreasing the number of product lines purchased over time is predictive of a customer who will defect. The reverse is also true; wherein a customer who increases the number of product line over time is predictive of a loyal customer.

The FMCG giant HLL has its marketing programmes oriented towards moving their customers up to a higher volume in the same product line or in the trial of a product line new to the customer.

Applications of Customer Migration Measurements

> *"A dictionary is a wonderful database of words, but a dictionary can't write a letter for you"*

Thus the most valuable measurements are those that can actually be used to improve the components they are measuring. The applications linked to customer migration measurements that can be used to improve the results may either be:

1. Pro-active Measures
2. Reactive Measures

Pro-Active Measures

The effective measures taken to develop measures to monitor customer satisfaction levels may provide sufficient customer inputs.

- *Direct customer relationship management*: the data captured during churn management can be used to identify features important to particular customers.
- *Personalized, continuous correspondence*: Mailing campaigns and phone calls to each customer can be directed throughout the life of the relationship.
- *Dedicated loyalty building programs*: Customers with sufficient increases in purchases and product penetration should be appreciated for their sincerity towards the products.
- *Follow-up activity*: Upon initiation of the product/service, the firm can compose a follow-up courtesy communication with the customer. For example, GE Cellular, has a follow up campaign as below:
    1. Contact customer by direct mail 1-7 days after service initiation with a welcome letter and referral coupons.
    2. Call the client 60 days after initiation to evaluate the relationship with a standard questionnaire.
    3. Call the customer 150 days after initiation to address any concerns.

4. Mail additional referral cards and discounts one year after initiation with a service contract for extending service for the next year.

Reactive Measures

With the migration measurements, customers with declining purchasing patterns can be targeted specifically to "reactivate" their historical purchasing patterns.

- *Communicate with effective programs*: A winning series of communications can be designed to modify the behaviour of the target groups.
- *Use your best service with the defecting customers*: Empowering service and support representatives to provide fast and effective response to most customers. For example, Ritz Carlton provides up to $2000 for its frontline employees for spot redressal of customer grievances.
- *Use complaints as an Information opportunity*: The Coca-Cola Company found that only one unhappy person in 50 complaints and the rest just switch brands. Unpleasant though they may, customer complaints form an invaluable source of information to the marketers. General Electric's toll free number handles 150,000 complaints a year and they believe money triples itself through the added business from the retained customer.
- *Audit for service gaps*: A service gap is any difference between what a customer might reasonably expect and actual service performance. Then a firm can naturally take steps to fill the gaps. In truth they are easier to fill than to find.

Retention Strategies for Online Businesses

With the intervention of technology in every walk of business practices it becomes essential to devise retention strategies for online businesses. On the Internet, customer retention means, giving the visitor something to remember them by. It is more about making he: remember them than about trusting them to remember us. The key tips may be as follows:

1. Add fresh content on a regular basis

2. Offer regular free publications (newsletters)
3. Provide signups for future notifications
4. Enable for data mining resources

Conclusion

Although measuring customer migration is an important tool for increasing growth and profitability, its value and performance can greatly be increased only when it is linked to other tools and processes such as:

- Integrated account management;
- Customer value grading;
- Employee loyalty/productivity analysis.

While attracting new business remains a critical part of any viable marketing strategy, the company without comprehensive plans to satisfy, retain and cross-sell existing customers begs for trouble. Therefore, a balanced strategy of finding new customers and keeping old ones is the key to profitability. In a word, intelligent customer retention strategies are synonymous with doing business today, for without them businesses in the new millennium will lose customers faster than they can gain them.

REFERENCES

1. Evans, Joel R. and Berman, *Marketing*, 7th Edition, Prentice Hall, 1997.
2. info@marketingadvocate.com
3. "*Curbing Wireless Customer Churn,*" Wireless Week (5 December, 2000).
4. Srinivasan, V., "*Keeping Your Customers*" http://ethailand.com
5. www.relationshipmktg.com

11

Retaining Customers

Innovative Marketing Strategies Integrating Life Time Value (LTV)

P.K. Panigrahi*

Introduction

Recently, customer loyalty and retention are being used extensively in marketing environment. Everyone wants to retain their existing customers rather than acquiring new customers. In this context, a lot of companies have started taking initiatives designing their programs. On the other hand, a significant number of companies design and implement their marketing strategies to acquire new customers rather than retaining the old customers. A few companies are implementing strategies to retain the existing customers. The cutthroat competition among companies necessitates the importance of having innovative marketing strategies integrating lifetime value of the customers.

This paper discusses lifetime value analysis and its importance of use in designing marketing strategies for customer retention. A model for building lifetime value of customer has been proposed. It also discusses how the validity of loyalty building strategies is tested using lifetime value analysis before heavy amount of money is spent on them. It shows how lifetime value helps the manager in taking valuable decision.

In the past, companies measured their economic success by taking a revenue market share orientation. Today, the salient metrics are share of customer wallet and share of current customer

* LIBA, Loyola College, Channai.

value. Innovative companies are beginning to reexamine their relationship with customers, including how much value each customer currently contributes to their overall revenues. Winning firms are beginning to evaluate their economics based upon their customers' overall lifetime value.

The two major objectives of good marketers with any kind of customer retention marketing are hold on to the most valuable customers and try to make less valuable customers more valuable. Retention marketing programmes are designed to react to and prevent customer defection while growing the overall valuation of the customer base. A byproduct of customer retention programmes is customer loyalty. Customers who are part of an active retention programme demonstrate higher loyalty to the business. A highly specialized version of retention programmes using a unique store of value to provide customer incentive is called a loyalty programme. Customer retention-oriented marketing approach using customer data, and especially customer behavior, to determine the targeting, timing, and content of marketing promotions is called Data-Driven Marketing. It is about allocating marketing resources. Customer profiles are used to select marketing approaches generating the highest profit, and to avoid promotions with the lowest profit. Past and current customer behavior is the best predictor of future customer behavior. Customer profiles using demographic characteristics are not nearly as effective in predicting the likelihood of the next visit or purchase as profiles of customer behaviour. Customers want to win at the consuming game. They like to "feel good" about decisions they make, and marketing promotions (discounts, sweepstakes, special benefits, etc.) are designed to encourage these feelings. Data-driven marketing is all about: Action—Reaction—Feedback—Repeat. Marketing with customer data is a highly evolved and valuable conversation, but it has to be back and forth between the marketer and the customer, and you have to listen to what customers are saying to you through their actions or non-actions. If customer data is organized and visually displayed in specific ways, it can "tell", or speak to, the dynamics of a business. The data is, in effect, speaking for the customer, suggesting how and when promoting to specific customers and flagging potential problems in the business.

The percentage of customers demonstrating a certain level of the behavior being profiled is called hurdle rate. Looking at hurdle rates for certain customer profiles over time is predictive of future strength or weakness in a business. The predictable patterns in customer behavior occurring from the first interaction with a business through the last, is called customer lifecycle. Lifecycles are usually required to determine Lifetime Value (LTV). Lifetime Value (LTV) is the net profit a customer contributes to a business over the entire lifecycle.

The Lifetime value concept has been horribly abused and misunderstood over the last several years. It is not necessary to figure out an absolute lifetime value for a customer or wait "a lifetime" to find out the value to use the concept in managing customer value.

Calculating Lifetime Value (LTV) or Lifetime Customer Value (LCV)

In practice there are two kinds of measurement (a) absolute and (b) relative. The second method is very easy to calculate and also powerful compare to the first.

Lifetime of a customer is the most important component in calculating LTV. Lifetime value is the value of the customer over the Life cycle. Lifetime Value doesn't exist without a life cycle.

If one is new to this LTV calculation and have not tracked the appropriate parameters, or the company is new and lacks meaningful operating history, he/she can look for "relative Lifetime value", link it to customer behaviour, and still get leverage from using LTV in business model to manage customer value.

(*a*) *Relative LTV Calculation*

Relative LTV calculation is a four decades old technique. It is still used by mail order and TV shopping companies today. Large sites with CRM analysts are using this technique, known as RFM, to predict customer value and response to promotions. RFM—stands for Recency, Frequency, Monetary value. It is a method of ranking a customer relative to all other customers in their likelihood to respond to promotions and ranking the customer's future value to the company. ROI—stands for Return on Investment. It's the amount of money spent divided by the net profit generated over a defined length of time.

Here relative LTV is calculated as a proxy for absolute LTV value.

Based on the input, the market responds. Customers change their behavior based on the market input. Sometime we get high percentage of repeat visitors (content visit or purchase) or buyers and sometime a low percentage. Repeat behavior indicates higher Lifetime value. It predicts future repeat behavior, regardless of what the actual monetary lifetime value is. A manager can switch money from low repeat item/area to the high repeat to get higher ROI. Here nothing is measured except the repeat behavior. In this way one can predict the relative lifetime value and loyalty of customers.

High RFM customers represent future business potential, because the customers are willing and interested in doing business with you, and have high LTV. Low RFM customers represent dwindling business opportunity, low LTV, and are a flag something needs to be done with those customers to increase their value.

Once you have scored customers using RFM, you will be able to: (a) Decide whom to promote and predict the response rate (b) Optimize promotional discounting by maximizing response rate while reducing overall discount costs, and (c) Determine which parts of the site or activities attract high value customers and focus on them to increase customer loyalty and profitability

(b) Absolute LTV Calculation—Lifetime Value Chart Calculation without Considering Referred Customers

Revenue Calculation

Let's keep track of first N number of customers during their first 3 years (Y_i, i=1, 2 & 3) with the company. Let the initial retention rate is R_1%. Let the retention rate changes in the second and third years to R_2% and R_3% respectively. Let's assume average frequency of visits or purchases of these customers change from Y_1 through Y_3. Let the number for Ist year be F_i. Let's assume the average purchases made by these customers during their visits in Ist year are P_i. So, the amount of money released from these customer's wallet in year Y_i is F_i*P_i. Let this amount be S_i. Now, the total revenue in year Y_i is $RV_i = S_i$*N_i.

Cost Calculation

Let's assume the direct costs (DC_i for i=1, 2, 3) for Ist year are estimated at D_i%of the total revenue (RV_i) for the Ist year Y_i. Let the cost to acquire one new customer through advertising and other forms of promotion is C_1 in first year and NIL in both 2nd year and 3rd Year. Now the total costs for 1st year (TC_i) is DC_i+ (N_i*C_i). Here N_2 and N_3 are the same customers out of N_1 customers who are continuing.

Profit Calculation

Gross profit for a particular year Y_i is calculated by substracting total costs of Ist year from total revenue of Ist year. $GP_i = RV_{i-}TC_i$. The discount rate for Ist year (DR_i) is used to discount future profits so that they can be compared and added to present profits. Discount rate over the length of Ist period can be calculated using the formula $DR_i = (1+j)^n$, where i = particular year, j = Interest Rate and n = Number of years. Discount rate is required to calculate NPV. As all of us know, NPV calculates the net present value of an investment by using a discount rate and a series of future payments (negative values) and income (positive values), NPV Profit for Ist year ($NPVP_i$) is calculated using usual NPV (net present value) formula $NPVP_i$= {values/$(1+DR_i)^i$}, where i = 1 to 3. Once NPV profit is calculated, the cumulative NPV Profit (CNPVP) for a particular year can be calculated easily.

Final Customer LTV Calculation

Finally, customer LTV is calculated by dividing the cumulative net present value profit by the number of originally acquired customers (N1 or N). In other words, lifetime value is the value of a newly acquired customer. The model of Customer LTV calculation is given below:

Model-1

	Y_1	Y_2	Y_3
Revenue			
Customers	N_1	N_2=R_1% of N_1	N_3=R_2% of N_2
Retention Rate	R_1	R_2	R_3
Avg. Frequency of Visits/ Purchases by Per Customer	F_1	F_2	F_3
Avg. Amount made by Per Customer Per Purchase	P_1	P_2	P_3
Spending Rate by Per Customer	S_1=F_1*P_1	S_2=F_2*P_2	S_3=F_3*P_3
Total Revenue	RV_1=S_1*N_1	RV_2=S_2*N_2	RV_3=S_3*N_3

	Y_1	Y_2	Y_3
Costs			
Direct Costs	$DC_1 = D_1\%$ of RV_1	$DC_2 = D_2\%$ of RV_2	$DC_3 = D_3\%$ of RV_3
Total Cost of Acquisition Of these same customer	$N_1{*}C_1$	$N_2{*}C_2$ $(C_2 = 0)$	$N_3{*}C_3$ $(C_3 = 0)$
Total Costs	$TC_1 = DC_1 + (N_1{*}C_1)$	$TC_2 = DC_2 + (N_2{*}C_2) = DC_2$	$TC_3 = DC_3 + (N_3{*}C_3) = DC_3$
Profits			
Gross Profit	$GP_1 = RV_1 - TC_1$	$GP_2 = RV_2 - TC_2$	$GP_3 = RV_3 - TC_3$
Discount Rate	DR_1	DR_2	DR_3
NPV Profit	$NPVP_1$	$NPVP_2$	$NPVP_3$
Cumulative NPV Profit	$CNPVP_1 = NPVP_1$	$CNPVP_2 = NPVP_1 + NPVP_2$	$CNPVP_3 = CNPVP_2 + NPVP_3$
Customer LTV	$LTV_1 = (CNPVP_1/N_1)$	$LTV_2 = (CNPVP_2/N_1)$	$LTV_3 = (CNPVP_3/N_1)$

(c) Introducing Retention Building Programs using Lifetime Value

After measuring the customer lifetime value, the next step is to manage customer value—to make money by creating very high ROI customer marketing campaigns and site designs. The manager has to design how to easily create future value and likelihood to respond scores for each customer, and provides detailed instructions on how to use these scores to continuously improve the profitability of your customers.

Typically, LTV numbers themselves have no particular significance if they are not used in comparison with other numbers to evaluate the effect of proposed strategies. The LTV values calculated using above model could be categorized to high, medium and low scores based on some business rules. It can be categorized from most profitable groups to least profitable groups. One has to come up with a strategy that makes customers happy, then they will reward you with something that you want, but which costs them next to nothing: loyalty.

Some of the Customized Strategies are as follows

Sending postcards, friendly greetings & emails etc. to the customers after a certain period (i.e. in between the customer lifecycle) suggesting for further visits/purchase.

Employee Satisfaction/Training: Training and motivating customer service representatives/employees to adopt various methods (computerized or manual) to "detect/identify" between old customer and new customer and deal according to the individual customer profile.

Getting Referral Customers: After building good relationships with the existing customers, representatives can collect some references from these existing loyal customers and then sending personalized letter or and coupon to these referred persons. If the referred persons visit to and purchase something from the business unit, then the referrer will be rewarded. Some types of promotional strategies should be adopted to get referral customers.

More customized strategies can be built up for your "gold" customers (customers with high LTV scores). One can spend more money on services on this type of customers to get more profit, more referral customers, and to increase the loyalty. One can think up new strategies for the customers who are falling bottom category i.e. very low LTV scores. They have to reactivated or archived. One can spend more money on marketing that are just below the "gold" customers so that they may move up.

Introducing membership cards and membership programs.

Better communications by the service people or employees.

Conducting satisfaction surveys.

Frequent buyer programs, which permit customers to build up equity.

Event driven communications that are meaningful to the customers' lives.

Databases that keep track of customer's purchases, preferences, complements and complaints, which are used to carry out loyalty building services and dialogues.

Integrating marketing programs where the advertising, direct communications, customer service, database marketing and sales programmes are all orchestrated together and designed to build loyalty.

Segmentation of the customer base by LTV groups, and different marketing programs designed for each segment.

(*d*) *Lifetime value chart calculation considering referred customers: LTV with Retention Building Strategies*

When one company adopts some retention building strategies, it is more likely that after a certain period (say 1 year), (i) the old retention rate will increase by XR_i% (ii) Referral rate will increase. Accordingly retained customers, frequency of visits, amount of purchases per visit, revenue, costs, as well as profits will increase. Of course one has to spend some money towards acquisition of this referred customer, which is generally little more than the old acquisition strategy. The gains in revenue may partially offset by increased costs, including staff training, referral incentives, and customer communications. However, it has been observed that referred customers, in general, have a better retention rate and spending rate than customers that walk in off the street. The net impact is significant.

In order to calculate the LTV considering the referred customers, the above Model-1 can be modified. Otherwise we can calculate the above chart again considering effect of only "referred customers" and the "difference of retention and corresponding values" of baseline customers. Then we can see the "increased" value of LTV of customers when we adopt retention-building strategies.

Lets assume that the referral rate is RR_i% for i = 1, 2, 3. The old retention rate of customers increased XR_i% simultaneously along with introduction of these referred customers. Now we can calculate the referred customers as well as total customers based on the referral rate and the increased retention rate. The values are self explanatory.

By comparing new customer LTV with old LTVs, we can find out what are the changes in customer lifetime value and how much profit earned for N customers. From these values, one can find whether the marketing strategies adopted are properly planned, and implemented. You can find out whether the strategies are suited to your customers or not.

Some Issues Relating to Calculation of LTV

(a) Calculation of Standard Lifetime of Customer

Consider a manager who has not been in business for a long time to know the lifetime of a customer. If this is the case then the manager should look for the defected best customers. These are the customers who have spent or visited the most and then of these, some of them haven't made a purchase or visit in some time (6-9 months, for example). When best customers who have stopped buying or visiting, the last purchase or visit was the end of their

Modified Model-1

	Y_1	Y_2	Y_3
Revenue			
Referral Rate (newly referred & also changing)	$RR_1\%$	$RR_2\%$	$RR_3\%$
Retention Rate (changed by $XR_i\%$)	$R_1 + XR_1\%$	$R_2+XR_2\%$	$R_3+XR_3\%$
Customers Retained	N_1 (Base Year)	$CN_2=(R_1+XR_1\%)$ of N_1	$CN_3=(R_2+XR_2\%)$ of N_2
Referred Customers	0 (Base Year)	$RC_2=RR_1\%$ of N_1	$RC_3= RR_2\%$ of $(CN_2+ RC_2)$
Total Customers	N_1	$N_2= CN_2+ RC_2$	$N_3= CN_3+ RC_3$
Avg. Frequency of Visits/ Purchases by Per Customer (changed by $X_i\%$)	$F_1=F_1+X_1$	$F_2=F_2+X_2$	$F_3=F_3+X_3$
Avg. Amount made by Per Customer Per Purchase (changed by $K_i\%$)	$P_1=P_1+K_1$	$P_2=P_2+K_2$	$P_3=P_3+K_3$
Spending Rate by Per Customer	$S_1=F_1*P_1$	$S_2=F_2*P_2$	$S_3=F_3*P_3$
Total Revenue	$RV_1=S_1*N_1$	$RV_2=S_2*N_2$	$RV_3=S_3*N_3$
Costs			
Direct Costs (% will not change, only value changes as RV_i changes)	$DC_1=D_1\%$ of RV_1	$DC_2=D_2\%$ of RV_2	$DC_3=D_3\%$ of RV_3

(Contd.)

(*Contd.*)

	Y_1	Y_2	Y_3
Total Cost of Acquisition of these same customer (No change)	$N_1 * C_1$	$N_2 * C_2$ $(C_2=0)$	$N_3 * C_3$ $(C_3=0)$
Additional			
Cost of Retention Marketing Programs (M_i)	M_1	M_2	M_3
Total Costs	$TC_1=DC_1+(N_1*C_1)+M_1$	$TC_2=DC_2+(N_2*C_2)$ $=DC_2+M_2$	$TC_3=DC_3+(N_3*C_3)$ $=DC_3+M_3$
Profits			
Gross Profit	$GP_1=RV_1-TC_1$	$GP_2=RV_2-TC_2$	$GP_3=RV_3-TC_3$
Discount Rate	DR_1	DR_2	DR_3
NPV Profit	$NPVP_1$	$NPVP_2$	$NPVP_3$
Cumulative NPV Profit	$CNPVP_1=NPVP_1$	$CNPVP_2=NPVP_1+NPVP_2$	$CNPVP_3=CNPVP_2+NPVP_3$
New Customer LTV	$NLTV_1=(CNPVP_1/N_1)$	$NLTV_2=(CNPVP_2/N_1)$	$NLTV_3=(CNPVP_3/N_1)$

life cycle. The lifetime of these customers is the difference between the last purchases or visits date and the first purchase or visit date. This length of time is considered as the "standard" customer lifetime. The average lifetime is probably much shorter.

Customer Lifecycles is a more Complex Version of the RFM Model: Customer behavior over time. Time is the most overlooked and underutilized tool in the Data-Driven marketing toolbox but one of the most powerful. Customer behavior changes over time and these changes are clues to the future. These changes over time are known as the customer Lifecycle; and the Lifecycle is used to calculate LTV. Without knowing the Lifecycle, it's impossible to find LTV. The speed or rate of behavior change is incredibly important to modeling interactive behavior, much more important than in offline models. Small changes over time are to be expected; rapid and accelerating changes are much more significant and a signal for action.

(b) Lifetime of Defected Customers who Return

Frequently, a customer will defect for a few years and then come back. Their life changed somehow and they left, and now they need you again. It is very important to define or to decide the time gap in which the customer has had zero activity so as to fall under defected customer category. It depends on the type of business (online/offline/Seasonal). It can be over 2 years or 6 months. Now the question is whether to consider this defected customer who starts up again, as a "new customer" or an "old customer". As an alternative, considering the customer number of these defected comeback customers, the current new behavior can be combined to the old behavior record and customer service database can be updated. In fact, this information (knowledge) about knowing how long on average a customer defects before they come back can be a useful promotional tool. It again depends on the type of business. In many situations, they will more likely behave like a new customer than a customer who has been with you the whole time. The behavior will ramp and fall off all over again. They're likely to be interested in different products, for example. The manager has to take a decision whether to consider this defected customers who come back as a new lifetime or not depending on the business in hand. In most cases, from a marketing perspective, and for the purposes of Lifetime Value, they should be treated as a new customer. Otherwise, all your customers will have "infinite" lifetimes, and you lose the relevance of the metric.

(c) Data requirement for Calculating Lifetime Value

Much of the data one need to complete the simple calculation of lifetime value, are not available. Sometime in a big company where many players are managing the marketing activity, it is very difficult to be agreed upon what data to be considered. Some of the data, which are important for lifetime value calculation, are what the average unit returned costs you in terms of overhead, what the average number of customer service calls per unit shipped are and what the calls cost, etc. This is a particularly difficult problem for offline retailers, who don't have a database that captures nearly enough relevant data.

(d) Calculation of LTV if the Operational Data is not Available or Unclear

Find out the average unit sold. Break up all the revenue and cost components that comprise the unit. Once you get to a profit/unit, just multiply by units sold to a customer over the "lifetime", minus overhead and promotional costs, and you get LTV. Average price, cost of goods sold, gross margin...should be easy to find. To get customer service costs, look at how many units you move annually, and divide by annual customer service cost. Do the same thing for returns, and so on, until you know the costs/unit sold of all the elements going into a sale. Don't forget credit processing, after sale support, etc. For example:

Net Profit per Unit Analysis

Average Sale Price	Rs. 40.00	100%
Cost of Goods Sold	(36.00)	(90%)
Gross Margin	4.00	10%
Credit Clearing	(.80)	(2%)
Revenue Ship & Handle	6.00	15%
Cost of Ship & Handle	(4.00)	(10%)
Call Center (1 call every 5 sales)	(.80)	(2%)
Returns and Processing (5% of Sales)	(2.00)	(5%)
Fraud/Merchandise Loss (1% of Sales)	(.40)	(1%)
Promotional Costs/Discounts/Ads	(.80)	(2%)
Net Profit per Unit	Rs. 1.20	3%

LTV Calculation and Customer Acquisition Cost Calculations

Say the average customer buys for 2 years, then stops for at least 1 year.

Therefore, we define the Lifetime of a customer = 2 years.

Let, over the 2 years, the average customer makes 16 purchases.

LTV of the average customer = 16 x Rs. 1.20 Profit per Unit = Rs. 19.20

Let, the average customer recruits 3 other customers.

The maximum acquisition cost of a new customer should be 4 x Rs. 19.20 = Rs. 76.80 to breakeven.

(e) Should we include Referral Customer Value in an Individual Customer Lifetime Value?

If it is done, then what are the referral customers worth? It's double counting. The referral customer can be used to know the acquisition costs. It should not be included in LTV calculations. The sum of lifetime values of all these customers should be equal to the business future profits. If someone includes the value of referral customers in lifetime value, then he/she is over estimating the profits.

(f) Negative LTVs

Sometime one can find some customer groups have negative LTV's. Although this very common, it is usually forgotten while doing LTV analysis. It literally means you would be more profitable if you had fewer customers.

Conclusion

Lifetime value is an analytical technique used to arrive at a customer's long-term value to the company. It is a useful concept in measuring customer retention. When a company loses a specific customer, the lost profit is equal to the customer's LTV. It is the present value of the profit stream that the company would have realized if the customer would have realized if the customer had not defected prematurely. The LTV represents the customer's net current value to the seller. Once one manager gets the LTV scores, he/she can categorize the LTVs as high, medium and low value based on business rules. The customers with high scores can be given more attention and effort. Customer retention marketing strategies can be designed by integrating lifetime value of the customers.

REFERENCES

1. *Customer Retention: Integrating Lifetime Value into Marketing Strategies*, by Arthur Middleton Huges, www.dbmarketing.com
2. *Creating Customer Life Time Value Through Effective CRM in Financial Services Industry* by Tapan K. Panda, Journal of Services Research, Volume 2, Number 2 (October '02 March, 2003).
3. *Mining Gold from Customer Data* by Deepak Halan, Indian Management, February 2003.
4. Newsletters, by Jim Novo, http://www.jimnovo.com

12

Customer Retention Strategies in Indian Hotel Industry

S. KALIYAMOORTHY*, S. PREM KUMAR** & V. PANDIRAJA***

Introduction

Customer retention is the key concept having much significance among the companies in the prevailing highly competitive business environment. Almost all the companies have understood and realized that 'retaining an existing customer is very difficult than acquiring a new customer'. A customer in today's market expects more value added service from the companies which offer different products or services to them. So, it becomes necessary for the companies to fulfill the customers' expected value added services by providing quality services to them in order to retain them. Because, there are lot of economic benefits a company receives when it is able to retain its existing customer base for a long time.

Companies consider 'Customer retention' as a key to business success. It has more impact on profits than market share, economics of scale and other variables that are considered to provide competitive advantage to a firm. In fact, it has been found that companies which reduced customer defections by 5 per cent could

* Director i/c, Alagappa Institute of Management, Alagappa University, Karaikudi-4.

** Faculty Member, Alagappa Institute of Management, Alagappa University, Karaikudi-4.

*** UGC—Junior Research Fellow, Alagappa Institute of Management, Alagappa University, Karaikudi.

boost profit from 25 per cent to 85 per cent. Therefore, now-a-days, the companies are serious in formulating different strategies and implementing them in order to retain their existing customers.

The success or failure of any business organization in future heavily depends on how it is able to retain its customer and deliver quality services to them.

The Indian hotel industry is a rapidly growing and dynamic one. Of course, it has a direct relationship with the country's tourism industry. It is a service oriented industry and the second largest foreign exchange earner next to textiles and garments. There are around 1000 classified hotels in India with the capacity of 60,000 rooms. Apart from this, there are many new projects coming up with the total investment of Rs. 1040 crore.

The competition in this industry is remarkable and this forces them focusing on retaining their existing customer base by providing excellent services to them. Of course, most of the hotels in the middle and higher segment have started implementing customer retention strategies. They, too, have realized that the biggest commercial challenge today is building profitable, long-term associations with clients.

This paper attempts to bring out the outlook of customer retention strategies with a special reference to the Indian hotel industry.

Customer Loyalty

The success of any business greatly depends on acquiring the right customers who will provide steady cash flows and a profitable return on the firm's investment for years to come. No doubt, all companies look for more profitable customer. Most of them put a lot of thought and labour into persuing that exclusive market segment that will find their offering irresistible. But only few realize that some customers are inherently more loyal than others.

Types of Customers

The potential customers can be identified by the companies by the following three ways:

- Some customers are inherently predictable and loyal in all kinds of situations. They simply prefer stable and long-term relationships.

- Some customers are more profitable than others. They spend more money, pay their bills more promptly and require less service.
- Some customers will find a company's products and services more valuable than those of its competitors. In simple words, companies' particular strengths will simply fit better with certain customers' needs and opportunities.

It is up to the companies which have to formulate suitable strategies in order to acquire the above kinds of customers and retain them for a long period.

Conversion of Existing Customer into Loyal Customer

Infact, it is very difficult to convert the existing customers into loyal customer. But, if companies want to service in the competitive environment for a long time with the capability of competing their rivals, it is very essential to have loyal customers. Here the question is how to own a loyal customer? To answer this question, the companies have to follow the following strategies.

(*i*) *Building a Superior Customer Value Proposition*: The companies should develop strategy on the development of a value proposition that offers key customers truly superior value in relation to competitive offerings.

(*ii*) *Finding the Right Customers*: The companies have to identify who are their target customers and to develop systems to acquire them selectively. Because, adverse selection can seriously diminish the value available to core customers.

(*iii*) *Earning Customer Loyalty*: The companies should treat customers like assets and do everything possible to retain these assets and increase their life time value. Pricing policies, product line, employee incentives, and service levels all engineered to enhance customer loyalty.

Customer Loyalty to Customer Retention

Customer loyalty is the brass ring of business. Loyalty is repurchase of a company's product or service. Every one is chasing it, reaching for it and of course, angling for it. Winning the loyalty purely depends on how the customer is satisfied with the product or service being offered by the company. Here, satisfaction becomes a significant factor. Companies should not expect that a simple customer satisfaction alone will drive customer loyalty.

Moreover, it is very important for the companies that they must know what reasons make the customers to switch on to the competitors. The general causes could be price, inconvenience, core service failure, poor employee response to service failure unethical practices, competitors issues, etc. Understanding these causes will be very much helpful to the companies to formulate strategies in order to prevent switching.

Customer are loyal because they believe it is in their best interest to be loyal or they feel switching is not worth the effort. Our company's brand must have the capacity to solve their problems and has to suit their needs better than competitors in our price bracket. When a brand rises the bar by improving quality

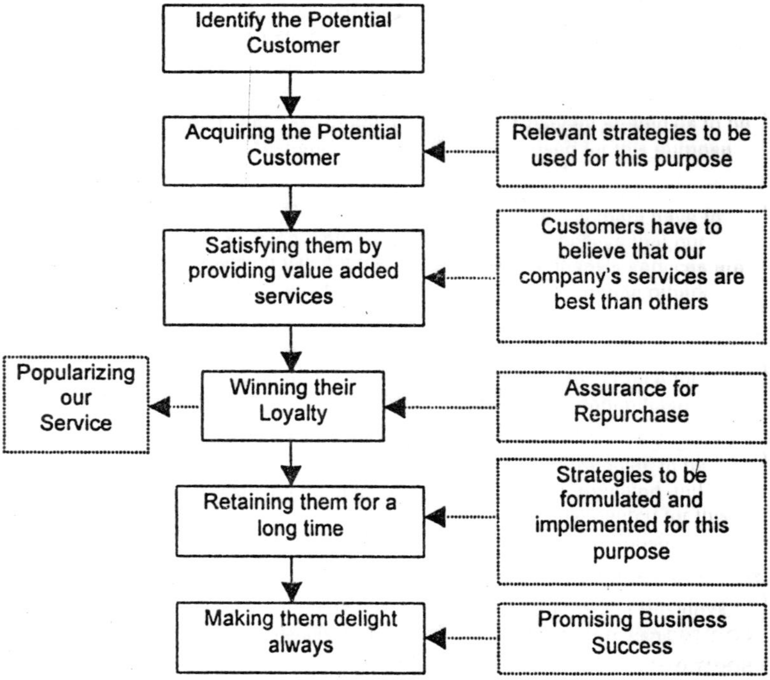

Fig. 1: Customer Retention Process

or service or convenience or any other thing which its customers appreciate, then that brand will gain more loyal customers until another brand meets the challenge. Moreover, the creation of loyal customers from served, target customers is simply a bonus. Therefore the companies must provide ever-increasing value in order to create and retain life long loyal customer in today's business. Because, customer retention is possible only when the customer is satisfied with the services and products of the company and is loyal to the company.

Customer Retention

Customer retention begins by delighting the customer with a dynamite product/service and a positive, consistent purchasing behavior. There is little business risk in investing in progressive value aimed at customer retention. Because, loyalty has been empirically demonstrated to bring enormous economic returns.

Customer retention has a powerful effect on the business bottom line. According to Harward Business Review Statistic, a 5 per cent increase in retention can result in a bottom-line profit increase of upto 75 per cent depending on the industry. The dramatic economic power of customer retention is revealed when viewing customers in terms of Life Time Value (LTV). The value of retaining customer makes perfect business sense when one considers that a consumer retained for life is more cost effect, requires less service, provides more business and contributes to new customer acquisition by offering positive referrals.

For the average business, studies indicate that repeat business account for 70 per cent of total revenues. Thus customer retention guarantees significant current and future economic benefit.

Strategies for Retaining Customers

In services marketing, the customer perception of service quality and satisfaction only results in conceptualizing customer retention. Researchers have identified the following stages are essential in order to retain customers.

Among the four stages, the last two stages have much significance. Because, after the segmentation process is over, the companies have to precisely identify the service needs of different segments. Only on the basis of these service needs, they can formulate their service strategies which must have the capability of meeting the service needs of different segments.

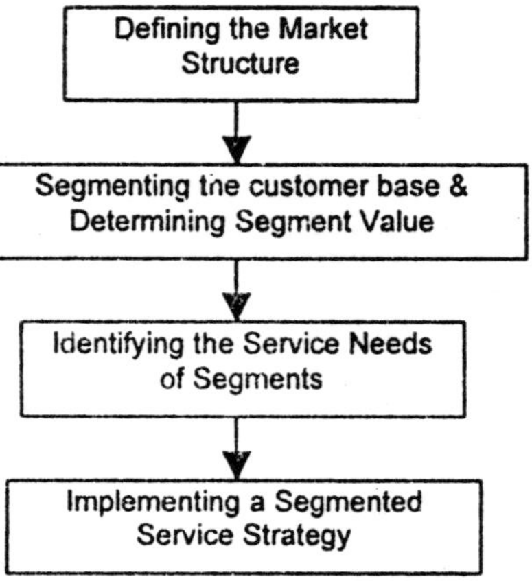

Fig. 2: Developing Customer Retention Strategies

Economic Benefits Received by Companies through Customer Retention

As discussed earlier, when the companies are able to retain their existing customer base, they will be able to enjoy the following economic benefits too.

- Savings on customer acquisition or replacement cost.
- A guarantee of base profits as existing customers are likely to have a minimum spend per period.
- Growth in per customer revenue over time.
- A reduction in relative operating costs as firms can spread the cost over many more customers and over a longer period.
- Free of charge referrals of new customer from existing customer and
- Price premiums as current customers usually do not wait for promotions or price reductions before they make their purchases.

The Indian Hotel Industry

The hotel industry in India is considered as an important industry as it is the second largest foreign exchange earner. Between the financial years 1991 and 1998, there had been a 100 per cent growth in foreign tourists. Receipts from foreign tourists alone were at US$ 1.45 billion in the financial year 1991 as compared to US$ 2.91

billion in the financial year 1998. At present India attracts approximately 2.5 million tourists every year which is just 0.4 per cent of the world tourists arrivals.

Table 1: Tourists Arrivals and Earnings

Year	*Tourist Arrival*	*Tourist Earnings (US $ million)*
2000-01	2,637,641	3,303
1999-2000	2,480,945	2,949
1998-99	2,387,457	3,053

Distribution of Rooms By Category

There are around 1000 classified hotels and the total room availability is pegged at 60,000 rooms. Presently, the total 5 star and 4 star room capacity alone in the four metro cities is close to 13,000 rooms. Mumbai and Delhi account for the bulk of the total room availability. In Mumbai, it is expected to increase by another 3100 in the next 2 to 3 years.

Table 2: Category Wise Distribution of Rooms

Hotel Class	*No. of Hotels*	*No. of Rooms*
1 Star	124	4,244
2 Star	296	10,584
3 Star	288	13,747
Heritage	42	1,012
4 Star	72	5,180
5 Star	54	7,518
5 Star Deluxe	42	10,734

The luxury hotels earn about two-thirds of their revenue from foreign tourists. Leisure travelers constitute approximately 76.5 per cent of the total tourists arrivals whereas business travelers constitute only 21 per cent of the total arrival. The remainder is accounted by the students. Therefore, future growth in premium segment will purely depend on high spending foreign tourists.

According to Indian Hotel Industry survey 2000-01, 57 per cent of customers in the Indian Hotel industry comprise of business guests. In the overall figures of business as well as leisure, 74.6 per cent of hotel customers are domestic while 25.4 per cent are foreigners. The survey has also indicated that business travel had grown over the last couple of years by atleast 10-15 per cent annually.

There was a temporary down turn in the industry during the year 2002 because of oversupply and week socio-economic conditions. It is strongly believed that this will slowly disappear because, globally, leisure and entertainments are seen to be growing industries. Hence, stable socio-political and economic conditions coupled with an improvement in infrastructure facilities (roads, airports, etc.) will improve the sentiments of tourists towards India. If so, the tourists arrivals can increase five-fold from the present levels.

Investment in Indian Hotel Industry

Between August 1991 and August 1998, 259 foreign collaborations were approved by the Government of India. Out of these 167 proposals were for equity investment to the tune of Rs. 280 crore. Presently, there are 127 proposals to set up various grades of hotels at a total investment of Rs. 1040 crore.

Strategies followed by the Indian Hotel Industry for Retaining Customers

Generally, hotel customers are referred to as guests as they receive hospitality by way of accommodation or food and drink for which they pay. If they are satisfied, they will return for receiving further paying hospitality. The important hotel products are (*i*) accommodation, (*ii*) food and (*iii*) beverage.

The economic viability of a hotel depends largely on the following three factors.

- The speed with which demand for hotel facilities can be generated.
- The capacity to ensure and retain customer satisfaction which will result in repetitive business and expansion of business, and
- The package, tenor of atmosphere, service and quality which together, constitute the hotel's standing and image.

Importance of Services Offered by the Hotels

As discussed earlier, there has been down turn in the hotel industry in India for quite some time. Even though this is what the precise situation, many new hotels are coming up day to day with the expectation that the industry will be alright within a short span of time. This leads to oversupply in the industry and of course heavy competition among the existing hotels as well as new ones. Therefore, hotels in India are forced to go for new strategies which will guide them in order to survive in the highly competitive environment.

Customer satisfaction is very important in order to retain the existing customers. Because, customer satisfaction is one of the most important factors which makes a customer to be loyal to a hotel. This, in turn, will help the hotel to retain him for a long span of time. A customer is satisfied only when his expected service quality is met by the service quality of a hotel. So, hotels have to provide excellent services to their customers in order to satisfy them.

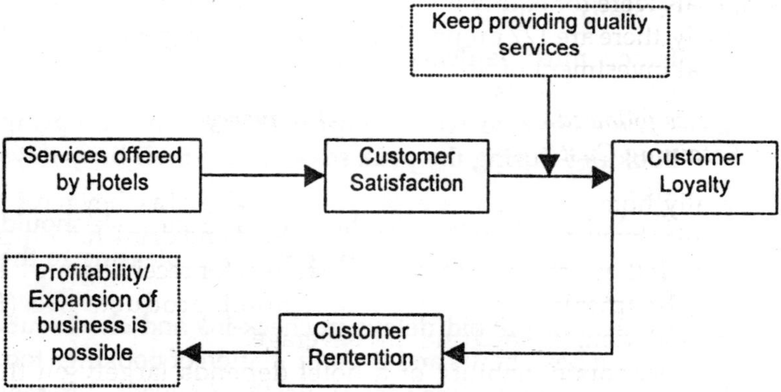

Fig. 3: Linkage between Services Provided and Customer Retention.

According to a study, good services at the hotel are the key in retention of guests. Hotels which have 70 per cent of occupancy are from repeat customers. Services include all areas starting from the first action of the customer to initiate the booking process to the time that she/he departs are essential and of course must be excellent.

Even though most of the hotels keep providing quality services to their customers, they are still not as expected by their guests in several fronts which have been disclosed by a recently conducted study by Federation of Hotels and Restaurants Associations in

India (FHRAI). This clearly indicates that the hotels in India must upgrade the quality of services being provided to their guests. So, the Marketing Managers in hotels, before developing strategies in order to retain their existing customer base, have to identify the areas where they lack in quality service, determine to what extent their service quality be improved and answer how they can provide excellent service to their customers.

Quality Services Required in Order to Retain Customers

The following are the areas where quality services are very essential with a view of retaining the customers by the hotels. Hotels have to realize that excellent service alone will help them achieving customer retention. Hotels, by considering the following areas where they are generally lack in quality service, will be able to formulate effective customer retention strategies and implement them successfully.

1. Hotels must be flexible in allowing early check-ins or late check-outs.
2. Hotels have to show helpful attitude in accepting bookings during the peak seasons and their busy days also.
3. The hotel staff, especially those on the front desk, should be well trained and must be polite and pleasing to the customers.
4. Hotels must avoid delays in check-ins and check-outs during peak hours and in confirmation of bookings too.
5. There should be free communication between different staff members and different department of hotels so as to deliver quality services to the 'guests' in time.
6. Hotels have to keep in touch and continue to inform the customers about any new products and services.
7. Hotels should avoid delay in billing and also mistakes in billing which occurs rarely at times.
8. Hotels must offer other incentives to the customers in order to retain the business. For example, they can offer some discount on food and beverage, free use of business centre, complementary local transportation, etc. at times. Most of these services do not cost the hotel much but will be helpful to improve the loyalty factor.

9. Hotels can introduce leisure and entertainment activities in the evenings in order to please the foreign guests.
10. Hotels have to introduce the following products/services so as to acquire new customers and also retain them.
    - Night City tours
    - Good bar/pub in the hotel
    - Innovations in F and B (Food and Beverage)
    - Creative menu selections
    - Cultural programmes and folk dances
    - Facility for late night swimming
    - Night club with dancing area
    - Ayurvedic treatment and massage
    - Pool/Billiards table
    - Library with a wide choice of Magazines
    - Health club with a gym, sauna, steam bath, Yoga and Jacuzzi.
11. Hotels have to give importance to recognize repeat guests and provide them personalized service.
12. Reasonable charges for business centres may be adopted.
13. Hotels must concentrate on
    - Personalized and flexible services
    - Efficiency in services required by business guests like message delivery
    - Trained and motivated personnel
    - Providing e-mail and internet facility in the rooms
    - Good business centre with 24 hours service
    - Periodical renovation of the property
    - Innovations in its products and offering and
    - Introduction of interactive televisions etc.
14. Hotels have to offer additional incentives to their loyal clients and should offer good loyalty programmes too.
15. From time-to-time, new things to be experimented to further customer care and satisfaction.
16. Supply of mineral water and liquor coupons for the guests at free of cost.
17. Fruit basket may be given on demand, the guest can ask for his choice of fruits from the room services, etc.

Conclusion

This paper has tried to briefly discuss customer loyalty, customer retention strategies, the Indian hotel industry, how customer retention is possible in the hotel industry, etc. From the above discussion, it is very clear that, for better growth in the industry, hotels in the different segments will have to offer new-value-added services to their guests. This is what the gateway of their success. Currently, guest retention and repeat clientele is the name of the game. If a hotel is able to achieve guest retention and repeat clientele, it will definitely win the game.

REFERENCES

1. Ravi Shankar and S.L. Sen, "*Hotel Marketing*", *Services Marketing—The Indian Experience*, Manas Publications, 1993.
2. Frederick F. Reichheld, *The Loyalty Effect—The Hidden force behind Growth, Profits and Lasting Value*, Bain & Company Inc., 1996.
3. K. Ramakrishnan, *Customer Retention: The Key to Business Performance*, Strategic Marketing Research Team, 2002.
4. *Achieve Links Business Travel*, January-February, 2003.
5. FHRAI Study on *Trends in Business Travel in India* (Sept.-Oct., 2002).
6. Channing Rollo, *Manager of Business Intelligence*, Clientlogic www.clientogic.com.
7. Mei Lin Fung, *Measuring the Values of CRM*.
8. True Dimond, *Customer Retention Strategies*, 9-7-2000.
9. Indian Hotel Industry Survey, 1999-2000.

PART II

Customer Service Quality

13

Customer Service Quality Dimensions

J. TAMILSELVI* & C. MADHAVI*

Introduction

Customers today are very hard to please. They are smarter and price conscious, more demanding and less forgiving. And all the more they are approached by many more competitors with equal and better offers. Hence, the challenge is not to have simply satisfied customers but highly delighted and loyal customers. Today, all businesses strive to differentiate themselves in this rapidly increasing competition. They all try to look for profitable ways in order to succeed in competition. Delivering high quality service is the only strategy that leads to success in this increasing competition. High quality in service means pleasing and creating delightful customers and not just simply prevent them from annoying.

Importance of the Study

The phenomenal growth of services in the recent years has led to growing interest in marketing services. Customer service is one of the core business processes which involve activities that enable the customers to receiver quick and satisfactory service and solutions to problems. Service becomes the mantra and many companies manage to deliver superior service. Quality has got various dimensions and serviceability is one among them. Because of the nature of service quality (Intangibility, Heterogeneity and Inseparability), it cannot be measured objectively. The foremost important service dimensions identified are Reliability,

* Faculty Members, Dept. of Business Administration, Annamalai University, Annamalai Nagar.

Responsiveness, Assurance, Empathy and Tangibles (Parasuraman, Zeithaml and Berry). Quality of service is ensured when the various dimension of quality are taken care. This study attempts to recognize the various quality dimensions of service from the customers and to know their importance attached to the product.

Objectives

The main objectives of the study are:

1. To identify the service quality dimensions.
2. To find out the order of preference of the service quality dimensions.
3. To identify whether the order of preference of service dimension varies from product to product.

Methodology

To study the above specified objectives, first attempt was made to identify the various quality dimensions of service from the customers.

In the first stage, pretest I was conducted with a sample size of 15, to identify the service quality dimensions. First, a brief description of service quality was explained to the respondents and the various dimensions of service quality were generated. From the responses nine majority dimensions were taken for the study.

In the second stage, pretest II was conducted with the same sample size of 15, for product selection. According to Stephen, consumer durables may be classified into four categories namely, (i) Housing and home furnishing, (ii) Appliances and personal care Equipment, (iii) Communication, Education and Entertainment products and (iv) Transport. The articles for each of the above category were listed and supplied to the respondents to enable them to understand the products under each category. To determine the products for the study, the respondents were asked to rank three products which they own in each category according to their importance, and also to specify the type of vehicle they owned. For the first three ranks, given to the various products by the respondents, weightage 3, 2 and 1 respectively were assigned. Through this ranking and assignment of points a single product with maximum weightage under each category was determined.

Thus, the products, refrigerators, almirah, computer and two-wheeler representing appliances, home furnishing, educational and transport segments respectively were chosen for the study.

In the third stage, pretest III was conducted with a sample size of 30, to find out the order of preference of service quality dimensions for all the 4 different products. Standardized questionnaire was prepared in which the 9 service quality dimensions were listed and the respondents were asked to rank the service quality dimensions based on the importance.

Corn-bach alpha was used to measure the reliability of the questionnaire and the alpha value for 4 products was found to be in the range of 0.84 to 0.91, which reflected on the high degree of internal consistency.

Sampling Design

The sample for the study was drawn from Annamlainagar by taking a random sample of 100 respondents. Among the 100 respondents, 79 were found to be fit for further analysis.

Tools for Analysis

The generated data had been duly analyzed using the statistical tools viz., rank correlation test for agreement and non-parametric multiple comparison test.

Analysis

To identify the importance of service quality dimensions the respondents were asked to rank the service dimensions for all the four products. Rank correlation test for agreement in multiple judgments was applied and the result was found to be significant at .1% level. (For refrigerator F value is 266.8 for d.f (9,702) at 1 per cent level). When the similar test was carried out for the products, almirah representing furniture category, two-wheeler representing transport, segment computer from educational products the F value is observed to be significant at 1 per cent level.

S. No.	*Product*	*F Value*	*d.f*	*L.O.S.*
1.	Refrigerator	26.68	(9,702)	< 0.001
2.	Almirah	28.81	"	"
3.	Computer	36.67	"	"
4.	Two-wheeler	30.92	"	"

Products/Ranks	*Refrigerator*	*Almirah*	*Computer*	*Two-wheeler*
I	Immediate attention	Assurance of service Reliability of service	Immediate attention Assurance of service Reliability of service	Immediate attention
II	Assurance of service Reliability of service	Cost of service Time taken for service Immediate attention	Friendliness of service Explanation of service rendered	Time taken for service Reliability of service
III	Cost of service Time taken for service	Infrastructure facility available for service Friendliness of service Appearance of service personnel Explanation of service rendered	Time taken for service Cost of service	Assurance of service Cost of service
IV	Infrastructure facility available for service Friendliness of service	–	Infrastructure facility available for service Appearance of service personnel	Infrastructure facility available for service Friendliness of service
V	Appearance of service personnel	–	–	Explanation of service Appearance of service personnel
VI	Explanation of service rendered	–	–	–

Further, to identify the order of preference, non-parametric multiple comparison test was also applied. In the case of refrigerators, the first priority was found to be 'immediate attention' which was followed by assurance of service and reliability of service came next while the infrastructure facilities available for service and friendliness of service personnel gained the fourth rank. The appearance of service personnel and explanation of services rendered registered the fifth and sixth ranks respectively. Similarly, priority for service dimensions for the other products as a result of non-parametric test is tabulated before page.

Findings

For all the four products, from the 'F' value it is observed that the importance of service quality dimensions varies significantly. It means that all the service quality dimensions are not given equal importance by the respondents. It differs from individual to individual. It is also found that the order of priority differs depending upon the nature of the product also. For example, the service dimension, explanation of service required (executed) has gained importance in the case of computers but in other products it was not so.

Recommendation

An understanding of the priority of customers' towards service is indispensable before enterprising to satisfy their expectation.

14

Improving Customer Satisfaction through Service Quality

C. JAYA & S. GAJALAKSHMI*

"Do less than customers expect and service is perceived as bad. Do exactly what customers expect and service is perceived as good.... But do more than customers expect and service is perceived as superior."

—John Tschohl

Companies that have the latest and greatest technologies still do not always have a great relationship with their customers. Many companies will survive and thrive very nicely by just focusing on quality customer service, customer retention, and customer loyalty. The loss of a customer could imbalance your bottom line and, if it becomes a frightening recurrence, might threaten the viability of entire company. Statistics repeatedly affirm that it costs five times as much to attract a new customer as it does to retain a current one. Quality is seen as residing in the expertise of the professional and in the specific professional-client interaction.

The point of service quality is to achieve customer satisfaction. Customers' level of satisfaction is dependent on their expectations and perceptions of the service experience.

* Faculty, Department of Business Administration, M.O.P. Vaishnav College for Women, Nungambakkam, Chennai.

Interrelationship of Customer Satisfaction and Service Quality

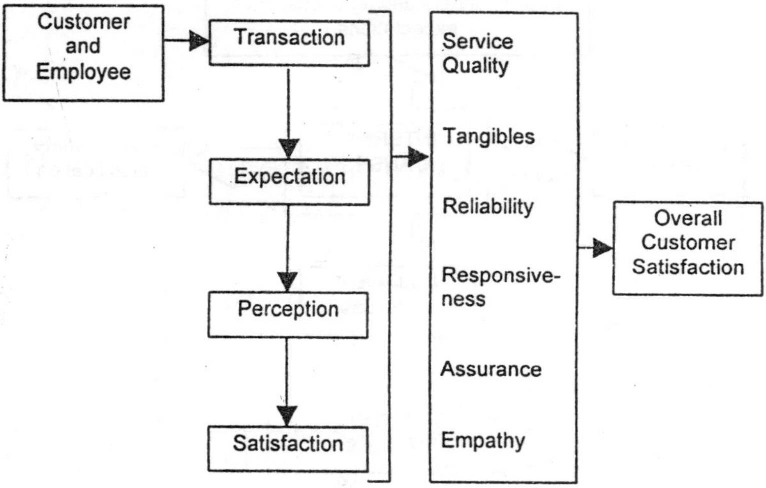

Managing Service Quality

The five important factors in managing service quality include, Customer expectations, Service delivery, Perception of service, Level of satisfaction and reducing the mismatch of customer expectation and Perception of service.

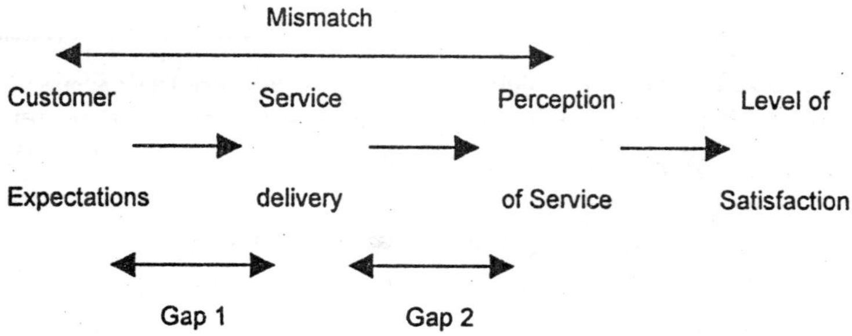

Managing Service Quality

Simplified "Gap Mode;" (after Parasuram, Zeithaml and Berry 1988)

Reasons for the Gaps

Gap 1

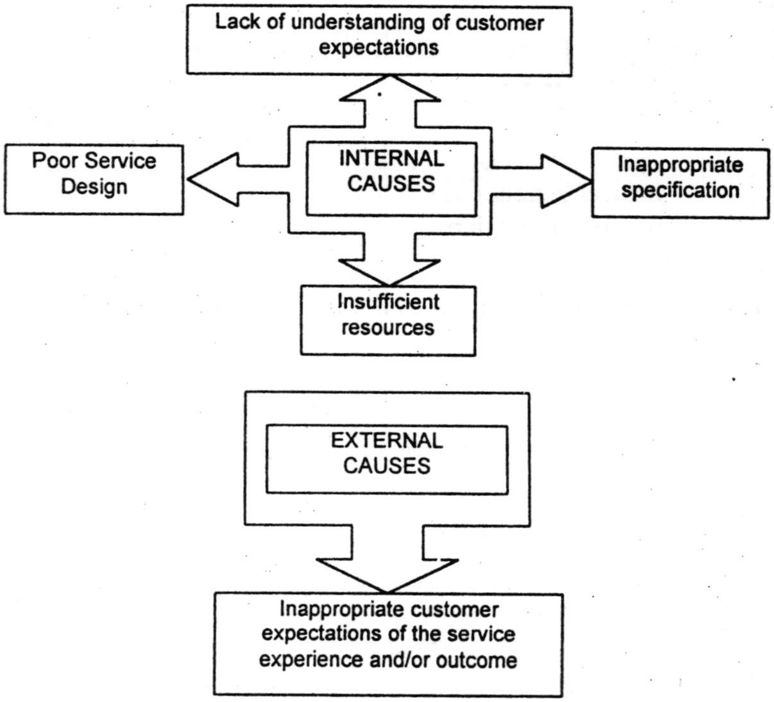

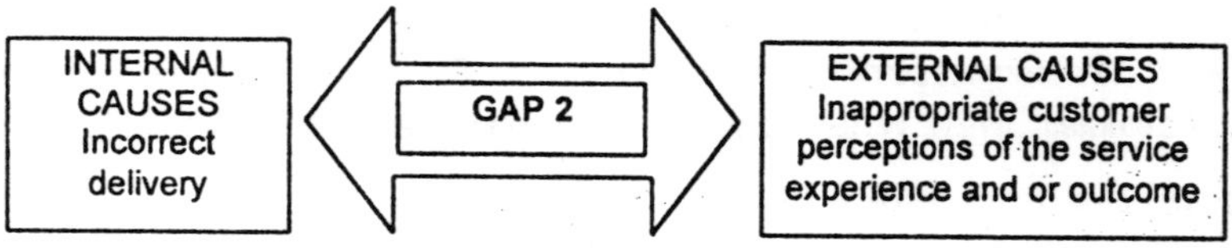

Measuring/Monitoring Customer Satisfaction and Service Quality (1)

A range of methods are available to measure and monitor satisfaction and service quality.

- Complaints and comments analysis
- Reactive
- Can facilitate through installing systems
- Capture serious dissatisfaction

- Customer questionnaires
- *Servqual* which captures expectations and perceptions on a 5 point Likert scale

Measuring/Monitoring Customer Satisfaction and Service Quality (2)

- Focus groups
- Customer advisory panels
- Critical Incident Technique
- Sequential Incident Analysis
- Servqual

Making Internal Customers Happy

Customer service is a major focus of many successful companies. And many of those companies have determined that making employees happy leads to legendary customer service. The techniques that can be followed to make the internal customers happy are:

Creating Forums to Share Information

The more employees know about the goals of the company as a whole, and how each department contributes to accomplishing those goals, the less likely they are to feel a need to "protect" themselves and their jobs by building walls around their "turf." Forums for sharing information can be as grand as a company-wide assembly or as modest as a chat in the hall. A shared lunch between two departments would qualify, as would e-mails and memos outlining what a particular department is doing and why.

Proactive Information-Sharing

Without waiting for employees to ask for information, it should be offered to them. It will help employees to shed their walls, which they have built. The first is clearly defining the business objectives and the payback expected. The second is wisely employing some form of knowledge management They need to know about the kind of internal, corporate knowledge to do their job effectively and efficiently.

Open Environment

Create, or contribute to, an open environment in which status is accorded to those who share freely and don't build walls. Rewarding behaviors–via compliments, pats on the back, commendations at meetings, lunch serving, bonuses, letters of congratulation, etc.—that lead to open information sharing. Treating employees like valued customers contributes to the company's success.

Equipping Employees

One simple way to keep employees satisfied is to use new work-force management technologies that give them innovative ways to schedule their time and match their skills against customer needs. When employees are happy, customers are happy. It's a simple philosophy that leads to top quality customer service.

There's an old saying,

> *"A happy customer will tell one person about his experience, but an unhappy customer will tell eight people about it."*

While customers often become frustrated with employees who aren't equipped to handle their needs, employees also experience frustration when their skill sets don't match.

Staffing Technologies

Use of technology in Staffing can play a key role in aligning employee skill sets with customer requirements—making sure the right employee, with the right skills, answers a customer's inquiry at the right time. By identifying the skill requirements for certain customers and matching skills with corresponding employee, companies can eliminate unnecessary frustrations for the customer and the employee. Incorrectly assigned employees who do not have the appropriate skill sets waste not only customer's time, but also their own time.

Skills-based Routing

Skill-based routing makes sure that employees are utilizing their expertise, feeling satisfied with their work and aren't leaving customers waiting. This in turn saves the company time, increases customer satisfaction and adds stability to workflow through efficiency of employee deployment and increased employee retention. Not all customers' needs are the same and not all employees can handle every type of need. Organisations can utilize technology to better understand customer wants and subsequently match that customer with the most appropriate employee. Automatic pre-qualification of customer needs insures the greatest level of success in setting the tone for consistently pleasant and effective customer-employee interaction.

Right Technology

The employee personifies an organization. He is the public face of a company and becomes the first destination for customers who respond to a direct marketing program, have a question about the status of an order, or need a product or information. Therefore, smart businesses want to make sure that the employee is able to respond to customer's inquiries quickly, cheerfully and with the right answer. The key to keeping customer service representatives happy, motivated, and productive is to deploy technology that makes their jobs easier. Technology can be used easily to staff appropriately, increase response times, and make sure that the right employee answers the right call at the right time. Interactions with the employee can often be the first point of contact that a customer has with a company; a positive, enjoyable experience can lead to high customer loyalty and repeat purchases over time. Clearly, the right technology can ensure that employees have the tools they need to help customers, and ultimately help the company.

Know Your Customers

> *"The sale merely consummates the courtship. Then the marriage begins. How good the marriage is depends on how well the relationship is managed by the seller."*
>
> —Theodore Levitt

Most customers' still want the human touch. They still want to talk with a person, interact with a "warm body", and get their problem resolved or purchase confirmed by a real person. The value of direct, personal communication cannot be underestimated. Personal relationships with customers—face to face or on the phone—allows gauging their mood, intent and level of satisfaction. You can also build trust, demonstrate accountability, answer questions, ask for feedback, dispel rumors and anticipate or solve problems. You can explain and sell new products or services, provide company updates and subtly up sell when appropriate. But most importantly, you can show that you care by learning more about your client and their business—which in the long run will enable you to serve their needs even better.

Improving Customer Satisfaction Through Service Quality-Strategies

This begins with basic information gathering and culmination in the execution of various strategies. Following is a template that, while not all-inclusive, can put the organization well on its way towards becoming more customer-centric.

1. In advance, find out who your end customers are? And find out what they want and expect? In other words "Anticipate their needs!"
2. Understand what you have to offer them that matches their wants?
3. Provide the goods and/or services to the customers in a manner that is enjoyable. Overcompensate your behavior.
4. Be sure that the customer perceives value from the experience.
5. During the process, make sure that the customer feels important and cared for? Don't "hover over them" and don't ignore them as well.
6. Study their actions, facial expressions, tone of voice, hand gestures and analyze what your interaction should be.
7. Ask them if they would like some more of this or another product or service.
8. When completed, ask them how they enjoyed the experience.
9. Analyze their answer and "brainstorm" how to make it better the next time.

Knowing What Strategy the Competitors use to build customer loyalty, and what's the very minimum that company can do to keep customers satisfied will provide the baseline for customer-focused efforts. An integral part of keeping customers happy knows which factors drive satisfaction and these can be determined in part by executing a survey program.

Conclusion

Continuing to deliver *quality* product and on-time *service,* pricing competitively, keeping up with marketplace demands and mastering the most current technology available in your industry will ensure service quality and customer satisfaction.

Companies with loyal customers enjoy repeat business, heightened "customer demand and improvements pertaining to margin. They can reduce costs for things deemed unimportant by customers and can demand premium prices for products and services perceived as vital.

15

Customer Service Quality
Creates Value

VENKATESH J.* & P. PERIYASAMY**

What is "Service"?

Several definitions of "*service*" exist. All of them emphasize the following:

A service is intangible, yet it provides satisfaction to the customer. Good service makes the consumer feel good. To understand "service". Therefore, it is necessary to understand what makes people feel good. People, not manufactured by machines perform it. It does not come out of a process in a factory, but is experienced during the interaction of one person with another.

Categories

The boundaries of the variety of service businesses are tending to get blurred. The service sector can be divided into four categories:

- Production Services, such as repairs, maintenance and transportation of goods, growing almost at the same rate as industry.
- Business services, like banking, insurance, advertising, accountancy, finance, market research, credit cards, software, business centres, etc., growing at rates faster than industry.

* Lecturer, Department of Management Sciences, D.J. Academy for Managerial Excellence, Othakkalmandapam, Coimbatore.

** Reader in Business Management, Erode Arts College (Autonomous), Rangampalayam, Erode.

- Consumer services, such as health care, travel, leisure, beauty care, entertainment, information, investments, education, consultancy, brokerage, etc.
- Public administration and defense. Although this is the function of the government, administration is an important activity within all organizations, manufacturing or otherwise.

From Transactions to Relationships

The goods economy tends to be relatively transaction-oriented. Management's attention is naturally drawn to the constant battle for attracting (rather than retaining) customers, and it is on that battlefield that Brand equity reigns supreme.

Now consider the "new" service economy. Services work differently in the marketplace than goods. Think about a typical service—retail banking. A bank customer opens an account, and has dealings with the bank over time. The customer does not reconsider his/her choice of bank at every transaction, although a bad experience might trigger thoughts of switching. This has led to a shift from a focus on consumer transactions to a focus on long-term, one-to-one customer relationships.

Old Economy	→	New Economy
Goods	→	Services
Transactions	→	Relationships
Attracting Customers	→	Retaining Customers
Product Focus	→	Customer Focus
Brand Equity	→	Customer Equity

Why Quality?

Entry barriers are minimal in the service business. The way to beat competition is to acquire product differentiation, which is reflected in quality. The better the quality, the more the customer is "delighted". Business is learn that "delighting the customer" means:

- fewer customer lost
- less time and money spent putting things right for dissatisfied customers
- less time and money spent on advertising and marketing to find mew customers

- less use of costly discounts and offers to attract new customers
- more time to devote to anticipating and meeting the needs of your best customers
- free (word of mouth) publicity from our best customers

Keys to Quality Service

The keys to quality service require attention in three areas:

1. *The Customer*—becoming aware of his expectations and experience, using insight, feed back, complaints and formal maket research
2. *People Management*—appropriate leadership that makes people skilled and empowered, sensitive to problems and response to the customer's needs, with the ability to build work teams
3. *Processes*—to constantly review them, in order to improve effectiveness, in terms of speed, accuracy and costs, as well as in terms of results achieved

Value-Added Quality Service

Quality is what the customer says it is. It is not what the provider says it is. Quality is measured by the extent of the satisfaction of customer. Quality is the Value-added offering that provides a more satisfying experience, which makes the customer come back for more of the term loyalty. It helps to gain a larger market share and it helps by way of word-of-mouth publicity. It takes time and effort to achieve and needs strategy.

The basic assumptions of a service provider should be that:

- Quality service brings in customers and generates profits
- Quality is to be maintained, no matter what it takes
- Quality means "willing that extra mile" for the customer's sake
- Quality can always be improved upon
- Quality is provided by people
- Quality is provided not only in the front line, but also in the back office

Levels of Quality

There are four levels of acceptable service. They are:

- Good
- Very Good
- Near Perfect
- Wow

Management consultants from the UK, uses the word 'Delight' for Wow. Both delight and Wow occur when the experience is far beyond expectations.

Costs of Quality

The costs of investing:

• Prevention	→	Costs of investigating and planning for prevention of failure, systems reviews, testing and controls, training of personnel
• Appraisal or Inspection	→	Costs of assessing quality achieved, monitoring, testing, feedback
• Internal failure	→	Costs of correction, redoing, scrap, etc., when failure occurs before customer contact
• External failure	→	Costs of failure after customer contact, compensation, warranties, penalties, losses, recalls, claims, including loss of customers.

Elements of Quality

Managing service quality requires attention to a number of related issues, such as, techniques to define and measure customer satisfaction, evaluating customer feedback, handling of complaints, benchmarking service quality, setting and achieving service standards, diagnosing service delivery problems, serving internal customers, empowering staff, using work teams to reinforce quality. A product is the outcome of a process. This is so in services too. The process is functional, interactive. The process has systems, technology and people. Outcomes, systems, technology and people, all contribute to quality.

Managing Five Quality Gaps

Here are five critical gaps that may occur, which affect the quality of service. Strategies to enhance quality must focus on ways to reduce these five gaps.

- *Gap 1*: is the one that exists between the management's perception of customer's expectation (MCE) and the customer's expectations (CEE). This gap can be bridged through better understanding of the customer. Surveys, feedback, complaints, etc., help.
- *Gap 2*: is the one that exists between MCE and the product benefits as designed (DPB). DPB includes parameters of delivery systems. The gap may occur while translating intended benefits into systems. The gap may occur while translating intended benefits into systems. The gap may arises because of constraints, limited resources or inaccurate evaluation of the systems' capability.
- *Gap 3*: is the one that exists between DPB and the actual product benefits as delivered (APB): This happens because of incompatibility between different parts of the systems, modifications made during operation, or errors made during delivery of service. This gap can be bridged through middle managers, supervisor, communication, control systems, training, etc.
- *Gap 4*: is the one that exists between APB and the communication of the service benefits (CPB). This gap may differ from the gap three because of the unique factors present at the time of delivery of service. Specific mention of, and drawing attention to some aspects of the service by the provider or by other users, cause differences in perception.
- *Gap 5*: is the one that exists between the perception of actual experience (CAE) and CEE. When CAE is better than CEE, quality is good.

It is to be assumed that these gaps always exist. Only then will one keep looking for them. If unattended, the gaps will widen. When noticed, these gaps can be bridged. The correction may be in product design, process, equipments or in people. The responsibility of managing quality rests at the top management level. This is so, despite the fact that quality is determined at the lowest level of operations, where service is made and delivered. Often, there is a tendency to say that quality has to be managed by 'those out there at the front'. It cannot be. Although the error takes place 'at the front', more than 80 per cent of errors are due to systems which only top management can change. Even for the remaining 20 per cent or less, caused by people at contact points, management must take the responsibility of training these people in the requirements of their respective jobs and building an appropriate culture of quality of service. Training has to be viewed as an investment quality.

Monitoring Customer's Needs and Expectations

Monitoring will try to identify critical areas of expectations, and see what elements could be built into either product features or processes, to satisfy those expectations. These elements would then be the parameters of quality.

Customer's needs and expectations can be monitored through:

- Market research and surveys
- Observation of customer behaviour and responses
- Data regarding offers from competition
- Complaints
- Personal contact with customers
- Focus groups
- Comment/feedback forms from users

The True Lifetime Value of the Customer

Key Insights	*Action Steps*
1. Monitoring customer lifetime value is essential to accurately gauge the health of the organization.	• Set up systems to collect and store the inputs required to calculate customer lifetime value. • If ours is a transaction—oriented business in which customers are essentially anonymous, set up the lifetime value database on a segment basis.
2. The lifetime value of a customer is usually analyzed best by considering a customer's contributions to profit over time.	• Examine our company's customer lifetime value calculations • What is the measure used—revenue, profitability, contribution, or other? • What is the time horizon employed? Why? • What discounting factor is used?

(Contd.)

(*Contd.*)

Key Insights	*Action Steps*
3. Calculating lifetime value based on retention probabilities systematically underestimates customer lifetime value, because it ignores the fact that customers can switch away and then switch back.	• Examine whether the calculations allow for customers switching out and then switching back.
4. Patterns of brand switching are the keys to accurately calculating customer lifetime value.	• Find out where our lost customers go. • Determine where our new customers come from.
5. Business-to-business lifetime value calculations often require the notion of share of wallet.	• Find out who else of our customers is buying from and the percentage of their business that we currently receive.

Role of Value Equity

Value is the foundation of the customer's relationship with the firm. The firm's products and services have to meet the customer's needs and expectations. If the customer does not receive value from the firm, the best brand strategy and the strongest retention strategies will have little effect. The value connection begins with the customer's expectations of the product or service, which are formed before the first purchase. It is very difficult to create something and force or convince the customer to value it, which is the reason why many products enabled through innovative technology are unsuccessful. The customer will value them only if the customer perceives the need for them.

Balancing the Customer's Value

We all hear and use the term "value" a great deal when it comes to what we want in products and services. It is a term that is difficult—but essential to pin down when a firm wants to understand how to obtain the first cornerstone of customer service quality. Value is the consumer's objective assessment of the utility of a brand based on perceptions of what is given up for what is received.

In knowing what different groups of customers mean by value, it appears that customers define value in four ways:

- Value is low price
- Value is whatever I want in a product
- Value is the quality I get for the price I pay
- Value is what I get for what I give up, including time and efforts

When Value Equity Matters Most

- When there are or can be difference between competing products
- Purchases with complex decision processes
- Business-to-business purchases
- Innovative products and services
- Firms wanting to recycle products in the maturity stage of the life cycle

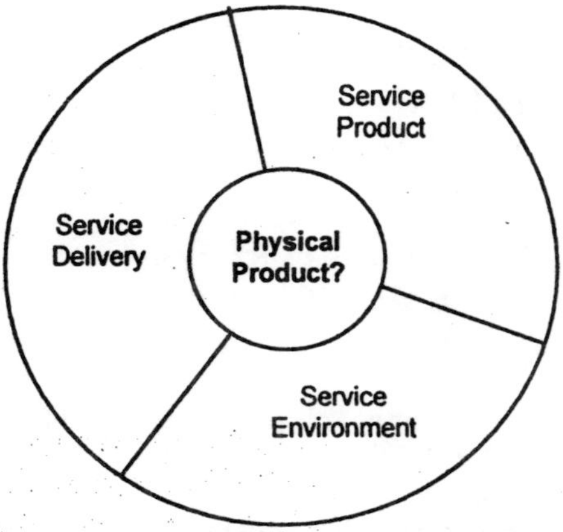

The Managerial Components of Quality

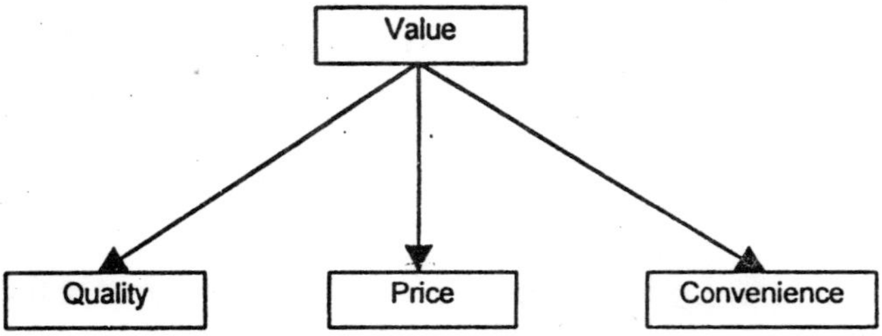

Drivers of Value Equity

Conclusion

Customer's expectations are attitudes held by customers towards a company. They relate to the product, to the service given, and to the professionalism of customer contact. There is always a degree of urgency, perhaps emergency, in the call for service. Tensions are created that build up with every moment of delay before the customer's problem is resolved. Customers are potential customers calling for service, are, therefore, seldom unprejudiced. There is influence, for good or ill, by the way the company has handled previous requests for service. So when a customer has had experience in dealing with the company, expectations are directly colored by the efficiency and smoothness of the earlier contact which relies on customer service quality will definitely creates value.

REFERENCES

1. Bernard Katz, *Customer Service into Customer Sales*, Jaico Publishing House, Mumbai, 2000.
2. S. Balachandran, *Customer-Driven Services Management*, Response Books, London, New Delhi, 1999.
3. Roland T. Rust, Valarie A. Zeithaml, Katherine N. Lemon, *Driving Customer Equity*: The Free Press, New York, 2001.
4. Zeithaml, *Services Marketing*, Tata Mc.Graw Hill, New Delhi, 2002.
5. S. M. Jha, *Services Marketing*, Himalaya Publishing, New Delhi, 2000.
6. The Journal of Marketing, Volume II, August, 2002.
7. www. indiamart com
8. www.google.com
9. www.jaicobooks.com
10. www.hinduonline.com

16

Small Scale Service Business Enterprises
A Study

SAI KRISHNA Y.*

Introduction

The S.S.I. sector in India covers a wide spectrum of industries categorized under small, ancillary, tiny, SSSBEs, Women enterprise and cottage segments, ranging from small artisans/handicraft units on one end to modern production units with significant investments on the other. This sector has acquired a pre-eminent place in the socio-economic development of the country, as it acts as a 'nursery' for the development of enterpreneurial talent. The sector produces a wide range of about more than 7500 products and services.

Industry related/business-oriented service enterprises were classified for the first time as small scale service establishments in 1985 and later, in 1991 re-defined as Small Scale Service and Business (industry related) Enterprises (SSSBEs).

Small Scale Service and Business (Industry Related) Enterprises (SSSBE)

An industry related service/business enterprise with investment up to Re. 0.5 million in fixed assets, excluding land and building, is treated as an SSSBE.

The service sector has grown to 8.3 per cent in the year 1999-2000 as against 8.2 per cent growth in the preceding year. The financing, insurance, and business services are expected to perform

* Lecturer in Business Management, P.B. Siddhartha College of Arts and Science, Vijayawada.

well with the growth rate improving significantly from 6.1 per cent in 1998-1999 to 10.5 per cent in 1999-2000. The Small Scale Sector's contribution to the economy is more than 40 per cent output in manufacturing sector and 35 per cent exports. The service sector in Small Scale Sector Business Enterprises—Medical and Educational establishments are 9.6 and 6.2 respectively. Total employment in service sector of SSSBEs is 16.5 per cent.

The very nature of service marketing requires that service organizations should devote more attention on offering efficient services to the customers. As the services are invisible, they can gain confidence and goodwill through efficient and prompt customer services only. The Small Scale Sector plays an important role in marketing various types of needs of customers. The best way of servicing and prospering in the competitive environment is through providing prompt, relevant and efficient customer service at reasonable cost. The main objective of this paper is to study the quality of services offered in Small Scale Sector at Vijayawada.

Review of Literature

The Central Statistical Organisation conducted a survey in 1991–1992, where the rural-urban break up of enterprises in the service sector as well as employment by segments and sector-wise distribution were studied. In another study the total establishments at all-India level and their location in various states and the gross value added per worker at all-India level was also studied.

However, there are perceptible data lags in the case of Service Sector Establishments in India. Hence it is intended by the researcher to cover up some of these gaps and undertake a study on efficiency in the service sector.

Objectives and Scope

The main objectives of this paper are:

1. To study the extent to which quality services (facilities) provided by the SSSBEs have resulted in increased customer satisfaction level.
2. To suggest improvements in the existing services or new service that will increase the customer satisfaction level by increase in quality of service.

The scope of the study is limited to how the customers feel about the SSSBEs services received by them. The respondents included the customers of SSSBEs.

Methodology

Five types of service sector establishments in Vijayawada city were taken for the study. These were (1) Repairs and Maintenance, (2) Hotels and Restaurants, (3) Mail Service, (4) Tailoring establishments and (5) Day Care Centers. After studying the services provided by these establishments, of which the customer is the main focus, a questionnaire was designed. A sample of 200 customers in total (40 customers for each five types of service sector establishments) was taken for the study. The quality of service levels was measured in terms of following variables[1], which were graded as poor, satisfactory, good, very good and excellent. The data collected was classified and ranking was given to the grade totals. Percentages were used for analyzing the data. The researcher took maximum measures to over come the limitations while preparing the questionnaire, collecting the data and analyzing it.

(*a*) Appearance of physical facilities, equipment, personnel and communication materials.

(*b*) Ability to perform the promised service dependably and accurately.

(*c*) Willingness to help customers and provide prompt service.

(*d*) Possession of the required skills and knowledge to perform the service.

(*e*) Politeness respect. consideration and friendliness of contact personnel.

(*f*) Trust worthiness, believability, honesty of the service provider.

(*g*) Freedom from danger, risk or doubt.

(*h*) Approachability and ease of contact.

(*i*) Keeping customers informed in language they can understand and listening to them.

(*j*) Making the effort to know customers and their needs.

With the increasing sophistication in products we find the product support service emerging as an important service

1. Delivering Service Quality—Zeithaml, Berry, Parasuram.

generating sector of the economy. A number of skilled, semi-skilled and manual workers are found getting employment facilities. These services improve the level of efficiency of the products. It is felt that a hazardous and unplanned development of service centers has very much been instrumental in aggravating the problems of the customers. It is against this background that Repair and Maintenance service is selected for the study.

Table 1: Opinion of the Respondents for Repair and Maintenance Service

Particulars	*Poor*	*Satisfactory*	*Good*	*Very Good*	*Excellent*	*Total*
Tangibles	12 (30%)	9 (22.5%)	8 (20%)	8 (20%)	3 (7.5%)	40
Reliability	10 (25%)	8 (20%)	9 (22.5%)	9 (22.5%)	4 (10%)	40
Responsiveness	12 (30%)	8 (20%)	9 (22.5%)	6 (15%)	5 (12.5%)	40
Competence	8 (20%)	9 (22.5%)	10 (25%)	10 (25%)	3 (7.5%)	40
Courtesy	10 (25%)	8 (20%)	7 (17.5%)	10 (25%)	5 (12.5%)	40
Credibility	13 (32.5%)	7 (17.5%)	6 (15%)	8 (20%)	6 (15%)	40
Security	10 (25%)	8 (20%)	9 (22.5%)	6 (15%)	7 (17.5%)	40
Access	12 (30%)	9 (22.5%)	8 (20%)	8 (20%)	3 (7.5%)	40
Communications	13 (32.5%)	8 (20%)	8 (20%)	9 (22.5%)	2 (5%)	40
Understanding Customer	12 (30%)	8 (20%)	8 (20%)	9 (22.5%)	3 (7.5%)	40
Total	112	82	82	83	41	400
Ranking	I	III	III	II	IV	

Source: Primary Data (Figures in the parenthesis represent percentage).

The transformation of industrial economy has made possible multi-faceted developments in the business environment. Hotel, that is a temporary home. It is a home away from home. It is always important in modern life of the man. Hence it is included in the study.

Table 2: Opinion of the Respondents for Hotel and Restaurant Services

Particulars	*Poor*	*Satisfactory*	*Good*	*Very Good*	*Excellent*	*Total*
Tangibles	4 (10%)	10 (25%)	7 (17.5%)	7 (17.5%)	12 (30%)	40
Reliability	7 (17.5%)	8 (20%)	9 (22.5%)	8 (20%)	8 (20%)	40
Responsiveness	11 (27.5%)	9 (22.5%)	8 (20%)	7 (17.5%)	5 (12.5%)	40
Competence	10 (25%)	7 (17.5%)	8 (20%)	9 (22.5%)	6 (15%)	40
Courtesy	6 (15%)	9 (22.5%)	8 (20%)	10 (25%)	7 (17.5%)	40
Credibility	12 (30%)	8 (20%)	8 (20%)	9 (22.5%)	3 (7.5%)	40
Security	12 (30%)	8 (20%)	9 (22.5%)	6 (15%)	5 (12.5%)	40
Access	7 (17.5%)	7 (17.5%)	8 (20%)	8 (20%)	10 (25%)	40
Communications	10 (25%)	7 (17.5%)	8 (20%)	10 (25%)	5 (12.5%)	40
Understanding Customer	8 (20%)	9 (22.5%)	10 (25%)	10 (25%)	3 (7.5%)	40
Total	87	82	83	84	64	400
Ranking	I	IV	III	II	V	

Source: Primary Data (Figures in the parenthesis represent percentage).

With the increasing pressure of work and decreasing efficiency, the department of posts failed in managing the mailing services which made it essential that an alternative system emerges to cater to the charging needs of trade as well as the domestic sectors. The courier service thus came into existence and became important for the study.

Table 3: Opinion of the Respondents for Mail (Courier) Services

Particulars	*Poor*	*Satisfactory*	*Good*	*Very Good*	*Excellent*	*Total*
Tangibles	12 (30%)	7 (17.5%)	6 (15%)	8 (20%)	7 (17.5%)	40
Reliability	9 (22.5%)	7 (17.5%)	10 (25%)	7 (17.5%)	7 (17.5%)	40

(*Contd.*)

(Contd.)

Particulars	*Poor*	*Satisfactory*	*Good*	*Very Good*	*Excellent*	*Total*
Responsiveness	12 (30%)	8 (20%)	8 (20%)	7 (17.5%)	5 (12.5%)	40
Competence	9 (22.5%)	8 (20%)	7 (17.5%)	8 (20%)	8 (20%)	40
Courtesy	10 (25%)	7 (17.5%)	6 (15%)	8 (20%)	9 (22.5%)	40
Credibility	12 (30%)	10 (25%)	9 (22.5%)	8 (20%)	1 (2.5%)	40
Security	11 (27.5%)	9 (22.5%)	8 (20%)	5 (12.5%)	7 (17.5%)	40
Access	6 (15%)	8 (20%)	10 (25%)	7 (17.5%)	9 (22.5%)	40
Communications	9 (22.5%)	6 (15%)	8 (20%)	11 (27.5%)	6 (15%)	40
Understanding Customer	12 (30%)	7 (17.5%)	8 (20%)	8 (20%)	5 (12.5%)	40
Total	102	77	80	77	64	400
Ranking	I	III	II	III	IV	

Source: Primary Data (Figures in the parenthesis represent percentage)

With the prosperous future of corporate culture the day-care culture is paving avenues for the safety, nursing and development of children. This will contribute to the social transformation process of the children.

Table 4: Opinion of the Respondents for Day-Care Centers Services

Particulars	*Poor*	*Satisfactory*	*Good*	*Very Good*	*Excellent*	*Total*
Tangibles	6 (15%)	8 (20%)	7 (17.5%)	9 (22.5%)	10 (25%)	40
Reliability	10 (25%)	8 (20%)	9 (22.5%)	7 (17.5%)	6 (15%)	40
Responsiveness	10 (25%)	7 (17.5%)	8 (20%)	8 (20%)	7 (17.5%)	40
Competence	7 (17.5%)	8 (20%)	8 (20%)	10 (25%)	7 (17.5%)	40
Courtesy	7 (17.5%)	8 (20%)	8 (20%)	8 (20%)	9 (22.5%)	40

(Contd.)

(Contd.)

Particulars	*Poor*	*Satisfactory*	*Good*	*Very Good*	*Excellent*	*Total*
Credibility	9 (22.5%)	9 (22.5%)	8 (20%)	10 (25%)	4 (10%)	40
Security	10 (25%)	10 (25%)	7 (17.5%)	7 (17.5%)	6 (15%)	40
Access	6 (15%)	7 (17.5%)	10 (25%)	8 (20%)	9 (22.5%)	40
Communications	8 (20%)	7 (17.5%)	9 (22.5%)	11 (27.5%)	5 (12.5%)	40
Understanding Customer	8 (20%)	5 (12.5%)	10 (25%)	10 (25%)	7 (17.5%)	40
Total	81	77	84	88	70	400
Ranking	III	IV	II	I	V	

Source: Primary Data (Figures in the parenthesis represent percentage).

This is another service area, which is playing a significant role in providing the employment for the skilled persons. The limitations of this service sector has paved the way for the ready-made garments.

Table 5: Opinion of the Respondents for Tailoring Establishment Services

Particulars	*Poor*	*Satisfactory*	*Good*	*Very Good*	*Excellent*	*Total*
Tangibles	8 (20%)	9 (22.5%)	8 (20%)	8 (20%)	7 (17.5%)	40
Reliability	9 (22.5%)	9 (22.5%)	7 (17.5%)	8 (20%)	7 (17.5%)	40
Responsiveness	14 (35%)	8 (20%)	7 (17.5%)	6 (15%)	5 (12.5%)	40
Competence	9 (22.5%)	6 (15%)	6 (15%)	11 (27.5%)	8 (20%)	40
Courtesy	6 (15%)	9 (22.5%)	7 (17.5%)	8 (20%)	10 (25%)	40
Credibility	8 (20%)	7 (17.5%)	9 (22.5%)	10 (25%)	6 (15%)	40
Security	10 (25%)	8 (20%)	9 (22.5%)	8 (20%)	5 (12.5%)	40
Access	7 (17.5%)	7 (17.5%)	9 (22.5%)	7 (17.5%)	10 (25%)	40

(Contd.)

(Contd.)

Particulars	*Poor*	*Satisfactory*	*Good*	*Very Good*	*Excellent*	*Total*
Communications	6 (15%)	8 (20%)	10 (25%)	10 (25%)	6 (15%)	40
Understanding Customer	6 (15%)	7 (17.5%)	9 (22.5%)	10 (25%)	8 (20%)	40
Total	83	78	81	86	72	400
Ranking	II	IV	III	I	V	

Source: Primary Data (Figures in the parenthesis represent percentage).

Table 6: Showing the Rating of Services by the Customers

Particulars	*Poor*	*Satisfactory*	*Good*	*Very Good*	*Excellent*
Repair and maintenance	112	82	82	83	41
Percentage	28%	20.5%	20.5%	20.75%	10.25%
Hotel and restaurant	87	82	83	84	64
Percentage	21.75%	20.5%	20.75%	21%	16%
Mail service (courier)	102	77	80	77	64
Percentage	25.5%	19.25%	20%	19.25%	16%
Day-care centers	81	77	84	88	70
Percentage	20.25%	19.25%	21%	22%	17.5%
Tailoring establishments	83	78	81	86	72
Percentage	20.75%	19.5%	20.25%	21.5%	18%

Findings

Results of the survey are presented in the table. Findings are summarized as follows:

- In repair and maintenance service units 112 responses out of 400 responses are rating them as poor which is 28 per cent and only 41 responses are rating them as excellent with 10.25 per cent. Very good is rated by 83 responses which is 20.75 per cent and 82 responses are rating the services as satisfactory and good with 20.5 per cent.
- In hotel and restaurant service units 87 responses out of 400 responses are rating the services as poor which is 21.75 per cent, 84 responses which is 21 per cent

responded the services as very good, 83 responses which is 20.75 per cent responded the services as good, 82 responses which is 20.5 per cent is rating them as satisfactory and only 64 responses i.e., 16 per cent rated the services is excellent.

- In mail services units 102 responses out of 400 responses are of the opinion that the performance is poor with 25.5 per cent, 80 responses with 20 per cent opinion that it is good, 77 responses with 19.25 per cent opinion that the services performed are satisfactory, another 77 responses with 19.25 per cent opinion that the services performed are very good, and only 64 responses with 16 per cent opinion that the services are excellent.
- In day-care service units 81 responses out of 400 responses are of the opinion that the performance poor with 20.25 per cent, 88 responses are in favor of very good with 22 per cent, 84 responses are in favor of good with 21 per cent, 77 responses are satisfactory with 19.25 per cent while only 70 responses i.e., 17.5 per cent is in favor of excellent rating.
- In tailoring establishment units 86 responses out of 400 responses are of the opinion that the services are rated very good with 21.5 per cent, 83 responses rated the services as poor with 20.75 per cent, 81 responses rated the services as good with 20.25 per cent, 78 responses rated the services as good with 19.5 per cent and 72 responses rated the services as excellent with 18 per cent.
- Of all the five units the highest rating for excellent category is given to tailoring establishments with 18 per cent, second by day-care centers with 17.5 per cent, followed by mail service units and hotel and restaurant units with 16 per cent and the least rating is given to repair and maintenance services units with 10.25 per cent.
- Highest rating poor is given to repair and maintenance units with 28 per cent, mail services being the second with 25.5 per cent, third being tailoring establishments with 20.75 per cent, hotel and restaurants being fourth with 21.75 per cent and day care centers with least in poor rating with 20.25 per cent.

Conclusions and Suggestions

- Management does not accurately perceive customer expectations.
- Management perceptions of customer expectations are not well translated into service specifications.
- Service specifications are not properly executed.
- Service execution (Service to be expected) is not communicated to customers.
- Customer does not perceive Service executed accurately.
- Unplanned development and expansion has been inviting multi-dimensional problems.
- There is no proper application of marketing principles in the small-scale service business enterprises.
- There must be training to the small-scale service business entrepreneurs about the consumer behavior, marketing, and management principles, and technical support-training etc., by support institutions.
- There should not be any gap between what is promised and what is performed.
- Communication between the customer and organization is not clear—give clear service specifications.
- There is every chance for the new player to enter the field and be successful either in existing services or new services, as customers rating poor is very high so improve the services that being offered now.

REFERENCES

1. Hellen Wood Ruffe *"Services Marketing"*, Macmillan India Ltd., 1995.
2. Holly Edmunds *"AMA Complete Guide to Marketing Research for Small Business"* NTC Business Books, Illinois, U.S.A.
3. S.M. Jha, *"Services Marketing"*, Himalaya Publishing House, 2003.
4. Dr. T.M. Joseph *"Management of Services"*, Himalaya Publishing House, 2002.
5. Vasanthi Venugopal, Raghu V.N., *"Services Marketing"*, Himalaya Publishing House, 2002.
6. SIDBI Report on Small Scale Industries Sector 2000.
7. The Indian Journal of Commerce, vol. 52, no. 1, January-March 1999.

17

Has Service Gone Out of Services?

The Case of Indian Higher Education Institutions

S.V. NARAYANAN* & P. RUPA RANI**

As the contribution of the services sector to the GDP of most economies is rising, the Sector is sought to be promoted by government and individual, in order to enhance the foreign exchange position and to Strengthen the institutions in the sector. One such form is the Higher Education Institutions (HEI)-Viz. Universities and related organizations. In recent times, in view of its vast HEI network, India has began to take steps in this direction through EdCIL—an educational consulting organization attached to MHRD—and by encouraging HEIs to enter into Memoranda of Understanding (MOU) with other HEIs across the globe.

On the other hand, Indian HEIs seem to have developed many dysfunctional features. They have depleting state-support for their finances, their academic programmes are perceived to be irrelevant, their approach archaic, and their output pretentious and cosmetic.

As jobs take precedence a recessionary economy in the drop-out rate has increased and HEIs appear to be running on rationalizations rather than on value-for-money basis.

Have HEIs no role to play in India? Are HEIs not part of services sector? Why do they have a poor image in general? What can be done about it? How can HEIs as part of the services sector, improve their performance and market themselves successfully? These are some of the questions that the paper hopes to answer.

* Senior Professor and Dean (Former Interim Vice Chancellor).

** Researcher (Ex. Lecturer) School of Management, Pondicherry University.

Services Sector

Essentially intangible, services are "Products" offered by one person to another. The services sector includes a variety of services, which are classified in various ways (such as: People/equipments-based, Client's presence, Personal/business-need, provider's goals/ownership, mind/body direction, continues/discrete delivery, customization, etc.). The contribution of the services sector to the GDP of economies is so significant that developed countries are also alternatively called service economies. For India too, it has crossed half of the GDP.

Although there are several industries within the services sector, the Indian government is prioritizing those industries that have the greatest and swiftest potential. In recent times, the government has begun to focus on Software, Tourism and Higher Education. The linkage is obvious: Software and Higher education could synergies into ITES; Tourism and Higher education could synergies to have educational as a Tourism motive-category; and the three, could synergies to trigger a business-multiplier.

Of these, work appears to have done on Software and Tourism, while little material is seen on Higher education as a marketable service. Hence this paper has examined it.

Higher Education

In India higher education network is vast. There are about 278 Universities under various categories (such as: Central/State, Open, Women, Language, Discipline-specific, Rural, etc.) Millions of students are taught thousands of courses by lakhs of teachers in HEIs located all over the country. The Central and State governments spend thousands of crores on these institutions. Apex institutions (like UGC, AICTE, MIC, etc.) try to ensure that quality does not deteriorate and standardization between institutions is made possible.

Thus the Indian Higher education system is not only vast but has great marketable potential too.

If they are marketable, why are HEIs unable to fill in all the seats, and why are students (from India and abroad) not so attracted despite the variety and lower expenses?

It is the thesis of this paper that the failure of Indian HEIs is due to their failure on the services front:

- Because they have forgotten that they are part of the services sector.
- Because, if they understand their goals well enough to improve themselves, they can promote themselves successfully.

Why is Higher Education Sought?

It appears that Higher Education is sought for these reasons:

1. To get a good job
2. To "complete" one's education
3. To "kill time" while awaiting (like marriage or job posting)
4. To gain knowledge
5. To obtain social status.

By contrast, HEIs seem to think otherwise. Therefore, they offer Curriculum-constrained knowledge through an inflexible delivery and evaluation system within a fixed time frame. The livelihood facet is largely ignored.

What HEIs Do?

Have decided on such as contrasting objective, HEIs concentrate on these activities:

1. Preparing the curricula
2. Selecting the students and teachers
3. Teaching the courses
4. Evaluating the students
5. Monitoring the processes and students
6. Administering the system.

Over a period of time, it is seen that procedures become more important than purposes and, on occasion, even persons and procedures become more important than principles! Bureaucratization and compromises result.

As this has taken away the services orientation from the services sector, the Public Image of HEIs has begun to dip.

What Service Orientation?

While balancing the stakeholder-interests is the corner-store of good governance, customer-satisfaction is crucial for organizational continuity in a competitive environment.

Dissatisfaction results when the Actuals are (or are perceived to be) inferior to the Expected (or promised). This is true of Higher education too.

Gaps

These vacant spaces cause unsuccessful service delivery:

1. *Customer Expectation and Management Perception*: The student may want a degree while the Universities thinks he wants knowledge!
2. *Management Expectation and Quality Specifications*: Expecting a high pass percentage with inferior students and teacher inputs.
3. *Quality—Specification and Service Delivery*: While knowledge acquisition is expected, the number of class-hours available may be inadequate to transmit it.
4. *Service Delivery and External Communication*: Impressive prospectus and brochures may not be matcher by reality, which could be quite unpleasant.
5. *Perceived Service and Expected Service*: As some HEIs have built up an image for themselves, expectation because very high *vis-a-vis* the reality and negative consumer-surplus results.

This is as true for students as for other stakeholders (like employees, suppliers, teachers, community, etc.)

By not caring to know whom the customers (and other stakeholders are) and what they want, HEIs allow things to go wrong. Incorrect "products" are offered with incorrect standards through incorrect delivery mode, and evaluated incorrectly. Promises, therefore, cannot be matched by performance. HEIs begin to lose their credibility.

This has affected HEIs in several ways. Industry is not keen to support them beyond tokenism. Society respects but does not admire HEIs. The nation finds them useful only for scoring brownie points in Human Development indicies. Students go through the grind for the degree, thinking of teachers as industrially unemployable. Governments, therefore, conclude that HEIs need not be supported with non-merit subsidies.

What New Developments?

HEIs were able to survive in the past because life was placid, finances were not stringent, and accountability was rationalized. Major setbacks to HEIs loom large.

1. Governments (buffered by recession, financial crunch and multiple allocation-needs) have defined funding for Higher education as a non-merit subsidy, and have slashed their budgetary support.
2. HEIs have been asked to fend for themselves on a limited support (a) by careful cost control (b) by marketing themselves better to generate the balance of their financial needs.
3. The external Recession, S—agcession if you (like Stagflation), causes students (a) To drop-out in order to take the immediately available jobs, (b) To be disinterested both in traditional disciplines and in knowledge per se. (c) To consider the postal (distance-education) mode. This reduces the fee-inflow and created idle-capacity.
4. The Stagcession also builds cynicism in the HEIs lowering the Morale; this could turn into irritability within the system.
5. The aggressive marketing of foreign HEIs in India is taking the sheen off the Indian ones.
6. There is an increasing view that it is the nexus of knowledge-skill-attitude and not degrees that enable employment and promotion. Coaching, Certificates and Diplomas—even if not recognized by the HEIs—have become more attractive than the offerings of HEIs.
7. The poor quality of financial management has made HEIs to reap the bitter harvest: a large portion goes towards salaries leaving little for even labs and libraries. There is not much left for Marketing. And the vicious cycle is on.

What is being Done?

HEIs are trying to come out of the morass by taking a few sporadic, tentative steps:

1. They offer a variety of "interesting" courses.

2. They enable interdisciplinary option to be taken
3. They permit self-paced study (to complete even faster, if possible)
4. They are upgrading their infrastructure.
5. They cater to extra curricular needs
6. They try to provide a peaceful, conducive, environment.
7. They facilitate combinational, add-on courses (like Dual Degrees)
8. They tie up with other institutions through MOUs to increase their reach and delivery.
9. They encourage healthy competition by offering financial and other prizes
10. They enable national minimal standards through National educational Tests (of UGC).
11. They seek certification on quality through national bodies like NAAC and NBA.
12. They seek international reputation through ISO routes.

These initiatives are welcome developments. However more needs to be done.

Bridging Service into Services

1. *Conduct a SWOT Analysis*: Positive HEIs should analyze the positive linkage between their Strengths and Weaknesses and to leverage on the Opportunities and overcome the Threats. Stakeholder's expectations, Demand-Supply differences as well as the related factors (quality, cost, competition and the like) have to be understood, analyzed, and productively interconnected. The Mission Statement can, then, follow.
2. *Develop Empathetic Goals*: The mission statement should balance the needs of different stakeholders (on education, career, finance, society, etc.), balance the Cost-Quality-Equity dimensions, and balance the needs of the present with the future scenario. Targets and commitments should flow from the Mission. The competencies to be developed should be clearly defined. Grand and Obfuscator, statements are dishonest and, therefore, avoidable.
3. *Differentiate the Services*: There are foreign HEIs and non-HEI (non-degree) institutions in addition to the 278

Indian HEIs; the number and variety of courses offered by them is mind-boggling. Also Distance education, despite its limitations, scores a convenience and cost parameters. The embarrassment of earning while "idling" and the financial constraints must goad HEIs to differentiate them in the market-place. They must answer the question—Why should I study/work serve this HEI and not another?

These are three ways in which HEIs could differentiate themselves and build their USP: (a) Products (such as: the programmes, courses, syllabi, etc.), (b) Faster/Better delivery/and evaluation (such as: good, innovative, reliable and resilient-in-a-crisis), and Image (such as: reputation, and post-service customer–relationships).

4. *Market the Idea*: Successful marketing for a service organization is a two-step process:

   (*a*) *Marketing it within the HEI*: The idea has to be understood along with its significance, pitfalls and possibilities so as to generate fine-tuned improvements and to elicit enthusiastic support for its promotion.

   (*b*) *Marketing it outside the HEIs*: Once the idea has gained acceptability and support within HEIs, it has to be promoted outside the HEI. By positioning and targeting the Services-quality Evaluation—Search (Prepurchase), Experience (Postpurchase) and Credence (Uncertain even after Postpurchase)—the various P's of marketing—product, price, place, promotion, people, physical evidence and processes—can, then be developed, coordinated and implemented with care.

5. *Ensure that the Determinants of Service Quality are Intact*: Researchers have developed ten determinants: Access (convenient availability and location), Communication (correct, understandable description), Competence (Knowledge—Skill—Attitude—Values of providers), Courtesy (Friendly, Considerate), Credibility, (Trustworthy and Caring). Assurance (Knowledge and courtesy, conveying confidence). Reliability (dependable

consistent, accurate), Responsiveness (helping quickly), Security (clear and risk-free), Tangibles (physical items indicate class finesse) and Empathy (personalized to individual's needs). HEIs must rate themselves on these feedback-based determinants and try to improve themselves.

6. *Incorporate Good Practices*: Well-managed service organization have:

   (*i*) Customer-Centric strategic concept, so that stakeholder-needs are prioritized and fulfilled,

   (*ii*) Top-Management's commitment (so that financial and service performance could be improved,

   (*iii*) High Standards (so that deficiencies are lowered to zero),

   (*iv*) Self-service Technologies (so that dependencies on traditional methods are reduced),

   (*v*) Monitoring systems (so that the gap between the factors considered important by the customer and its actual performance could be narrowed),

   (*vi*) Swift and friendly Complaint-Redressal Processes (so that grievances and removed, customers are retained, ideas are churned, and a good name spreads),

   (*vii*) Satisfied employees (so that productive and enthusiastic activities are created and supported).

In the ultimate analysis. Higher education must not forget:

1. That it has to be a useful service
2. That it has to be compete
3. That it has to build a reputation
4. That it has to better itself.

These things are possible only if the Service Providers of HEIs realize the need and overcome their traditional mind-set, so that HEIs become debureaucratised, socially relevant institutions. Service would have come back to the Services Sector.

Recapitulation

Many of the institutions in the Service sector seem to have forgotten the services concept: of being useful to stakeholders. HEIs, which are expected to play a key role to promote exports and to sustain them well, have forgotten this. By understanding the urgency and implementing the lessons from successful service organizations, HEIs could reinvent themselves for the common good. Service would have returned and well.

REFERENCES

1. Brady, D., "*Why Service Stinks*", Business Week, October 2000. pp. 119-28, highlights the major complaints: inaccurate information; unresponsive, rude, ignorant staff; delays.
2. Zeithaml V.A. and M.J. Bitner, *Services Marketing* (New York: McGraw Hill, 1996).
3. Kotler, P., *Marketing Management* (New Delhi: Pearson Education (Asia), 2003), XI edition, p. 446-47 suggests that Intangibility could tangibilised by Place (location, arrangements). People (presentable, helpful). Equipment (modern gadgets), Communication (material, pace, efficiency). Symbols (for image-building), and Price (compensatory in crisis).
4. Payne, A., *Essence of Services Marketing* (New Delhi: Prentice Hall India, 1993).

18

HR Torque for Customer Captivity

G. SUDHA,* C. MADHAVI* & A.S. RAMESH**

Introduction

Customer service is the most critical factor in determining an organization long-term success and also its survival. People within the organization have the basic role in developing and maintaining relationship with customers. Everyone in the organization must realize the fact that their work is towards satisfying customers. The marketing department can integrate the activity towards the customer satisfaction. A company with strong customer satisfaction and loyalty can survive better even in a tough economy. Now HR departments are focussing their efforts on improving customer satisfaction. The employees are given training and coaching programmes by that they can develop and nurture positive, lasting relationship with clients. A landmark, 1999 analysis of 800 sears Roebuck revenues stores, demonstrated that for every 5 per cent improvement in employee attitudes, there is an 1.3 per cent increase in customer satisfaction and a raise in half-percentage in corporate revenue. Now the focus is towards service employees because:

(*i*) They are the organization in the customer's eyes, and
(*ii*) They are the marketers

Investing on the employee to improve the service is parallely as important as making a direct investment on improvement of a product. Because satisfied employees make satisfied customers.

* Faculty Members, Dept. of Business Admn., A.U.
** Faculty Member, Dept. of Business Admn., D.DE., A.U.

It is not possible to achieve a customer satisfaction unless service employees are happy on their jobs. Studies by Ryder Truck prove that when the company put pressure on employees through certain negative human resource practices, employees reacted with low motivation and dissatisfaction, and there is a connection between employee tension levels, poorer quality service, and negative customer reactions.

People within the organization have the basic role in developing and maintaining relationship with customers. Everyone in the organization must realise the fact that their work is towards satisfying customers. The marketing department can coordinate integrated activity towards customer satisfaction. Obviously, people within the organization form the basis for building customer relationship.

Setting Satisfactory Service Standard

An organization is expected to render services in all three phase viz., presales, during sales and after sales. During presales when the customer develops expectations, the organization must ensure quality and availability of the product in time. During sales, when the customer experiences the sales process, the organization must provide the customer an opportunity to inspect, and treat them with courteous attentiveness, prompt reply etc. During after sales, when the sales are finalised, the organization must provide supporting services such as speedy replacements, simplified complaint procedure, efficient maintenance and repair services and so on. Such services, which are provided immediately and instantly will bring total customer satisfaction.

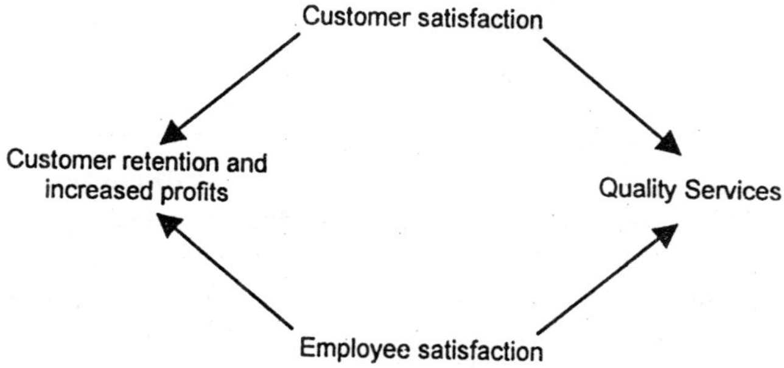

A satisfied employee will deliver quality services which inturn gives customer satisfaction and ends with customer retention and increased profits for the organization. Also a satisfied employee informally by his or her direct contact with the customer can increase the business of the organization and can held to maintain the existing customers.

Employee Behaviour is the Backbone for Service Quality Dimensions

Service employees has a direct influence on service quality dimensions.

Reliability: Most of the time delivering the service in the correct time is in the hands of the front line employees. Even though automation is entered into all fields, if error occurs, it is rectified by employees only.

Assurance: The assurance dimensions of service quality highly depends and on employees ability to create a climate of trust and confidence. The reputation of the organization will help, but in the end, individual employees with whom the customer interacts confirm and build trust in the organization from its reputation and ultimately destroy trust.

Responsiveness: It is the duty of the employees to make the customers feel that they are treated in a good manner. They have to do it through their personal willingness to help the customers.

Empathy: It is difficult to imagine how an organization would deliver "carring, individualized attention" to customers independent of its employees. Empathy implies that employees will pay attention, listen, adapt and be flexible in delivering what individual customers need. Organizations that leave this quality dimension to chance are likely to find extreme variation on this dimension across employees and customer experiences.

Employees as Boundary Spanners

The employees those who are in the front line position are known as boundary spanners because they operate at the organizations boundary. They are making the link between the external customer and internal operations of the organization. They are the persons who understand, filter, interpret information to and from the consumers boundary spanning positions. As this job develops stress among the employee it requires a mental maturity. In addition to mental and physical skills, boundary spanners require high levels of emotional labor. The term 'emotional labor' was coined by Arlie Hochschild which means that the labor that goes beyond the physical (or) mental skills needed to deliver quality service. It means delivering smiles, making eye contact, and engaging in friendly conversation with people.

Factors Related to Employees

There is a gap between the actual service delivery and customers expectations about service designs and standards. To some extent the gap arises because of the HR practices prevailing in the organization. The key factors related to employees are:

(*i*) Ineffective recruitment
(*ii*) Role ambiguity and role conflict
(*iii*) Poor employee-technology-job fit
(*iv*) Inappropriate evaluation and compensation and
(*v*) Lack of empowerment and teamwork.

Hire the Right People

Hiring is the first and most critical factor in building customer friendly environment. It is comparatively easier to start with the right personalities than to teach those skills to whoever walks in the door. One cannot select a person just because he gives a better answer in an interview. It is not sure that he is going on his words, when be becomes an employee. So HR people have to make sure that they are selecting the person who has the right inspiration, which they can reinforce through training. A good customer service person will try to work hard on customer behalf and he is the person who balances his own interest and the organizations interest with the customer interest.

Develop People to Deliver Service Quality

Though a person with right personality is selected, he needs some guidance to channelize his positive qualities towards customer satisfaction. So, proper training has to be given to employees on various skills such as communication, balancing stress, resolving conflicts, interpersonal relationships etc. Training program should also include "active listening". It is also important to give training on hard skills because the service employees must be in a position to answer (or) advise the customers, regarding the raised queries by the people. The service employees must have a good working knowledge of whatever the product he is selling.

Provide Needed Support Systems

To be efficient and effective the service workers require internal support systems. Everyone in the organization has a customer and then measuring customer perceptions of internal service quality, an organization can begin to develop an internal quality culture. Right equipment and right technology are to be provided to the service employees. Internal processes are driven by rules, tradition, cost efficiencies, or the needs of internal employees. Providing service- and customer oriented internal process can there imply a need for total redesign of systems known as "process re-engineering". Since Service personnel in the delivery of quality service is on the front line, an organization's internal processes be designed with customer value and customer satisfaction.

Retain the Best People

Organization that hires the right people, trains and develops them to deliver service quality, and provides the needed support should also work to retain the best ones. Employee turnover, especially when the best service employees are the ones leaving, can be very detrimental to customer satisfaction, employee morale, and overall service quality. Employee who delivers service day in and day out need to understand how his work fits into the overall goal of the organization. Employees are also customers (valued customers). So, the organization should treat the employees feel valued and their needs are taken care of, they are more likely to stay with the organization.

Conclusion

Services are being delivered by people to people. So, the service performance chiefly depends on HR strategies of the organization. They have a greater impact on service quality perceptions to a larger extent. It is highly essential to match the customer's wants and needs with service employee's ability to deliver. Service jobs are frequently frustrating, demanding and challenging. A team work environment will help to reduce stress among employees. To satisfy the customer one has to first satisfy the employees of the organization.

REFERENCES

1. *CRM—A Step by Step Approach,* H. Peern Mohamed, A. Sagadevam, Vikas Publication, New Delhi, 2002.
2. *Managing Human Resources,* Wayne F. Cascio, McGraw-Hill International Edition, New Delhi.
3. *Organisationsal Behaviour,* Fred Luthans, McGraw Hill International Edition, New Delhi.
4. *Services Marketing,* Valarie A. Zeithaml, Mary Jo Bitner, McGraw Hill International Edition, New Delhi, 1996.
5. *Work Force,* May, 2002.

19

Impact of Improving Customer Service in Indian Banks

M. SWAMINATHAN*

Customer has always been at the centre stage of any business organization. Its capacity to keep the life time running of business houses can never be undermined. Customer service is the most important factor on which the success of the banking sector hinges. In the walk of intense competition amongst banks on the one hand and between banks and non-financial institutions on the other quality of customer services has assumed a larger dimension.

Customer and client approach banks with the objective of availing various kinds of services offered by the banks to satisfy and meet their individual needs. Thus, interaction between a customer and a bank commences and continues till the customer service the end product of the desired service. In the entire process of such an interaction, how the banker treats the customer and the methods and means employed to satisfy the customer form the core of the customer service.

The changes in Indian banking sector have been phenomenal, since the reforms were initiated in 1991, from regulation to liberalization, from planned Economy to market economy, from licensing to deregulation with global economies, the changes have been swift, one of the advantages which customers obtained was the much needed freedom of choice in the banking services.

Technology drive has benefited the customer in terms of faster, improved, convenient banking services and variety of financial

* Reader and Head, P.G. and Research Dept. of Commerce, A.V.V.M. Sri Pushpam College (Autonomus), Poondi (TN).

products to suit their requirements. In the new digital market place, now with a deregulated environment—the market is changing so fast that banks are finding it extremely difficult to cope with the demands being made by customers for faster and cheaper financial products and services in line with their needs and preferences. The range of service offered by e-banking includes,

- Automated teller machines (ATMs)
- Direct Deposits
- Pay-by-phone
- PC Banking or House Banking
- Credit cards
- Point of sale transfer/debit cards
- Stored value cards or smart cards
- Electronic Data interchange (EDI)
- Electronic or Digital cash
- Direct credits
- Electronic Fuind transfers
- Real time Gross settlement system

The quality, range and price of these electronic services decide a bank's competitive position in the industry. Technology in banking has been used in four major ways.

1. to handle a greatly expanded customer base.
2. to reduce substantially the real cost of handling payments.
3. to liberate the banks from the traditional constraints on time and place.
4. to introduce new products and services.

Impact of Improving Customer Services in Banks

Customer Satisfaction

The most important objectives of customer services in banking sector is:

(*a*) to retain the existing customers, and
(*b*) to add new customers.

To fulfill the above objectives, the banker should satisfy their customer by way of providing valuable services. Satisfaction of customer is of paramount importance for any business organization. It determines the future cash in flows to the business. The banking sector has to depend on it's existing as well as new customer to keep itself growing. Attracting new customer involves considerable acquisition costs, such as advertising, promotion follow up and set up costs. The operating cost is also higher than the existing ones. The longer any business keeps a customer, the more profits are likely to flow in. In case the customer is not adequately satisfied and defects the business not only incurs a loss due to unrecovered costs but it also misses an opportunity to make profit. Satisfied customers improve the business bottom line only through continued relationship but also through referrals and positive word of mouth feed back of WOM behaviour.

Cost Reduction

Customer service does not mean merely service with smile; it means improving productivity, reducing costs and coming up efficiency, while under pricing those services which are not liked, it would be the principal endeavour to bring down costs, so that competitive and efficient survival and success are ensured. Due to improving customer services, drastic cost reduction for distribution and customer service. The internet dramatically lowers distribution cost for information and dramatically improves the ability to keep information current.

Profitability

Profitability will have notable impact on improving customer service as only efficient service will fetch profit along with satisfied customers. Referring to the banks' relationship with a customer, particularly a borrowing customer, the annexure has noted that "Each relationship must produce enough profit to service capital. This should be the objective of all account managers." All this is possible, if only the focus of the budgeting system in banks is shifted from deposits to profits.

The positioning of the bank in a new perspective becomes acutely relevant with more foreign banks and banks in the private sector entering the banking arena. It has been expressly stated that private sector banks are allowed to be set up to compete with the existing banks and improve the efficiency of the latter through competition. It is good that such a challenge is in the offing.

With so many impacts and benefits from Electronic banking services rendered by banking sectors, there are some bottlenecks.

Adoption of Technology: Statistics reveals that out of 40,000 bank branches in India, only about 5,000 are computerized with local Area Network. Most of the public sector banks are not in a position to adopt technology as such.

Customers Acceptance: it is also problems of modern customer service, fear of technology puts the average customer away from electronic delivery channel.

Cost of Technology: Cost of technology is more and is still not within the reach of the middle class or even the upper middle class.

Lack of Preparedness: The banks are not only behind the bend in developing a customer-friendly on-line presence but most of them are woefully unprepared for the blissfully unaware of the underlying changes in banking.

Suggestions

To improve the customer service in the banks the following measures should be considered:

1. Computerisation of maximum network
2. Customer education
3. Customer meets and cells
4. Human resources development.

Conclusion

Managing with change is the greatest need of the hour as our tools are changing fast. But the rules of the game remain same. Previously, we had a supply based economy, so all that really mattered was production. That was an era of Sellers' Market. But now the situation has changed a lot. We have entered into an era of Buyers' Market.

The market forces are in favour of the customer. The one who cares for them will eventually win. Size location of past history does not matter any more. What matters quickly you can adopt yourselves to the changing world at internet speed that itself is fast changing.

20

Customer Service Excellence through Total Quality Management

D. ARAVAZHI* & SM. CHOCKALINGM**

Introduction

Survive and prosper in the new millennium and beyond, all businesses need to establish mechanisms enabling them to exert conscious and sustained effort continuously to improve their operations.

This has to be coupled with an acute awareness of changes in customers' requirements, competitiveness and broader variations in the business environment. In an increasingly competitive market, firms with a strong continuous improvement culture and external focus are more likely to survive and prosper. Total Quality Management (TQM) is considered an important catalyst in this context.

TQM has been the focus of many organisations due to its contribution to success. With today's ever increasing pressure from the consumers/customers in relation to demand for quality goods and services, firms are facing tough time especially in providing the quality goods and services than their competitors. It has now become increasingly important for firms to introduce and implement the concept of TQM in their operations. The increased use of this concept in Japan, USA and other developed countries prompted the developing countries like India also to follow this concept to reap the advantages of the same.

* Senior Scale Lecturer in Commerce, Periyar Arts College, Cuddalore.

** Professor and Head, Department of Commerce, DDE, Annamalai University, Annamalai Nagar.

A large number of contemporary organizations across the globe have adopted Total Quality Management (TQM) to satisfy customers through quality products and responsive services in order to gain competitive advantages. TQM first took its roots in improving quality of physical products, as the measurement of quality performance of such products was easier.

A country's economic development evolves through a three-stage process from agriculture to manufacturing to services. The service sector contributes to the economy by absorbing surplus labour released from the agriculture and manufacturing sectors due to automations. The service sector plays a positive role in maintaining the economic stability and such a sector is growing at a very rapid rate. The sector covers many organisations such as health care, education, banking, insurance, hotels, transport, tourism, municipalities, power supply and distribution, police, telecommunications, judiciary, professional societies, consulting companies etc.

Therefore, today, we observe a large number of organisations engaged in providing services are implementing TQM. To implement TQM effectively in service organisations requires an analysis of the unique characteristic of the service operations, the role of clientele of services as well as that of the providers of services; and the application of appropriate quality management concepts, tools and techniques.

> "Total Quality Management (TQM) is an approach to improving the effectiveness and flexibility of business as a whole. It is essentially a way of organizing and involving the whole organization, every department, every activity, and every single person at every level. TQM ensures that the management adopt a strategic overview of quality and focus on prevention rather than inspection".

The Concept of Total Quality Management (TQM)

According to International organisation for standardisation (ISO). "Quality means the totality of features and characteristics of a product or service that bear on its ability to satisfy stated or implied needs". In simple words, quality means meeting the customer or client needs everytime.

All the three words, total, quality and management are

important in understanding TQM. It involves everyone and everything in the organisation (total), provides customers with what they expect (quality) and quality is managed in (management) rather than inspected in, built in or even organised in TQM is the development of a total organisational way of life, involving everyone in an organisation putting quality first to continually meet agreed customer requirements now and in the future.

Objectives of TQM

Meeting the customer's requirements is the primary objective and the key to organisational survival and growth. Customers are never regarded as people to whom the company presents its product in a take it or leave it spirit. Relationship with the customers is considered as a supreme act of faith. It is believed that if customers are satisfied, they will continue to patronise the company, which, in turn, will make it survive and grow.

The second objective of TQM is the continuous improvement of quality. The management should stimulate the employees in becoming increasingly competent and creative. They should keep doing better. As long as things are not perfect, there is room for improvement: new products can get to market faster, new adjustments in processes can cut down on time and coat, and the environment for work can be made more satisfying.

Thirdly, TQM aims at developing the relationship of openness and trust among the employees at all levels in the organisation.

Need and Significance of Total Quality Management

Total Quality Management is the need of all modern organisations. This realisation first came in Japan where it was felt that quality cannot be ensured by inspection and test alone; every department and the individual had a role to play in the achievement of quality. Thus "Quality Control" which was basically restricted to testing and inspection of the end product gave way to "Quality Assurance". In addition to inspection of the product, quality assurance also involved the inspection of the production process and equipment.

Total Quality Management goes a step further as its aim is to actively involve all the employees in the pursuit of quality and to infuse in them the spirit of continuous improvement to satisfy the ever-changing needs of the customers. It intends to achieve desired quality rather than control and prevent defects in the goods produced. TQM is the sum total of the quality of various aspects of the business system, namely, product design and development, production, purchase, marketing, financing, etc. It also involves all technical and administrative systems and procedures, which can ensure the desired quality on a consistent basis. This is why, organisations all over the world have become conscious of the need of total quality management.

The importance of TQM lies in the fact that it encourages innovation, makes the organisation adaptable to charge, motivates people for better quality, integrates the business arising out of a common purpose and all these provide the organisation with a valuable and distinctive competitive edge.

Benefits of Total Quality Management

The following benefits can be derived from a sound TQM programme:

(*i*) Total Quality Management brings quality consciousness in the enterprise, which encourages production of quality products.

(*ii*) TQM helps in providing greater satisfaction to the customers by meeting their requirements. If the customers are satisfied, the sales are increased.

(*iii*) It creates a good public image of the enterprise by helping it to provide goods and services of higher quality to the society.

(*iv*) There is better utilisation of materials, machines, capital, human resources, etc.

(*v*) Wastage's are reduced to the minimum. As a result, cost of production is reduced and profitability is increased. Even the customers could be provided goods at lower prices. The competitive position of the firm in the market is improved.

(*vi*) The employees are committed to higher quality and feel highly motivated. Their morale is also higher because of the public image of the firm and its goodwill in the market.

TQM in India

India awakened to the adoption of the concept of TQM in the late

1980s though 'Quality Control' had been emphasized since the adoption of the industrial policy resolution, 1956. The quality control efforts did not prove to be adequate to raise the quality of Indian products and to increase their exports. But this scenario changed with the announcement of Industrial policy, 1991, which talked of integration of Indian economy with world economy. The introduction of liberalisation measures such as delicensing of industries and removal of restrictions of the entry of foreign capital and technology into the country had the immediate effect of opening up Indian Industry to international competition as also increased competition from within. In an extremely competitive environment, only the fittest can survive and for survival, every organisation has to embark upon a workable quality improvement process. This illustrates the significance of continuous quality improvement by the Indian Industry.

Conclusion

With the integration of Indian economy with the global economy, we can survive and prosper only by successful competition. Success in competition is possible by ensuring excellence in the quality of product and service offered to the customer. This is preciously what is provided by TQM.

21

Revitalising Customer Service through Technology and Quality Movement

V.N. SUBRAMANIYAN*

QUALITY IS STRENGTH

The statement is enough to register into the minds of customers for better product acceptance. Whenever quality is given priority, satisfaction tends to move towards the arena of consumer's mind.

When customers are in need of quality, service at affordable cost is within their limit. They seem to create demand of their own. To develop service levels of an organization which will assist customers in specifying, acquiring, fixing on returning products. Besides technology also moves on a par with quality to upgrade utility level of customers.

The goal of quality management is to meet the ultimate objective of customer's satisfaction customer service and qualities are synonymous term. Organizational commitment to quality has to be developed through the process of educating the internal customers. i.e., the people who make up the organization.

Ex: Orchid Chemicals

Orchid chemicals and pharmaceutical limited has been a remarkable success story of a first generation enterprise in the Indian pharmaceutical industry and notched upon a turnover of US $90 million.

Orchid is driven by a set of five core values:

* Lecturer, Dept. of Business Administration, Shree Chandraprabhu Jain, College, Meenjur, Chennai.

- Respect for fellow humans and premium of intellect.
- Quest for international standard.
- Customer satisfaction through quality and service.
- Harmony with environment.
- Creation of wealth for all stakeholders.

At Orchid, quality is way of life for global presence; orchid's quality initiative covers all aspects including product quality, operational quality, environmental quality and good quality of life for its people.

Orchid has been awarded the prestigious ISO 9001:2000 and ISO 14001 certifications for its world class quality management and environmental management systems.

Polaris Software Lab

Polaris software lab is India's leading software solutions provider, specializing in providing quality and customized IT solutions to several multinational clients in Banking, Financial services and Insurance (BFSI) segments.

Quality

Quality at Polaris is an inherent characteristic. The company has always maintained a razor sharp focus on quality. The reason why such tremendous focus on quality is shown because of a simple core philosophy, it cannot improve unless it can measure and for this purpose, the company has a measurement/metric systems aligned to the corporate business goals. Indeed, this is a corner stone of the company's dedication to quality. All Polaris internal facilities are designed to provide only the best quality to associate, so that this quality is passed onto clients in form of superior solutions.

CMM Level 5 certification and ISO 9001:2000 are ample testaments to the quality standards followed at Polaris.

ITES

Call center business is one of the fast growing sectors within the spectrum of ITES. It is a facility that has customer relationship executives to handle Customer queries, complaints or calls to acquire new customers, collections, telemarketing campaign etc.

Their objective is to:

- Increase customer satisfaction level, enhances customer relationship which in turn increases revenue.

India's Quality Achievement

Medium sized Chennai based Indian company *Sundaram Brake Lining* (*SBL*) which was awarded the prestigious and highly coveted Deming's prize considered to be the noble prize in the global quality world.

Kodak

In Japan the concern for quality starts with the CEO, whereas in the United States quality has been the primary concern of lower level mangers and quality engineers.

Cobly H. Chandler Kodak C.E.O. started his career as quality control engineer. His philosophy was

"Quality pays for itself many times over"

Kodak's strategy is driven by research and development as well as concern for productivity and quality.

Conclusion

It's the overall quality and technology that drives the organization towards demand market which is based on service levels. The quality movement which drives every organization towards global market seems to increase its competitive advantage for better market acceptance.

22

Customer Quality Service

K. Sentamil Selvan*

Introduction

The most important asset of any organization is its customers. An organization success depends on how many customers it has how much they buy and how often they buy. Satisfied customers will increase, buy more and buy more frequently.

Increasingly, manufacturing and service organization are using customer satisfaction as the measure of quality. The importance of customer satisfaction is not only due to national competition but to world wide competition. This fact is reflected in the Malcolm Baldrige National Quality Award, where in customer satisfaction accounts for 30% of the total points.

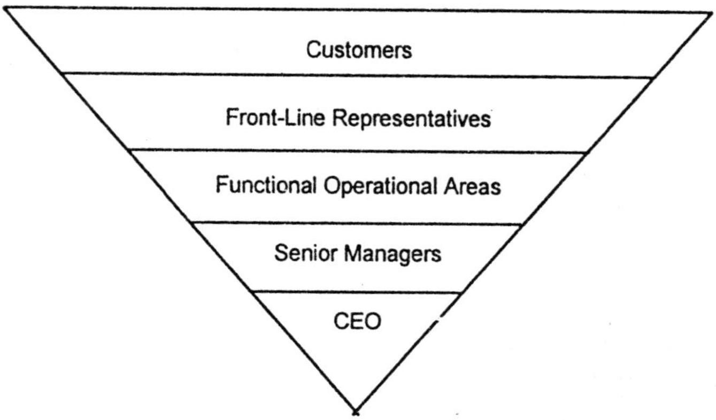

Customer Satisfaction Organizational Diagram

* Senior Lecturer, Dept. of Management, V.R.S. College of Engg. & Tech., Arasur, T.N.

TQM implies organisational obsession with meeting or exceeding customer expectations to the point that customers are delighted. The successful TQM programs begin by defining quality from the customer's perspective. Customer satisfaction not increasing profits must be in the primary goal of the organization. It is the most important consideration because satisfied customers will lead to increased profits. Customer needs are represented by the circle and square depicts the product or service offered by the organization. Total satisfaction is achieved when the offer matches the need or the circle is super imposed on the square. The goal is to cover the expected performance level better than the competitors.

That part of the square that lies within the circle is perceived by the customer as satisfying, and the part of the square outside the circle is perceived as unnecessary. It is important that the organization listens to the voice of the customer and ensure that its marketing, design, production, distribution processes truly meet the expectations of the customer.

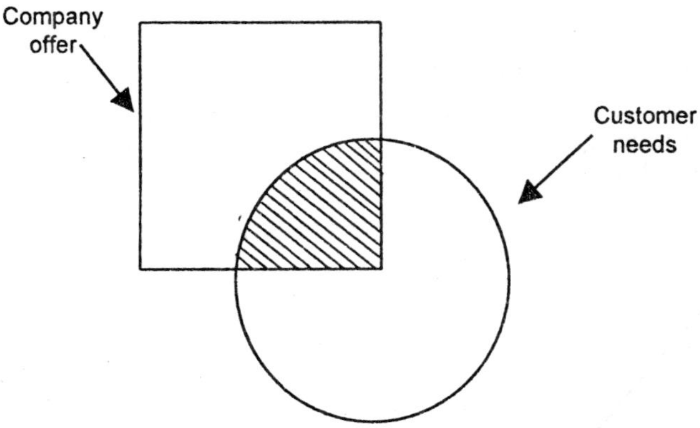

Customer Satisfaction Model

Customer satisfaction seems simple enough and yet, it is far from simple. Customer satisfaction is not an objective statistic but more of a feeling attitude. Although certain statistical patterns can be developed to represent customer satisfaction, it is best to remember that people's opinion and attitudes are subjective by nature. Because customer satisfaction is subjective it is hard to measure.

Customer Perception of Quality

One of the basic concepts of the TQM philosophy is continuous process improvement. This concept implies that there is no acceptable quality level because the customer needs, values and expectations are constantly changing and becoming more demanding.

An American Society for Quality (ASQ) survey on end user perceptions of important factors that influenced purchases showed the following ranking;

The factors of *Performance, Features, Service* and *Warranty* are part of the product quality service. Therefore it is evident that product quality and service are more important than price. Although this information is based on the retail customer, it appears to some extent to also be true for the commercial customer.

Performance

Performance involves *"Fitness For Use"*—a phrase that indicates that the product and service is ready for the customers use at the time of sale. Other considerations are

(*i*) *Availability*—which is the probability that a product will operate when needed.
(*ii*) *Reliability*—which is freedom from failure over time.
(*iii*) *Maintainability*—which is the case of keeping the product operable.

Features

Features are secondary characteristics of the product such as attributes of a product or service are psychological, time oriented, contractual, ethical and technological.

Service

Organisations that emphasize, service never stop looking for and finding ways to serve their customers better, even if their customers are not complaining. Intangible characteristics are those traits that are not quantifiable, yet contribute greatly to customer satisfaction. Providing excellent customer service is different from and more difficult to achieve than excellent product quality.

Warranty

A warranty forces the organization to focus on the customers definition of product and service quality. Warranty generate feed back by providing information on the product and service quality. It also forces the organization to develop a corrective action system. Finally, warranty builds marketing muscle and encourage customer to by a service buy reducing the risk of the purchase decision and it generates more sales from existing customers by enhancing loyalty.

Price

Today's customers are constantly evaluating one organizational products and services against those of its competitors to determine who provides the greatest value and update each customers perception of value in relation to each product and service.

Reputation

Total customer satisfaction is based on the entire experience with the organization not just the product. Customers are willing to pay a premium for a known brand name and often become customers for life. Investment in customer retention can be a more effective bottom-line approach than concentrating on lowering operational cost.

Concluding Remarks

A quality is essentially dynamic in nature that leads to continuous improvement Review of performance and the effectiveness of the quality system should be a continuous process carried out at levels in the center. Principally, this is a review by senior management to ensure that process employed really satisfied customer needs and expectations and the center's mission.

This review should include:

- Suggestion for improvement
- Results of Internal Quality Audit
- Results of Review at Operational Levels
- Any Complaints.

To conclude the following concepts should be kept in mind and use.

- Quality improvement is a key business performance area essential for success in today's world.
- Qualitatively improvement begins with management leadership.
- Productivity improvement also improves quality, quantity improvement also improves productivity.
- Participation is a kay to qualitivity improvement.

REFERENCES

1. Johnsons Aimie, Edo Son, *"Productivity and Quality Improvement"*, IFS Publication, UK, 1988.
2. David J., Sumanath, *"Productivity Engg. and Management"*, TMH, New Delhi, 1982.
3. William F., Cristopher, *"A Hand Book for Productivity Measurement and Improvement"*, Productivity Press, Portland (1993).

23

Customer Service Quality

HENRY ONSARE OKONG'A*

Introduction

The 21st Century has seen the economic mantras of almost all business enterprises shifting centre stage and finally settling at the power of the customer. The choice-empowered customer is now in a commanding position to the throne, to borrow an expression from military literature, dictating terms and proclaiming kingship. There is no any other way except for bankers to wake up to this new and emerging reality and realize as such.... that, to be competitive, one must necessarily have to be customer focused. For the same reason, bankers' missions are no longer product, profit, or even market-oriented, but only focused on customers' supremacy.

Customer Service

In a service industry like banking, the quality of customer service holds key to success, particularly in today's era of cut-throat competition. This is especially true when compared to other sectors engaged in the production of tangible commodities. Bank Services are unique by nature, in the sense that they are produced and delivered at the service centres themselves i.e. branch level. In view of the vast expanse and diversity of banking services, customer service is also of varied dimensions—accessibility, costs, returns, speed, product range, operational efficiency, technology, courtesy, punctuality, accountability and a host of other elements associated thereto. The level of customer service is therefore,

* Dept. of Bank Management, Alagappa University, Karaikudi, T.N.

measured and determined by those varieties of services, rates and charges, systems and procedures, mechanization and automation, computerization, competitive efficiency, customer overtures, complaint redressals, and more important, staff skills, attitudes and responses. Essentially, good customer service in banks should have three basic tenets at the entry or contact points i.e courtesy, accuracy and speed.

Since the interface between the customer and the staff is very narrow, being across the counter, the nature of service has an overwhelming impact on customers' psychology and therefore, makes them oversensitive towards the service i.e. either for the best or to the worst. Normally, the business relationship between bankers and customers is not a one-time shot, but later a relatively permanent and enduring relationship, which requires to be nurtured and nursed with better and efficient service.

Despite so many measures initiated at different levels to improve the standard of customer service in Indian banks, the level of satisfaction as perceived by various segments of customers has been abysmally low. This is due to the fact that customer service is a fast changing phenomenon. What may be customer expectation today may not be the case tomorrow. Hence, to meet customer expectation in the strict sense of the term and commensurate with the changing times is indeed very difficult. As the 'bells' for improving customer service continues to ring louder, so is the level of customer complaints regarding poor service. The zooming customer complaints at an alarming pace have made bankers wary about containing the mounting tide of customer dissatisfaction by its very sensitive nature, the issue of customer service had been a subject of considerable debate and constant focus, especially in the post-nationalisation era. This period witnessed quantitative explosion of bank branches and subsequently changed the banker-customer relationship, as a result of which customer service reached the lowest ebb in India's banking history. Public sector banks, for instance, though achieved to some extent the dual objectives of social justice and balanced economic growth, their quality of service deteriorated badly. This is evident when considering the geographical coverage across the length and width of the Indian sub-continent, with an exponential rise in the number of customers. They were hardly well equipped with sufficient manpower and other infrastructural facilities to meet the awesome demand to render good customer service, especially at the time of nationalisation. India has 66000 bank branches as at present to serve 1000 million people i.e. one branch for every 15000 citizen approximately.

Another aspect which contributed significantly to customer dissatisfaction was the rising expectation of customers. The phenomenal developments in communication technology and the consequent widening of the level of awareness led to the rising customer expectation and also radically altered the customer perceptions about the service delivery standards. Adding to the injury was the efficient and personalized service rendered by foreign and new private sector banks, which came about as a result of liberalization and the subsequent opening up of the banking sector.

Committees and Commissions

The declining quality of customer service and the imperative need to improve the standards of service had been a serious concern for the Government as well as the Reserve Bank of India over the years. The first organized effort to tackle the issue was the constitution of the Talwar Committee whose recommendations were accepted and implemented in right earnest. Given the dynamic context and rising expectations of customer service, the level of customer satisfaction suffered yet another downturn, leading to the constitution of the Goiporia Committee. The working group carried out an extensive study and came out with major recommendations, which were also readily accepted and implemented. However, these committees failed to bring about any perceptible improvements in service quality because they didn't take into account the infrastructural inadequacies and the availability of supporting systems. Moreover, no punitive measures were suggested for failing to implement the recommendations. One major reason that can be cited from such regulatory frameworks is that mere impositions of fiats do not suffice. It is imperative that all such instructions/directives must be backed up by the active participation of the employees at all levels. Therefore, unless and until individual bankers properly perceive the necessity of improved customer service, as the only means to achieve sustained business growth; make their internal systems and procedures adequately responsive to the changing requirements; and ensure commitment of all the staff members towards the benchmark, improvement in the quality of customers service still remains an elusive milestone.

Causes for Inefficiency in Customer Service

There are a number of causative factors responsible for the deteriorating standards of customer service in banks. Some of these factors are briefly discussed below:

Awful and Archaic Systems and Procedures

Those systems and procedures, which were framed many years back, pose visible hindrance to the delivery of better quality service. Most of the basic systems and procedures existing in banks today were framed keeping in view the legal, accounting and safety considerations which have long become outdated and do not aptly back up the process of prompt and efficient customer service.

Poor Approach

In an environment where the customer is the king, the new mantra for banking companies should be upgrading themselves from mere 'service providers' to value-based service providers. Such a new approach is not only necessary but also required in order to design systems whereby service is rendered after identifying customer needs.

Indifferent Employee Attitude Leads to Indifferent Service

The main dominant cause for the indifferent attitude of the employees towards the customers is the job security, which plays havoc with the service they render across the counter. Queues at the counters for unduly long period for carrying out over a simple banking transaction reflects more of the indifferent employee attitude towards customers.

Technology Upgradation

Undue aparthy towards technology has taken its toll in the form of poor quality of customer service in some banks compared to foreign banks. Indian banks are admittedly slower in adopting technology as a superior tool for better quality service. The entire banking industry is almost becoming fully synonymous, and indeed is, with information technology. Bank customers have become over sensitive, just like investigative agencies, plumbing for more and detailed information on the developments in banking in order to enable them identify and choose the best and modern service available in the market. In such an environment, only those banks which invest heavily in technology will be able to achieve the economies of scale; become low cost producers and thereby achieve a high degree of customer satisfaction. The state of the art technology also offer opportunities to banks to improve their products and services further, thereby giving greater customer value.

Developments in Customer Service—Issues & Dimensions

There is no denying that multifarious and concerted efforts have been made to improve customer service. The most important that needs reckoning in the sphere of customers service relates to the advent of technology—ATMS, Tele banking, internet banking and other technology based services. Banks have adopted the latest IT to cater to the customer service in a better way e.g shared payment network system (SPMS), whereby a customer of one bank can use his ATM card at another bank's ATM, both being in the same network. Ambitious programmes have been launched country-wide towards partial and total computerization of branches and technology up gradation, which hopefully have turned the Indian banking system to be a little bit efficient, speedier and customer-oriented. Besides, banks have opened specialized and highly professionalised branches like industrial finance, SSI & NRI branches, with a view to provide personalized services and at the same time meet the ever-increasing demands of customers. To provide customer–friendly services, banks' front office personnel have been trained for achieving near perfection in customer service across the counters. They have even set up customer grievance redressal cells at major centers to attend to customer grievances, but still complaints seems to be on an increasing trend.

The emerging banking scenario, being in the throes of rapid changes, has been minced by fierce competition, high levels of customer expectation and most prominently, the technology driven-service. Now the question that remains unanswered is: how can these Indian banks cope up with the transition and face the challenges of this new market reality. An explanation to this dilemma and definitely an answer, lies in the improvement of service quality through a new and an undiscovered route of service quality, customer satisfaction and delight.

Therefore, there is a greater need, more than ever before, for a second thought of the basics of customer service, recognizing the primacy of the customer and discovering new routes between customer service and customer delight. Usually, bank customers prefer one product over another because of better value. A satisfied and delighted customer is the best insurer for the banker, best unpaid publicity agent, who engineers creation of new customers, which means more business opportunities.

Hence, bankers ought to make more and concerted efforts in generating customer delight by:

- Constantly surpassing the expectations of the customers;
- Constantly striving to provide additional customer value atleast in every business transaction;
- Holding the customer in high esteem as though he is the only person who matters for the successful performance of the bank; and
- Continuously being alert of the changes in customer expectations and delivery gaps in order to identify opportunities and areas of customer delight.

First, bankers need to have an idea about their market share, who their customers are, which category they plan to satisfy and in which way. Unlike in the past, customers of today have many options at their command, and with the new players in the market, they have every right to be choosy. Thus, customer services should not be a mere rhetoric, but must be pursued in the right earnest and spirit. For this to happen, bankers need to keep their hands closed, pull their heads together and so their souls, so that not a single 'drum beat' of the changing customer expectations sneeks out of their fingers. By so doing they develop the desired skills and create sensitivity to gauge customers' perceptions. However, one major drawback in obtaining the right perception from customers of all genre is the existence of silent millions who quit/

shift without complaint. Hence, unless there is a reawakening in banking circles that customers can no longer be taken for granted, and that key to survival lies in the individual banker's response to improved service quality, any bank is bound to slowly pass into oblivion.

> "Bankers' efforts at service excellence should be designed in such a manner as to ensure that customers are not just satisfied but delighted with what bankers do for them".

24

Contingency to Provide Excellence Service to Customer

"Facilitating Services are Mandatory of Today's Firm"

P. VIKKRAMAN*

Introduction

In today's competitive business world customer loyalty and customer satisfaction are becoming more difficult and but it is important to maintain customer satisfaction. Keeping your customers satisfied is the key to ensuring they come back. And better to improve making sure they keep coming back is as we will see vitally important to the top to bottom line. So customer satisfaction doesn't only apply to the end user of your organisation products or services; it also applies to the people in your organisation, and how they work together to produce products and services.

Improve customer satisfaction does not have single dimension. It must be multidimensional factor that is a both to external and internal customers. The sample principles that apply to keeping external customers happy apply to keeping internal customers happy, too.

So, what is an internal customer? Think about a track-and-field relay team. When one running passes the baton to a teammate, they are engaging in internal customer interaction. Both runners are part of the same team yet the second runner's ability to run a good race and make a successful hand-off to the next member of

* Faculty, Institute of Management, R.V.S. College of Engg. & Tech., Dindigul, T.N.

the relay team depends on how smoothly the firm runner passes the baton (Thus satisfying his or her internal customer). These relationships affect not only the next log of the race, but the success of the entire team. If your team wants to win the race against your competitors, you need to work to make sure that your hand-offs are smooth and effective. As you can see, internal relationships have a profound impact on your organisation's ability to run a good race and to provide your customers with the kind of service that will keep them coming back for more.

We will discuss about how for measuring and increasing customer satisfaction. Present about specific tools to increase customers satisfaction. Think of it as a blue print to achieve external customer satisfaction and loyalty.

Later we will provide valuable concepts and tools for you to use, whether you are a manager, team leader, team member, sales person. Engineer or quality professional. The approaches presented below are adaptable to a service or manufacturing setting, as well as profit or non profit organisations both large and small.

Unfortunately, many companies wait until problems are full-blown before they concern themselves with customer satisfaction. By then, it is often too late. Focus on customer satisfaction long before the loyalty of your customers ever comes in question.

Organisations spend a lot of time tracking customer satisfaction. Unfortunately, the employees responsible for tracking satisfaction are not always those responsible for making the necessary changes to increase satisfaction.

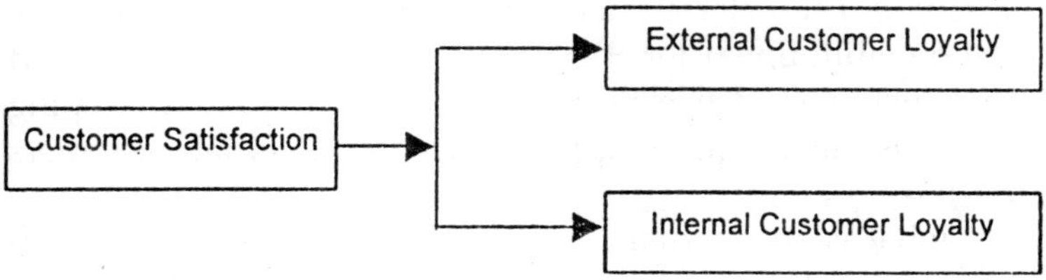

Let us take a close look at the dynamics involved in creating external customer loyalty by satisfying internal customer first.

Role of Employees

To succeed in this new approach to customer service, a firm should decentralise, empower its employees, set high standards of service, and most importantly all this must get the wholehearted support of top management.

It's very difficult to follow this approach in an orthodox, highly centralised organisation. When roles are very tightly defined, customers are more likely to receive answers like 'that's not my department, ask my supervisor, I don't know etc. If the problem is not fixed where it arises, it snowballs into a much bigger and complex problem, which later on consumes enormous time and resources of the organisation.

Retailer Nordstrom's approach to customer service, though perhaps overly emphatic is worth taking a closer look here.

- Warm-up cars of the customers in the winter
- Pay for customer's parking tickets
- When the customer is trying a new shirt, iron his old shirt.

Its legendary now, that when a customer asked for a coat that was not available with Nordstrom, the sales clerk ran to an other store and gave the customer a 30 per cent discount or, allowed a terribly busy executive to try out a new jacket in the airport in between fights!.

It is impossible to serve the customers so lavishly (as in case of Nordstrom) unless employees are empowered to do so. But empowerment without proper training would only create chaos. Training not just in one activity but 'cross training' which would help employees handle different situations. Cross training is a sure way to stop employees from yelling I can't fix this or I don't know. In Xerox, cutting across functional areas, everyone is trained no handle '*Customer Complaints*'

- Do they put customers first?
- Do they boss around?

New Approaches To Customer

Knowing fully well, the sources of satisfaction are diverse, the new definition offered to customer service is "*what ever enhances customer satisfaction*". This includes spectrum of activities right from design of product, use of product, to the salvage of product.

This new approach even includes finding out the gap between the way customer expects to be served and the perceived service received by him. For long, managers at British Airways (BA) thought 'Care and Concern' is what customers expect. But they were in for a major surprise when, customers said they expect 'Spontaneous & Flexible' service—a classic case of gap between managers awareness and customer expectation. The whole computer industry believed 'faster the better'. In a Platinum council meeting (a forum which ensures free flow of information from customers on a constant basis), Michael Dell to his surprise found out that customers really wanted 'a stable product that doesn't change. Bulk of his customers didn't care for a 2 per cent faster or a 3 per cent slower computer.

Satisfying Customer Service is Everybody's Job.

Most of the above mentioned activities are performed by the front line executives. But leadership in customer service, unless seen as 'everybody's' job in the firm, is very difficult to attain. It includes everyone, right from the CEO to the clerk who finally handles the customer. The CEO of Xerox spends one day a month with the customers, trying to understand them.

Provide Adequate Infrastructure to Customer

For the kinds of service that the above mentioned service leaders are offering, a firm needs to put in place a suitable service infrastructure. Putting in place a physical infrastructure requires enormous resources. Segmentation can offer some relief here. Customers can be effectively segmented based on the 'urgency of service' (or delay they are willing to tolerate) and cost. Dell has found a solution for this by 'Segmenting—segmenting based on the customer's service needs'.

Product—Service Relationship

Since the new definition of customer service includes the spectrum of activities right from design of product, its use, and its salvage, it is very important to understand the product-service relationship.

- Computers that help complex operations of a bank or a insurance firm must run smoothly or a high cost aircraft engine cannot afford to breakdown. They require multiple backup and need really quick-quality service.

- For products like a car, washing machine, photocopier etc., support like repair people, spare parts, service expertise etc., matter most.
- Product augmentation has increased the complexity of servicing them. Today, products come with so many optional features, many of which really don't add any value. Service quality will improve if many of these redundant optional features are done away with.
- Design simplication reduces cost and time of servicing. In fact with properly designed manuals, customers can be induced towards 'Self service'.
- Eliminating marginal products will reduce service complexity and add to your profit.

Sales-Service Relationship

Increasing sales increases the pressure on its service infrastructure. So the moot question to be addressed is: should service infrastructure be put in place expecting sales growth or service infrastructure to follow the sales curve? Probably one leapfrogging another seems to be a sensible approach.

How to Improve the Internal Customer Satisfaction through Adequate Services?

Gaining, keeping, and maintaining customer loyalty through customer satisfaction efforts starts with activity along your organisation's internal chain events.

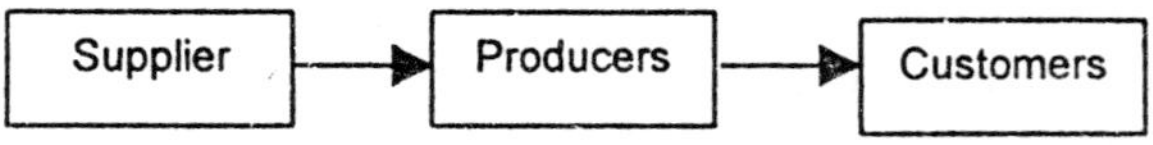

On an External level there is a Supplier-Producers-Customer relationship between organisation and a final customer. For example:

Company A supplies materials. Services or information to company B, which incorporates those inputs into a new purchase or goods or services for company C, the end user (or customer).

Each of these internal events or process overlap each other at the hand-off points between internal customers, producers and suppliers.

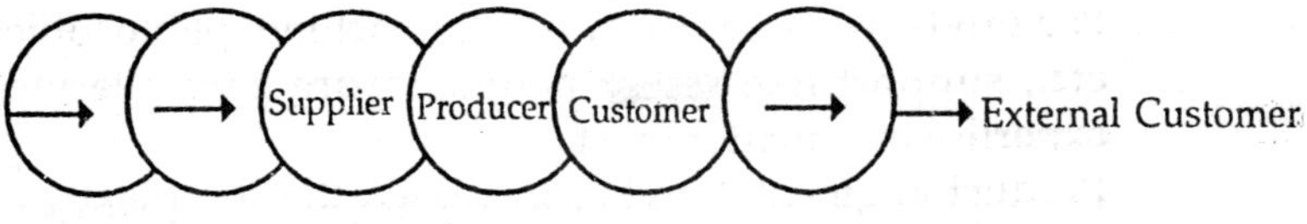

The goal of any customer satisfaction effort should be to improve external satisfaction levels by first improving internal customer relationships. One of the key ingredients for determining and managing customer satisfaction, both inside and outside the organisation, is feed back.

How To Build Up Customer's Feedback?

Customer feedback speaks in many voices from a whisper to a shout. If you haven't set up a system of communication with your customers, you may not have a means of recognizing and interpreting the warning signs of low satisfaction levels. Instead you may see the end results, such as: reduced sales, high rates of customer turnover, and so on. Low satisfaction levels end up costing your organization money in two ways.

- Loss of revenue from former customers, and
- Investment in advertising, marketing, and sales efforts required to replace their business.

While you could consider these signs a type of customer feedback, they aren't exactly the type of feedback that's best for your organization. To maintain customer satisfaction, you must manage the customer feedback loop.

How To Build Up Loyalty?

Vital to creating and maintaining customer loyalty is the knowledge needed to capture that seemingly elusive prey.

Satisfaction + Effective Feedback Management = Customer Loyalty

Customer loyalty is the result of satisfaction and effective feedback management inside and outside of the organisation. It is more than just a concept—it can be measured in Rupees and Dollars.

Improve your current customer and per cent of loyal customers and supports your company, try to reduce number of customer considered sense sitters. Avoid number of lost customers and think about replacing of each lost customer.

Customer feedback satisfaction and bottom line results like those above can all be managed by focusing on internal customer satisfaction first.

How to Measure External Customer Satisfaction through Excellence in Service?

It is little value to know that customer satisfaction levels need improvement if you don't have the tools to improve them.

This six-step model directs you and your team toward the fulfillment of your goals. It begins with measuring external customer satisfaction and ends with measuring the results of your actions.

Measure External Customer Satisfaction

As any carpenter knows, there's a sound reason for the adage, "*measure twice cut once*". Carpenters recheck their measurements, because if they act on a questionable measurement, they waste time and valuable materials, with customers, if action is taken on a hunch, a small problem easily becomes a larger one. Measure customer satisfaction before you take further action.

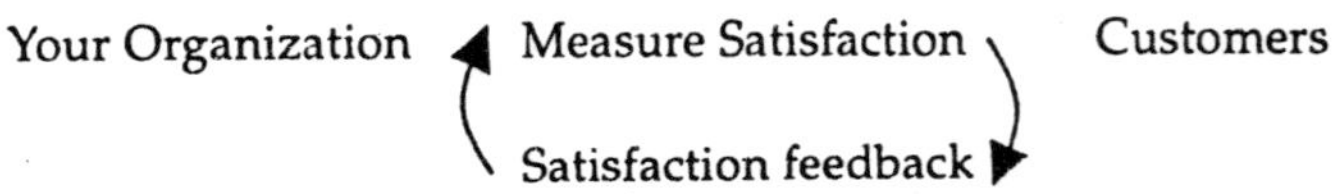

Within this first step are four key sub steps:

(*a*) Identify your customers' requirement areas
(*b*) Determine your surveying methodology
(*c*) Develop survey/interview questions
(*d*) Survey/interview your customers

How to Build up the Internal Chain

Just like a relay team, your team relies on a series of hand-off relationships. The smoothness of these relationships affects your group's success in delivering what your external customers want. Mapping out hand-off relationships, and specifying who passes what off to whom, creates a powerful, customer-oriented atmosphere in your organization.

Locate the Critical Links

Deciding the relationships that are crucial to external customer satisfaction is vital for improving customer satisfaction. We'll look at the three valuable tools determining the critical links you should improve.

Analyze the Critical Links

Knowing that a person is ill does very little in helping a doctor to make a diagnosis. At this stage of the process, learn valuable techniques to separate symptoms from problems, and focus on important issues at the critical links.

Resolve Critical Link Issues

Here you will learn skills and techniques helpful for you and your team to make changes to improve the quality of your internal chain of relationship and to improve your output as an organization.

Evaluation of Changes

Evaluating your changes and their results justifies the time, effort, and money going into making satisfaction-oriented changes.

Admit Changes

After evaluation you have to admit changes for the benefit of customer service outcome will be customers satisfaction.

Implementation

Implement changes physically into field are product and service. For the benefit of customer satisfaction.

Measure External Customer Satisfaction

Why is it important to measure how satisfied your customers are? Have you ever kept a running mental tally of how satisfied you are with a product and service. We want to know the satisfaction level of the external customer.

Customer satisfaction is a result of your product or service meeting a certain set of customer requirements some of the ingredients that make up this set of customer.

How to Measure it?

There are several measurement tools you can use with relative ease:

1. Interview/Survey
2. Focus group
3. Customer satisfaction feed back method.

Interviews/Surveys

Surveys allow you to zero in on specific issues. If you want to know whether or not your external customers are satisfied with shipping practices, then you can write interview/survey questions that pertain to delivery.

Here are four sub-steps you can take to develop useful interviews and surveys:

Step A : Identify your customers' requirements areas
Step B : Determine your surveying methodology
Step C : Develop survey/interview questions
Step D : Survey/interview your customer

How to Build up the External Chain

From the time your organization starts producing its product or service to the time you deliver it to your external consumer, the product or service being changed for consumption goes through an internal chain of events.

In that chain, everybody is a customer, a producer, and a supplier. When you accept the baton from a teammate, you are a customer, when you run with it for your leg of the relay, you are a producer—making some change or adding value to the baton. When you pass it off to the next member of the team, you become a supplier.

If you identify the chain of events in your organization and note where internal customers relationships exist, you can increase your definition of customer requirements for each link in the chain, setting the stage to identify, links where difficulties have developed, and make changes at those critical links.

The chain of internal relationships is represented visually in a format we'll refer to as a map. The map shows major work process as circles, and the relationship between these process (between customers, producers, and suppliers) as the areas where the circles intersect.

Locate the Critical Links

Critical links are specific points where the causes of external customer satisfaction issues occur. After mapping the chain of internal events, determine where the critical links are. '

The approach you choose will depend on whether you are tying to implement an internal customer service climate or pinpoint a specific internal customer satisfaction issue.

The three possible approaches are:

1. Measure all the links in the chain, then select the one with the lowest level of satisfaction—the critical link.
2. Measure from the outside in. Work back from the measure of external customer satisfaction through each link in the internal chain.
3. Have the customer pinpoint the critical links.

Analyze the Critical Links

After you have located the critical link, determine the nature of the problem and its true causes. In medicine, proper diagnosis and treatment begins with a list of symptoms. To make sure the treatment is thorough, a doctor then determines what is behind the symptoms. This same in-depth diagnosis is necessary to improve the well-being of an organization too, if it is to succeed at delivering customer satisfaction.

To determine the root causes of problems arising at a critical link, we have provided you with a set of tools for separating the causes of a problem from its symptoms.

Evaluate Changes

Why Evaluate?

There is really only one way to justify the cost, time, and effort that goes into improving your organization's internal customer service atmosphere, and too make sure that the changes you have made are the right ones. Measure customer satisfaction again. If satisfaction has improved, you are on the right track.

However, we do not live in static work, and cannot control all the variables in the relationship between changes at a specific critical link and changes in external satisfaction levels. It is possible that the changes made at the critical link are positive and are directly related to improvements in external customers satisfaction, However, that connection doesn't show because something else is affecting their overall satisfaction with your organization.

The method you use to evaluate the effects of change will depend partly on the approach used to locate the critical link.

Admit Changes and Implementation

After evaluation you have to admit changes for the benefit of customer service out come will be customers satisfaction. Implement changes physically in to field are product and service. For the benefit of customer satisfaction.

Conclusion

We come to conclusion customer services/customer satisfaction is required for success of business. Service leaders have proved beyond doubt that "Service Pays but for the firms to develop competency in service and to use it as a source of competitive advantage" use service to bridge the performance to satisfy internal customer and external customers. They have to change the way they look at service. Unless they take a holistic approach towards service to include activities, right from product design, its service to salvage and address the key issues discussed above, a total customers service is only the contingency for to provide excellence service the customers. It is applicable for both profitably and non-profitably organization. For example 2003-2004 Railway budget is titled by our Railway Minister is "Customer Satisfaction Railway Budget".

> *"Customer Satisfaction Is Affordable and Profitable Because a Satisfied Customer Becomes Excellent Sales forever".*
>
> *"We have come to Conclusion Customer satisfaction is required for cusses we have a road map for achieving it".*

25

Customer Excellence Service in Various Industries

V. SACHITHANANTHAM* & M. SYED ZAFAR**

Today, the markets are undergoing a dynamic change, which forces the firms to adopt innovative strategies to retain their customers. One such strategy is providing world-class services to the customers. More and more firms introduçing different techniques to outperform their competitors.

Our paper highlights some of the best examples, which are offered in Indian market. Each and every industry follows an unique way of satisfying their customer and thereby retaining them for long-term relationship.

Few examples are: Banking Industry are providing basic services like accepting deposits and lending loans but in the present scenario they are giving service like Tele banking, internet banking etc. In Automobile industry they are providing services like you can travel all over the country with out any fear of breakdown. If anything happens you can avail of the 24/7 hrs mobile highway service facilities. In IT industry, the customer need not go to the shop for purchase of IT spares the product reaches the doorstep of the customer by accepting an order over a phone call.

One of the major pillars of Indian Economy is agriculture. For development of Agriculture business Cooperative banks play a vital role. The major part of the funds of Cooperative banks is utilised for promoting the customers who are basically agriculturist and village people.

* Lecturer in Business Administration, DDE. Annamalai University.

** Reader in Business Administration, DDE, Annamalai University.

At present the Cooperative banks provide various services to the account holders like green card loan for purchasing agriculture inputs etc. To compete with the competitors Cooperative banks also have scheduled bank Reorganization by RBI.

The new generation banks and MNC banks have created too much of hype in the market and projected that their organizations are offering world class services which the Indian consumers have never experience. However, the population living in rural areas are deprived of this "service" advantage. The only alternative is gearing up the cooperative banks to grow high in the service ladder and ascertain their level of relationship with their customer.

Hence, a survey (at macro level) was conducted to identify the level of awareness among the customers of cooperative bank with regard to the services offered by the new generation banks. The study revealed some fascinating results which are discussed in the following pages.

A sample of 50 customers were conducted to elicit information pertaining to research objectives. A structured questionnaire was distributed and their opinion was recorded. The respondents were contacted on random basis.

90% of the respondents expressed their satisfaction with the services extended by their bankers (Refer Table 1). The following are the main reasons they have attributed for their satisfaction (i) Customer service (44%), (ii) Maintaining good rapport, (36%), (iii) Proper guidance (14%), (iv) others 6% (Refer Table 2).

Table 1: Satisfied with the Present Service

No. of Respondent	Yes	No
50	45	5
In Percentage	90%	10%

The survey also revealed that 10% of respondents are unhappy with their present bankers. The following are the main reason for dissatisfaction (i) ATM facilities, (ii) status, (iii) Loans (Personal, car loans) etc.

Table 2: Reason for Customers Satisfaction with Present Service

No. of Respondent	*Customer Service*	*Maintaining Good Report*	*Proper Guidance and Help*	*Others*
50	22	18	7	3
In Percentage	44%	36%	14%	6%

Awareness about the new generation banks was also explored. 76% of the respondents revealed that they were aware of new generation banks (Refer Table 3). In spite of high awareness level customers still continue to patronize cooperative banks. The study highlighted that (i) Good rapport, (ii) Timely help, (iii) Cordial relation, (iv) Sentiment, (v) ATM problem, (vi) No guidance in other banks are some of the important reasons for their continued support (Refer Table 4)

Table 3: Awareness about New Generation Banks

No. of Respondent	Yes	No
50	38	12
In Percentage	76%	24%

Table 4: Patronage for Cooperative Banks

No. of Respondent	*Good Rapport*	*Cordial Relation*	*Timely Help*	*No Guidance in other Bank*	*ATM Problem*
50	24	13	7	3	3
In Percentage	48%	26%	14%	6%	6%

Table 5: Switch Over to New Generation Banks

No. of Respondent	Yes	No
50	38	12
In Percentage	76%	24%

Conclusion

The study clearly indicates that in spite of high awareness about the new generation banks the customers express their loyalty to their present bankers (Refer Table 5). Hence, switching over to the new generation bank is a point to ponder and only sustained effort may yield the expected result.

26

Customer Service Scenario (War) among Fixed Line, GSM and CDMA

M. SIVASUBRAMANIAN* & K. SOUNDARARAJAN**

The business entry of Reliance Info and Tata Indicom into Wireless telephony arena has signaled the onset of revolutionary services in terms of the customer service satisfaction. The customer service war is this time noticed in CDMA (Code Division Multiple Access) based limited Mobility Services and the Global System for Mobile communication (GSM).

In this scenario, as a customer we will be getting much more service than what we are rightly getting now. CDMA and GSM operators have been reducing their prices frequently. Which creates business with other competitors like. BSNL/MTNL. Further the GSM operators have started protecting their subscribers base by introducing new consumer schemes.

Operators will offer technology such as unified messaging service, which allows subscribers to send SMS embedded with graphics in real time. Several other applications such as text-to-speech e-mail, web chat and checking of flight and train schedules have also been introduced by Hutch. He said. Hutch also brings cricket video replays to its subscribers in its capacity as one of the World Cup.

In GSM market one kind of the leading Bharti cellular limited, launched MMS (Messages with picture and voice) which is one kind delivering the finest value to customers. This paper is

* Reader in Business Administration, DDE, A.U.
** Lecturer in Business Administration, DDE, A.U.

intended to highlight the services offered by the CDMA & GSM, and how customers are getting more value oriented services at the lowest cost.

The SMS habit is also growing first. Cellular companies handle on an average 1 lakh SMS calls a day. With WLL services in full spate, telephony in India is likely to be transformed beyond recognition in the coming months. Reliance Infocom has an initial rollout plan to network 673 towns and cities in the next 45-60 days. Reliance has also developed schemes to minimize the adverse impact of the lack of roaming. The regulatory authorities insist that WLL (limited mobility) services have to be confined to the SDCA (short distance charging area) as per the license condition. But call forwarding, coupled with multiple cities, may minimize the adverse impacts. Reliance is aiming at a 25 per cent market share or getting 10 million subscribers within one year, something which needs to be seen.

BSNL has also announced nil incoming call charge on two of its most popular tariff plans. "There will be no charge for incoming calls from all networks, be it fixed or cellular."

In the last eight months, we have seen two new cellular service providers and two limited mobility service providers enter or about to start operations. Obviously, the increased competitions put downward pressure on pricing as the new entrants engage in market share activities.

We witnessed a tariff crash in both ILD & NLD services which is worth around Rs. 12,500 crore. To counteract cellular operators announced a cut in cellphone to cellphone long distance tariffs by two-third to a flat rate of Rs. 2.99 per minute which is lower when compared with the earlier cost of Rs. 9 per minute.

In Kolkata, recently BSNL launched the scheme of extending the service of Internet access and cable TV through their existing telephone cables. This confirms that due to intense competition customers are getting more value addition.

The days of the fixed handset might be numbered. A trend that seems to have caught on in the past few months is the phenomenon of people surrendering their land line (fixed) phone connections and replacing them with wireless-in-local loop (WLL) fixed wireless terminals (FWTs) or their mobile version. According to reports, nearly 15 lakh Bharat Sanchar Nigam Ltd. (BSNL) connections have been surrendered over the past two years.

Similarly, a very large nationwide financial institution is moving on to the Reliance Infocom network. The reason is Reliance's 40 paise per minute long distance rate between Reliance phones anywhere in the country. There are other reasons too. For home users who have more than one phone, it makes sense to surrender one and purchase mobile connections. Many people are doing so and keeping the landline primarily for internet access. But the biggest reason yet is the fear that landline telephones are becoming more expensive and do not provide the host of features that GSM or WLL does, like SMS, MMS, roaming and even e-mail and internet access.

The mobile phone industry is growing at a much faster pace than fixed line in India, though it will take time in India, for the total number of mobile phones (over 11.5 million GSM phones and around 5.5 lakh WLL) to outgrow the nearly 40 million landline connections installed till date.

Basic telephony is clearly in a tangle as more and more people, plug into the mobile revolution. New land phone connections have registered a negative growth of 24.7% during the first nine months of the current financial year for basic phones and WLL against the same period last year. It has been accompanied by a 73% growth in new cellular phones during the same period. During April to December of last financial year, 26 lakh new basic telephone connections were added, while only 19 lakh new telephone connections were added during the same period this year. According to Dot officials, of them, about 7 lakh are WLL phones. Therefore, if we consider only fixed line connections, the total growth in new basic phone connections is negative 54% per cent. According to the survey, the cellular segment grew by 73.7 per cent. During the first nine months, 33 lakh new cell phone connections were added against 19 lakh cellphones during the same period of the current fiscal. The total growth in the mobile phone connections was 110.5 per cent during this year as WLL phones are basically mobile phones. The shift from fixed to mobile telephony in India is in line with International trends. In the last 10 years, the number of mobile telephones have already overtaken fixed line telephones.

The result states that in future the customers will be more interested in GSM & WLL technology than in landline. This is not an end as anything may happen in the world. To retain its customers the corporate has to give the excellent service with updated technology.

27

Taking a Company to Service Excellence

R. ANAND*, G. UDAYASURIYAN** & S. ARULKUMAR*

Introduction

In today's international competitive market, companies want to capture and maintain the market share in their respective industries. The most difficult part of taking a company to service excellence is not generating the ideas but rather execute the ideas—and continuing to execute the ideas that allow a company to continue in the dynamic state of service excellence.

The key areas to maintain the dynamic state of service excellence and checklist are:

Organization Structure

The organizational structure is not simply a framework but may regard as the "Grammar" of an Institution/Enterprises/ Company. It's quite true because it defines the place, positions work, method execution of a personal either as an employer, employee/manager or a service support personnel.

Such a live structure in the context of service excellence should have certain factors enabled within it.

It should posses a service strategy, which should be known to act the employees.

It should put forth method, which could include or ensure participation of both (a) Front line service delivery personnel and (b) Back office service support personnel's who could originate and put forth ideas to increase customer satisfaction.

* Lecturers, Dept. of Management Studies, D.D.E. Annamalai University.

** Reader, School of Management, Annamalai University.

It should opportunities or generate opportunity for participation of all the peoples in the organization.

It should ensure the sufficiency, execution of exercise of opportunities on. (i) Job rotation, (ii) Job Engineering, (iii) Practice of Employees, Customers Management Techniques, (iv) Promotions, (v) Job enrichment, (vi) Development of employees Conceptual skills.

It should measure the success or failure of the ideas either subjectively or objectively and the workable balance among power groups in support of the service strategic should be evaluated.

The Right People

A proper selection of personal therefore should be ensured in accordance with highest degree of synchronization with the job descriptions, job specification and the services skills and attitude recollect for customer contact position.

Selection of personal should be genuine, ethical, far of bias and should ensure maximum utilization of all tools and techniques of the selection process.

Opportunity

Sufficient opportunity for the development and exercise of conceptual skill should be emphasized so as to cope up to the customer's expectations. This could be accomplished only if there is Sufficient staffing level. Proper Allocation of Authority and Responsibility. Sufficient incentive schemes supporting the companies service strategy and sufficient reward and recognition schemes for customer satisfaction. Establishment of performance standard for both routine and non-routine situations. Monitoring whether the service offerings are continuously in tune with the customer's needs; through establishment of proper feedback systems.

Performance

"One can expect more If he Inspect More" similarly "The one who is praised loses and the one who is appraised benefits".

Hence there should be good appraisal standards, which should predominantly rest on customer service and satisfaction. So it is good to have service standards based on customer's expectations.

Customer satisfaction has to be given top priority in the context of (i) Performance appraisal, (ii) Promotions, (iii) Job descriptions and various other factors.

It is also advisable to ensure whether the daily supervision activities gear performance to deliver service as number one priority and under extraordinary operating conditions too customer satisfaction remains at the top priority. The company's management style should be reckoned whether it plays "The same strokes for All Flocks". It treaties employees in the manner that the company would like its customers treated.

Level of Commitment

Service excellence is not simply "What you do with people" but it includes "What you do to people", also and hence it requires a greater degree of commitment.

There should certainly be interdisciplinary groups compressing majority of skeptical personalities too so as to look at service excellence. Playing "Different strokes for the same flock" is essentially necessary.

At the managerial level personnel's executing "high competence" and "variable commitments" should be placed who would pass act messages, responsibility, extend support, educate his subordinates and would provide feedback Gis cross the organizational chain and would eventually connect the top executives or top management to the lowest designates of the company, seeking and ensuring commitment of the entire structure.

Care should be taken that time commitment and priority to service excellence is provided and if do not interferes with other initiatives of the company on any account/grounds. A strong service strategy should be laid down upon agreement favoring service excellence. Provision should be made that the senior executives are able to monitor the crisis and lay down a course of action is rectifying them.

Training and Development

"Everyone has peak performance potential and one should just need to know where they are coming from and next them there". There should be a comprehensive overall training plan for all employees in support of the service strategy, emphasizing. "Technical, Behavioral and conceptual skills on new methods, procedures and products.

These skills should hold proper and essential balance among them. It should also be ensured that the training, techniques, used have achieved the instructional objectives at the most cost-effective manner. On the whole the overall training plan should also include both the internal and external agencies who are in line and intact with the company's business performance.

Advertising and Sales

"In reality fakes blow their own trumpets" but

"In business one who does not blow his own Trumpet becomes a fake"

(*i*) *Advertising message* should have a positive impact on employees attitude and customer's to buy it. The message should feature both personal and material services. It should have a theme, a logo, a trademark or a symbol which would enhanced easy memory/ remembrance of the company in the minds of the customer. The message should have liveness and continuity. Service benefits should be translated into advertising message in a keen and clean way so that the customer can easily understand the benefits of the product.

(*ii*) *Service guarantees* should be meaningful to the customers and should be used effectively. The service guarantee in proportion and projection should support the service strategy. The work of the sales force should be monitored that they sell "service first" and service second. Proper solution for breakdown and faults! Should be laid down so as to proceed and perform an undisturbed service.

Product/Service Perception

Emphasis should be laid on whether the product and service being delivered is of sufficient quality and is supported by the (a) services strategy, (b) prices, (c) the customers support, (d) Advertising message, (e) public relations activity. The employee's perception of the product and service should be tested and evaluated regularly soliciting the customer's opinion.

Measurement and Evaluation

Measurement makes a thing finite and

Evaluation elucidates its excellence.

The service delivered and customer satisfaction could be measured internally and externally. Internally it could be measured through quality assurance inspection, audits, employee's services, self-audits, etc. Externally through customer audits, customer satisfaction surveys, customer comment cards, etc. Dates perusing financial amenities in terms of profiles and revenue opportunity or market damage should be obtained in the peer view of customer satisfaction.

Resolving Failures

"Failures are the first step for success but not always" unless resolved. The customer's comments, inquiries abed complaints should be handled when first expressed rather than allow it to escalate. A regular business plan or profit plan for handling complaints and inquiry should be laid down in units and all staffs in the units should be adequately trained so we need to attend to the complaints and inquiries effectively; for selling and cross selling opportunities there by providing a proper feed back network for resolving the problems.

Conclusion

The journey to service excellence is not easy; the road has no end. It requires commitment and perseverance over time, but it rewards are great.

REFERENCE

1. Linda M., Lash. The complete to guide to "*Customer Service*". John Wiley & sons, Inc. 1989.

28

Customer Service in BSNL

Issues and Strategies

S. MUTHUKUMAR* & N. PANCHANATHAM**

Introduction

One of the major trends in the India in recent years has been a dramatic growth of customer service. The reason is that changing customer expectation, competitors are seeking customer service as a competitive weapon with which to differentiate their sales. The trend of customer service builds a strong foundation in our Indian market. There are many service sectors that had tremendous development in application of customer service, such sectors are banking, communication, insurance, transportation, hotels, hospitals, educational institutions etc. In our India, telecommunication sectors play a significant role in providing excellent services to the customers. The revolution of communication and information technologies made tremendous changes in the field of customer service through the telecommunication sectors. The Indian telecom service sectors such as BSNL, VSNL, MTNL, Bharati, Reliance, and Tata telecom are leading telecommunication sectors in providing services to the customers. Among that BSNL is a government of India enterprise, which provides better and excellent services to the customers through the location of Customer Service Centres with fully computerized in their various telephone exchanges and periodical telephone adalaths to redress the grievances of the customers. The aim and scope of this research paper is to present the significant changes in the issues and strategies of customer service in BSNL based on the literature review and observation.

* M.Phil Scholar.

** Reader in Business Administration, Annamalai University.

Customer Service Concept

Philip Kotler and Gary Armstrong stated that "customer service process are all the activities involved in making it easy for customers to reach the right parties within the company to obtain service, answers and resolution of problems". (1997, p. 578)

Ben M. Enis viewed that "Customer service is paramount because customer satisfaction is the key to successful attainment of the organization objective, e.g. profit, return on investment, increased market share, winning the election or whatever". (1997, p. 323)

Therefore, the concept of customer service is an instrument, which monitor the level of satisfaction among the customers with

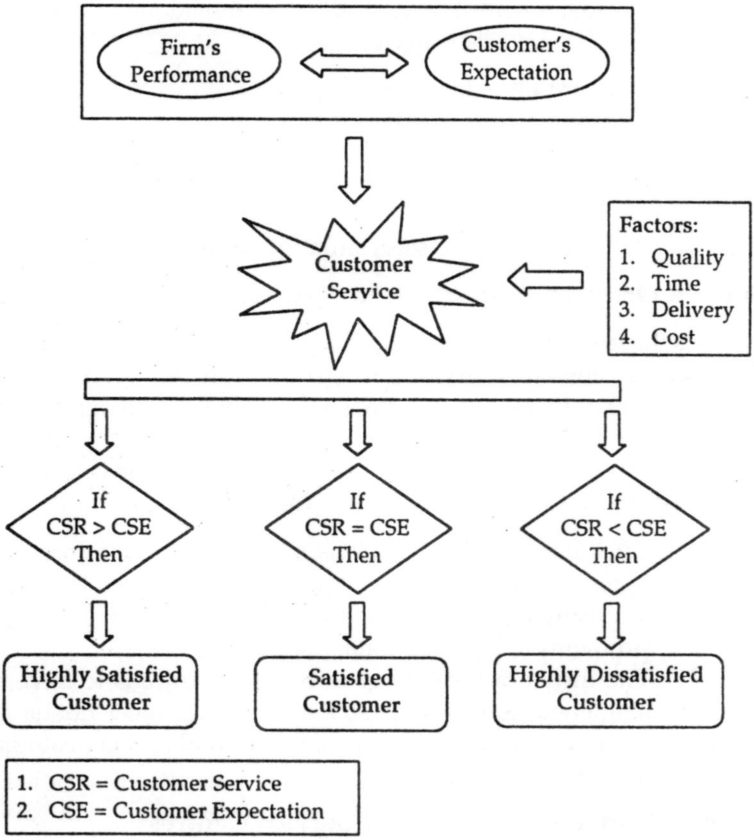

Fig. 1: Relationship of Customer Service with Customer Expectation and Satisfaction.

their expectations based on the marketing factors. R. Michael Donovan suggested, "Customer service is a competitive weapon that can easily differentiate one supplier from another. A lot of task today is centralized on quality, new processes and system, continuous improvement and the like, but it must be aimed at customer satisfaction or it isn't worth much over the longer term"(www.rmdonovan.com). The customer service is only determinant factor, which affect the level of customer's expectation and satisfaction and developed harmonious relationship between them. This relationship has been explained in the Figure 1.

Benefits Over the Customer Service

American Management Association International stated several benefits over the customer service are,

1. Deliver better, faster service.
2. Increase customer satisfaction.
3. Gain repeat business.
4. Increase your credibility with customer and your value to your organization.
5. Better manage stressful situation. (www.amanet.org)

Service Orientation of BSNL towards Customer

BSNL is the leading telecommunication sector, which ensures better and excellent customer service through establishment of Customer Service Centres in various locations of telephone exchanges. The Customer Service Centre acts as a separate functional department deals with resolution of customers' problems. The objectives of locating this Customer Service Centre are:

1. Customer Service Centre is a convenient, comfortable place to interact effectively with customers in a friendly atmosphere and to attend to most of their requirements/ problems in a professional manner.
2. The thrust of the Customer Service Centre is to have a single window concept so that customers does not have to go to different persons/locations and all his dealings are handled at one place.

Facilities offered by Customer Service Centres

BSNL offered several facilities through the Customer Service Centres are:

1. Application form for New Phone Connection.
2. Registration of New Phone Connection.
3. Accepting requests for additional accessories phone plus services and shifts.
4. Handling of complaints on Telephone Services.
5. Sale of Telephone Directories literatures useful to the subscribers.
6. Issues of duplicate Telephone bills and receipts of payment of Telephone bills by cheque/cash.
7. Reconnection of Telephone lines disconnected for non-payment of dues.
8. Copy of waiting list register of Telephone exchanges of SSAs.
9. STD/ISD/Local PCOs.
10. Fax/Telex facilities. (http://www.tamilnadu.bsnl.co.in)

Functional Conditions of Customer Service Centres

The functional conditions of Customer Service Cetres are:

1. Customers Service Centres are to function at all Telephone Exchanges of capacity more than 1500 lines.
2. As on date there are 166 such exchanges having justification.
3. Out of this 47 Telephone exchanges are provided with Customer Service Centres.
4. The supervision is to be done by a responsible officer and the officials manning the Customer Service Centres are having good personality, pleasing manners and aptitude of helping others.
5. They are trained in various aspects of departmental working, relevant rules and regulations to meet the customer needs. (www.tamilnadu.bsnl.co.in)

Computerization in Customer Service Centres

In order to enhance operational performance and provide better customer services, various works and services are being computerized progressively by BSNL telecom sector. The following services are being covered under computerized plan,

1. Issue of duplicate bills.
2. Registration of new lines.

3. Waiting list positions of new lines.
4. Booking of complaints and disconnection/reconnection of phones.
5. Electronic exchanges in Headquarters of Telecom Districts are equipped with Interactive Voice Response System (IVRS) where in faults are booked and computer announces changed numbers when customer dials 198 and 196 respectively.

In addition to the Customer Service Centres, each head of SSA (Secondary Switching Area) conducts periodical Telephone adalaths and open house sessions to redress the grievances of the customers.

Result

The study reveals that the trend of customer service made tremendous development and unexpectable changes over the BSNL through the location and computerization of Customer Service Centres in India. The study also proved that BSNL Customer Service Centres take care of various customer service activities and provide solutions to various customers' problems effectively.

Conclusion

In the conclusion, the author has studied the various issues and strategies of the customer service in BSNL in the current scenario. This research paper viewed that BSNL having carried out the customer services through Customer Service Centres successfully and hopes that it will extend its operations across national boundaries with intend to meet the global competition in the future. This study also serves as a guideline to others who wish to conduct further work in this aspect and provides effective information to everyone.

REFERENCES

1. American Management Association International, URL: http://www.amant.org/seminars/cmd2/5165.htm
2. Ben M., Enis, 1997, *'Marketing Principles—the Management Process'*, California, Goodyear Publishing Company.

3. R. Michael, Donovan, URL: www.rmdonovan.com
4. Philip Kotler and Gary Armstrong, 1997, *'Principles of Marketing'*, New Delhi, Prentice-Hall of India Private Limited.
5. URL: http://www.tamilnadu.bsnl.co.in/corporateinfo/lookback/win.htm.

29

Marketing of Interface Services

C. SAMUDHRA RAJAKUMAR* & R. SRITHARAN*

Introduction

As competition intensifies, consumers may view product benefits as service. Intangibility, perishability and variability are the characteristics associated with service. To explore the possibility of positioning product as service, "Categorisation of the offering" can be used. This is viewed as a pure-tangible product, a tangible product with accompanying services and hybrids. The basic idea of this paper is that as more and more brands enter a category, the focus of consumers is likely to shift from core products to specific benefits and hence perception on benefits is vital for marketers.

Need Analysis

Exploring the needs of the consumer is an important aspect of customer product interface. The need analysis helps the firms to findout which aspect of the offering needs to be highlighted to win over competition. For example, the core benefit of detergents is to remove dirt and secondary benefits might be harmless to hands, fragrance etc. Core and secondary benefits assist a marketer to understand the trend towards specific consumer interface. Linkages between benefits and offer categorisation is shown in the following figure.

The core benefit of any malted food drink is to provide nutritious value but taste and flavour could be the secondary benefits. In some specific cases the secondary benefits could be

* Faculty Members, Dept. of Business Administration, Annamalai University, Annamalai Nagar.

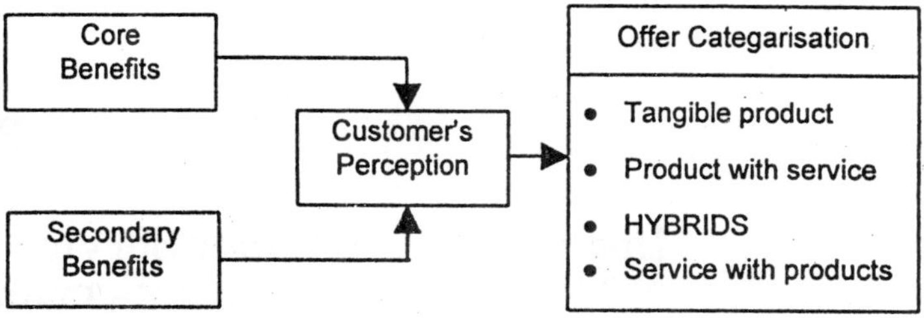

converted as a basis for differentiation. This increased differentiation is central to customer product interfacing and is vital in increasing the perceived value of the brand.

Home shopping/ Tele shopping networks are the best example of Hybrid category. Here, the core benefit is making the product available at your doorsteps and the secondary benefits are the main features associated with the product. In addition to after-sales-service, for hybrid category, pre sale service plays a major role in motivating the consumers to buy the advertised product. 'Vender Interfacing' is the secret behind their success.

Examples for service with products are airlines, holiday trips etc. Past experience is the influencing factor for future preference. Creating and maintaining positive image perception is the strategy adopted by firms operating in this segment.

Customer services interfacing enable a firm to positively reinforce the image of the product/service in the minds of consumers. Customer product Interface aims at increasing the contact between consumer and the company. Providing information on time, enhancing delivery system and building confidence are some ways to enhance CPI.

Conclusion

CPI provides a strategy to augment the differentiation of a product/service with a view to have an edge over competitors. This also helps to increase brand value and utility to the consumer. To conclude, firms use CPI to reduce the gap between the expectation of the customer and the product. This provides an opportunity to the corporates to create products or services to match the needs of customers.

30

Improving Customer Service in Public Sector

N. Markkandeyan*

As public sector organizations move toward providing better service, they must anchor their strategies in the knowledge that government service delivery is more complex than the private sector. Poor quality and service in public organization may result in complaints to politicians, privatization, tax resistance, restructuring and downsizing of staff and so on. Here are some trends that are impacting customer service in government.

Trends Impacting on Customer Service

1. *Customer Expectations*: In the fierce competitive private sector, ways are constantly being sought to improve customer service and thus gain a competitive edge. Buy now; play later, free delivery, electronic ordering, payment by credit card, extended hours all set the expectations of customers.
2. *Downsizing*: All levels of government have been significantly reducing the levels of staff in order to reduce budget deficits. This has had three implications for customer service:
   (*a*) Less people available to deal with customers.
   (*b*) Poor morale among those remaining due to uncertainly and increased work loads.
   (*c*) The people that have remained do not necessarily have the knowledge and skills to provide excellence in customer service.

* G.T.N. Arts College, Dindigul (TN).

3. *Fiscal Constraints*: Reduced resources also mean fewer offices, shorter hours and fewer services—all that can negatively impact on customer service.
4. *User Fees:* More and more departments are charging their customers user fees to recover some of the costs of services. Customers tend to be more patient if the service is free but along with fees they expect better service.
5. *Twenty-four Hour Society*: Customers are beginning to expect service at any time or any day. Extended shopping hours and the ability to buy 24 hours a day are becoming more common. Customers would like to get government services at their convenience.
6. *Want it Now*: People have been conditioned to expect results in one-hour, e.g., one-hour photos, one hour cleaning, one-hour glasses. People expect to get what they want within a short period of time and don't like to wait.
7. *Electronic Communications*: Organizations and the public are becoming accustomed to using electronic communications technology. Fax machines and on-line systems are now available in many businesses and a good number of households. People would like to use this technology in their dealings with the public sector.
8. *Customer Service*: Many companies provide training to their employees and staff in customer service. The business media constantly focuses attention on the importance of customer service. This awareness in the public at large increases the demand for better customer from all organizations.

Therefore despite reduced resources in public sector organizations, the demand for high levels of customer service is likely to increase.

The Quality Concepts

Investing in quality improvement reduces costs and increase sales.

- Doing things right the first time (zero defect).
- Designing products and services to meet customer's needs.
- Setting product and service standards.
- Measuring performance.

The Service Concepts

- Finding out what customers want.
- Designing a service to meet customers' needs.
- Providing customers with extraordinary service.
- Setting service standards.
- Measuring service performance.
- Empowering staff to meet customers' needs.

The Internet and Service Quality

The basic rule in providing excellent customer service is to make it as easy, convenient and pleasant as possible for your clients to do business with you. This means you must make it easy for customers to:

- find you or your unit, branch or department
- find the information they need
- get in contact with the right person
- get the service the need
- pay for the service
- receive follow-up service and support.

The Internet can be used to improve customer service in the public sector. Here are just some ways:

1. Your clients and the general public can use the Internet to find you and get information about your programs and services. If you have a Net presence, this can be done 24 hours a day, 7 days a week, from anywhere in world without long distance charges.
2. The Internet is a great tool for professional development, research and networking. This means that staff can be more informed and therefore can be more helpful to their clients.
3. By putting as much information on-line, the work load on your staff should decrease as they have to handle fewer routine inquiries. This allows them to provide better service to those customers that have unique needs or problems.
4. Putting your newsletters, reports and policies on-line will not only provide your clients with an option to get this information at their convenience, but can also save

significant amounts of work and costs associated with traditional information dissemination. Give your customers a choice of getting the information on-line or via traditional methods.

5. The Internet can be used to survey your clients to assess their needs, get input on proposed plans, and to obtain evaluation on existing programs and services.
6. The Internet can be used to work more effectively and conveniently with partners involved in projects. Committees may not physically have to meet as often, but still can work together electronically and exchange documents. This could save significant time and costs for all involved.
7. The Internet can be used to provide better customer training and support. This can be done through e-mail, FAQs, on-line documents and interactive problem solving.
8. Putting statistical and comparative data on-line, can allow your client organizations to develop and implement more effective business plans.
9. Create a moderated newsgroup were your customers can exchange and share information, and engage in discussion of important issues and problems facing their organizations.

Why a World Wide Web Site

So why would you want a World Wide Web site for your government branch or division? There are six major reasons for having a web site:

1. *Image*: Some 72 per cent of companies said they have a web site to enhance their image. So if you are a public official who is concerned about your unit's image, you may want to put up a web site. After all, it's a cool thing to do and shows you are innovative and at the leading edge.
2. *Marketing*: About 75 per cent of companies said they use the web to provide product and price information to their customers. So if you are selling products or services directly to consumers, a web site can be an important marketing tool.

3. *A Business*: Creating a web site and charging individuals, companies and other organization to list on your web site can be a business in itself. Income can be earned from listing fees, or as a percentage of the business earned as a result of listing on your web site.
4. *Public Information*: This is the most common application by the public and non-profit sectors. The goal is to provide current and relevant information to your clients, stakeholders, partners and the general public in an easily accessible and convenient format.
5. *Save Money*: Many organizations are using the web as a means of saving money. A web site can result in significant savings due to reduced long distance phone charges, less staff to take calls and answer questions, and reduced printing and mailing costs.
6. *Enjoyment*: Another good reason for setting up a web page for your unit is as a learning experience or for the fun of it. The best way to learn about the technology is to actually do it yourself.

A World Wide Web site offers government departments and branches a number of benefits. These include:

1. *Improved Communications*: The World Wide Web site can provide information 24 hours a day to many customers. Electronic message can be sent any time and responded to by your staff.
2. *Better Service and Support*: Rather than just relying on staff during business hours for assistance, a web site can provide answers any time.
3. *Improved Efficiencies*: Less staff time will have to be devoted to personally answering questions and solving problems.
4. *Expandability*: The Internet is evolving. Today it is mainly a static information dissemination service. However, software is becoming available to do dynamic linkages to databases. Most branches can start small and expand their services as the technology and resources become available.
5. *Consistent with Directions in Information Technologies*: The Internet is experiencing an explosive growth rate. Your

use of a web site is consistent with the direction millions of companies and organizations are going.

6. *Setting an Example*: The government wishes to encourage the use of technology to improve the efficiency and effectiveness of its operations and those that they fund. Your web site could be a model for your public sector clients.

Conclusion

A real concern about the Internet is the lack of security for confidential data. Extra care needs to be taken when using the Internet to transfer data of a confidential nature. Some form of encryption needs to be used. All departments have policies and procedures regarding privacy and this need to be extended to the Internet. Extra precautions need to be taken to establish secure "firewalls" to protect their data. All government departments have identified performance indicators and measures of success in their business plans. The same should be done with their Internet-based information systems. Government units should be able to monitor and evaluate how successful their Internet systems are in providing better service to their customers. Developing and operating an Internet presence in the public sector will definitely improve the customer service.

31

Dimensions of Service Quality

A. BHAVANI* & G. SRIDEVI*

Sooner or later, today or tomorrow, we are suitably rewarded for our excellence. Our dedication, commitment, optimisms play an incremental role in generating excellence which is the result of perception. An individual or an institution succeeds in thriving if there is no boundary for quality. Sky is the limit for perfection. Innovation makes a new ways for achieving perfection. This makes it essential that we assign a transcendental priority to the total quality management. It is in this context that almost all the organizations have been found making innovative efforts to develop a new perception of quality, which helps them in achieving the desired results.

Service quality is crucial to both the customer and the service firm. Service firms use quality in maintaining competitive advantage and customers use service quality in maintaining competitive advantage and customers use service quality to differentiate between competitors.

The definition of quality started from an emphasis on product quality and has been extended to include services. While the importance of quality is recognized everywhere the concept seems to refer to several different areas, namely, quality of the output quality of the process, quality of the delivery system and quality as general philosophy of the organization. We understand that

* Lecturers in Business Administration, A.V.C. College of Engg. Mayilladuthurai, Tanjore Distt.

the quality is holistic philosophy and should be included at every stage in the organization. Quality is a difficult concept to define in a single definition.

Quality can be Viewed from Two Points of View

1. *From the viewpoint of the service provider*—to set up standards or specifications in the manufacturing process as well as the output which is totally objective and technical in nature.
2. *From the viewpoint of the customer*—service quality occurs only when the service firm provides services to the specifications that satisfy their needs. The idea of quality here is subjective and will be strongly linked to the needs and expectations of the customer.

The following are some of the more popular definitions of service quality:

- Fitness for purpose
- The totality of features of service that meets the needs
- The difference between customer expectations and performance delivery
- Meeting or exceeding what customers expect from the service

Various Dimensions of Service Quality

The dimensions of service quality refer to process quality as judged by consumers during a service delivery and output quality judged after a services performed.

A service firm delivers to customer a service package, which consists of some physical aspects and some intangibles. Christian Gronroos suggested that the quality of service as perceived by the customer has two dimension—technical or outcome dimensions and the function of process related dimensions. Technical dimension describes what the customers get and when they get it, while functional quality describes how they get it. Berry Parasuram and Zeitham who conducted extensive research in service quality identified 10 criteria used by consumers in evaluating service quality.

Dimensions and Definition	*Examples of Specific Questions Realised by Customers*
Tangibles: Appearance of physical facilities, equipment, personnel and communication materials.	• Are the bank's facilities attractive? • Is my stockbroker dressed appropriately? • Is my credit card statement easy to understand? • Do the tools used by the repairperson look modern?
Reliability: Ability to perform the promised service dependably and accurately	• When a loan officer says she will call me back in 15 minutes, does she do so?
Responsiveness: Willingness to help customers and provide prompt service.	• When there is a problem with my bank statement, does the bank resolve the problem quickly? • Is my stockbroker willing to answer my question? • Are charges for returned merchandise credited to my account promptly? • Is the repair firm willing to give me a specific time when the repairperson will show up?
Competence: Possession of the required skills and knowledge to perform the service.	• Is the bank teller able to process my transactions without fumbling around? • Does my brokerage firm have the research capabilities to accurately track market developments? • When I call my credit card company, is the person at the other enable to answer my questions? • Does the repairperson appear to know what he is doing?
Courtesy: Politeness, respect, consideration and friendliness of contact personnel.	• Does the bank teller have pleasant demeanor? • Does my broker refrain from acting busy or being rude when I ask questions? • Are the telephone operators in the credit card company consistently polite when answering my calls? • Does the repairperson take off his muddy shoes before stepping on my carpet?

(*Contd.*)

(*Contd.*)

Dimensions and Definition	*Examples of Specific Questions Realised by Customers*
Credibility: Trust, worthiness, believability, honest of the service provider.	• Does the bank have good reputations? • Does why broker refrain from pressuring me to buy? • Are the interest rates/fees charges by my credit card company consistent with the services provided? • Does the repair firm guarantee its services?
Security: Freedom from danger, risk or doubt.	• Is it safe for me to use the bank's automatic teller machines? • Does my brokerage firm know where my stock certificate is? • Is my credit card safe from unauthorized use? • Can I be confident that the repair job was done properly?
Access: Approachability and ease of contact.	• How easy is it for me to talk to senior bank officials when I have a problem? • Is it easy to get through to my broker over the telephone? • Does the credit card company have a 24-hour, toll-free telephone number? • Is the repair service facility conveniently located?
Communications: Keeping customers informed in language they can understand and listening to them.	• Can the loan officer explain clearly the various charges related to the mortgage loan? • Does my broker avoid using technical jargon? • When I call my credit card company, are they willing to listen to me? • Does the repair firm call when they are unable to keep a scheduled repair appointment?
Understanding the Customer: Making the effort to know customers and their needs.	• Does someone in my bank recognize me as a regular customer? • Does my broker try to determine what my specific financial objectives are? • Is the credit limit set by my credit card company consistent with what I can afford (i.e., neither too high nor too low)? • Is the repair firm willing to be flexible enough to accommodate my schedule?

In the subsequent research they found a high degree of correlation between most of these variables and consolidated them into five broad dimensions:

1. *Tangible*: Are those factors that the customers can see, hear and touch. It includes the appearance of physical facilities, equipment an appearance of contact personnel. Tangibles are used when assessing the physical qualities before the service is experienced.
2. *Responsiveness*: It is the willingness and ability on the part of the service provider to respond to the needs of the customer and serve him promptly. Responsiveness is an important dimension for those customers who require some service over and above what is usually provided.
3. *Empathy*: This includes providing, caring individualized attentions to customers. It is described as "the human touch". Empathy includes features like approachability, sense of security. Empathy and responsiveness, though closely related, differ in this point—responsiveness shows willingness to meet customer needs and empathy indicates willingness to go beyond customer needs.
4. *Assurance*: Represents the employee knowledge and courtesy and their ability to inspire trust and confidence. A favourable assessment of assurance will indicate that the customer is satisfied as the staff understood his needs and met them.
5. *Reliability*: It is the ability of the service firm to perform the service accurately and dependably. To the customer it will ensure whether the promise made by the service firm has been met. Reliable service performance is a customer expectation of the service. In fact, most customers regard reliability as the most important of the 5 dimensions of the service performance.

32

Customer Service Excellence

T.R. ANANDHI* & S. ANURADHA**

Banking System occupies an important place in a nation's economy. The Banking system in India grew tremendously after independence in terms of office, magnitude of bank deposit and bank credit etc.

The Industrial Credit and Investment Corporation was set up on 15th January 1955 with Head Office at Mumbai. The banks issued capital has been taken up Indian Banks, Insurance companies and others, certain individuals and corporation of United States, the British Eastern Exchange Banks and certain English and other Common Wealth Insurance Companies and other Companies and general public in India. ICICI has been raising resources from within the country as well as from outside. It has obtained loans from government of India, the World Bank and from Reconstruction Loan Corporation of West Germany.

Initial Resources—17.5 crores { 12.5 crores in rupees; $ 10 million foreign currency }

There has been a remarkably significant increase in financial assistance rendered by ICICI in recent years.

* Lecturer in Commerce, Theivanai Ammal College for Women, Villupuram.

** HOD/Commerce, Theivanai Ammal College for Women, Villupuram.

Financial Assistance by ICICI

Particulars	*1970-71*	*1980-81*	*1990-91*	*1998-99*
Loans Sanctioned	44	310	3740	34220
Loans Disbursed	29	180	1970	19225

Service Given by ICICI

1. Free Net Banking
2. Free ATM
3. Free Mobile Banking etc.

ICICI direct.com—Facilities online Trading

ICICI Bank.Com.

It is the Internet Banking Channel of ICICI bank. It offers you' the convenience of banking transaction from the comfort of your home or office. It's like having a bank branch on your computer. By logging on to ICICI Bank.com, you can view and transact on your

(*a*) Bank accounts
(*b*) Credit Cards
(*c*) Demat accounts.

ICICI Bank Credit Cards

Credit Cards make life so easy. You can subscribe to Credit Cards Alerts. These Alerts are sent to you by e-mail, and are also stored Credit Card Alerts inbox.

Status India's Top Symbols

There is no denying it. Being seen in the right clothes on the right set of wheels or with the right gadget, has a magical sesame effect. It open doors. In some cases even gateways.

An A&M—AC Nielsen Survey (Credit Card Survey)

The study surveys some 2400 respondents in eight cities Delhi, Mumbai, Chennai, Kolkata, Bangalore, Hyderabad, Pune and Ahmedabad. In each city the target sample of 210 males was balanced to ensure there were two salaried mean for each self employed male. For the 90 women surveyed in each city, there was one working women for every two house wives.

Methodology

Each respondent was asked to pick 10 objects (from a given list of 30) that he/she considered the "most powerful status symbol", and then rank them. Points were awarded in reverse order. (10 points for a symbol ranked first, and 1 point for tenth). Once every response was in each symbol, national power scores were calculated by taking an average across all the cities and people, weighted by the actual proportion of people who have cars in the cities. Similarly, separate power sources for each gender and city.

An A&M—AC Nielsen Survey

Year	*Points*
2001	3.29
1997	2.27
1994	2.38

Analysis of Preference of Credit Cards

Sex	*Rank*	*Points*
Male	No. 4	3.52
Female	No. 6	2.74

Credit Cards jumps for places to No. 6. Men assigned their symbol a score higher than the women. But then, plastic is getting common. West matters these days is the specific brand.

Citi Bank is still the most prestigious card though it has lost some prestige share (from 45 per cent in 1997 to 25 per cent now) American Express is the one not to leave home without 16 per cent of respondents. ICICI makes an impressive debut with an 8 per cent share of spontaneous mention. City wise Citi Bank is more preferred in Mumbai and Bangalore, while in Delhi and Chennai American Express and Citi Bank enjoy equal status. SBI is popular in Hyderabad. Pune plumps for Citi Bank VISA and SBI.

S. No.	*Banks*	*Percentage*
1.	Citi Bank	25
2.	American Express	16
3.	VISA	14
4.	ICICI	8
5.	Standard Chartered	7
6.	SBI	7
7.	HSBC	6
8.	Others	17

Conclusion

Awareness with regard to Credit Cards should be created in rural areas also. This can be done by an awareness Programme by Representatives of Banks through the help of Self Help Groups, NGO's Advertisement (through Radio, Television Magazines) etc.

33

Critical Dimensions of Achieving Eternal Customer Satisfaction

J. JAYAKRISHNAN*, C. SAMUDHRARAJAKUMAR*
FRANK SUNIL JUSTUS** & B. NATARAJAN**

Introduction

India is experiencing a transition phase where large number of organisations are in the process of changing attitude towards customer-centric. With a proliferation of brands, the critical question in today's marketing context is "how to maintain market share and profit". The simple answer is ensuring eternal customer satisfaction.

The concept of customer satisfaction has undergone radical changes in recent times. It is an ongoing process which need to adopt itself to the changing expectations of the customers as well as to the competitive strategies devised by other firms. This paper stresses the concept that satisfaction starts with consumer's perception about benefits and features of the product. If any mismatch occurs between expectation and product the process of satisfaction will never take-off. In this context, understanding domains of customer satisfaction has become essential.

Satisfaction is an outcome of the interaction between the expectations of a consumer and performance of a product/service. In the first phase 4 types of satisfaction need to be understood by the marketers followed by 4 elements of satisfaction.

Clear understanding of domains of satisfaction helps the firms to formulate competitive strategy which significantly influences the perceptions. The diagram depicts four areas of satisfaction, *viz.*, Product, Peripheral, Ambience and Psychic.

* Faculty Members, Management wing, D.D.E. Annamalai University.
** Faculty Members, School of Management, Annamalai University.

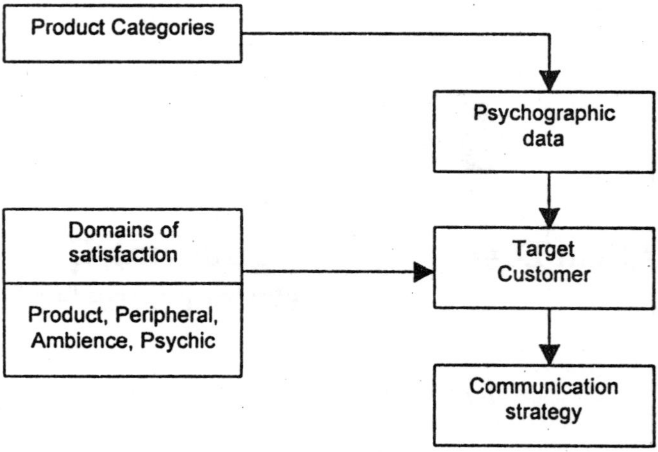

Product Satisfaction

This centers around the product's basic features, which could be applied to durables and consumables.

Peripheral Satisfaction

This is concerned with creating product/service differentiation when identifying the differences between brands is difficult.

Ambience Satisfaction

This is a combination of both tangible and intangible factors which influence the consumer's experiences in his encounter with a product or service.

Psychic Satisfaction

This area of satisfaction is focused on the 'self-esteem' and 'goal achievement' traits of customers.

The marketers needs to understand the following 4 elements to meet customer satisfaction.

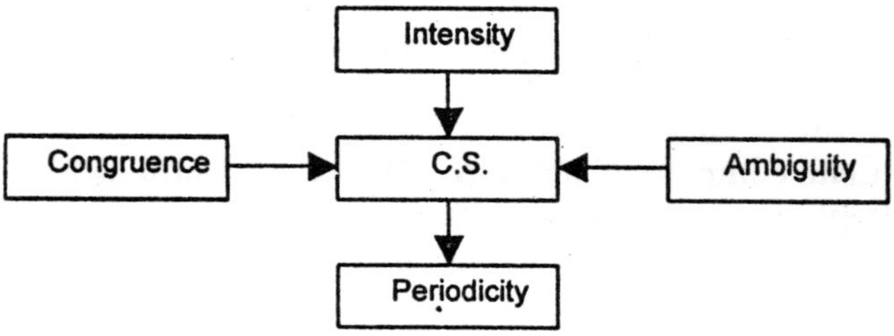

The third dimension is satisfaction trap.

This involves: (i) measuring the wrong parameters associated with satisfaction, and (ii) Adding factors which can augment satisfaction but may not result in retention.

Conclusion

Satisfaction is concerned with updation of products which serve the needs of customers. Customer satisfaction is a concept which is not to be viewed in isolation, measuring customer satisfaction and translating into meaningful strategies in key factor for ensuring success for a product or service.

34

Quality Customer Service in Automobile Component Industry

R. ARUNMOZHI* & S.B. NAGESWARA RAO**

Introduction

This chapter discusses the customer service relationship between the Auto Component Industry and Automobile Industry. The Auto component industry has a simple beginning in the fifties catering to the requirements of the makers of Ambassador and Fiat cars. The commencement of commercial vehicles production in India in the sixties and seventies—and Japanese investments in passenger cars in the Eighties enlarged the components Industry. In the Eighties there are more than 400 Auto component Industry with wide range of products for different segment of the Automotive Industry.

The entry of foreign auto major in India made Auto component industry to increase the capacity expansion and modernisation programme. Soon the foreign auto major realized that the Indian market was not as big as it appeared to be. Their plans went haywire. The Auto Component Industry inventories piled up.

Silhouette of the Industry

There are about 400 small and medium sized component firms supplying for 24 Automobile companies. To meet the international quality requirements and for tapping the global markets, many ancillary unit, have entered into joint ventures with foreign

* Lecturer, Dept. of Business Administration, Annamalai University.

** Professor & Head, Dept. of Business Administration, Annamalai University.

component majors. At present there are about 225 active collaborations of which 67 are with Japan, 40 with U.K., 44 with Germany and 31 with U.S. International component manufacture have already entered India due to cost advantage, especially the availability of low cost skilled labour.

Performance

It is an Industry with a turnover of over Rs. 20,000 crore and an investment of over Rs. 11,500 crore, offering direct employment to over 2.5 lakh persons. It is a vital industry that caters to the transport sector, which is the backbone of the economy.

Industrial Buyers

Auto component manufactures have two kinds of buyers. Original Equipment Manufacturers (OEM) and the replacement market. The replacement market now forms about 65 per cent of the demand. The relative importance of the OEM and replacement market varies across products depending upon factors such as life of components, quality and materials used, average age of vehicles and so on. The replacement market generally yields higher margins. OEM market is dependent on the demand for new vehicles.

Industry Classification by Groups

The Auto Component Industry can be classified into 3 distinct group. First are the MNCs operating with wholly owned subsidiaries. Delphi and Visteon are in this category. Second category, which are owned by Indian promoters with foreign collaborators holding a minority stake in return for technology transfer, Example: MICO.

The third ones are players who do not have any relationship either for finance (or) technology with foreign ones. Examples are Sundram Fasteners. Auto component Industry is faced with two critical issues at the moment. The first in how to divide space for itself in the domestic market that has been opened upto overseas companies. The second is how to survive in the current recessionary environment. Indian companies doing well are confined to low technology products such as castings, forging, sheet metals, brake linings, pistons, piston rings, wheels and oil pumps. The MNCs are not interested in these lines, companies such as

Delphi and Visteon are more interested in hi-tech areas such as climate control systems, engine management systems and emission control products.

Conclusion

The task of an Automobile Component Industry is to manufacture the product according to Automobile Industry specification which include.

Quality and inspections to be followed.

Once the product is manufactured, it is checked for specifications. If the Product Quality is satisfied it is delivered to the Industry. In the Automobile Industry the products are again inspected, based on the level of rejection and quality the Auto Component Industry will be ranked. In order to retain the supplier status the Auto Component Industry will have to work towards zero defective component. Some Indian Auto Component Industry (Sundram Fasteners) supplying to overseas market (General Motors) are showing continuous excellent performance every year.

The Auto Component Industry can have an Admirable Customer Service Relationship with Automobile Industry, provided if it follows the following.

- Technology Transfer
- TQM

REFERENCES

1. The Survey of Indian Industry, 2003.
2. The Business Line.

35

Creativity as an Excellent Tool in Achieving Customer Service Excellence

PROF. A. SENGUTTUVAN* & T.G. SAMBANTHAN**

Excellence in customer service can be achieved by observing the following types of quality in an organisation.

- Transcendent Quality
- Product-Based Quality
- User-Based Quality
- Manufacturing-Based Quality
- Value-Based Quality

This paper makes an attempt in identifying the avenues in which creativity can be applied to achieve the above types of quality. In addition to providing the methods of applying creativity, it also discusses the constituent abilities of Creativity and about some of the simpler techniques of creative thinking.

This paper also analyses the potential chances of applying creativity in order to achieve Total Quality Management as a means of attaining excellence in customer service.

Finally this paper provides the advantages and disadvantages of applying creativity to achieve excellence in providing customer service in the organisational environment.

Introduction

The most important requirement for achieving excellence in customer service is to maintain quality. Philip Crosby defines

* Professor & Head, Department of Computer Science & Engineering, Madha Engineering College, Kunrathur, Chennai.

** Professor & Head, Computer Centre, T.T.T.I. Taramani, Chennai.

(Ref. 1) quality as 'Conformance to requirements', while it is true that the requirements of individuals may differ from novice to the expert and thus the term quality will have subjective interpretation. The quality of a product may have the following interpretations (Ref. 2) for an end-user.

Transcendent Quality

It is the innate or inherent excellence of the product as observed by an individual. It varies from person to person based on the background of the person.

Product-Based Quality

The presence or absence of a specified product is the most important factor to determine this type of quality.

User-Based Quality

This quality can be decided based on how far the product is able to meet with the user's expectations.

Manufacturing-Based Quality

This quality is decided based on how far the product conforms to its design specifications.

Value-Based Quality

This quality depends upon the perception of the end-user and primarily thrives on personal satisfaction or dissatisfaction. This quality is decided by perceptibility and preferences of the concerned individual.

Though these qualities apply to products, they can readily be adapted to customer service excellence. This paper analyzes the various techniques of creative thinking that can be applied for attaining excellence in customer service.

Creativity

It is found (Ref. 3) that creativity is not one ability, but a whole cluster of abilities. The most important of these abilities are as described below.

Fluency of Ideas

Fluency is the ability to come up with a large number of ideas or solutions to a given problem. Fluency works primarily through the process of associative thinking. One idea leads to another, second idea to a third and so on. Fluency can be improved by trying to get answers for questions like 'How would you make your student more interested in Computer Graphics?' etc.

Flexibility

It is the ability to come up with a variety of ideas or concepts to a given problem. For example, to answer the question, 'What are the uses of brick? One can tell us (i) Used as a constructing material (ii) as a weapon to attack instead of telling as (i) used for building bridges (ii) for houses etc.

Originality

It is ability to come up with unusual but appropriate responses. For example, use of brick (i) as a substitute for pillows (ii) hiding place for jewellery. Originally is the vital element of creativity. Try to get answers for questions like, 'Suppose that your child has no gift for music, but loves it. How would you help him to become a good musician?'.

Guessing Ability

It is the ability to go to the roots of a phenomenon by unravelling its causes. It makes good guesses about the causes and consequences. This is considered to be a vital ingredient of Scientific Creativity.

Sensitivity

It is the ability to spot the uncommon; to be sensitive to feelings, sight, smell, sound, etc. Try to get answers for questions like 'Why some experts in designing efficient algorithms have aversion to working with computer terminals?'

Elaborating Ability

It is the ability on a theme. It involves working out the implications of a bright idea by a combination of analytical, evaluative, and associative thinking. Try to get answers for questions like, (i) Elaborate upon the paradoxial proverbs 'Stitch in time saves nine' or 'Haste makes waste'.

Creative Thinking Techniques

Brainstorming

This method is an unstructured process for generating all possible ideas about the concept of maintaining quality within a limited time-frame through the spontaneous contributions of participants. When ideas are suggested, there should not be any hasty attempt in finding out how far the ideas are practical or feasible? All ideas, irrespective of how illogical or logical, must be recorded with participants (being disallowed, to criticize or evaluate during the brainstorming session).

Reverse Brainstorming

This method is quite similar to brainstorming, except that criticism is allowed. In fact, this method is primarily based on finding fault by asking the question "In how many ways can this idea fail?" Since it has a pessimistic tone, enough care must be exercised to maintain the group's morale. This method is considered to be very effective in stimulating innovative thinking. This method involves the identification of all possible pitfalls and to have a discussion on methods of overcoming these problems.

Synectics

This method can be applied to solve problems through one of the following four analogical approaches (Ref. 4).

(*i*) Personal Analogy
(*ii*) Direct Analogy
(*iii*) Symbolic Analogy
(*iv*) Fantasy Analogy

Two steps are involved in this method as shown in figure 1. The first step enables the strange ideas to be converted into familiar ideas. This can be implemented through generalizations or models consciously reversing the order of things and rearrange the problem into a readily acceptable or familiar perspective, thereby eliminating the strangeness. After having eliminated the strangeness, the second step can be initiated by making the familiar strange through personal, direct or symbolic analogy which may ideally result in a unique solution.

Gordon Method

This method can be applied only to the members of a group who are not aware of the exact nature of the problem. This prerequisite helps in ensuring that the solution is not clouded by preconceived ideas and behavioural patterns.(Ref. 5) This method is started by mentioning a general concept associated with the problem. A number of ideas may be expressed as responses. Thus a concept is developed, followed by related concepts through appropriate guidance. The whole process, thus helps in getting the actual problem revealed, enabling the group members to make suggestions for implementation or refinement of the final solution.

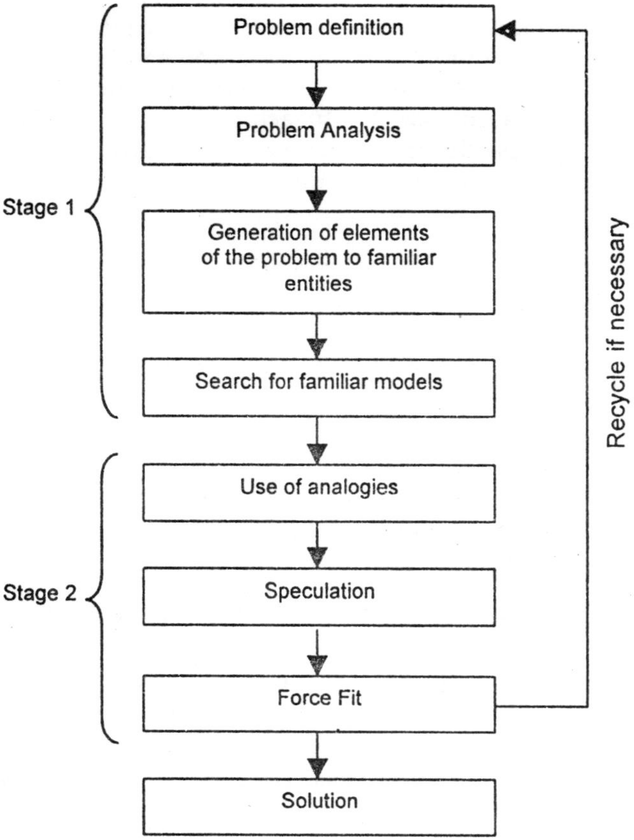

Fig.1: Synectics Process

Checklist Method

In this method, a new idea is developed through a list of related issues or suggestions. The list of questions or statements can be used to guide the direction of developing entirely new ideas or concentrating on specific 'idea' areas. The checklist can be in any form and it can be of any length. This checklist may explore the possibilities of adaptation, modification, magnification, substitution, rearrangement or realignment, interchanging of components, reversals, positive and negative transposition, combinations or permutations, blending, assorting and other manipulations.

Free Association

Even though this method is found to be the simplest one, it is deemed to be the most effective method. This technique is helpful in developing an entirely new slant to a problem. At the outset, a word or phrase related to the problem is taken down, then other such words consecutively (with each new one to the ongoing thought processes), thereby creating a chain of ideas ending with a new product idea as an emerging one.

Forced Relationships

This method aims at forcing relationships among some product combinations. In this technique, questions are asked about objects or ideas with an interest to develop a new idea. The new combination and eventual concept is developed through a series of five steps as given below:

1. Isolate the elements of the problem
2. Find the relationships between these elements
3. Record the relationships in an orderly form
4. Analyze the new relationships to find new ideas or patterns.
5. Develop still newer ideas from these patterns.

The following table illustrates the suggestive fields which can be used to explain the Forced Relationship Technique.

Table 1: Illustration of Forced Relationship Technique

ELEMENTS		
Forms	*Relationship/Combination*	*Idea/Pattern*

Collective Notebook Method

In this method, a small notebook with a statement of the problem (alongwith relevant details and empty pages) is distributed to all the members of the group. Members consider the problem and its possible solutions, recording ideas at least once, but preferably three times on daily basis. At the end of the month, a list of the best ideas, is developed alongwith suggestions (Ref. 6). This method can also be applied with a group of persons who record their ideas; give their notebooks to a central coordinator who will summarize all the contents of the notebooks. This summary becomes the topic of a group discussion by the group members. Emphasis will be laid on the creative outlook that is to be displayed by the group members during the discussion.

Heuristics

This method primarily thrives on the concerned individual's ability to discover through a progression of thoughts, insights and learning. This method is quite popular due to the fact that persons must settle for an estimated outcome of a decision rather than certainty. A specific type of this method is known as Heuristic Ideation Technique (HIT) (Ref. 7). This technique involves locating all relevant concepts that could be associated with a known product area and generating a set of all possible combinations of ideas.

Scientific Method

This method is applied in different fields of research. It consists of principles and processes, conducting observations and experiments and validating the hypothesis. In this approach, the individual defines the problem, analyzes the problem critically, gathers and analyzes data, developing and testing potential solutions and finally chooses the best solution.

Value Analysis

This method identifies methods for maximizing value to the new idea or concept developed (Ref. 8). To maximize value of the idea developed, critical questions are raised and possible answers are found. In a value analysis procedure, regularity is maintained to develop, evaluate and refine ideas.

Attribute Listing

This method is an idea-finding technique that requires the individual to list all the attributes of an entity or problem and then look at each from a variety of viewpoints. Through this process, originally unrelated objects can be brought together to form a new combination and creative potential uses for the entity or object concerned.

The Analytical Bootstrapping Creativity (ABC) Method

The problem analytic strategy is more an approach to alternative generation than a well-specified technique. It consists of the following steps.

Step 1 : Group members should privately write down ideas on their own.
Step 2 : Collectively analyze the problem, delineating the structure of its solution space.
Step 3 : Generate and report ideas resulting from problem analysis along with those produced in Step 1.
Step 4 : Analyze ideas and alternatives, especially those not clearly implied by the recognized solution space. Ascertain the rationales for these proposals, augementing the solution space as appropriate.
Step 5 : Generate and report ideas suggested by the enlarged solution space.
Step 6 : Consolidate and organize all solution alternatives.
Step 7 : Select several alternatives for further evalution and choice.

The Analytical Bootstrapping Creativity (ABC) method enables a thoughtful, thorough exploration of the solution space.

The Normal Group Technique (NGT)

In this method, a group is convened to discuss the ideas and evaluate and select solutions. NGT is a structured group meeting that follows this format.

A group is convened to discuss a particular problem issue. After the problem is understood, individuals silently generate ideas in writing. Each individual, in round-robin fashion, then offers one idea from his or her list. Ideas are recorded on a blackboard or flip chart; they are not discussed at this stage of the process. Once all ideas are elicited, the group discusses them. Anyone may criticize or defend any item. During this step, clarification is provided as well as general agreement or disagreement with the idea.

The Delphi Technique

This technique is a group process that anonymously generates ideas or judgements from physically dispersed experts. Unlike the NGT, experts ideas are obtained from questionnaires or via the internet as opposed to face-to-face group discussion. The Delphi technique is useful when face-to-face discussions are impractical, when disagreements and conflict are likely to impair communication, when certain individuals might severely dominate group discussions, and when groupthink is a probable outcome of the group process.

Matrix Charting

This method explores new opportunities by listing important elements for the product area along two axes of a chart and then asking questions regarding these elements. The answers must be recorded in the relevant boxes of the matrix.

Big-Dream Approach

This method requires that the individual's dream about the problem and its solution are quite ambitious and result-oriented. While practising this method, every possibility should be recorded and investigated without any prejudice for all the negative factors involved or the resources required. Ideas should be conceptualized without checking the practical constraints and this idea is developed as a feasible solution.

Parameter Analysis

This method consists of parameter identification and creative synthesis as two different phases (Ref. 14). Figure 2 indicates this method. Parameter identification phase involves analyzing variables in the situation to determine their relative importance. These variables become the focal points of investigation, while the other variables are set aside. After having identified the primary issues, and the relationships, a viable solution is developed; the whole process of such a solution development is called as "Creative Synthesis".

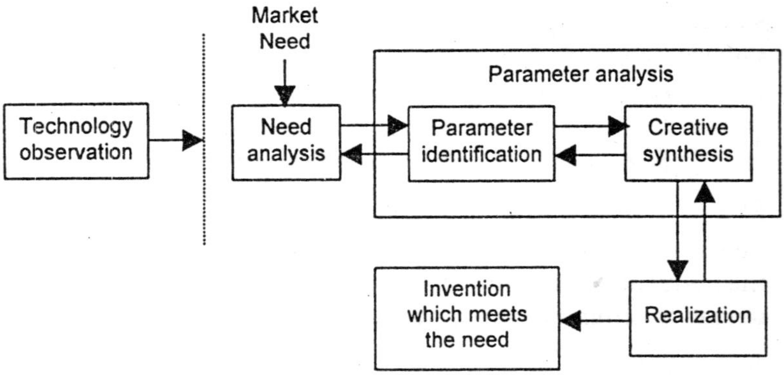

Fig. 2: Parameter Analysis.

TQM Through Creativity

The following tools help in improving the creativity of skillful managers who want to maintain quality at all possible levels by following the concept of Total Quality Management.

Flow Chart

It is a graphical display of a sequence of activities and decisions.

Fishbone Diagram

It is a cause-and-effect diagram that helps TQM Managers to visualize important cause-and-effect relationships.

Pareto Analysis

This method involves in constructing a bar chart by counting and tallying the number of times significant quality problems occur. The tallest bar on the chart representing the most common problem, demands prompt attention.

Control Chart

This is a visual aid showing acceptable and unacceptable variations from the norm for repetitive operations. This chart is used to monitor actual versus desired quality repetitive operations.

Histogram

A histogram is a bar chart showing whether repeated measurements of a given quality characteristic conform to a standard bell-shaped curve. Deviations from the standard imply the need for corrective action.

Scatter Diagram

This diagram is used to plot the correlation between two variables.

Run Chart

This is also called as a time series or trend chart. A run chart tracks the frequency or amount of a given variable over time. Significant deviations from the norm imply the need for corrective action.

Advantages of Applying Creativity to Achieve Customer Service Excellence

1. Exhaustive list of possible solutions can be found out.
2. Since creativity may result in getting novel solutions, it may help in reaching the relatively unthinkable solutions.
3. The Utility of the concept 'serendipity' may help in getting other possible solutions.
4. Some of the creative solutions may lead to enjoy the status of monopoly and thus eliminating competitions.
5. Creative solutions in achieving customer service excellence will make ordinary business persons as entrepreneurs. Thus creativity is a very important characteristic that is to be possessed by entrepreneurs.

Disadvantages of Applying Creativity to Achieve Customer Service Excellence

1. The normal customer who may have the mentality to resist the change may not have a liking for creative approaches.
2. Employees who may not have experience in implementing creative solutions may spoil them due to bungling.
3. Some of the Creative solutions may take some time in having an impact on the customers. Persons who are responsible in making policy decisions, should be willing to wait till such time and should not resort to hasty decisions.
4. Creative solution developers (who are supposed to be experts in applying creative techniques) may not be

readily available in a specific industry. To develop creative solutions, a person must both be knowledgeable in creative techniques and possess expertise in the particular domain.

Concluding Remarks

This paper makes an analysis of the various types of quality and different techniques of applying creativity to obtain creative solutions.

Since excellence in customer service is a context-sensitive concept, it is upto the individual to choose a specific technique and derive a creative solution.

This paper also discusses the factors which will lead to achieve Total Quality Management (TQM) by following creative techniques and thus achieve customer service excellence. In addition to all these details, it also lists the advantages and disadvantages of applying creativity to accomplish excellence in customer service.

REFERENCES

1. Philip B. Crosby; *"Quality Without Tears—The Art of Hassle-free Management"* (New York; Plume, 1984), p. 64.
2. Ron Zemke, *'A Buffer's Guide to TQM Training 30'* (April 1993): pp. 48-55.
3. Pradip N. Khandwala *"Fourth Eye Excellence Through Creativity* (Second Edition)" (1988) A.H. Wheeler & Co., pp. 142-59.
4. W.J. Gordon, *"Synectics: The Development of Creative Capacity,"* (New York: Harper & Row, 1961), pp. 37-53.
5. J.W. Haefele, *"Creativity and Innovation"* (New York: Van Nostrand Reinhold, 1962), pp. 145-47. Sidney J. Parnes and Harold F. Harding, A Source Book for Creative Thinking, (New York: Charles Scribner's Sons, 1962), pp. 307-23; and Souder and Ziegler, "Review of Techniques" pp. 34-42.
6. J.W. Haefele, *"Creativity and Innovation"* p. 152.
7. Edward M Tauber, *"HIT—Heuristic Ideation Technique,"* 'Journal of Marketing (January 1972), pp. 58-70.
8. *"A Study on Applied Value Analysis of General Electric"*, pp. 66-67.
9. A. Senguttuvan and T.G. *"Sambanthan: Inculcating Creativity in the Curricula of Technical Education"*, Vol. 1. Proceedings of Integrating Technology into Teaching and Learning, First Annual Conference of SETRAD held in February, 2002, pp. 301-05.

36

Customer Care

Operational Excellence

SELVARASU A.* & NAGESWARA RAO S.B.**

Of late, employees' direct contact with customer can help the customer to meet his needs. Such need could be a demand for quality or special features of products and services. The need could also be a demand to meet an emergency or the call for an innovative solution to an unresolved problem.

To operate the process of customer-care companies as a whole should transcend its resources to meet the demands of customers. The aim of companies should be to provide the best possible solution to the customer always, even if this means at times having to suggest alternate products or services and losing business. Hence, winning customer's trust and loyalty for the future should be the outcome of caring customers.

In order to have operational excellence, companies should continue to develop a set of procedures, methods, patterns of work and culture, which can be followed by every one concerned. Giving concession to customer on commercial issues should be the last best thing on earth to satisfy the customer. Therefore, keeping up to the promises with customers by way of operational excellence can take the companies to the cream layer.

As a marketer of products and services one should see either the growth or at least the existence in their own industry. It is possible only when he covers the whole on one side and parts on the other. The efforts put forth to reach the whole of any industry speaks by itself as effectiveness. The outcome of an exercise seduce

* Lecturer, Department of Business Administration.
** Professor and Head, Annamalai University.

into parts can be said as efficiency. A blend of effectiveness and efficiency is termed as Excellence. For instance offering products and services to customers as they need, want and desire is effectiveness and easing up the pressure by extending solution to the purchase is efficiency. Bringing problem-free offers to customer and operating it successfully can be said as operational excellence with customer care.

Objective

It is to construct a model on operational excellence by caring for customers. The other important aspect is to indicate the relevant constituents of consumer behaviour.

Review of Literature

In order to seek information about the topics related to the objective, seven different stages of excellence are identified. These stages of excellence are in the area of manufacturing, marketing, customer, operational, human, promotional and behaviour. The relevant information is presented in this section.

Manufacturing Excellence

Sethuraman Kannan and Tirupati Devanath (2000) have taken up a study on the art of keeping pace with the manufacturing excellence in an Engineering industry. The company included for the study is Lucas—TVS Limited. It is argued that the path to the success of the industry is by adopting manufacturing excellence in the company. Gupta B. M. and Kashikar S. S. (1997) have identified that the manufacturing excellence can be achieved through waste reduction. Ramamoorthy S. E. (1992) has focused that understanding quality is must for Excellence. Chatterjee Pradeep K. (1993) has recommended that quality excellence is essential for improving the productivity.

Marketing Excellence

Hindustan Lever (1998) believes in Marketing Excellence and practices over the years with huge amount of success. The art of managing the position of excellence is by admiring the marketing excellence within its reach that is wherever it is done and whichever company is proved the concept. Basu Debashis (1998) has acclaimed that there is price through Excellence. Singh S. K. (1997)

has opined that the pursuit of Excellence is shunned. Singh N. P. (1997) has foreseen the powers beyond Excellence and Innovation in 21st Century. It is predicted that the level of excellence achieved by one firm should direct the same to aim for higher level of it. Singh Kanwaldeep (1997) has lamented that cooperatives are the islands of Excellence. At the same time the success of cooperative movement in one particular category of industry need not have the same level of excellence. Every industry can have its own level of excellence with the introduction of cooperatives. Nautiyal Suresh (1995) has suggested that in advertising new levels of Excellence must be sought with.

Customer Excellence

Parasuraman A. (2000) has stroke the balance while achieving marketing excellence by reaching the customers. It is desirable to keep the customer as the superior and deal with them in the manner in which they expect. The concept of marketing excellence can only give short term success if the Customer Service is left unchecked. The two sides of the same success coin are the superior customer service on one side and the marketing excellence on the other.

Operational Excellence

Saraangi G.B. (1994) has directed that operational excellence can only improve the capital adequacy of an organization. It is indicated that activities that are formally carried out should follow the standardised ways and means. The deviation in the activities must be addressed and measured periodically. The concept of leap frog from bench marking must be implemented for the betterment of standardization. Sahay K. B. (1998) has looked up the claim of excellence over Green Revolution is a Myth. The impediments in the success of the green revolution are not because of the contribution to agribusiness but due to the operational excellence farmers nurtured in the fields.

Human Excellence

Meyer Christopher (1994) has brought out the importance of achieving excellence through Team Work. The synergies of the team work are legitimated. Siddiqui M. Yunus (1984) has identified that biotechnology can make Human Excellence. Singh Rahul (1993) has picked up the impact of fear of Excellence.

Promotional Excellence

Mukhopadhyay Sukumar (1999) has stressed upon the retention of the position as excellence is difficult. There are several danger signals blow across the path of Excellence. The steps should be measured when moving ahead with the value of excellence. Bhatnagar R. G. (1999) has indicated that Excellence in Corporate Governance is the order of the day. Khedkar Uday P. (1996) has argued that measuring Excellence need not stop with numbers alone. It should further add social dimensions to its strategic moves towards excellence. Sarkar Jayanta (1996) has commended on Indian industries to have identical thrust for Excellence. Shukla Archana (1998) has argued that creativity is the key to Excellence.

Behavioural Excellence

George Katona has developed an index of consumer sentiments. This index is claimed to represent the confidence consumers have in the economy. It is justified that the psychological variables are needed to better understand the spending behaviour of consumers and their effect on economy. It is also found that income is an explanatory variable in the study.

Francesco Nicosia has focused on the complex decision process in place of purchase by customers. The process is said as a flow of communication on specific attributes. The attributes start from Firm to consumer and results into formation of attributes. The consumption can be reached only after the attribute is evaluated and purchase is made.

Howard has depicted the consumer behaviour as problem solving experiences. The problems are specific to the extent of familiarity with customers. There are three different levels of problem solving are addressed. These are Extensive (unknown), intensive (familiar) and routine (unfamiliar) problem solving behaviours.

Engel, Kollat and Blackwell have introduced the level of involvement of customers and the significance of their experiences. Higher the level of involvement there is extended problem solving behaviour and vice-versa.

Conceptual framework

The concept is laid down with its components as shown in Figure 1 and 2 as to how the operational excellence can result into customer excellence.

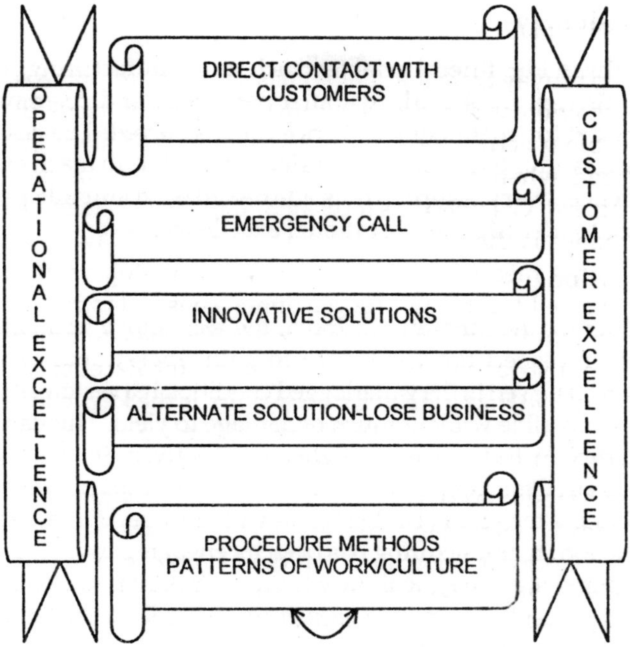

Fig. 1: Reacing Customer Excellence-Conceptual Framework.

Fig. 2: Scope for Reacing Customer Excellence.

Methodology

With these identified variables such as manufacturing, human, marketing, promotional, customer behaviour and customer care, the model for customer excellence is constructed. The case study method is adopted in order to design the model. To reach customer excellence, every component is addressed with suitable product/ service to identify the operational excellence.

Discussion

Considering the farmland in India, the technology adaptation has widely replaced the workforce to gain operational excellence (Harvester). Even in the waterlogged condition harvesting of the crop is made possible without much of damage to yield. This can be said as quality in harvest with higher productivity in the farmland operations. Other scope for excellence in these kinds of production is by reducing the waste. United States with the operational excellence production/manufacturing has been by engaging only five per cent of the population on agriculture whereas in India it is started declining from 65 per cent. A country of *manufacturing excellence* can be Germany with its technology that is 'German formulas'.

Kone Elevators Limited has claimed that *human excellence* is fruitful only when there is teamwork in executing the orders collected by marketing effort. The service maintenance persons regularly attend to its products that are in operation in different places. The company also conducts short term training programme about the precautions and safety modes while using the elevators and lifts for the users as well as the buyers. It all account for the success of the company to remain with order for 1500 numbers of lifts in the years to come with human excellence by teamwork. The country of human excellence can by Japan in first place and Korea in second place that is they worked hard and proving it.

Maruthi Udyog Limited market its Cars by extending the service facility anywhere in the country. Customers can attend to proper maintenance of their vehicle with easy-going service facilities. In the case of Ford Motors, it is the team selling approach followed to market its products. At the time of completion of an sale order, employees from each one of the departments are called and then they will be introduced to a customer so that he can have his transaction very easily. A photograph used to be taken at the time of delivery. These kinds of approaches in *marketing excellence* can make the customer feel someone as special person. Similarly, Eureka Forbes is marketing "Acqua-guard' water purifier with excellence in its marketing approach. The marketing approach is aimed at the intelligent quotient of a person and its relation with drinking pure water. This approach takes the product at the best possible price from the company. A country of marketing excellence is undoubtedly the United States because they introduce new marketing mantras.

Table 1: Customer Care by Operational Excellence

Customer Care	*Operational Excellence*		
	Before	*During*	*After*
Manufacturing: Harvester	Quality	Waste	Productivity
Human: Kone Elevators	Teamwork	Delivery 24 Hs	Safety
Marketing: Maruthi/Ford	Service/ Team selling	Photograph	Member
Promotional: MRF	Corporate Governance	Protect interest of Distributors	Social Dimension
Economy: Staple Goods (Health Drink/Soft Drink)	Lowest Price	Maxi Quantity	Easy Refill
Psychological: Telecom Services (Mobile Phone—Reliance)	Plus-plus value added services	Provide the Best	Accommodat ive Billing
Familiarity: Software/Bikes (Microsoft Windows—Hero Honda) Unknown—Familiar—Unfamiliar	Add-on Gifts	Quick Installation	Complete information
Involvement: Television (Samsung Bio/LG High Golden eye) FMCG Low	Innovate/ New Reposition	Acceptable Warranty Tie-in	Fulfilment of promises Exchange

MRF limited has the highest level of corporate governance with social dimensions by which it tries to *promote* its excellence. A country of promotional excellence is India as it gives lot of business opportunities for others.

The process of customer behaviour has to be taken care of by the marketer. The question is as to whether marketer has to care for the customer after the purchase or during the purchase or before the purchase. The intersect model out of the identified variables of customer behaviour (economical-psychological-familiarity-involvement) with reference to customer care can be constructed.

The economic behaviour of customer has three related factors that can be taken care of by marketers such as the lowest price, the maxi-quantity and the easy refill. These three strategic operations can be had before, during and after the purchases respectively. In the case of staple goods the marketer adopts these strategies viz. Health Drinks, Soft Drinks, Tooth paste. Toilet soaps, etc.

The psychological behaviour can be brought out as excellence with the plus-plus value added services, providing the best solutions and accommodating the bills. These particular phenomena can be observed in the Reliance telecom service even before its services are made available to customers. As long as the problem solving behaviour of customer is taken care, then there is every possibility of making the service more effective and the most efficient.

The concept of behaviour in relation to *familiarity* and the extent of involvement plays crucial role in the customer excellence. When the customer is familiar about the product/service then he need to ask for additional information only. Hero Honda brings out bikes with special features to the existing products of its excellence. Similarly, Microsoft also brings out software that exists over a period with improvement in the interest of customers. In this situation marketer should be in a position to give the required information precisely.

The interest of customer makes his purchase more involved with products or services. The extent of involvement in the purchase determines the amount of time spent in the market place. Samsung as well as Lucky Gold bring products with customer friendly features in it. For instance, Samsung brings durables with Bio-products and Lucky Gold with Golden Eye by caring customers. This is to place the products in the mindset of customer excellence.

In essence, the operational excellence can be achieved with the set of procedures and guidelines in the area of manufacturing, human, marketing, promotional and behavioural aspects of customers. The customer excellence is derived by following the strategies in making the purchase useful in many dimensions.

REFERENCES

1. Sethuraman Kannan, Tirupati Devanath (2000), Lucas—TVs Limited: A Journey Towards Manufacturing Excellence, Vikalpa, Vol. 25, No. 2, p. 43.
2. Parasuraman A (2000), *Superior Customer Service and Marketing Excellence: Two Sides of the Same Success Coin*, Vikalpa, Vol. 25, No. 3, p. 3.
3. Mukhopadhyay Sukumar (1999), *Excellence and Danger*, Business Standard, 28/02/99.
4. Bhatnagar R. G. (1999), *Excellence in Corporate Governance*, Observer of Business & Politics, 05/08/99.
5. Shukla Archana (1998), *Creativity: A Key to Excellence*, Indian Journal of Industrial Relations, Vol. 34, No. 1, p. 1.
6. Sahay K. B. (1998), *Green Revolution: Claim of Excellence a Myth*, Statesman, 21/02/98.
7. Hindustan Lever (1998), *Marketing Excellence, Economic* and Political Weekly, Vol. 33, No. 21, p. 1221.
8. Basu Debashis (1998), *Price Through Excellence*, Economic Times, 21/10/98.
9. Singh S.K. (1997), *Pursuit of Excellence Shunned*, Times of India, 18/08/97.
10. Singh N.P. (1997), *Beyond Excellence and Innovation in 21st Century*, Abhigyan, Vol. 15, No. 1-2, p. 35.
11. Singh Kanwaldeep (1997), *Cooperatives: Islands of Excellence*, Times of India, 11/09/97.
12. Gupta B.M., Kashikar S S (1997), *Excellence in Manufacturing Through Waste Reduction, Productivity*, Vol. 38, No. 3, p. 462.
13. Sarkar Jayanta (1996), *Quest for Excellence and Indian Industry*, Dateline Business, 04/07/96.
14. Khedkar Uday P. (1996), *Measuring Excellence: Not by Numbers Alone*, Times of India, 29/06/96.
15. Nautiyal Suresh (1995), *Advertising must Seek New Levels of Excellence*, Observer of Business & Politics, 04/04/95.
16. Saraangi G. B. (1994), *Improving Capital Adequacy by Operational Excellence*, Financial Express, 20/10/94.
17. Meyer Christopher (1994), *Excellence Through Team Work*, Economic Times, 25/10/94.

18. David L. Loudon; Albert J. Dela Bitta (1993), *Consumer Behaviour,* McGraw Hill International, New Delhi.
19. Singh Rahul (1993), *Fear of Excellence,* Indian Express, 31/01/93.
20. Chatterjee Pradeep K (1993), *Quality Excellence for Productivity Improvement, Productivity,* Vol. 34, No. 2, p. 288.
21. Ramamoorthy S. E. (1992), *Understanding Quality Must for Excellence,* Observer of Business & Politics, 05/12/92.
22. Siddiqui M. Yunus (1984), *Biotechnology for Human Excellence,* Yojana, Vol. 28, No. 6, p. 35, Education, Vol. 17, No. 1, p. 47.

37

Customer Profitability and Service in Supply Chain Marketing

M. JEYAKUMARAN* & G. UDAYASURIYAN**

In recent years, marketing practioners and academicians alike have embraced such concepts as one-to-one marketing, relationship marketing, targeted marketing, interactive marketing and so on and have increasingly talked about the importance of building relationships with customers.

The basic premise behind this concept is that if a firm can address and target individual customers, it can improve its profitability by serving these customers differently.

The customers driven under this new paradigm, firms increasingly need and should develop the capability to evaluate profitability at the customer level to formulate their marketing strategies better. Single period customer profitability in the context of supply chain marketing benefits the customer in all ways. Attempts have been made to build customer profitability models in direct marketing context but it was not successful, supply chain marketing firms deal with customers, supplying products and services with good quality and economically which has been successful. Direct marketing faces the huge problem of getting the order and execution of order, the costs of purchasing, inventory, order processing delivery and services are cheaper in supply chain marketing.

The model of supply chain starts from large wholesaler/ distributor to redistributor and to retailers then finally ends with the end user (Customers).

* Lecturer in Business Administration, Annamalai University.
** Reader in Business Administration, Annamalai University.

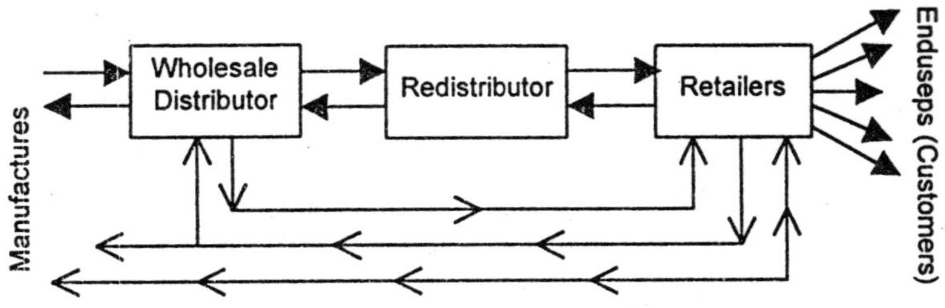

Transaction Flows in Supply Chain

The super markets and chain stores who come under retailer category purchases the commodities directly from the wholesaler or manufacturer and having their own redistribution facility to serve several of its own retail outlets exclusively.

Features of supermarkets and chain stores and their benefits to the customers are

- Quality products at cheaper rate
- Excellent service
- Product availability
- Menu-based Pricing
- Round-the-clock service
- Uniform price level in all Retail outlets.

Conclusion

Customers are rewarded economically and non-economically in the system of supply chain marketing. Nowadays customers are well aware of market situation, so firms should develop the capability to reward the customers with excellent service and understand that "Customer is the king in the Markets".

REFERENCE

1. Journal of marketing (A Quarterly publication of the American Marketing Association), July 2001.

PART III

Customer Relationship Management

38

Zero Customer Defection

H. SLADE*

e-CRM

Introduction

Twenty-first century power shifts to "customer". So, there are a lot of surveys world over, directly and indirectly, in every branch of business and administrative activities and services. Governments are not spared.

Bottom line is just 'Profit'. Profit may be anything but it should be profitable to the society and the nation at large. So, necessary tuning up is needed, if one has to see the light of the day in the present century.

In developing underdeveloped countries, one can observe how insignificant contribution the state gets from the workforce and how the customer, the user of the services of all kinds is treated. So the companies in advanced countries are trying to re-invent to be customer-friendly. They all "strategise' with unique selling proposition (USP) to be better termed as Unique Marketing Proposition (UMP). Good companies sourcing 'relationships', try to create extraordinary business/service results. Aim is to work on healthy competition to give customers varied services, depending on the capabilities (being upgraded every now and then) in the system, with an eye on ROI (return on investment) and try to ensure value for investment potentially and fully exploited by prudential re-inventions.

Customer looks for ease and flexibility and does not accept cumbersome structures any longer. He wants immediate service,

* Dept. of Bank Management, Alagappa University, Karaikudi (TN).

so you will have to build 'internal relationship chains' to augment and supplement the services, positively effectively and in shortest time-span.

Customer has no time to wait for you, as you are no longer a monopoly. He is just bent upon crushing all monopolies and he needs JIT (just in time) services and he does not want to wait and expects everything yesterday! So training and development department should suitably rehearse the personnel in the activities and prompt effectiveness otherwise, customer is lost any moment, if there is poor to very poor adaptability to his needs. Service providers to individuals like banks, insurance companies, hotels, etc. should clearly know customers are not intruders and they are the very meaning for the service. This will help the note that customer plays "withdrawal strategy" when he finds the service provider is just disgruntled. Customer is more sure wed a person with enormous common sense, timely assessor of factors, highly-result-oriented.

Banking Scenario

In the banking services, no doubt, the banker has learnt from time to time that a customer might be a borrower at one place but he is also a depositor at another place. In both cases he is a customer. When he observes the bankers integrity he will definitely appreciate the same and he will bank on such banks only.

Economic reforms initiated by the Government of India in the early nineties had brought about a sea-change in operational environment of financial sector and functioning and outlook of Indian banks. Features such as liberalization, deregulation, globalization modernization, information technology explosion etc. witnessed by financial sector in the transition phase of reforms have attached prime importance to the quantitative customer service in Indian banks. Customers today want you to set measurable business goals and develop strategies to achieve them. Hence, there is innovative use of information and technology. Technology leads to implementation of new strategies innovated creatively. Innovation and technology development continue incessantly.

Urbanization has caused the problem of time management which has led to major innovations such as Automated Teller Machines (ATMs), home banking, relationship banking, banking-on-wheels, tele-banking, single window concept, specialized NRI/ SSI branches, personal banking, anytime banking, anywhere banking, electronic funds transfer, on-line terminals to customers, SWIFT, Bank net, smart card, shared payment network system, e-CRM, etc. which are responding well to the customers expectations and needs.

e-CRM Concept

Markets are becoming saturated communication channels delivering marketing messages are becoming saturated. Increasing competition has made customer relationship management (CRM) an important consideration for organizations as CRM can position an organization to compete in this competitive climate.

CRM is the seamless coordination between sales, customer service, marketing, field support and other customer-touching functions. It integrates people, process and technology to maximize relationships with all customers and partners-e-customers, traditional customers, distribution channel members, internal customers and suppliers. At its core, CRM provides an organization with an understanding of the customer. This understanding enables the organization to cultivate a one-to one relationship with the customer that is based on their needs. Once this relationship is established, marketing communications become more relevant to the customer. The relationship also becomes stronger over time, implying that aggressive marketing by competitors is less likely to result in the gradual marketing and destruction of the confidence of long-standing customers, thereby ensuring zero customer defection.

Evolution of e-CRM

The phenomenon of building relationships with customers via the internet is known as, electronic customer relationship management (e-CRM) focuses on Electronic channels, mainly on the internet and on technologies that enable automated and electronic management of customer relations. On the other hand, traditional CRM focuses on the use of traditional media such as telephone, fax etc. Corporates are catching on the internet bandwagon to launch new marketing sales, and service initiatives. This is especially true given the fact that the number of net users is growing significantly. Organizations are, therefore, shifting their business models and a web strategy has become the norm of the day.

Role of e-CRM

The idea of CRM is to help business use technology and human resources to gain insight into the behavior of customers and value of those customers. If it works as expected, a business can:

- Provide better customer service
- Cross-sell products more effectively
- Help sales staff to close deals faster
- Simplify marketing and sales process
- Discover new customers
- Increase customer revenues

The list is only indicative.

The e-CRM strategy must address customer optimization across three dimensions.

Acquisition

Through which an organization increases its customer base.

Expansion

Through which an organization increases the profit per customer.

Relation

Through which an organization increases the amount of time its Customer stays with it.

Hence the strategy of e-CRM in customer acquisition, expansion and retention ensuring Zero Customer Defection is unparalleled.

Today, most organizations are moving from a product-centric model to a customer centric one. Organizations now realize that they need to device a winning web strategy that not only addresses customer needs and expectations, but also integrates customer Information throughout the organization to have a single shared view of the customer. The goal is to create one verified database of customer information that is integrated seamlessly between both front and back office functions. The realization that customer are key to profitability and business success has driven the need to create a customer-centric organization. On the Net, the competition is only a mouse click away. Organizations need a new, approach—e-CRM-to leverage the internets unique strength for capturing customers. During the late 1990's was the most important period for the CRM Industry. Companies realized that they could make more money by providing better service to their customers, hence they started researching ways to expand their base and developed applications for marketing, campaign-management and call centres. Instead of focusing primarily an customer acquisition, businesses must work to develop long-term relationships with their customers. They must treat very transaction as an opportunity to create loyalty, cross-sell products and develop new ideas and opportunities. e-CRM makes it possible to learn more about customers and provide a highest level of service than ever before by leveraging the internet and other new technologies.

Benefits of e-CRM

Data Rationalization

By conducting a data rationalization exercise (looking at the data collected to make better, more intelligent decision) enterprises can increase revenue and decrease costs.

Revenue Enhancement Attributable to New Software

Blended sales and service call centres, interactive selling tools, customer collaboration and tools that let customers select and configure products without direct salesperson involvement are examples of effectiveness focused applications.

Process Change

The elimination of non-value-added activities can significantly reduce the cost of processing certain transactions.

Conclusion

Business competition has increased manifold and is increasing by the day. Companies are unable to cut costs beyond a certain limit, and have, therefore, to count on customers for enhancing their bottomlines. Customer loyalty is beginning to wear thin, given that rival companies are pampering customers with all kinds of inducements (and the customer is enjoying every moment of it). Such, and other developments in the market place have made the customer the KING, and as in any monarchy, the King must be flattered. E-CRM is, therefore, far more important today than in the just bygone era when the supplier was the king and the Customer was at the suppliers mercy.

39

Development Stages of e-CRM

D. Mahesh*

Introduction

With an ever-increasing competition and customers becoming restive, selective and even indifferent to marketer's pressures, it is not uncommon to observe firm's losing their market share. One of the common characteristics of successful enterprise/firms in the last decade is that they have been more responsive to customer needs than their rivals. Lessons from these organizations are that they implemented CRM strategy to build—long-term customer relationship. CRM is the seamless co-ordination between sales, customer service, marketing field support and other customer-touching functions. It integrates people, process and technology to maximize relationship with all customers and partners—e-customers, distributional channel numbers, internal customers and suppliers. CRM results in a number of benefits to an organization like increased sales revenues, increased margins, improved customer satisfaction ratings and decreased administrative costs.

Evolution of e-CRM

The phenomenon of building relationship with customers via the internet is known as electronic CRM (e-CRM). The objectives of the CRM and e-CRM are the same—the difference is the medium used for providing services to the customer. e-CRM focuses on electronic channels mainly on the Internet and on technologies that enable automated and electronic management of customer relations.

* Lecturer, B.B.A., K.S.R.CAS., Tiruchengode (TN).

Objective of e-CRM

- It provides better customer service.
- It helps sales staff close deals faster.
- To discover new customers.
- To increase customer revenues.
- To simplify marketing and sales processes.

e-CRM is now actively considered by organizations across the globe as an integration of database marketing with technology. Recent survey suggests that the e-CRM market is likely to grow by 700 per cent in the next four years and is estimated to generate revenue of $3 billion by the year 2004. The biggest challenge faced by marketers is to know the effectiveness of their e-CRM programs. It also provides an insight into developing strategies for increasing e-CRM effectiveness. This paper discusses the approaches to e-CRM, benefits, analytical and tactical e-CRM, present Indian market and Dimensions of e-CRM to be competitive in the area of e-CRM.

The awareness of CRM in India is extremely low, it is important to stress the benefits of CRM as a concept before seeking to sell the CRM software. Once this is done, technology can be leveraged as the differentiator in effective CRM implementation. In the same way the organization has to ensure that the product offering is customized to suit the size and nature of the target customers business.

Approach to e-CRM

Once an organization has identified the e-CRM solution best suited for its needs, it can consider the following approach for its e-CRM strategy.

Step 1 : A business and marketing process consultant.

Step 2 : Technical consulting for database design, extraction and transformation. And loading of data into the organization's warehouse.

Step 3 : e-CRM application implementation, integration and project management.

The following are the basic e-CRM tenants cross-channel co-ordination, customer profiling, one-to-one marketing and continuous assessment can achieve higher response rates on their marketing programs. Companies implementing the e-CRM will have far easier times attracting, retaining and expanding profitable relationships with customers.

Benefits of e-CRM—Data Rationalization

A data rationalization exercise looking at the data collected to make better, more intelligent decisions; enterprises can increase revenue and decrease costs. Most of the firms are attempting rationalization projects-across the supply chain, across multiple business units. A team was assembled to define a consistent approach to more than 1,000 global accounts and identify business metrics, functionality and data required for each interaction channel and user group. A significant positive cash flow within 12 months resulted, beginning with cost reductions through the elimination of redundant activities and greater e-self-service capabilities.

To achieve its goal of creating a loyal community, based on trust and accessibility, enhancing both revenue from new channel and continuing to provide the high quality customer service, customers have come to expect and revamped its call centers.

Process Changes

The elimination of non-value added activities could significantly reduce the cost of processing certain transactions. For example, Ford streamlined its processes and implemented technology to expedite fleet sales. Ford could legally present only the manufacturers suggested retail price, not the price negotiated by the fleet buyer with the dealer. Ford implemented a sales configuration application. It enabled dealers and fleet buyers to work together over the internet when specifying cars and it enabled the dealers to maintain value-added content and pricing rules as negotiated. The new process enabled streamline product configuration and 'e-order' verification. One fortune 500 companies are trying e-CRM implementation for the fourth time, primarily because its sale force resisted all previous efforts to share customer data. Despite the growth of e-commerce, up to 60 per cent of web transactions are not completed largely low companies have sufficient real time, online customer support.

Analytical and Tactical e-CRM

Campaign management consists of 3 major parts, Planning, Executing and Monitoring.

Planning—Customer Profiles

Information regarding the demographics and psychographics of the customer for targeting the campaign.

Past Consumer Behaviour

Information on how customers reacted in the past to offers of products and services.

Marketing Costs

Data about the historical costs on similar campaigns. Various components such as data warehousing, data marts and their analytical applications provide the e-CRM information for this activity of campaign management. The information must be supplied with the ability to

- Analysis presentation
- Design the campaign
- Project result with good communication
- Prepare to execute the campaign

Executing

- Actual revenues and costs
- Key metrics
- Fulfillment status of keeping up orders.

The understanding of what customers are responding to and which products they are buying. Certain actions are needed to ensure a successful completion of the activity. They are:

- Managing fulfillment
- Capturing customer interactions
- Tracking costs and revenues
- Budget and actual cost

The activities in the monitoring the campaigns-based on correctional steps during the campaign analyst have all the tools and resources to manage the process by pulling all tactical and analytical components into a single environment.

Present Indian Market

Looking specifically at India, the e-CRM market here is estimated at between Rs. 50crore and Rs. 100 crore. Every projection in e-business in speculative, and is churned out mostly by the market players themselves, or those with a vested interest in the market. So in the absence of a totally neutral study.

Since e-CRM is in a stage of infancy in India, the most recent technologies-high bandwidth may not be required by most clients at this stage. But even with the currently available limited bandwidth early phase CRM can be effective for most organizations. Organizations present want to invert in initial phases of e-CRM and investment in subsequent phases depends on the gains of previous phases. International studies show that 53 per cent of the global e-CRM market comprises outsourced services.

Software accounts for only 12 per cent, integration 22 per cent, training 8 per cent, and consulting 5 per cent. These above statistics hold great meaning for Indian e-CRM service providers. India's well-established status as a leading market of outsource IT services. It is by catering to e-CRM services market that Indian e-CRM companies can stay afloat and necessary investment in "educating" the Indian market on e-CRM

Dimensions of e-CRM

The e-CRM strategy must address customer optimization across three dimensions:

- Acquisition—Through which an organization increases its customer base
- Expansion—Increases the profit/customer
- Retention—Increases the amount of time its customers stay with it.

Conclusion

In 2001, 76 per cent of the companies' insight surveyor reported achieving minimal improvements as a result of implementing e-CRM systems. CRM tools will become less an issue of competitive advantage and more a matter of basic survival.

For vendors, 2002 will either be a banner year (or) the year they disappear from the market place. Based on the data gathered, CRM spending growth will get back on track and increase 35-45 per cent over 2001 levels. As the industry evolves, both from a buyer and vendor perspective, the promise of e-CRM will become a reality.

REFERENCES

1. *Intelligent Solutions Making CRM Tech.*, DM Review, December, pp. 12-16.
2. www.wheelhouse.com
3. *The Craft of CRM*, December 7, p. 46, www.infoworld.com

40

e-CRM in Service Excellence

G. GANESAN* & D. RAJAGOPALAN**

Introduction

In today's competitive business world, achieving total customer satisfaction, delighting the customer is a key element in setting the business goals and objectives of the corporate. Improving performance in service delivery and responsiveness to the customers has become a source of advantage in many industry and service sectors. CRM is being increasingly used to identify, attract and retain most valuable customers that help businesses to sustain profitable growth. Mainly, successful companies are achieving long term performance in CRM by gaining deep insights about their customers which helps them design product/service offerings that match or exceed the customer expectations which in turn help in building customer trust and gain loyalty.

Issues

One of the most vital issues companies face is how to manage the thousands of rows of customer data and attributes stored in different repositories in the organization. As companies begin implementing CRM solutions namely, sales, marketing, service, contract management but they are uncertain about how to fill in gaps in customer data, or what to do with multiple sets of data for the same customer. Another issue involves company culture and absolute need to get employees to embrace a more customer-centric world as a "warm and fuzzy" would when in reality it is

* Lecturer in commerce, Periyar Arts College, Cuddalore.
** Senior Prof. of commerce, Pondicherry University.

driven by numbers and analytics. And here's the connection back to data quality. If the data is good and available, you have got a crystal clear view into which customers you need to focus on.

Economists say services now accounts for nearly 50 per cent of our GDP and their growth at 8 per cent to 10 per cent per annum is outpacing both industry and agriculture. The extent that growth in services pushes up the average rate of growth, in spite of industry and agriculture showing signs of stagnation, it is good news for our economy. But we need to pause and critically analyze service sector's growth. This paper addresses e-CRM strategies to explore the possibilities in order to achieve preactive and proactive service excellence.

e-CRM

It is a customer-centric on-line business model that optimizes the customer experience across all phases of the on-line customer life-cycle using a personalized and customized approach to interact with prospects and customers. e-CRM is a multifaceted strategy that helps companies understand, anticipate and manage customer needs. A major thrust of it involves segmenting customers and offering appropriate and differentiated services for each of these levels. It mainly uses the electronic media to integrate and simplify customer-related business processes, drastically reducing costs of customer-facing operations while achieving CRM's primary goal is to enhance the customer experience.

The Six "e's" of e-CRM

The "e" in e-CRM not only stands for "electronic" but also can be cross channel integration and optimization, the six "e" in e-CRM can be used to frame alternative definitions of e-CRM based upon the channels which e-CRM utilizes, the issues which it impacts and other factors. The six "e's" are briefly explained below:

1. *Electronic Channels*: New electronic channels such as the web and personalized e-Messaging have become the medium for fast, interactive and economic communication, challenging companies to keep pace with this increased velocity. e-CRM thrives on these electronic channels.

2. *Enterprise*: Through e-CRM a company gains the means to touch and shape a customers experience through sales, services and corner offices—whose occupants need to understand and assess customer behavior.
3. *Empowerment*: e-CRM strategies must be structured to accommodate consumers who now have the power to decide when and how to communicate with the company and through, which channel, at what frequency. An e-CRM solution must be structured to deliver timely pertinent, valuable information that a consumer accepts in exchange for his or her attention.
4. *Economics*: An e-CRM strategy ideally should concentrate on customer economics, which drives smart asset-allocation decisions, directing efforts at individuals likely to provide the greatest return on customer-communication initiatives.
5. *Evaluation*: Understanding customer economies relies on a company's ability to attribute customer behavior to market programs, evaluate customer interactions along various customer touch point channel, and compare anticipated ROI against actual returns through customer analytic reporting.
6. *External information*: The e-CRM solution should be able to gain and leverage information from such sources as third party information networks and web page profiler application.

In addition, e-CRM must address customer optimization along three dimensions: a) Acquisition: increasing the number of customer for the company's product. b) Expansion: increasing portability by encouraging customer to purchase more products and service. c) Retention: increasing the amount of time that customer stays.

An e-CRM strategy must be able to identify the expansion potential for each customer. A company should be able to identify the opportunities to cross-sell and up-sell to the same set of customers. The cost of acquiring customers is nine to ten times more than the cost of retaining existing ones. An e-CRM solution should also establish a central mechanism to determine which customer should receive which investment at the relationship level.

Key e-CRM Features

Regardless of a companies objectives an e-CRM solution must possess certain key characteristics:

- Driven by a data warehouse.
- Focused on consistent metrics to assess customer actions across channels.
- Built to accommodate the new market dynamics that place the customer in control.
- Structured to identify a customer's profitability or profit potential, and to determine effective investment allocation decisions accordingly, so that most profitable customers could be identified and retained and the resources could be invested in relationships, which are most profitable.

Evolving to e-CRM

A company evolving to e-CRM should have done the following:

1. Define its business objective; this would be specific and different for different businesses.
2. Assess its current position with respect to the environment and determine its current level of "sophistication" along the e-CRM continuum. Define new business processes and align its existing strategy and existing processes in line with the new realities.
3. Define a technical architecture and the criteria's associated with this architecture.

Traditional brick and mortar companies usually start their dire-marketing efforts through simple list pulls and "one shot campaign", and then gravitate to a data warehouse and software for executing multiple, targeted campaigns that run simultaneously and utilize sophisticated capabilities. The diagram below depicts the path that typical brick and mortar companies usually follow toward e-CRM, along with the characteristics that mark each stage:

Various Stages in Evolution to e-CRM

1. Single enterprise view of customer
2. Integration of customer channels

e-CRM

3. Strong customer Metrics
4. Reduced cost peer interaction

⟶

1. Multiple, outbound channel
2. Campaign ROI metrics

Behavior-based Marketing

3. Many campaign running simultaneously
4. Higher effectiveness rates.

⟶

- Single channel
- Outbound only
- Simple metrics

Database Marketing

- <25 campaigns a year
- 2 per cent average response rates
- 20 per cent of customer deliver
- 100 per cent of profits.

Implementation of e-CRM

e-CRM implementation is more than system automation. Implementing e-CRM necessitates much more than merely automating the related functions and addressing the infrastructure requirements for its implementation on the web. It requires a fundamental change in the culture, philosophy, attitudes and operations of an organization and hence, the needs to initiate a change management process to move from a product-centric focus to a customer-centric one. With this view, the implementation strategy should look at,

- Gathering, storing, sharing/retrieving and tracking customer database repository, analyzing this information and deciding upon the relevant course of actions.
- Seamless integration of all customer communication channels with the customer database so as to respond in customers preferred channel.

- Automating and streamlining on-line customer service through installing the necessary software and hardware.

Steps in Implementation of e-CRM

1. Getting a first hand feedback from customers preferably through an unbiased third party would be vastly useful in identifying problem areas in the customer relationship management cycle, a key input for any e-CRM implementation exercise.
2. Successful e-CRM implementation warrants the need for a well-planned infrastructure in place that allows captures, storage and analysis of customer data.
3. An organization must select the e-CRM software based upon the incremental ROI that it will bring to the organization. Sans this exercise, the benefits of e-CRM implementation could take anywhere between three to six months and the business returns could start flowing in over another six to twelve months more.
4. There is an increasing need in the country for institutions offering high-class e-CRM training programs to organizations, as this could save enormous cost and time to these organizations on learning and implementing the same.
5. Organizations need to select the e-CRM vendors cautiously and must prefer those that offer sufficient training, incentives, etc., to their employees/representatives, and bring in with them a rich and diverse experience in the field.

Market potential of e-CRM in India

CRM is one of the fastest growing segments of technology. Coupled with the increased usage of net, this augurs a highly optimistic scenario for the e-CRM industry. The available projections for e-CRM market sizes vary widely depending upon the levels of optimism and perceptions of the related agencies. While the META Group estimates the global e-CRM market to reach $ 15 billion by 2004, the leading market researcher. Data Monitor forecasts the e-CRM services market size to be worth $ 130 billion by 2005. Keeping aside whether these projections are conservative or optimistic estimates, one fact emerges clearly *viz.*, the market for e-CRM growing exponentially.

India is emerging as the hot spot for the e-CRM services for the reasons that are obvious as mentioned previously. Industry experts estimate the domestic e-CRM market size at close to $45 million to $50 million. Growing at an average annual rate of around 30 per cent to 35 per cent, this market is expected to be worth around $300 million over the next three years. It is believed that in the long run, India definitely has the potential to capture almost a fifth or more of the global e-CRM market.

Conclusion

Competitive environment, eroding margins, need to reduce costs, finding and keeping customers are the prime drivers for organizations to embrace e-CRM. The e-CRM is a most exciting strategy that emerged from the networking technology revolution of the nineties. Today, a well-executed e-CRM strategy can result in a number of quantitative benefits including greater ability to sell and cross-sell, improved customer retention besides reduced cost of service.

REFERENCES

1. Stanley A. Brown, *Customer Relationship Management—A Strategic Imperative in the World of e-Business,* Price Warehouse Coopers.
2. Jagdish N. Sheth, Atul Parvatiyar and G. Shainesh, *Customer Relationship Management—Emerging Concepts, Tools and Applications,* Tata McGraw Hill.
3. Philip Kotler, *Marketing Management*—The Millennium Edition. Prentice, Hall India.
4. The Economic Times—Various issues.
5. The Hindu—Various issues.

41

A Framework for Measuring: Effectiveness of Customer Relationship Management (CRM)

D. MALMARUGAN*

Introduction

"If you can measure it, you can manage it" Customer relationships can be measured qualitatively and quantitatively, there are two basic approaches to obtaining customer inputs.

1. *The planned approach*: The planned approach entails corporate initiatives to seek out both internal and external customer inputs on a proactive basis. This includes customer surveys etc.
2. *The event-driven approach*: The event-driven approach entails being ready to accept customer inputs when the customers reaches out to the company. This might include having a toll free number available when a customer is in trouble with your product, specifically monitoring and managing complaints, gathering information when there is a warranty claim etc.

Qualitative Measurement

Qualitative measurement probes the environment surrounding an observed phenomenon. The techniques are:

1. *Focus Group Interviews*: Focus group interviews are repeated interactive discussions among randomly

* Lecturer in Management, K.S.R. College of Arts & Science, Tiruchingode.

selected customers of your product, coordinated by a moderator.

The discussion will be on the usage of the product/service, attitude towards the need addressed by the product/service, attitude towards players in the market for that product, exposure to promotional aids and concluding on the customers expectation being met.

2. *Advisory Panel*: Customer Advisory Panel (CAP) are also repeated meetings of small group of customers. The subject matter for the meetings is a company's relationship with its customers; unlike the focus group, where a group meets once and is disbanded, CAP Membership is a long term to develop community of action within the panel.
3. *The Critical Incident Technique—CIT*: CIT uses detailed narratives to uncover the essence of moments of truth i.e., interactions between the customer and the company.

   CIT proceeds by asking customers to identify significant interactions and to relate their experiences. The information is generated by an open ended Question of a general form such as the following, which is from a mail questionnaire addressed to retail store customers. Describe an outstandingly good or bad experience at our store, as it happened.

   The survey could be conducted by mail, telephone or even by face-to-face interview.

   It is not only unwise but potentially dangerous to make major changes in customer relationship management policy based solely on a Qualitative study.

Quantitative Measurement

The process of quantifying the link between the "Voice of the Customers" and internal process measures is called internal metrics.

Internal metric is an easily measured activity inside the company. Such as coverage response time to a customer such as average response time to a customer enquiry, average time to handle a repair etc.

These internal metrics have an impact on the customer satisfaction. So, selecting the internal metrics that affect customer satisfaction for every industry is critical and then measuring it is done.

Customer perceived value is driven by quality and price. Quality drivers are:

1. *Product Usability Drivers*: Product usability is the capacity of a product or service to satisfy the essence of a customers need, want or expectation.
2. *Service Strategy Drivers*: The service strategy drive is all those plans and policies you make in anticipation of the customers arriving to purchase your product or service.
3. *Service Environment Drivers*: The service environment drive is composed of physical surroundings like ambient conditions, spatial layout, signs and symbols that facilitate the delivery of your product or service.
4. *Service Delivery Drivers*: The service delivery drive, is everything that actually happens when the service strategy is carried out by the employees.

The facility drives are liked to the business process of delivering the expected value to the customers. Internal metrics are identified and measured in terms of the customer perceived value.

Attribute impact diagrams can be drawn as illustrated.

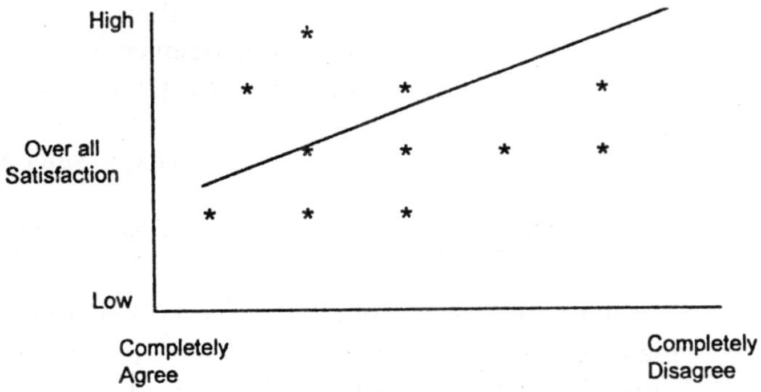

Attribute of Measure

Strategic decision matrix is a tool to measure the impact

Impact	Low	High
High	Critical Improvement Areas	High Leverage
Low	Lower Priority for Improvement	Lower Leverage

Attribute Performance

So that quadrant in which attribute performance is low and impact on customer satisfaction is high is the area for critical improvement where both are high there is higher leverage for profitability, the other areas are given lower priority for improvement.

Conclusion

Thus measuring the internal metric which is linked to external customer satisfaction is a path to sustainable development and higher profitability.

REFERENCES

1. CRM by J. Anton, R.A. Feilberg.
2. *Measuring Effectiveness of Relationship Marketing* by A. Lindgreen.
3. Leonard Berry—*Relationship Marketing*.
4. Jagdish Sheth—*Handbook of Relationship Marketing*.
5. www.crm2day.com
6. www. crmdaily.com

42

Customer Lifetime Value (CLV) Through CRM

A Case Study

J. PAUL SUNDAR KIRUBAKARAN*

Introduction

Relationships have proved to be the central element in the success of business since time immemorial. CRM goes beyond the transactional exchange and enables the marketers to estimate the customer's sentiments and buying intentions, so that the customer can be provided with products and services before he starts demanding. It is possible through integrations of four important components i.e. people, process, technology and data. Organizations have realized the lifetime value of a customer. CRM has once again acquired the highest place in every strategist's priority list. The product life cycle approach strategy is now obsolete and it gives way to customer lifetime value (CLV).

The concept is the marketer to analyze the cost of acquiring, serving and retaining a certain set of customers in the market. The paper throws light on some of these issues in financial services industry. Today it is facing an uphill task of re-orienting itself with changing technology and varying customer demand. The concepts of CLV are analyzed with credit management strategy and billing system for a financial services industry.

CRM principally revolves around marketing and begins with a deep analysis of consumer behaviour. It uses IT to gather data, which can be used to develop information required to create a more personal interaction with the customer. It produces a method

* H.O.D., Commerce (CA), K.S.R.C.A.S., Tiruchengode (T.N.).

of continuous analysis and refinement in order to enhance CLV with a firm. The concept of PLC is giving way to the concept of customer life cycle focusing on the development of products and services that anticipate the future need of existing customers and creating additional services that extend existing customer relationships beyond transactions. According to Gartner Research—through 2005, 90 per cent of successful CRM initiatives will balance needs of improved customer experience with improved customer organizational collaboration (0.8 probability). Today, particularly for the industry "best" 3-C's i.e. Cooperation, communication and courtesy has changed from customer acquisition to retention.

In recent years, CRM is being enlarged to include an integrated perspective on marketing, sales, logistics, and technology for engaging in customer satisfaction. Practitioners are calling it Customer Relationship Management (CRM) and are interested in all respects of interactions with customers to maintain a long-term profitable relationship with them. It would be applicable for effective CRM (Customer Relationship Management) in the new millennium.

Customer Relationship Management is the establishment development, maintenance and optimization of long-term mutually valuable relationship between consumers and the organizations. In additions to creating and keeping new customers. So the concept of PLC is giving way to the concept of customer life cycle focusing on the development of products and services that anticipate the future need of existing customers and creating additional services that existing customer relationships beyond transactions. A good CRM program addresses the changing need of customers by developing products and services that continuously seek to satisfy the lifestyle and need patterns of individual customers.

According to Berry (1983) formally introduced the term, CRM to the literature but several ideas of relationship marketing had emerged much earlier. Two influential writings in the 1960s and 1970s a provided impetus to relationship marketing thinking, particularly in business-to-business context.

The second impetus was provided by John Arndnt (1979), who noted the tendency of firms engaged in B2B marketing in developing long-lasting relationship with their key customer and key suppliers rather than focusing on discrete exchange and termed as "domesticated market".

In recent years, CRM is being enlarged to include an integrated perspective on marketing, sales, customer service and recent technologies for engaging in customer satisfaction. Practitioners are calling it customer relationship management (CRM) and are interested in all aspects of interactions with customers to maintain a long-term profitable relationships with them.

Today's business are facing fierce and aggressive competition while operating in both domestic and global market. This uncertain environment has forced organizations to restructure themselves in order to enhance their chances of survival and growth.

The term CRM has become a buzzword, with the concept being used to reflect a number of differing themes and becomes a "catch-all" phrase (Brodie *et al.*, 1997).

Customer Relationship Management—Service Sectors

Globalization and Deregulation combined with advances in IT, have radically changed the managerial context of service sectors. The origin of CRM was initially in the industrial context; the service sector is also focus on maintaining and enhancing customer relationships.

Success of a service provider is dependent on long-term relationship that develop between the provider and customer.

According to Berry (1983), CRM defined as "Attracting, Maintaining and enhancing customer relationship in multi-service organizations. He stressed that the attraction of new customers should view only as middle level of marketing process. He outlined five strategy elements for practicing CRM;

- Developing a core service around which to build a customer relationship
- Customizing the relationship to Individual customer
- Core service with additional benefits
- To encourage customer loyalty through pricing services
- Marketing to employees.

Lifetime value analysis provides a basis for getting the annual marketing budget approved. More and more companies today are using CLV analysis to test and improve their retention strategies.

Benefits to Service Sector

For service sectors, strong customer relationships are important because of their inherently interpersonal focus, and relative lack of objective measures for evaluating service quality. Previous study has focused on the benefits of customer loyalty as viewed from the perspective of the firm, typically in B2B contexts. Customers who have developed a relationship with a service business expect to receive satisfactory delivery of core service there exists different types of relational benefits through effective CRM, with service sectors. The second set of relation benefits reported by respondents can be described as psychological benefits. Customers realize that there is often a feeling of comfort and security in having developed a relationship with the service provider. For their regular customers many service provides may tailor their services to meet particular needs. In some cases customers may perceive this as preferential (or) special treatment.

In today's deregulated world, members of financial services sector are continuously forced to seek new ways to gain on their competitors and to outdo one another in terms of effectively reaching to retail customer's demand for increasing financial products and services. CRM is of utmost importance to financial services industry for survival and growth. To retain customers in today's competitive environment financial sectors are increasing the depth of relationship through implementation of CRM program knowledge focused organizations collect data on their customer to provide them with a framework to build an understanding of their market. Capturing customer data, in developing on ability to store, share, analyze and transfer vast amount of data at low costs, data warehousing and data mining software applications make it possible for organizations to analyze customer behavioral patterns, individual profitability and LTV (Life Time Value) of their customers.

CRM delivers value to the business organizations finding out the type and nature of customer, buying patterns and delivering a product of their choice increases the ROI and makes the marketing strategy more scientific. It is based on the assumption that creating satisfied customer always serves as a sustainable competitive advantage for the organization. Data analysis can direct the strategic marketing communication, the standardization of service quality delivery, establish a basis for meaningful interaction through 'either personal (or) web based dialogues, the development of quality financial products and a large number of customers that can be translated into long term profitable relationship with source of revenue (i.e., payment by customers).

A customer expectation with regard to service delivery levels and product quality is essential for establishing a long-term symbolic value Relationships. Customers expected life cycle, performance measurement mechanism and corresponding service mix offering are crucial for success of a financial service provider. In addition to the creation of measurement system to monitor the progress augments the customer value model. This integrated approach can help in calculating customer life time value (CLV) by calculating and analyzing all relevant costs of customer acquisition and retention and corresponding revenues generated from each customer categories CLV creation consist of a process of adhoc segmentation and data analysis against customer requests, targeted rentention activities etc., is aligned to CLV, identification of customer categories for cross selling and up selling of financial services and product portfolios aligned to the concept of CLV.

Conclusion

Financial service sector is confronted with rapid modernization and inflated competition in today's world. Since profits are drying up in the face of increased competition and customers are moving very fast from one firm to another on service and complete solution provision dimension, it becomes important to have an integrated CRM strategy across the whole organization for generating higher CLV. Integration of process, people, technology and information will offer a greater value to the customer.

REFERENCES

1. *"Service Encounters and Service Relationships"*, Implication for Research—Journal of Business Research, 20(1), pp. 13-21.
2. *Developing Buyer-Seller Relationship*—Journal of Marketing, vol. 51, No. 1, pp. 11-27.
3. *Determination of Long-Term Orientation in Buyer-Seller*, Journal of Marketing, pp. 1-19.

43

Strategic Role in CRM to PRM in Corporate Renovation

G. DHANASEKARAN*

Introduction

In recent years the concept of CRM has taken an important role in the business world. Customer service, once a low-ranking corporate priority, was often handled by front office and Customer Relations Departments. Corporate Sectors are working towards giving the true meaning to CRM and have customers close to their hearts and attempt to gain higher returns on investment for their entities. Understanding that a massive new market is available to be explored, the worlds leading management and business software vendors continue to introduce value added packages and keep focused on this fast growing CRM market in order to secure a substantial share. There is a lack of consensus about what CRM really means and a growing uncertainty about the alliance of CRM and technology.

This paper sets out to explain in layman terms, the fundamental meaning of CRM from the Organization. It attempts to justify that CRM is management. Philosophy and it would understand and manage relationship of each partner thereby contributing to the well being of family as a whole, this would call all partners to work together to add value to themselves. This process will eventually shift the focus on CRM to PRM (Partner Relationship Management) where every Partner will understand, build and manage relationship with each other and contribute to a corporate renovation.

* Lecturer, B.B.A., K.S.R.C.A.S., Tiruchengode (T.N.).

What is CRM ?

Jennifer Pratt in CRM talk says that CRM as is a management approach (or) model that puts the customer at the core of the company's processes and practices. She argues that CRM leverages cutting-edge technology, integrated strategic planning, up close personal marketing techniques and organizational development tools to build internal and external relationship, that increase profit margins and productivity within a company.

CRM in Practice

For years, companies have focused much of their effort on cutting costs and improving efficiency within their organizations. They have attempted to streamline the internal processes, often automating elements of 'back-office' functions such as logistics and finance.

The common benefits about CRM is that the term relates to a set of new applications and systems, which were introduced for greater efficiency have converted the traditional customer care approach to a more "high-Tech" approach, CRM is more appropriately described as e-CRM, which involves not only the idea of internet access via PC, but also wireless devices such as mobile phones etc., problem resolution systems fact into the overall service fulfillment category, as do workflow automation and field service dispatch systems, considering the above scenarios, the corporate concerns are:

- How well the organization effort is defined?
- Its degree of acceptance across the organization of efforts.
- Under which category does on organization fits in better, based on real use of CRM?

The traditional CRM has information base that is very often used by the front line office of marketing, sales and customer service, its due to limited inter-department communication and also different information about the customer, so perform much more effectively than the traditional CRM levels provided there is adequate acceptance of CRM across the company and required leadership from the senior management is given for such implementation.

CRM to PRM (Corporate Renaissance)

It is a customer centered process, which ideally bring in a high return on investment, finally reflects the performance of the organization. High ROI and retention of customers will basically depend upon the satisfaction level of the customer.

Example

The role of a travel agent who arrange overseas travel to a customer. The organization sources the business, co-ordinates to put-together the total business packages by securing service from Airlines, Hotels and similar entities to give the best to the customer. Similarly travel agent is an important customer of the Airline and the Hotels. While the travel agent will have to understand, manage and develop its customers, and the airlines too have the understand and manage their customer.

Under the circumstances, the future CRM will keep another step forward to treat all value providers as partners of the value generating and sharing process and would convert itself to PRM instead of CRM. This would become the core management philosophy in any organization (or) group of individuals engaged in a value creation and sharing. The future definition of CRM (PRM) would be RM is a partner centric management philosophy where the value creators of any activity are equal partners and work in an alliance to understand and develop relationship that would create value for themselves.

Characteristics of PRM

All departments of the organizations, customers, suppliers and service providers, include human resources, marketing, manufacturing and finance.

- A greater opportunity to create and share value
- Global by a few clicks
- Stronger platform to create value for the customer.

Technical Aspects of PRM

PRM would be a total e-based operation, which will convert PRM to e-PRM, and this does not mean that it just has an electronic base of operation. The e-PRM would hold a Partner Contact Centre (PCC) that integrates all Partners required generating and sharing value, through a multichannel gateway. It would also hold platform to use data to produce a research and analysis of transactions scenario. This is frequently used to support management decisions.

It also hold software that aggregates fragmented buyers and/ or sellers to increase a market efficiencies beyond the exchanges of goods and multiple enterprise to work together online a dynamic for adding and sharing values. Integration of electronic interactions including e-mail, chat, collaboration, voice-over-IP (VoIP) with voice interactions, and fronting the interaction engine with a desktop PRM application features that could be integrated in the e-PRM operation.

In the PRM implementation all people including the top management have to be on board. It's a team effort that leads to understand adequately the benefits of positive changes that PRM can bring in.

Conclusion

The most difficult challenges are the increasing customer demands and expectation and rapid changes in the technology. These changes are further threatened by current global recession. The need to be a "master" is greater than before. The service providers and suppliers manage an effective and efficient relationship, this is only way to add value to every party involved in any transaction and lead to a corporate renaissance.

REFERENCES

1. www. crmcommunity.com
2. www. brendler.com
3. www.goldmine.co.uk

e-CRM in Educational Institutions

G. SATHYANARAYANAN*, K. ANANDHAN** & M. KAMARASAN***

Introduction

A customer is a person who seeks service and benefits from an organization and is ready to pay for it. Customer is the most important resource for any organization. Customer Relationship Management is a term which is not only used by business organizations today to maintain such good relationships with their present and old clients and associates, but the terminology is now being used by almost any type of organization to create beneficial environment in today's competitive world.

Among the several techniques of marketing management, Customer Relationship Management is the most prominent these days. In today's competitive scenario an institution or a company can exist only be satisfying their respective customers by delivering the necessary goods and services. Customer Relationship Management is all about satisfying and retaining the customer by providing the desired perquisites. The relations that are maintained are a kind of trust that the institutions provide to its customers and fulfill it.

Academic institutions are themselves not different to any other organizations. They are themselves profit making firms who impart education for money and try to grow as any other organizations. Whether they are government owned or self-financed private institutions; almost all educational institutions are profit-making organizations. Such organizations focus

* Lecturer, Engg. Wing, DDE, Annamalai University.
** Programmer, Engg. Wing, DDE, Annamalai University.
*** Programmer, Dept. of Comp. Sci. & Engg., Annamalai University.

on not only to impart state of the art education to their students, but they also have to maintain relations with their working staff, administrators, companies, vendors and of course with their primary customers—students. CRM plays an increasingly important role in maintaining such relationships in these organizations.

In this modern and electronic world, customer relation management has become more innovative and beneficial for the customers. Computers and many other electronic mediums and their advancement has assisted management practices of relationship maintenance and made them more confined towards customer benefits. This task of customer satisfaction done with the help of such electronic tools is called e-CRM, which may well be considered as the modernized or advanced system of customer relation management.

CRM Service Foreseeable

Educational Institutions deeply committed to improve customer satisfaction. The lay down of e-CRM shows, how useful is it creating a new database from an existing customer records and other sources to catch down marketing efforts—and decide where to start. The customers and stakeholders of educational organization include: Students, Companies, Administrators, Employees and Staff, Employer groups and Political Parties, Agents and affiliations, Providers and Vendors, The Media.

CRM is based on knowledge—identifying the customer needs, an organization has to provide refined products and services that keep them satisfied throughout the life cycle. Before CRM, educational organizations' customer satisfaction efforts were somewhat blind because they didn't have a way to collect and track customer encounters with the existing system. The basis of CRM for any organization is an integrated sales and marketing database that collects and consolidates customer data from all of the organization's touch points. It should include:

- Internal information captured from your organization's accounting and student's records.
- External information captured from outside data sources.
- Computed information from software to analyze and enhance the data.

Because the CRM solution for educational organizations involves working with complex, student, payer and provider information, as well as procedural and diagnostic codes, those involved in designing the program and building the database.

CRM program must also be embraced and promoted by top management and supported with a comprehensive annual CRM plan to ensure organization-wide success. Customer loyalty and retention are based on maintaining mutually beneficial, ongoing dialogues with your students and prospects. The success and cost-effectiveness of direct mail efforts depends on getting the right message to the right individuals at the right time. These tools can assist in identifying students and prospects likely to need certain services based on the requirements, profiles and other risk factors. With such information in hand, the institution can develop event trigger communications that raise to send a message.

A successful 360 degree customer view enables everyone within the organization who has customer contact to have a total picture of that customer's relationship. Customer Relationship Management (CRM) is the set of technology—enabling solutions that make this view possible.

e-CRM and Its Bang in Educational Institutions

The effect of e-CRM to the various customers/stakeholders of the education business are discussed below.

Students as Customers

Is higher education synonymous with cutting-edge business processes? It is safe to say that most universities lag a few years behind the business world in adopting envelope-pushing business technologies and practices. A more useful question might be: are there new technologies and business practices that could significantly improve the business and success of higher education? Today there are available and affordable technologies that can help universities very easily improve productivity across the institution to increase profits, and enable further investments in attracting faculty, funding new programs offering more facilities, and boosting productivity to free up time for additional projects to accelerate enhancement.

Higher education—often a business degree—is part of the profile of most present and future business leaders. So it's surprising, when universities do not see themselves as businesses first—in a very competitive market. Do they hire intelligent people who can maintain business-like operations? Absolutely. Do they purchase technology that can increase staff efficiency and benefit the education process? Of course they invest in technology. So where does the problem reside?

Most university-level schools, both publicly and privately funded, are organized into departments that act on some level to attract, service, educate, manage, or graduate a student. The problem isn't that these functions are distinct, but that they fail to interact or leverage information in the most efficient manner as the student progresses from one step of the education process to the next.

Traditional University Process

Recruiting/Admission

Higher education begins the process by trying to attract new students. Often this effort revolves around sending individuals to physically recruit students at a number of pre or high schools. Interested students listen to the recruiter who makes a presentation and then the students fill out a paper form with brief contact information. If interest is piqued, there are a number of options for the student to proactively obtain information and request an application: calling, making a visit, mailing, looking at a static Web site, and e-mailing. However, in the majority of schools, each of these communications tools is handled as a separate means of the admissions function.

Registration

Once the admittance review is painstakingly completed for each student, the education process begins and the functions of the registrar, faculty, and some level of student support take shape. These areas also act independently, often requiring the student to visit each department in an educational scavenger hunt to collect: Counseling and requirements, Grade and transcript information, Course offerings and availability. Financial aid, Schedules and activities, Exams and new applications.

Education

In addition to the rigors and demands of academic pursuit,

students know that every quarter or semester, they must run the gauntlet of registration, including the validating, yet time-consuming search for documents and class availability, so that the school knows that the checks-and-balances process has been completed and continuity is intact.

Suggested University Process

Recruiting

Marketing programs drive prospective students to engaging, interactive Web pages where a student can learn anything about the school and gain the experience of attending it, or provide personal information. (Even if students don't fill out a form, cookies are set, and make a student to recognize while return, and collect information about the pages they visit, which allows the program to make subsequent visits more customized and relevant to their interests.) All communication and interactions are documented and coordinated between recruiters and students, wherein all efforts are tracked to measure the effectiveness of particular individuals.

Admissions

Online applications can be electronically submitted across numerous communication channels (Web form, fax, e-mail, mail), making them readily available to the staff managing admissions. Staff and students can cooperatively complete online forms together for more successful processing. The growing volume of e-mail flowing into departments is automatically filtered and routed to specialists handling specific inquiries or issues. A detailed audit trail of this process is created so system users can easily access this information when handling future interactions.

Registration

Deadlines for classes or professors to submit grades are proactively sent via e-mail and logged into the system; follow-up mail is automatically sent to anyone who has not acted on a specific embedded link or action. Students can reach out to counselors, professors, financial aid officers, and transcript departments in person or directly from any telephone or computer, while the university collects data at all touch points (Web self-help, e-mail,

Web forms, chat, VoIP, fax, phone, wireless, and face-to-face meetings) to ensure proper servicing of any requests.

Profiling

Millions upon millions of up-to-date data packets (student profiles) are collectively available to every department within the university, each with the ability to run reports on multiple variables. Even the alumni department has permission to access this information to manage intelligent donation campaigns and further extend the campus to past students.

So what does this mean for the university and more importantly, students? Students are immersed in electronic communication to enhance their physical worlds and expect to have these options available anywhere they do business. Teenagers are shopping online before their parents and experiencing what it means to be a wired consumer.

The solution is that, Students can be perceived as customers. Embrace this idea and search for means to communicate in real time, a way that is second nature to this generation. And watch what a conscious transition to viewing students as customers does for the reputation—and the enrollment activity—of the university.

Companies

Companies come to educational institutions for recruiting students in campus selection procedures. Companies are so amongst the most important clients of such education organizations. Keeping continuous and direct contacts with these companies will enable institutes to maintain good and healthy relationships and improve contacts and services to them. Companies may be kept in contact through telephones and Web based services.

Administrators

Administrators keep the things going on in institutes; they plan for the present and future of the institutes. Enabling administrators to have a good contact with the organization from anywhere so that it would improve effectiveness drastically, by providing e-mail services, phone line support and access to Virtual Private Networks.

Employees and Staff

Employees, faculties and staff form the backbone of an education institute. By providing great support and services, staff's would not only benefited but also be obliged to deliver the same quality services. By this way the employees can even be benefited from such e-CRM services as they feel more attached, and emotionally involved in delivering good education services to students and others.

Employer Groups and Political Parties

Every educational institute is in gratitude and obligation of different employee groups and political parties, which influence their functions to a lot of extent. Maintaining good relations with these groups will enable smooth functioning of these institutions and e-CRM can enable direct and worthy ways of contact channels with them.

Agents and Affiliations

Almost all education institutions are supported by agents and affiliations. Institutions are helped by financial agents for funds from time to time and may take help of insurance agencies as such. So it becomes equally important to keep in touch with all of these agencies in order to get a long term service and support. Electronic means of relationship management may help in vast sense to keep friendly relations with all of these agencies.

Providers and Vendors

Education institutions are provided services themselves by a number of vendors dealing in equipments, systems, furniture, civil, engineering and development etc. If care is taken to build fine relations, great pre and post sales services are guaranteed to be delivered. Healthy relationship maintenance through the use of latest electronic means will result into prompt support and services being offered by them.

The Media

Academic institutions are many times interested in advertising, publicizing, promoting and marketing for them. In doing this, the institution can maintain and be in contact to various media based service providers who help them for this purpose. e-CRM plays an increasing important role in maintaining and making new such productive, profitable rewarding and fruitful relationships, which benefit these organizations on short and long runs both.

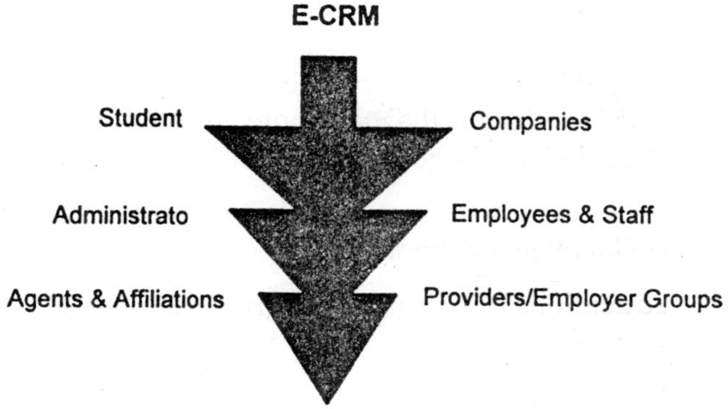

Fig. 1: Channel Flow in an Educational Institution (e-CRM)

The e-Learning Market

The initiative is deploying tracking and automation tools to manage the interaction between the University and both its existing and prospective students. When a University is providing global learning services to students enrolled in more than 500 countries, the University has to face the challenge of being responsive to client needs 24 hours per day, 7 days per week. The most efficient, cost effective way to manage the 24 × 7 challenge is to deploy effective automation tools, as opposed to running three shift student service desks or employing online tutors in different continents. The aim of such a system is to provide effective and efficient service to existing and prospective students at minimal variable cost.

The deployment of e-Customer Relationship Management (e-CRM) software (referred to by Million and Miles) as Learner Relationship Management (also known as e-care or e-service) will ultimately enable the use of a single toll free number integrated with an email based enquiry tracking system that will exploit the fundamental strengths of the Internet in enhancing communication and managing information. Using structured, intelligent databases, the knowledge generated by solving student problems/ enquiries is being progressively stored and made available so that, wherever possible, students with equivalent or similar problems can have their enquiries dealt with immediately through the self-help, automated response capacity, thereby facilitating effective first point of contact resolution (Fig 2).

In e-learning approach, many teaching staff make use of discussion groups, which entail students posting reflections via the asynchronous computer mediated communication (CMC) system. The teaching staff also post comments, which are aimed at engendering student engagement and ensuring that the focus and depth of the online threaded discussions are appropriate to achieve the learning outcomes. In the same vein, members of the teaching staff respond to student questions posted to the discussion group. These contributions are often quite complex and typically serve to enhance the quality of interaction. Development of a detailed response to a searching student query naturally takes time. A positive feature of the system is that the communication is on a one-to-many basis, so that all students may benefit, not just the one who asked the initial question. Further, our experience demonstrates that other students often comment on the issues raised thereby enriching the depth and quality of the dialogue. The value of these contributions is particularly useful where students are giving examples of applications in different cultural contexts. Such interactions may take place in conventional classroom settings, but the difference is that they are ephemeral and not documented for detailed reflection as they are in the CMC system.

At present, the effective use of CMC is presently constrained in an important way. It is still a function of what Daniel recently referred to as the cottage-industry model, which entails the traditional working practices of universities, wherein the same academic staff member usually does everything, including teaching, providing academic support and assessment for a group of students. In effect, the current applications of fourth generation Internet-based delivery tend to generate resource allocation models similar to tutorial-based on campus teaching. Indeed, it is still a fear of many academics initiating an online teaching program that they will be overwhelmed by e=mail requesting support from individual students. While such fears can be allayed by the use of one-to-many communication systems such as bulletin boards, mailing lists and threaded discussions, the underlying resource model is not significantly different from conventional on campus teaching, with a staff member being necessary to manage groups of approximately 20 students to maintain a reasonable quality of interaction and academic support. In contrast, the fifth generation

Intelligent Flexible Learning Model has the potential to deliver major economies of scale in managing teaching and academic support through the exploitation of automated response systems (Fig 2).

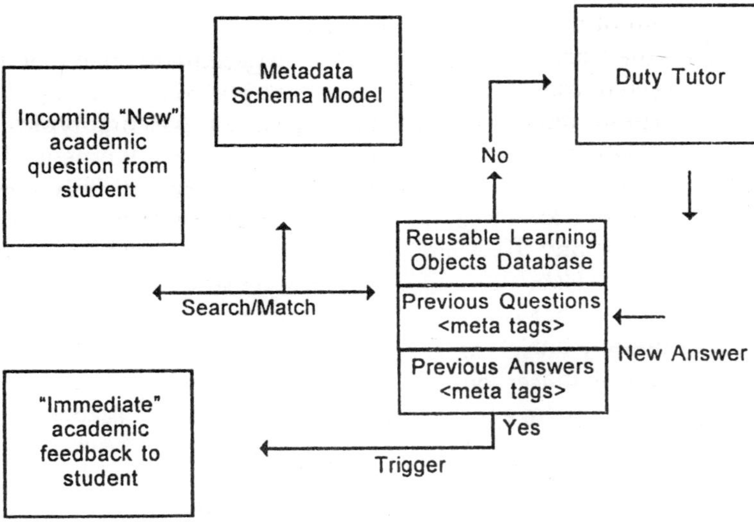

Fig. 2: Representation of 5th Generation Academic Productivity Enhancement System.

Conclusion

The e-CRM solution is a comprehensive, end-to-end education plan specific CRM offering. Information about members and customers, including their history of interactions with your organizations, is tracked within the system—from sales to marketing to service to knowledge. The outcomes are improved acquisition, increased retention, and expansion and deepening of current customer relationships.

Furthermore, e-CRM allows organizations to: Consolidate and analyze large volumes of information in real-time. Continually optimize your business model to reflect and meet education and customer demands. Move from reactive to predictive in meeting customer needs and educational market trends. Increased response time to customers. Do report generation in minutes.

REFERENCES

1. *Marketing Management*, Philip Kotler.
2. *Customer Relationship Management: Emerging Tools and Applications*, JN Seth, Atul Parvatiyar & G. Shainesh.
3. *Principles of Internet Marketing*, 1st Edition, South-Western College Publishing.
4. Gruen TW, '*Relationship Marketing: The Route to Marketing Efficiency and Effectiveness*'.
5. Berry LL, '*Relationship Marketing of Services: Growing Interest, Emerging Perspectives*'.
6. *Improving Customer Satisfaction, Loyalty and Profit: An Integrated Management and Management System*, Jossey Bass Press, 2000.
7. *A Conceptual Model of Service MQuality and its Implications for Future Research*, Journal of Marketing, Fall, pp. 41-50, 1985.

45

Cementing the Customer Bond in Banks through e-CRM

Namita Gopal* & C.S. Srividhya Pratibha*

Introduction

Customers are the wheel behind which business revolve. All businesses need customers in order that they may exist. Customers also realize their importance and together with the environment they are putting more and more pressure on their suppliers to gear up with new methods and technologies to deal with them.

Banks are major operators in the service industry and like all other businesses are depicting their desire to woo new customers and try hard to retain the older ones in the dynamic hard pressured changes that are prevalent all around. There is a complete shift in focus as how banks look at customers.

The evolution of marketing can be seen as under:

- 1960's Mass marketing
- 1970's Segment marketing
- 1980's Transaction marketing
- 1990's Relationship marketing
- 2000's e-CRM

Banks and other financial services institutions are increasingly facing stiffer competition, resulting in shrinking profit margins and increasing pressure to compete on the basis of price. In addition, the continuing development of new banking channels, personal financial management software and in particular

* Lecturers, Department of Business Administration, M.O.P. Vaishnav College for Women, Nungambakkam High Road, Chennai.

technologies such as the internet have made consumers more self-sufficient, with more sources of information on financial market activity and access to a wider range of financial products.

Many financial services institutions are responding to the challenge of carrying out business in such an environment by developing customer relationship management (CRM) strategies. Here the underlying rationale is that the introduction of channels combining CRM-enabling technologies—such as for example, interactive marketing, sales automation and customer service—can be used to develop a single customer view contributing to customer retention, defending and expanding existing relationships, and increasing 'wallet share'.

Bank Frame e-CRM is a set of tools designed to support an enterprise-wide CRM business strategy that will optimize profitability, revenue and customer satisfaction. This is achieved by personalizing the relationship with every customer and organizing a bank's marketing activities around specific customer segments, thus enabling better customer understanding, increased customer access, more effective customer interactions and integration across all customer channels and back office enterprise.

Key Drivers of e-CRM Initiatives in Banking

e-CRM is being implemented throughout the banking industry because banks realize that the competitive advantage gained from improved customer knowledge, reduced operational risk, and more informed selling opportunities, is too great to be ignored.

e-CRM technologies are being adopted in every industry, but there are imperatives in the banking industry that make them particularly relevant:

Identifying Profitable Customers

Banks need to know as much as possible about their profitable customers. In order to get to know them, they are increasing investment in real-time segmentation, profiling and related applications, as well as in data mining, analytics and other business intelligence tools. These measures facilitate the bank increasing their efficiency in extracting customer information from disparate applications.

Gaining a Single Customer View

The new generation of e-CRM systems can integrate richer packets of internal and external data to give a 'single view' of a customer in real-time. A single view is becoming critical for banks offering a growing range of products across multiple channels such as call centers, websites, interactive TV, independent agents, branches, in-store outlets, and in-house sales staff. Banks are realizing that to achieve "real" relationships with their customers—rather than just a bit of casual cross selling—they need to invest in e-CRM capabilities.

Reducing Operational Risks

Technologies such as e-CRM also promise to reduce operational risks, in particular, risks that occur when there is lack of communication between departments within banks. For example, e-CRM technologies can be used in the commercial sector to highlight links between credit risk entities that are not necessarily obvious across originating business lines and which can lead to credit concentrations or failures in collateral management.

Leveraging Intelligent Sales

Banks have portfolios of products. They are looking at CRM systems to help them sell those products that complement a customer's financial situation. Banks have a 'trust advantage' over other financial institutions when they offer financial planning—but they find running these services time-consuming. Sophisticated CRM systems help banks overcome this problem in two ways. The systems integrate customer data, but some also use rules-based systems to transfer expert knowledge from one part of the bank to another. The hard-won knowledge of specialists can be used to complement the advice of less expensive customer contact staff.

Drivers for e-CRM in Retail Banking

Customers have increasing demands. It is no longer just an issue of brand loyalty—customers want more. They demand speed, convenience, and glitch-free service, and off-site cash access. They want lower fees, competitive rates and banking options that suit their needs. To satisfy these customer needs, banks must learn to mimic leading consumer-goods retailers. To better understand the customer, banks must also learn to gather and use customer information and incorporate it via sophisticated database marketing techniques. In retail banking, the specific drivers for e-CRM implementation are:

The Need to Create Virtual Customer Intimacy

Retail banks must constantly strive to keep up with improving technologies in order to reach and retain today's demanding customer. While technology resource development can be fairly complex and costly, it is an absolute necessity. Many large banks are currently in the process of installing sophisticated information management capabilities to aid in establishing virtual customer intimacy. To successfully achieve this intimacy, banks must combine today's technology with existing human knowledge and know-how—giving them the ability and foresight to address customer requirements almost before the customers are aware of them.

Competitive Pressure

Competing in the retail banking industry is not getting any easier. It is more complex, more difficult and more costly to attract the desirable customers that banks look for. Retail banks will need to learn how to multitask when it comes to successfully competing for business. Tomorrow's leading retail bank will have to focus on retaining current customers while simultaneously looking for new ones and expanding their business. These banks should also expect to feel increasing pressure from non-bank competitors, such as online brokerage and insurance companies.

The Influence of the Internet

Most retail banks are in the dark when it comes to know what impact Internet banking will have on their industry. Will it act as a replacement delivery channel? A customer service vehicle? A marketing tool? Retail bankers will have to plan their Internet strategies carefully. Timing should be a major consideration. A bank that becomes involved in internet banking too early runs the risk of becoming obsolete and outdated in the eyes of the customer. While a bank that waits too long may find that it has lost the initiative, as well as the best potential customers.

Drivers for e-CRM in Corporate Banking

Corporate customers have outgrown the business models that most financial service institutions have long adhered to. Most corporate customers can no longer be adequately managed through a single, high-touch relationship manager. The diversity of the product offerings, as well as the global nature of many customers, is too much for one person unless that individual is equipped with superior technology.

In order to compete successfully in today's marketplace, it is imperative to leverage either a deal or product/line business account relationship into additional financial service sales, while keeping a consistent view of the customer soundly at the center.

To achieve this capability, financial institutions have put pressure on:

1. Front-office applications
2. Decision support systems.

Decision support systems need to monitor customer-level transactions and accounts within the relationship against the financial institution's business strategy for profitability and risk management. Financial institutions that choose to remain product-focused may find some of these solutions appropriate for selected business requirements, particularly in the front office, to remain competitively positioned. Key differentiators for success in the banking industry are:

- Development of mobile sales solutions for customer acquisition and origination
- Creation of new models for understanding customer risk profiles
- Fostering convergence of self-service channels
- Making provision for decision support technologies

Some Comments

Meera Sanyal, COO, ABN Amro Bank says, "Net Banking is a hygiene product today and enhances our customer value proposition".

A.K. Purwar, Chairman, SBI says, "The consumer is going to be wooed with new product launches, innovations and faster credit delivery".

Conclusion

e-CRM in banks has enabled banks to get a global presence. They have become customer-focused organizations and can no longer get away with making excuses about manpower hassles. Their product innovation and structuring capabilities have got a major boost with the advent of e-CRM. The environments, which they operate in, have become more challenging with robustness and financial resilience the buzzword all around.

There are however some drawbacks which are common to all e-CRM dependent businesses. There is no personal interaction between the customer and the supplier. Businesses have become impersonalized with vary powerful means of communication like body language and judgment skills becoming non-existent. Banks are not able to gauge their customers at all since the complete process has become over the computer screen.

e-CRM Payoffs

- Increased Sales Revenues
- Increased Margins
- Increased convenience
- Improved customer service ratings
- Decreased administrative costs
- Ability to introduce new schemes at a faster rate
- Facility to the customer in his increased mobile business life
- Improved speed of dissemination of information
- Reduced subjectivity in operations.

46

CRM in Hotel Industry

S. GAYATHRY* & G. RENUKA*

Consumer today is no longer the King, he has emerged as an Emperor

—Alyque Padamse

One of the most dynamic Information Technology topics of the new millennium is the area of CRM. At the core, CRM is an integration of technologies and business processes used to satisfy the needs of a customer during any given interaction. The new millennium is in the midst of explosive change witnessing rapidly changing market conditions, volatile equity markets, reconstructed value chains and new global competitor. Customers themselves are changing and natural customer loyalty is a thing of the past. As a result, the concept of CRM has taken the center stage in the business world for sustainable competitive advantage. Long-term success requires a greater CRM strategy. Hence, CRM—The management mantra of the new millennium has gained predominant importance in today's market. AMR Research Inc. predicts that CRM market will reach about $16.8 billion by the end of 2003, and a Compounded Annual Growth Rate (CAGR) of 49 per cent over the next five years.

CRM is the process by which an organization maximizes customer information in an effort to increase loyalty and retain customers business over their lifetime. It consists of activities that an enterprise performs to identify, select, acquire, develop and retain increasingly loyal and profitable customer.

* Department of Commerce, M.O.P. Vaishnav College for Women, Chennai.

It is the process of:

- Acquiring
- Satisfying
- Retaining
- Growing

profitable consumers.

It requires a clear focus on the service attributes that represent value to the customer and create loyalty. This encompasses:

- Developing long term relationship with customers
- Allocating the market based on the customers value
- Deriving maximum possible revenue from the customers over a life time

Objectives of CRM

- Long-term and profitable relationship with customers
- Closer contact with customers
- Maximization of market share

Evolution of CRM

In the pre industrialization era developing direct customer relationship was the only means to carry out business transactions. This was due to the fact that economy was agriculture driven. Farmers, artisans, traders, labourers etc. were customers of each other, which lead to direct relationship building. After the industrial revolution, factory systems and manufacturers as intermediary came into existence and led to transaction based trade relationship. The evolution of marketing is summarised as follows:

- 1960's Mass marketing
- 1970's Segment marketing
- 1980's Transaction marketing
- 1990's Relationship marketing
- 2000's e-CRM

Over the years the management approach that views customer relationship as key assets of the organization has gained increased prominence. This customer asset management approach has been referred to as "Relationship Marketing", otherwise popularly known as "CRM".

CRM in India

The Indian industries to cope up with global competition have started practicing CRM. But adoption of CRM by Indian companies is at an infancy stage. The CRM enabled companies include TATA Telecom, TVS Electronics, TATA InfoTech etc. India even has a CRM Foundation in New Delhi founded with the purpose of assessing and improving CRM practices.

3 C's of CRM

- Cooperation
- Communication
- Courtesy

Types of CRM

CRM allows a company to address all of the types of customers it serves at different points of time in their life cycle and to choose the marketing program that best fits a customer's attitude towards the company and willingness to purchase its products and services. There are four types of CRM

- Win back or save customers
- Attract new and potential customers
- Create loyalty among existing customers
- Up-sell or Cross sell services

Win Back or Save Customers

This is the process of convincing a customer to stay with the organization at the point they are discontinuing service or convincing them to rejoin once they have left.

Attract New and Potential Customers

Prospecting is the effort to win new, first time customers. Apart from the offer itself, the three most critical elements of a prospecting campaign are

(*a*) Segmentation
(*b*) Selectivity
(*c*) Source.

It is essential to develop an effective need based segmentation model that allows the organization to effectively target the offer.

Without these focused approach, the organization either fails to achieve an adequate acceptance or rate an offer or spends too much on promotions, advertising and concessionary pricing. It is advisable to achieve a 95 per cent confidence rate before embarking on a prospecting effort. Selectivity is as important to prospecting, as it is to win back. Needs based segmentation defines what the customer wants from the organization and the profit based segmentation, defines how valuable the customer is and helps the organization to decide how much it is willing to spend to get the customer.

Create loyalty among existing customers

Loyalty is the category in which it is most difficult to gain accurate measures. The organization is trying to prevent customers from leaving by:

- Value Based Segmentation—which allows the organization to determine how much it is willing to invest in retaining the customer loyalty.
- Need Based Segmentation—to offer a customized loyalty programme.
- Predictive Churn Models—using vast amount of demographic data and usage rate available for the existing base of customers, which helps in forecasting customer attrition. Through the use of advanced data-mining tools, an organization can develop models that identify vulnerable and potential customers who can be targeted for the loyalty campaign or offered alternative products.

According to Mc Kinsey, the repeat customers generate over twice as much gross income as new customers.

Cross-Sell or Up-Sell Services

The purpose is to identify complementary offering that a customer would like. Customers need based segment, usage pattern and reaction to the previous contacts or interactions determine the nature of the offer. Once the composition of the offer is determined and the contact medium is agreed to, then the organization directly presents the offer to the customers. Up selling is similar, but instead of offering a complementary product, the organization offers an enhanced one.

Threat to CRM

The biggest threat to CRM is that management focuses on short-run profits rather than long-term vision. CRM is an expensive, time consuming and complex proposition. Even in the best case, this tool is an opportunity to rise above minor advantages and develop an actual relationship with the customers. Companies that are the most successful at delivering what each customer wants are the most likely to be the leaders of the future.

CRM in Service Industry

Service industries are playing increasingly important role in the overall Indian Economy. Interest in the need and measurement of service quality is thus understandably high and most important. Service quality is an elusive and obstruct construct that is difficult to define and measure. In addition, to-date, the important relationship between service quality customer satisfaction and purchasing behaviour remain largely unexplored. Though the origin of CRM was initially in the industrial context, the service industry is also focused on maintaining and enhancing Customer Relationship. There is an awareness in the service industry that building better and deeper customer relationships requires new processes, new analytic, and new integration of systems to enable their employees to work harder and smarter to capture customer information. Everyone in the service industry adopts CRM.

Hotel Industry—An Insight

Hotel

Hotel is a place where all who conduct themselves properly and who being able and ready to pay for their entertainment, accommodation and other services including the boarding thus making it a temporary home. It is a home away from home where all amenities and facilities are available but chargeable.

Motel

Motels serve the needs and requirements of these travelers and meeting the demand for transit accommodation. Some of the important services offered by the motels are parking, garage facilities, accommodation, restaurant facilities, public catering and recreational facilities.

Hotel and its Typology

The recent changes in the perception to the hotel business culture make possible a large-scale variation in the different categories or hotels.

I. Classification on the Basis of Nature

1. Residential hotels
2. Commercial Hotels
3. Resort Hotels
4. International Hotels which includes
   (*a*) Five-star deluxe (*b*) Five-star
   (*c*) Four-star (*d*) Three-star
   (*e*) Two-star (*f*) One-star
5. Floating Hotels are found located on the water surface.

II. Classification on the Basis of Standard and Control

1. **Approved Hotels** are of international standards where the accommodations are available as per certain criteria laid down by the Department of Tourism. Ministry of Tourism and Civil Aviation and Government. They will be given official recognition.
2. **Unapproved Hotels** lack the official recognition, but are in par with approved Hotels in providing services.

Hotel Industry—Available Opportunities

The Hotel Industry is making an outstanding contribution to the process of transforming the national economy of our country. In the Indian economy, there are tremendous opportunities for the development of hotel and tourism.

The marketing environment for hotel is found highly volatile and competitive. This necessitates innovative marketing strategies. A fair blending of core and peripheral services would simplify the task of capitalizing on the opportunities. The promotional strategies and creativity in advertising would make the entire process cost effective.

Role of Human Element in Hotel Industry

People or human beings are the most important around which the entire Hotel Industry operates. Induction and training need to be given for the people working in the industry. Especially, the front line staff, in general, need a special training so that they are in a position to operate and maintain the sophisticated communicative technologies for delivering quick and quality services to the guests.

Customers of Hotel Industry

In marketing Hotel services, it is important to know about the different types of customers visiting hotels with diverse aims and objectives.

- Non-customers
- Prospective/Potential customers
- Actual customers
- Light customers
- Heavy customers

A particular guest visits a particular hotel frequently and ultimately, and thus forms a habit of visiting the same hotel. This helps in increasing the occupancy ratio of hotel rooms in addition to its positive impact on restaurants, bars and cafeterias.

In the hotel industry, the projection of a fair image is found important. The main task before the hotel companies is to satisfy the customers by offering them the services as per their expectations. The problem faced by the hotels is to establish a fair match between services expected and services offered. If the hotels make sincere efforts to understand the behavioural profile of customers, the task of identifying their expectations will be simplified.

Behavioural Profile of Hotel Customers

The users of hotel services come from different regions/strata/economic categories. Behaviour is not found static as it changes over time and specially in tune with the demographic, geographic and socio-economic changes. Understanding the behaviour of customers is thus found quite time consuming particularly, in the hotel services, the life styles occupy a place of outstanding significance.

In studying the behavioural profile of the customers, it is significant to conduct an in depth study of their psychology. Their attitudes, intentions and desires need to be analysed. An attitudinal change in customers is found difficult when they are found liberal to a particular hotel. The knowledge of customers' attitude can provide a sound base for initiating qualitative improvements in services offered by hotels.

The marketing decisions cannot be right unless the marketers make an in depth study of the expectations of customers. In marketing hotel services an experienced receptionist is supposed to know that business guests returning around 6.30 p.m. from a hard days work tend to be over-critical and impatient in waiting just a moment for the keys. He/She is supposed to know that they had a busy schedule and so cannot take it out on their wives, and so may blast off at the hotel staff. Here, a few words of empathy like 'Have you had a tough day?' would bring positive results. In hotel marketing, empathy plays an outstanding role. It is a key thought process or ability in successful marketing.

Marketing of Hotel Services

The major difference is marketing hotels as against other consumer products is that after a customer has spent money in hotels, he/she has nothing substantial to show except bills for his/her money as benefits as compared with buying tangibles, such as television or a refrigerator. If the goods remain unsold, it is possible to go for a sale programme as and when the circumstances favor. But if the rooms of a hotel remain vacant, it is unlikely that the same can be sold tomorrow. This makes it essential that marketing practices for the hotel services be given a transcendental priority.

The services are required to be planned, controlled, automated, audited for quality control and are also to be regularly evacuated to ensure quantitative-cum-qualitative improvements in the hotel services.

The inclusion of modern sophisticated facilities like

- Air-conditioning
- Four channel music
- Cold drinks
- Fridge
- Telephone & Communication facilities
- Television
- Luxurious beds
- Round-the-clock room servicing

- Coffee shop
- Swimming pool
- Health clubs
- Comfortable shopping arcade
- Garden
- Amusement centers
- Car parking
- Conference hall

have changed the traditional concept of hotel management.

CRM—In Hotel Industry

In the hotel industry, the formulation of product-mix becomes significant. Apart from product mix, the behavioral management helps in excelling competition. The communication with a sweet smile may be helpful in having a fair match of expectations and realities.

Image and atmosphere plays a significant role in CRM in Hotel industry. In the five star hotels where the customers do not mind the price, but the quality, the marketing practices need emphasis.

The changes in the life style and income are also found important for innovating the marketing decisions and giving customers good benefits for the cost incurred.

Customers Expectations from the Hotels

Customers do come to hotels for various purposes and they expect certain services on each occasion. The table will summarise the customers' expectations on various occasions.

Today, the hotel industry thrives on the customer services and satisfaction. So for as the hotel is concerned, the product a customer buys covers the feelings pleasure, satisfaction received from available services like restaurants, function rooms and other centers as a part of hotel service.

The customer expects the following from the Hotels

Reception	• Welcome desk • Counter • Enquiry
Boarding	• Restaurant • Bar

(*Contd.*)

(*Contd.*)

	•
Lodging	• Bedrooms • Amenities and facilities for a comfortable stay
Entertainment	• Radio • Television • VCR • VCP • Dance, Music, etc.
Shopping	• Shopping Arcade
Communication	• Telephone • Fax • Magazines • Newspapers • Reservations • Immigration
Function	• Function Rooms • Conference Hall • Wedding Hall
Medical	• First Aid • Ambulance
Personal care	• Hair dressing • Beauty Parlours • Play grounds • Jogging • Gym • Peddle tennis.

And the perception of satisfaction is so fluctuating that it keeps changing. This calls for improvisation in existing strategies to retain customers.

Weddings	• Status • Ego • Sentiment • Price • Security
Holidays	• Price • Value for money • Comfort • Health
Product Launch	• Investment • Status • Value for money

Attractive and well equipped accommodation to be máde available at reception desk. The reception desk is also required to maintain a file of service facilities giving additional information on each room, such as location, size, decor, furnishing, facilities etc.

A file containing the history of its customers like Name, Residential and Official address, Date of birth, E-mail ID, Nationality, Likes and Dislikes of past, present and future prospects must be maintained.

Objective of the Study

Services are produced and delivered by the same institutions. Success of a service provider is dependent on long-term relationships that develop between the provider and customer. Service is the end product of the Hotel Industry. Success of the Hotel depends on providing satisfactory services to its customers. Hence this paper attempts to study the CRM practices and philosophies adopted by certain Five Star and Three Star Hotels in Chennai and also the customers' reaction to the same. List of Hotels will include:

Methodology

Information for the study was collected from both Primary and Secondary sources.

Primary Data was collected by interviewing the Marketing and Sales Managers, Training Managers, Bar Managers, Customer Relations Officer, Personnel Managers, Chefs, Bell Captains, Receptionists, House Keepers, Room Boys of the following Hotels

1. Under the Five Star category
   - Taj Coromandel
   - Park Sheraton
   - Chola Sheraton
2. Under the Three Star category
   - GRT Grand Days
   - Hotel Henkala
   - Hotel Breeze

Information from the customers of various hotels was collected by using a questionnaire. 20 questionnaires were distributed for pilot study. 125 questionnaires were distributed, 100 were collected and chosen for the study.

Secondary Data was collected by referring various books and journals.

Outcome of the Study

The study revealed many interesting points, which are worth considering.

Information Collected from the Employees of Hotels

Influencing the Aggressive Hotel Customer-Views of the Customer Relations Officer

- It is not difficult to influence the regular customers as experienced receptionists, housekeepers; waiters know the way to tackle them. But the task is really more complicated when the customers are abnormal or are found aggressive. Some of the customers visiting the restaurant, cafeterias create disturbance and generate inconvenience. The front line staffs bear the responsibility of managing them properly.
- There are number of occasions where guests are found tensed, over pressed with personal/official problems. The hotel personnel in general and the front line staff in particular are well trained to identify the aggressive customers.
- If the problem is related to restaurant, the waiters are supposed to deal with them. They will watch their orders. The style of placing orders would confirm their observation regarding the guests. They will watch their style, way and dialogues. It will re-confirm the observations of customers being done by the staff/ management personnel. Mean while, the observation should be transmitted to the sales executive who will make necessary arrangements outside the gate, if circumstances necessitate so. Even the problem is related to a room where the guests are found creating nuisance and making it inconvenient to others to stay comfortably, the treatment is by and large the same.

A minor lapse on the part of the hotel management staff may result in a major loss to the business. The potential guests outside the hotel are not going to accept the faults of customers. It is really a difficult task to convince the customers. Hence, the most effective solution is to tackle the problem patiently, of course, at initial stage. This will also simplify the task of projecting a fair image and minimizing the problems created by abnormal aggressive customers.

Menu Fatigue-Opinions of the Chief Chefs

- Restaurant is an important part of a hotel. People who stay in hotels prefer to eat outside. Business executives generally stay in hotels and are found eating in the restaurants of the same hotel. The guest found staying in hotels regularly, often claim that they suffer from illness or the problem of indigestion. This is called as Menu Fatigue. This has to be checked with immediate effect.
- Most of the business executives usually do not get time to eat during usual meal hours. Many more people are going to work flexi-hours. It is very natural that those who work odd hours would prefer to eat at odd hours and hotel restaurants would fail in catering for this will suffer financial loss.
- Various social and technological changes are destroying the usual meal hours. The main issue is to understand the guests and making provisions accordingly.
- Recently there is a new trend set in the food habits around the globe. More and more people are found eating chinese and Indian food. Many more are going for fast foods. In America, consumption of hot and spicy food is increasing at a fast pace. The same trend is found in European countries. People, all over the world, by and large prefer vegetarian food for non-vegetarian items we call it a swing in the eating habits and taste patterns.

Changing Drinking Habits—Observations of the Bar Manager

- The Japanese who initially abstained from drinking, are today heavy consumers of whisky.
- The British were found satisfied with traditional beer. Today, they prefer large and real ale.
- The Indian culture did not appreciate drinks. Today, large section of them has opted to make drinks a part of their dietary habits.

- In many ways, drinking habits have now changed. The demand is increasing in almost all parts of the globe. The cocktails are now preferred by the new generation.
- There is also change in the place of drinking. They are not satisfied with old pubs. They prefer to go to new style restaurants.

In view of these considerable changes in the drinking habits, hotel bars, restaurants accept these changes and attempt to spot new trends.

Information Obtained from the Customers of Hotels

The customers frequently visit the hotels for boarding have ranked their preferences of services offered by the hotels as below

- Quality of the food
- Good atmosphere and environment
- Behaviour of the staff
- Parking
- Good reception
- Variety in the menu
- Quick service
- Round the clock service
- Entertainment
- Special discounts

The customers frequently visit the hotels for lodging have ranked their preferences as listed below:

- Good house keeping
- Room service
- Pick and drop facilities
- Laundry facilities
- Swimming pools
- Travel and tourist information
- Medical and first aid facility
- Shopping arcade
- Gifts and discounts
- Bar, health club and beauty parlour
- Netscape

General suggestions given by the customers:

- Greetings for the special occasions of regular customers

- Nativity of the place to be maintained
- Feedback of the customers should be obtained and implemented immediately
- Customers' grievance to be handled amicably.
- Customers should be informed about any new offers and schemes.

Limitation of the Study

- The sample size was only 100.
- Study was conducted only in and around Chennai.
- Random Sampling was adopted.

Conclusion

Offering world services to the customers/guests is a pre-requisite for the development of the hotel industry. The main task before the hoteliers is to make a combination of quality services at different stages so that the potential customers/guests are transformed into heavy/habitual guests. Customers expect refined services and decent behaviour. The success rate of a hotel is coiled in the essence of transforming casual visitors into regular visitors.

The task before the hotel marketers is to make the industry profitable and at the same time satisfy the customers, in the face of their expectations. The Hotel Industry in India is growing gradually, which necessitates handling of the problems in the right perspective. The application of marketing principles in the right fashion is the need of the hour.

To implement CRM successfully, the top management will have to change the entire organizational mindset. CRM requires commitment and understanding throughout the company, not just in marketing. A strong core service performance supplemented by effective Customer Relationship Management by the company will yield fruitful results to both the organization and the customers. Its success greatly depends on implementing at the right stage, targeting the right customers, in the right perspective.

A customer is the most important visitor on our premises,
He is not an interruption on our work; he is the purpose of it,
We are not doing him a favour by serving him,
He is doing us a favour by giving us an opportunity to do so.

—**Mahatma Gandhi**

47

Features and Future of e-CRM

C. SAMUDRARAJAKUMAR* & K.TAMIZH JYOTHI**

Introduction

Customer Relationship Management has been the corner stone for most of the organisations as the cost of acquiring new customers is far higher than cost of retaining existing customers. Besides there are other added advantages such as referral sales and customer loyalty. Because reducing customer defection (by 5%) will result in increase in profits (25% to 85% depending from industry to industry).

In today's competitive arena companies must address the issue of retaining customers in order to survive and prosper. Vendors from all corners have rushed to introduce CRM solutions. Among 175 companies surveyed by Informations Week Research (Jeff Sweat, Sep. 2000) in US that have developed CRM, 81 per cent are doing client support and services, and 59 per cent sales and fulfilment. Among all companies contacted just 28 per cent are tackling online sales and fulfilment and only 20 per cent are creating customised messaging for their customers. This indicates that the majority of the companies, which are implementing CRM, are yet to realise the full benefits.

What is CRM?

CRM in effect implies building long-term relationship with the customers and understanding their needs and responding through multiple products and services through multiple channels. A good CRM solution should allow for:

* Reader in Business Administration, DDE, Annamalai University.

** Lecturer in Business Administration,. DDE, Annamalai University.

- Differentiate customers
- Differentiate offerings
- Keep existing customers
- Maximise lifetime value
- Increase loyalty.

What is e-CRM?

In simplest terms e-CRM provides companies with a means to conduct interactive, personalised and relevant communications with customers across both elements and traditional channels. It utilises a complete view of the customer to make divisions about messaging offers and channel delivery. It adheres to permission-based practise, imparting individual's preferences regarding how and whether they wish to communicate with you and it focuses on understanding how the economics of customer relationship affect the business.

Why Employ e-CRM?

Company is need to take firm initiatives on the e-CRM frontier to:

1. Optimise the value of interactive relationships
2. Enable the business to extend its personalised reach
3. Co-ordinate marketing initiatives across all the customer channels
4. Focus the business on improving customer relationship and earning a greater share of each customer's business through consistant measurement, assessment and "actionable" customer strategies.

Features of e-CRM

Introspective of a company's objective an e-CRM solution must posses certain key characteristics. It must be:

(*i*) Driven by a data warehouse.

(*ii*) Focussed on consistent matrices to assess customer actions across channels.

(*iii*) Built to accommodate the new market dynamics that place the customers in control.

(*iv*) Structured to identify a customer's profitability or profit potential, and to determine effective investment allocations decisions accordingly, so that most profitable customers could be identified and retained and the resources could be invested in relationships, which are most profitable.

(*v*) The loopholes in traditional CRM packages can be as follows.

(*vi*) Customer centric metrics is non-existence—most CRM offerings have weak metrics and measurement capabilities.

(*vii*) Contemporary customer facing systems such as sales force automations and customer can have their own IT set-up. These systems rarely interact with each other.

Gaps with Existing CRM Solutions

Corporate are presently applying the same norms of CRM across industry while the consumer behaviour is surprisingly different for different products and services. The result is disastrous, as the individual needs are never fully addressed. Thus the same individuals expectations from a cellular phone operator may be different from that of a car manufacturer.

This is being explained through a series of examples that will be further expanded to show the roadmap for future CRM solutions.

Illustration 1: Car Owner's Expectations—Missing service option

For instance a new car buyer will like to be reminded on the due date of mileage automatically that his car is in need of a service.

It he recommended change for new tyres is at 30,000 running kilometres and for some necessity, one of the tyres of a new car had to be changed at 5,000 km, it is consumers expectations that he be reminded when which tyre needs to be changed. Thus consumer will like to be reminded at the end of 30,000 running km that these of his tyres need to be changed while one of the early burst replaced tyres need to be changed at 35,000 km.

Future of CRM Solutions

Unlike in the past future CRM solutions will be heavily characterized by:

1. Proactive rather reactive.
2. Personalized care to each individual.
3. Heavily technology driven.

4. Product and service specific rather than a genuine CRM solution across products and services.
5. Shall work on extensive of product and service offerings beyond the primary product/service sole.
6. CRM solutions should work on collaborative arrangement among different service offerings so as to the complex needs of individuals.

While source of the aspects such personalised cares have been touched above, other concepts have been explained below. For this, wherever applicable, illustrations described above have been used to explain the future trend of CRM solutions.

CRM Based on Proactive Rather than Reactive Model

Presently, for any routine queries that have been addressed earlier CRM solutions, without human intervention, try and resolve the same. User nevertheless still has to be in queue to log in a routine complain for the same to be addressed.

In a proactive model, for whole range of routine issues/queries and complains, user will no longer have the trouble of going to the customer care desk. Technology shall take care of routine tasks/ issues/queries and shall be able to approach the customer's care much before the problem becomes acute or has actually occurred. Some of the technological factors are

(*i*) Pervasive computing
(*ii*) Data warehousing/Determining.

Let us revisit the cases in illustrations and take a hard looks how organisations shall be addressing customer requirement at various stages.

Illustration 1 Revisit: Car Owner's Expectation—Missing service option

The centralised system in the car will keep communicating with the database of authorised dealer of car manufacturing or main service database being maintained by the manufacturer himself.

Car manufacturer himself may intern collaborate with the tyre manufacturer who shall keep a track on the mileage run by each car. Using data mining techniques tyre manufacturers will know when the tyres are due for replacement, service dealer will know when the car is due for servicing and a car dealer may know when the car is likely for sale again. Through pervasive computing car's internal devices through pervasive computing and data warehousing will be able to communicate to car dealer about car's health. The car dealer intern will know the health of the car and customer-buying factor for a new car preposition to the same dealer. With this information each of the agencies will approach the customer accordingly.

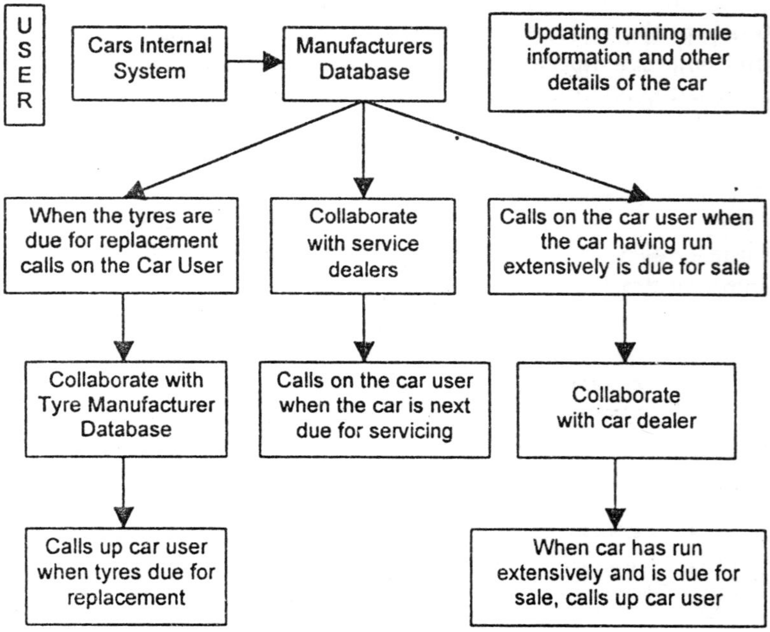

Car Owner's Expectation: Missing Service Option

e-CRM Architecture

The primary inputs to this module are mainly from the e-CRM assessment and strategy alignment module. During this stage the company will try and develop a Connected Enterprise Architecture (CEA) with the contexts of tho company's own Customer Relationship Management strategy. The following is a set of technical e-CRM capabilities and applications that collectively and ideally comprise a full e-CRM solution:

- Customer analytic software
- Data mining software
- Campaign management software
- Business simulation
- A real time decision engine

Conclusion

e-CRM is not what an organisation is doing on the web, but how effectively it utilises the online channel to improve customer satisfaction. e-CRM integrates customer channels and leverages customer information for personalized value proposition. The next phase of e-CRM revolution is knowledge-enabled CRM which is managing customer knowledge to generate value added products and to have sustained relationships.

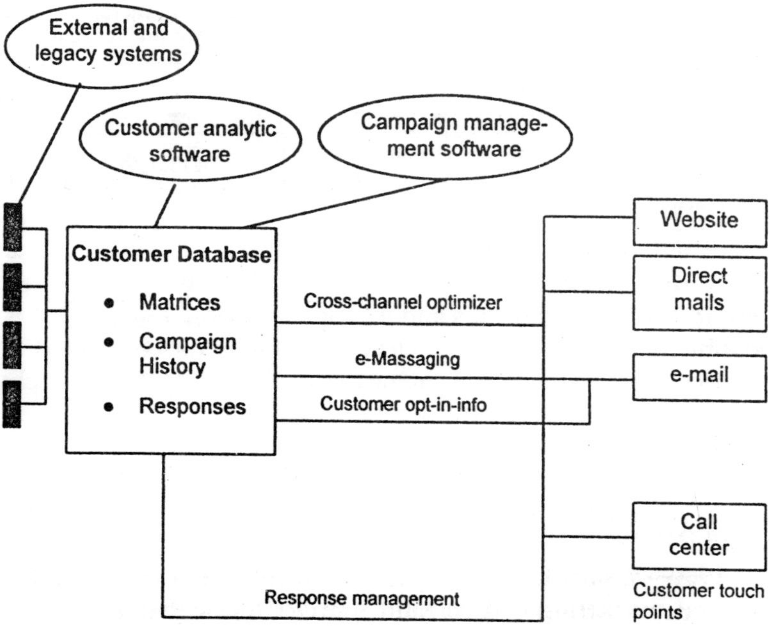

Basic Component and Architecture of an e-CRM Solution

48

Future Perspective of CRM

C. SAMUDHRA RAJAKUMAR* & K. ANANDANATARAJAN**

In todays competitive world, achieving total customer satisfaction, and delighting the customer is a key element in setting the business goals and objectives of any corporate. Improving performance in service delivery and responsiveness to the customer has become a source of competitive advantage in many service sectors. Customer Relationship Management is being increasingly used to identify, attract and retain most valuable customer that help business to sustain profitable growth. CRM mean different things to different people. It is possible to develop a greater understanding of it by looking at its origin and the principle that drove its development. By then examining the present day definition of what it means and example of who does it well, it is possible to understand more clearly how it could be applied to our own business. By looking at the future of CRM, we more clearly see where the benefits may be derived and where we should see CRM developing over the next few years.

Looking back at a snapshot history of marketing, one can see the following clear development and progression over the last four decades.

1960—Era of Man marketing, when Gibbs SR toothpaste being the first marketing of this kind with its black and white T.V. Compaign.

1970—Saw the beginning of segmentation, direct mail campaign and early telemarketing such as publishing.

* Reader in Management Studies, D.D.E., A.U.

** Lecturer in Management Studies, D.D.E., A.U.

1980—Where Niche marketing made millionaires of those who where best as it. You only need to think of sock shop. Tie Rack and Anita Roddick of the Body shop.

1990—Relationship marketing. The explosion of telemarketing and call centers, all set up to develop relationship with customers. The recognition of the true value of retention and the use of life time value as a business care.

Business issues remain the same—differentiation; loyalty; profit margin; segmentation; channel.

Until recently services have progressed nowhere as fast as it should have or as fast as we would have liked to think it. Almost every one talks about the importance of people.

Whilst business vision are still important, long term (5 year) business plan cannot work but they still exist.

The vision 15 most ago that IT and the internet would replace people in managing relationship, will not happen in the foreseable future.

The view that CRM has to be a single system vision is a fallacy. It is a way of conducting business which can in some instances—be facilitated by single system.

More and more questions are being asked about the ROI of implementing CRM—particularly by large retailer with multiple access channel.

Interestingly, Wastman software conducted a study recently of the UK's top 1000 companies asking what they saw as the most important element in successful CRM. The result where:

- Proactive customer management
- Product quality
- A single telephone number
- Web address for all enquiries

So what does the future hold? The astronomic development rates of technology are what many people see as the key driver. However, they need to look beyond this to the changes in customer expectations.

Business operations will also need to develop.

Sales marketing and service delivery will need to become one, or at the very least, act like once.

Future customer contact models will be based heavily around access.

So there is a balancing act between what the customer expect, what the technology enables and how far business are willing to go in allowing the customer to manage the relationship.

However we must bring ourselves back to the principle of CRM. It is not about developing a web portal. It is not about automating contact center services. It is about enabling customer access: Providing choice and allowing the customer to manage the relationship. It is also about centralising and creating easy access to customer information. So that the relation can be better understood, managed and maximised. The bigger an organisation and the older its legacy system, the harder it is to develop an effective CRM strategy.

In terms of what the future holds:

- Customer will play a significant role in managing relationship.
- Service model will continue to change (skills, remuneration, volumes framaction types).
- Develop end to end customer process.
- Be interactive.
- Provide seamless and integrated choice for customer use.
- Recognise customer individuality
- Re think telephone automation.

CRM can and does work. More quickly but be nimble and adaptable.

49

Analytical CRM in Service Sector

K. HARI* & R. SURESH*

Introduction

Customer Relation Management in general deals with people and processes with in an organization that captures all the information about the customer from all touch points. These touch points may be actual meeting with the customer, electronics channels like Telephone, e-mail, fax, website etc. The CRM system gathers all information irrespective of which channel the customer uses, integrates the data and provides an integrated view of the customer.

There are two major components to CRM systems. The Front End which acquires/captures customer information which is also called the operational CRM. The data will be integrated and a data-warehouse will be created. The Analytical CRM tool will use the data warehouse and convert data to customer knowledge. So to get full benefit of the CRM we need both the operational component and analytical component.

The paper discusses some of the analytical components and how customer data can be converted into customer knowledge. Analytical components include data warehousing and data mining.

Customer—The Core of Business

Your company's revenues, profits and market-share and even your salary income ultimately from one source: your customers! No matter what products and services you provide, be it a bathing

* Lecturers, Sri Chandrasekhrendra Saraswathi Viswa Maha Vidyalaya, (Deemed University) Kancheepuram.

soap, data processing system, medical services, customers are the heart of your business. When you get right down to it, the one single thing a company needs to be in business is a customer.

- You don't need money to be in business,
- You don't need to have an idea to be in business,
- You don't need a shop, factory or office location to be in business,
- You don't need personnel to be in business,
- You don't even need a product or service to be in business.

Mass marketing, used conventional methods of advertisement and promotion. The new approach of relationship marketing is based on the belief that people do not buy things but they buy solutions to problems. In order to succeed, companies need unique insight into customers and their problems. When things are viewed in this perspective, "Relationship" bond with customers becomes the key to attracting and holding them.

CRM

Relationship marketing is also known as customer management and of late as customer relationship marketing or CRM. This is the latest tool in the marketing management kit.

Its scope includes:

- Creation
- Development and
- Enhancement of individualized customer relationship with carefully targeted customers and customer groups resulting in maximizing the total customer life-term value.

CRM calls for companies to organize their business around their customers, and to interface and interact with customers, presenting a unified message and purpose. Aided by advances in information Technology, CRM is emerging as a pivotal strategy for business success in the twenty first centuries. Far more than just the latest path phrase or reinstatement of age old principles of business, CRM has the potential to reshape companies while also enhancing revenues and profits and boosting customer retention. This new CRM approach reflects the need to create an integrated cross functional focus on marketing—one which emphasizes keeping as well as wining customer. Thus, the focus is shifting from customer acquisition to customer relation and ensuring an appropriate amount of time, money and managerial resources be directed for both of these key tasks.

CRM recognizes that marketing starts after the sale is over and not during and when sale is completed. This results in improved customer retention and has a sizeable effect on company's bottomland. This approach leads to:

- Greater customer loyalty
- Enhanced retention
- Identification of most causes of defection and related key service issues
- Development of corrective actions to improve retention

(Given below is a brief study for predicting the Customer Churn for a Telecom Sector (DoT))

Title: A study on customer satisfaction in telecom service with special reference to DoT in Kanchipuram

Objective of the Study:

(*a*) To study the satisfaction level
(*b*) To study the switching behavior

Area of the Study: Kanchipuram

Sample Size: Total number of respondents considered as target respondents numbered around 700.

Data Collection: The questionnaire was administered through personal interview. Judgement sampling method was followed assuming that the particular sampling unit will contribute best to the research questions.

Data Analysis and Interpretation: Out of 700 respondents, 640 filled in questionnaires were received. All responses were treated as representation of the population.

Table 1: Number of Respondents Having Telecom Service in Kanchipuram

Telecom Service	*Number of Respondents*	*Percentage*
Landline connections	332	51.9
Mobile connections	180	28.1
Both	128	20.0
Total	640	

Source: Primary data

Table 2: Income-Wise Classification

Income Level/Month	*LAN*	*Mobile*	*Both*	*Total*
<5000	44 (6.48)	8 (1.3)	19 (2.9)	71 (11.1)
5001–10000	98 (15.3)	38 (5.9)	53 (8.3)	189 (29.5)
10001–15000	101 (15.8)	95 (14.8)	28 (4.4)	224 (35)
> 15000	89 (13.90)	39 (6.1)	28 (4.4)	156 (24.4)

Source: Primary data, figures within bracket indicate per cent.

Table 3: Occupation-Wise Classification

Occupation	*LAN*	*Mobile*	*Both*	*Total*
Private Employee	27 (4.2)	25 (3.9)	14 (2.2)	66 (10.3)
Govt. Employee	71 (11.2)	13 (2.1)	39 (6.1)	123 (19.2)
Business persons	132 (20.6)	92 (14.4)	45 (7.1)	269 (42.1)
Professionals	102 (15.9)	50 (7.8)	30 (4.6)	182 (28.4)

Source: Primary data.
Figures within bracket indicate per cent.

Table 4: Satisfaction Level of LAN Users

Factors	*Highly Satisfied*	*Moderately Satisfied*	*Less Satisfied*
Rental	2.7		
Service			0.8
Tariff		2.2	

Table 5: Preference of the Respondents

Preference	*Number of Respondents*	*Percentage*
Switching	251	75.6
Not switching	81	24.4
Total	332	

Source: Primary data

Table 6: Reason for Preferring Mobile Phones

Preference Factor	*Number of Respondents*	*Percentage*
Better Service	61	24.3
Expected to rise in tariff	82	32.7
Accessibility	89	35.4
Status symbol	19	7.6
Total	251	

Source: Primary data

Findings

- Most of the Respondents having Landline Connections
- The income level of more than 10,000 used LAN and Mobile Connections
- Mainly business persons were used both LAN and Mobile connections.
- From the Weighted Mean Analysis, we inferred LAN users were highly satisfied with Rent. Less Satisfied with their service.
- Nearly 75 per cent of LAN users would like to switchover to mobile connections.
- Various reasons are behind this, out of which Accessibility is the main factor followed by expectations in the hike in tariff.

Simply stated, "CRM is a business strategy in which every one in the organization is focussed on the customer and all processes and system are built with this concept in mind". CRM revolves round the following three elements

- Customer database
- Integrated mix of methods and media
- Measurable customer goals.

Customer Database

Customer marketing requires companies to be highly customer-oriented. But customer orientation is only possible if the company has a lot of information about customers and can communicate with them personally. Customer data is the life blood of CRM.

Certain key information on customers and prospects are:

Customer identity and characteristics—basic data such as names, addresses, telephone numbers are a must. Characteristics such as type of business, number of employees, sex, date of birth, family size etc. are also important and necessary to gather.

Products purchased/requests/interests. It is also important to store this information. Data using RFM Techniques—RFM stands for—

R : Recency—When the customer had a connection.
F : Frequency—Number of calls used.
M : Money—How much they paid.

Media and activity which influenced transaction, be it sales visit or response advertisement which led to sale. History of customer relationship—complete history of relationship with each customer or prospects in customer base. If all transactions in customer database including the medium which stimulated that transaction are recorded, then the company can get a clear idea of how much value has been received for money spent on advertisement and other promotion activities. Generating the data and building the database is the beginning.

Understanding the Customer

CRM begins by building a marketing base. The company must then apply different tools to access and message the information. This process is known as data-warehousing. It must be noted that quality of data is an important precursor for kick starting the process.

Data-warehousing comprises two stages

- Collection and storage of customer data
- Use of this information: if used smartly, the organization can come up with some segmentations and offerings differently for each segment.

Technology needed for data warehousing has, likewise, two components:

- Database software, which helps store, collected information
- Software to play around the data stored.

Date warehousing contains some of the following important activities:

- Subject Oriented
- Integrated
- Encoding:
- Time Variance
- Non-volatile

Numerous software providers are available today for CRM solutions. These covers practically every aspect of CRM and differing needs of organizations. CRM as assumed further significance on account of the speed and interactivities of the internet. Customer servicing on the Internet enables companies to reach out and provide real time assistance to the customer round the clock, across the globe; anytime, anywhere.

Conclusion

CRM software allows the company to interact with existing and potential customers. The Internet is the world's first really democratic medium that forces companies to listen to customers instead of talking down to them. While there are number of techniques available to the business manager of today, some of them are more popular than others. However, all or most of these techniques revolve around post facto analysis, some of the popular techniques used globally are:

- Regression analysis
- Discriminate analysis
- Cluster and factor analysis
- Conjoint analysis
- Topology analysis and pattern recognition
- Neural Networks and Data warehouse.

REFERENCES

1. S. P. Batra, "Marrying the Customer: A CRM Approach", Productivity. Vol. 42, April-June 2001.
2. Nickolas Tzoka & Michael Sareu (1997), "Top Value Transformation in Relationship Marketing", CRM Focus Resources.
3. Inmon Williams, Building a Datawarehouse, John Wiley, NY, 1996.
4. Kimbal Ralf, Dataware housing—Route to mass customization, John Wiley, Ny, 1996.
5. J. A. Berry, Data Mining Techniques, John Wiley, 1998.
6. Quinlan Ross, C4.5 Programs for M/C Learning, Morgan Kuffman, 1994.
7. Gregory Piatesky-Shapiro et al., Advances in Knowledge Discovery & Data Mining, AAAI Press NY, 1998.
8. References from the 37th National Convention organized by CSI Bangalore, by Prof. S. Chandrasekhar FORE School of Management.

50

e-CRM in the Indian Context

Prospects and Problems

R. SANKARANARAYANAN*, S. ARAMVALARTHAN* & R. VENKATESKUMAR*

Introduction

In the present age of hyper-competition, companies have to be extra smart in managing their relationship with customers. It is commonly said that it costs a company six times more to sell a product to a new customer than it does to sell to an existing one. This has motivated companies to maximize existing customer relationships. The main way to maximize value from existing customers is to know who the best customers are and motivate them to stay that way. Customer relationship management is "the infrastructure that enables the delineation of and increase in customer value, and the correct means by which to motivate valuable customers to remain loyal-indeed to buy again." It is a business strategy to select and manage the most valuable customer relationships.

e-CRM

CRM applications enable effective customer relationship management. To succeed today, companies must carefully manage customer relationships via an overall business system that enables internal processes, people, information and technology to provide positive customer experiences. e-CRM may give the solution in this regard. e-CRM refers to electronic customer relationship

* Faculty Members, Thiagarajar School of Management, Madurai (TN).

management. It is the set of activities to sell, support, manage and retain customers who do business through the company's web channel.

e-CRM Areas

e-CRM is divided into three areas:

- Marketing
- Services
- Sales

Marketing

Marketing aspect of e-CRM is divided into three parts:

- Analytics
- E-marketing
- Personalization

Analytics

Analytics help an organisation to understand the customer. Analytics software creates information from data gathered from a number of customer touch points. Combining demographic data with sales information from customer records can indicate how purchases vary by demographic group. Online activity records convey what particular groups of customers buy, what web pages they tend to visit and their tastes. Hoover's Online used analytic software to analyse Web site traffic, create customer profile and classify customers by market segment. They were able to analyse where people were going and promote areas that they were ignoring.

e-marketing

e-marketing software is used to keep track of which marketing campaigns succeed and which fail. It is also used to plan future marketing programmes. The analytics stage answers such questions as "Of the people who bought BPL television sets, how many also bought BPL VCD players?" In the e-marketing stage, a company uses the answers to allow it to offer discounts on VCD players via e-mail to customers who bought TVs.

Personalisation Software

Personalisation software allows businesses to offer products uniquely relevant to the individual visitor to a Web site by creating a web experience tailored to that individual's taste. Amazon.com uses this software to inform people who purchase a book or CD that people who previously bought that book or CD also bought books by another author.

Statistical correlation techniques are used to find other Web site visitors with similar patterns of behaviour. The behaviour of these like-minded people is used to make recommendations for further purchases. Personalisation software also uses neural network based artificial intelligence to model web site visitors on the basis of their "clickstream" (a sequence of web pages selected by a visitor) and purchase behaviour. Personalisation is superior to blindly e-mailing coupons to potential customers because it is more closely connected to that person's interests. Telecom majors like BPL Mobile in Mumbai and Modi Telestra in Kolkata have deployed tools to sift data for insights into customer behaviour and extract patterns which can be used to predict anything form a high usage customer to a potential defaulter.

Sales

Today's sales person must not only be proficient in traditional sales skills but he or she must be able to explain and sell increasingly complex, bundled products and/or customised solutions. In this fast moving global business environment, businesses improve the productivity of their sales forces by delivering relevant information and knowledge to the sales representatives. The information should satisfy the current, specific dictates of the sales situation just-in-time. Just-in-time know-how is the byword of the sales process. It must be relevant to the current situation. It must be presented in an appropriate form. It must be available for immediate use by the sales representative. If sales representatives know what they need and there is a repository of useful information, they can readily access the information when they need it. However, in many instances, they "don't know what they don't know." Information may be available within the company that is critical to the sales situation but sales representatives are unaware of its availability and there is no mechanism for linking the source to point of need. The solution must deliver know-how based on events within the sales process and also on the account planning, forecasting and order processing databases created by sales force automation tools.

An exhaustive task analysis of Apple Computer's (NASDAQ: AAPL) sales process revealed that customized presentations and access to Apple's knowledge base are critical to the success of the sales representatives. Existing training resources, presentation content and knowledge bases were transformed into the Apple Reference and Performance Learning Experience and Presentation Library (ARPLE). Originally available only on CDROM, ARPLE II is available online to Apple employees, authorized resellers, developers and value added resellers around the world. Internal studies indicate that Apple sales representatives save an average of 11 hours per month because they no longer have to physically search for information. Eleven hours translates into more time in front of potential customers, and as much as 3 or 4 more sales calls per month. More sales calls translated into increased revenue of $224 million that generated a return on investment of 387 per cent over a four-year period.

Customer Service

Enterprises can achieve competitive advantage and differentiation through customer service. Customer service personnel providing support to customers require operational integration with field service personnel and the sales force. e-CRM can help in integrating these groups with the operational organisation as a whole and the sales force.

Many organizations such as Silicon Graphics and Sun Microsystems are using the Internet to provide customer support. The ability to provide immediate answers to problems on-line, through resolution guides, archives of commonly encountered problems, electronic mail interaction (and in the future audio and video support) builds customer confidence and retention. Monitoring how customers use this support information also provides insights on improvement areas in current products. The list of issues encountered with products can be a significant source of product feedback for the design of new products.

Five E's of e-CRM

e-CRM embraces five "e's". They are:

1. *Electronic Channels: e-CRM* relies on new electronic channels such as the web and personalized e-messaging. These have become the medium for fast, interactive and economic communication.

2. *Experience:* Through e-CRM a company gains the means to touch and shape a customer's experience through sales, services and corner offices. The people manning these operations should understand and assess customer behaviour.
3. *Empowerment:* Nowadays, many customers have the power to decide when to communicate with the company, how to communicate with the company, through what channel to communicate with the company and at what frequency to communicate with the company. e-CRM strategy should be structured to deliver timely, relevant and information that a customer expects in exchange for his attention.
4. *Economics:* An e-CRM strategy ideally should concentrate on customer economics. It should result in smart asset-allocation decisions by directing efforts at individuals likely to provide the greatest return on customer-communication initiatives.
5. *Evaluation:* Understanding customer economics relies on a company's ability to attribute customer behaviour to market programs, evaluate customer interactions along various customer touch point channels and compare anticipated ROI against actual returns through customer analytic reporting.

Steps to Build a Successful e-CRM Initiative

Building a successful e-CRM initiative involves three steps:

Step 1: Segmentation

Specific customer should be identified and the strategy should be focused towards the targeted customers. Pareto's analysis can help here. On the basis of this, we can generalise that 20 per cent of customers provide 80 per cent of the sales. A company should identify them and target them. Customer lifetime value is the key factor that needs attention. An organisation should take appropriate measures to assess their customers' lifetime value.

Step 2: Personalisation

The whole activity of e-CRM is a combination of people, tools, past data, new information (both primary and secondary), behavioural pattern preferences, attitudes, values, responses and above all learning to achieve one-to-one relationships with customers. By integrating all these, a company can develop a personal dialogue effectively with its customers. Its a crucial but critical activity. Here utmost care should be taken to respect the ultimate privacy of the customers.

Step 3: Evaluation

After successfully building a strong rapport with the customers one can evaluate the results of one's strategies.

(1) Customisation

When a customer is lost or has switched his loyalty, the company should re-establish the contact with the same customer. If the company thinks that it would be advantageous to regain the customer, it should get back to the same.

The company already has the requisite information to develop an appropriate profile of the customer. This is possible because of the advancement of information technology. This profile would help the company in understanding the buying patterns of the customers. This in turn will enable the company to design more suitable and customised product or service to offer. The company can make a proposal to its former customers to reconsider their offer and thus the lost customer can be won back.

(2) Differentiation Strategy

In this case, customers are segmented on the basis of status. The status can be existing customer, lost customer and new customer. The potential of each of these will be different. Differentiation is the ability to provide unique and superior value to the customer in the terms of service, quality, special features and after sales service on the lines of individual requirements.

As the customers are segmented, every segment of customer should be addressed in a unique way. This strategy can be used to woo back the lost customers or attract new customers.

Emerging Opportunities for e-CRM In India

Several developments taking place in India augur well for e-CRM. Important among them are:

- India emerging as one of the top Internet users
- New telecommunication service providers with increased bandwidth

India Emerging as One of the Top Internet Users

In 1999 total number of Indians online were 2 millions. In US, there were 80 million. China had 9 million. In 2003, it is projected that there will be 70 million Indians online, compared to 90 millions in all of Europe, 170 millions in US and 80 millions in China.

Table 1: Internet User Bases (in millions)

Country	*1999*	*2000*	*2003*
Australia	5	6	8
China	9	17	80
Japan	22	29	58
Europe	33	42	90
USA	80	103	177
India	2	9	70

Source: Goldman Sachs.

This tremendous growth is likely to offer enormous potential for e-CRM initiatives.

According to the Boston Consulting Group Report on e-commerce, the Internet revolution could raise e-commerce transaction revenues in India to Rs. 195,000 crores by 2005. B2C e-commerce transaction volumes in 2005 are expected to reach Rs. 750 crores for the telecom services sector, Rs. 550 crores for consumer electronics, Rs. 450 crores for travel, Rs. 450 crores for automotive, Rs. 300 crores for financial services, Rs. 150 crores for books, and Rs. 100 crores for music.

The following are examples of companies that have already made use of the opportunity:

- Korean consumer electronics subsidiary LG India has about 25 per cent of its dealer sales online (via an ICICI payment gateway), and purchase orders are fed into the ERP system for production planning soon.
- Essar Steel auctioned a part of its steel output in July-August 2000 and realized Rs. 400 more per tonne than it normally would.

- Car manufacturer Maruti's Extranet links it with 215 dealers and 300 suppliers. It has tied up with Bank of America, Corporation Bank and ICICI Bank for payment gateways.
- Cisco India accepts all orders only via its Web site, and has improved configuration accuracy from 40 per cent (offline) to 100 per cent. 80 per cent of technical questions are answered online. e-training has reduced employee training costs by 60 per cent.
- Amul has leveraged its Web site to build a database of 110,000 customers; it receives 15,000 e-mails a day. The company uses e-mail to conduct market research, gauge customer expectations, and promote new products like ice cream flavors.
- Sony India uses the Net to conduct speedier and more cost-effective market research on products like digital cameras, and to drive potential customers to product showrooms.

New Telecommunication Service Providers

Reliance, Bharti and Tata have entered into the telecommunication business on a large scale. The increased bandwidth and improved technology is likely to improve the speed and quality of communication.

e-CRM in the Commodities Sector in India

Most commodity players deal with four major customer groups-dealers, institutional buyers, influencers (like architects ion the case of cement) and the final consumers. e-CRM can help lock in at least the first three.

Indal is trying out e-CRM. The company sells ingots, sheets and coils, extrusions and foils. Almost 80 per cent of the company's sales are to end-users (about 500) and balance is through dealers. Cost of production is high. So, the company cannot compete on the basis of price. It has to compete on the basis of quality and price. CRM is critical. Indal is tracking the customers' buying pattern, season, cost of service and customer line profitability. e-CRM will serve multi-location and multi-product customers.

DCM Shriram Consolidated, Indal, TISCO and Ballarpur Industries have implemented e-CRM solutions. The immediate benefit will be fall in sales time and better inventory control. It will also develop better dealer relationships. This is very important because it is the dealers who know the end-user requirements and can call the shots.

Ballarpur Industries Limited (BILT) hopes that e-CRM will transform the company into customer centric company from a production driven company, The earlier model of selling to dealers is no longer good enough as the company could not know what end use the paper is put into and who the customer is—whether he is a printer, a SOHO, a retailer or a diary manufacturer. The company has implemented Optivision, a paper industry specific solution from Honeywell. With this, it can follow the entire cycle of an order. Better end-use understanding of paper would enable the company to source a specific product form anywhere. Till 1999, only 2 per cent of BILT's sales were to end-users. Today, direct sales to end-users are up to 40 per cent.

Today, companies like Asian paints, Birla White, Grasim, Indo Rama and TISCO are looking at CRM solutions to bridge the gaps in relationship management. Thus, there are very good prospects for e-CRM in India.

Problems often arise as dealers are not very comfortable with change and infrastructure is very poor. Also, the dealers in small towns may not like the idea much. These problems have to be sorted out. In this context, BILT is educating the dealers on e-CRM through special programmes.

Consumer Goods and Pharmaceuticals

The vast distribution network consisting of about 1.5 million retail outlets poses problems as well as opportunities. Smaller segment regional players are growing faster thanks to better relationship management, as the terrain on which they focus is small. The only way to face this challenge is to go for e-CRM.

The launch of Automated Mobile sales Solutions and the creation of networks bring data on real time basis for faster decision-making are the first steps in introducing e-CRM.

Banking and Financial Services

Banking majors like Citibank, HDFC, ICICI and IDBI have already initiated the implementation of CRM solutions.

Retailing

Some oil companies have successfully implemented Smart Card Loyalty Programmes. Others can follow this.

Retailing companies can try Multiple Access points for shopping.

Airlines

Airlines have implemented frequent flier programmes.

Automobiles

TELCO has started implementing e-CRM solutions. Its Web enabled value chain management software has helped to reduce its inventory from 65 to 20 days.

Perceived Problems

1. It may be difficult to reach the people in rural areas. But the firms can concentrate on urban areas first and then move on to rural areas.
2. It may be difficult to serve non-English speaking customers. But this may not be a problem as the software applications in different languages are developed.

Conclusion

Increasing competition and decreasing customer loyalty have made the retention of customers crucial for the success of a business. As a result, customer relationship management has assumed significance. Developments in communication technology especially the Web technology has led to the emergence of e-CRM. The Indian market offers excellent opportunities for the exploitation of e-CRM. Business enterprises have to make use of these opportunities to survive and succeed.

REFERENCES

1. All India Management Association, *"Global Competitiveness"*, 2002.
2. Boston Consulting Group—India,*"e-commerce Opportunities in India"*, 2001.
3. Dyche, Jill, *"The CRM Handbook"*, Pearson Education Asia, 2002.
4. Hemamalini Suresh, *"Customer Relationship Management"*, PSG Institute of Management Publications, 2002.

Website:

The Customer Relationship Management Primer—CRMguru.com

Customer Relationship Management in Pharmaceutical Industry

UDAYASURIAN*, K. SUNDAR** & K. MARAN***

The liberalization, globalization and privatization have forced the competition into Indian industrial arena. Globalization is an irreversible process. In other words in an era of market on orientation, only such of those concerns which have a real concern for customer would survive in the long run. Of course, the purpose of every enterprise is to make profit, now and forever. The customer is the means to achieve this end. The relationship between the company and customer have a definite bearing on the bottom line. The stronger the relationship, the longer the corporate life of the company. In this context, a complex problem of building up, smoothing and maintaining the relationship is answered by the concept of customer relationship management (CRM). The CRM starts with deep knowledge of customers, their habits, desires and the needs by analysing their cognitive affective behaviour and attributes. The CRM concept helps in designing and implementing market strategies in order to develop a ever lasting relationship with customer. The write up highlights how the concept may be applied in pharmaceutical industry.

Indian Pharmaceutical Industry—A Bird's-Eye View

Indian Pharmaceutical market is worth about Rs. 7,40,000 million with a healthy growth rate of 10%. There are around 16,000 companies in the organised and the unorganised market,

* Reader in Management Studies, Annamalai University.
** Faculty Member, DDE Commerce Wing, Annamalai University.
*** Faculty Member, Sai Ram Engineering College, Chennai.

competing for a space in this pharmaceutical arena. It is a highly fragmented market with aggregated market share of the top five players not exceeding even 20%.

Indian Pharmaceutical market is one of the few markets that focused on process patents and not the product patents. Consequently, India has emerged as brand generic market where there are about 30,000 brands in all in the country. In such a case, any attempt to build brand differentiation would be a futile exercise. There are about Rs. 5,00,000/- registered medical practitioners in India as per the Indian Medical Association. Out of total doctor population as much as 60-65 per cent, are general practitioners with the basic MBBS degree. In chronic therapies like hypertension, once a patient starts on a particular medication, he is expected to continue the medication for life. Thus the lifetime value of a single patient of those ailment is very high. The specialist doctors like a Cardiologist Physician, Gynecologists and Pediatrician form the bulk of specialist. Thus the higher specialties form the remaining 35-40 per cent. They constitute an important segment. Product promotion though advertisement being against the ethical code, the medical representative is the major means of product promotion. The other media like direct mail, journal advertisement, conferences etc., play a limited role. Since it is the doctor who influences the patient and thereby influencing supply chain, the CRM initiative in pharmacy industry has to orbit around the doctor, the write up elaborates process of a CRM initiative for pharmaceutical industry.

Starting A CRM Initiative

Having understood the major characteristics of the industry, the Identification, Differentiation, Interaction and customization model as suggested by Don Peppers and Mathra Roger would be used to understand to a CRM initiative.

1. *Identification*

The CRM initiative should start with identifying medical practitioner. There are several sources through which the list of doctors may be gathered.

- *Medical Representative*: Medical representatives are prime source through which the list of doctors may be gathered. They can provide a list of doctors by virtue of their direct with the doctors themselves, stockiest, retailers, peers and so on.

- *Membership Directories of Associations*: There are several associations of doctors based on their specialty besides Indian Medical Association. They are one of the sources of information about doctor fraternity.
- *List of Conference Participants*: Vital details can be collected about the participants through sponsorship of conferences.
- *Doctor Referral*: Doctors may be persuaded to recommend the fellow practitioners.
- *Govt. Data Bank*: The details of doctors employed in government service may be gleaned through government data bank.
- *Medical and Research Institutions*: The names and profile of the medicos pursuing higher studies i.e. P.G. Diplomas, Post Graduation courses and doctoral researcher may be drawn from the medical institutions. The address of students undergoing internship may be gathered from medical colleges concerned. These are good sources to begin with. Telephone directory as well may be tried. Thus a complete list of doctors may be prepared. The collection of details is an ongoing process. Continuous updating should always take place. This list can be mined for getting various details of doctors, age wise, specialitly wise, area wise, sex wise, service wise, institution wise and so on. This serves as a vital input for our strategic marketing decision making process.

2. *Differentiation*

The second phase of customer relationship initiative comprises differentiating medical practitioners in terms of volume of business a company gets or expects to get from them. Typically medical rep. would group the doctors using ABC method as 'Core' Important and Others based on the volume of business he gets or expects to get. In a typical pyramidal fashion, the doctor occupying top slot who are fewer in number would be commercially important segment and the importance would linearly decline as one goes down the pyramid. The number of doctors on lowest rung of pyramid would be more. However, absence of any formal mechanism to measure precisely the revenue generated through a doctor hinders the process of grouping the doctor interms of revenue generation. Therefore the doctors have to be grouped soly with the help of inputs supplied by medical representative. The point to be noted is that the whole basis of differentiation to be done on the subjective terms of the perception of the local M.R.

3. *Interaction*

The main focus of phase III is to collect private information about the doctor i.e. hobbies, dislike, family details etc., through direct and indirect intervention. The information to be collected may cover the following area.

- *Personal Information*: date of birth, marriage anniversary, details of children, qualification, experience.
- *Hobbies and Interest*: Activities during spare time, T.V. channels watched, general interest, magazine read, favorite vocation destinations, type of movies watched.
- *Professional Interest*: Types of medical journal read, professional membership of associations, participation at conference.
- *Ownership Details*: House hold durables and vehicles.

The aforesaid information may be collected through the following ways.

- Company may make arrangement for interaction with the doctors through medical representatives who can collect most of the information from his day-to-day interaction with the latter. The medical representation should convince the doctors of the benefits that would accure to them from the information sharing.
- The company may mail structured questionnaire requesting details from the doctor. It may offer a token gift for each respondent to increase the rate of response. The information thus collected is then incorporated to the basic database built in the first place. What is more important is that companies should demonstrate its sincerity in actually using the data. Thus a complete master database of medical practitioner is to be built.

4. *Customization*

Under this phase the company should make use of the data relating to medical practitioners. The master database of doctor is more important to customize the interaction with doctors. The company should pass on the entire data relating to the doctor before MRs. make a visit to clinics. They should be well trained beforehand as to how to use the data to company's advantage. The field force should immediately report back the impact of their interaction with the doctor to the company so that the latter can update the master database. Thus updated master database would be the key driver to foster a learning relationship. The company may undertake the following measures for strengthening the relationship.

- Greeting doctor on his birth day, new year and wedding anniversaries from the corporate office.
- Delivering birthday cake, or bouquets at the door steps on the birth day.
- Arranging dinner for the doctor and his family on important errands.
- Presenting gifts based on his interest and hobbies and presenting durables like A/c machine, furniture, refrigerator, etc.
- Sponsoring the doctors participation in national and international conferences.
- Reimbursement of expenses incurred in subscription of journals of doctor's speciality and fees paid for membership in various associations.
- Sponsoring journal clubs conducted by medical practitioners.
- Arranging membership in prestigious clubs.
- Arranging sight seeing trips for doctors during vacation.
- Conducting special health camps inviting doctors of a particular locality in various places.
- Conducting Continuing Medical Education (CME) camp for medical practitioners for updating them on recent development in their fields.

All these measures bring the doctor fraternity closer to our marketing net and develop a sort of intimacy.

5. *Patronage Programme*

The company may design a patronage programme which would reward the doctors who contribute more to revenue generation by their patronage. But the concept of obviously rewarding doctors in return for their prescription being against medical code, programme is to be so designed as to reward the doctor clients indirectly. The doctors have to be graded into different categories in terms of pre-set level of prescription and accordingly they should be put in a pyramid. Those occupying the top slot of pyramide would be lesser in number than those at the bottom in a pyramid structure. Different package of privileges under different brand names may be instituted for different grades of doctor clients. All the doctor clients should be made aware of the objectives and exclusively of such programme. All promotional activities and inputs should reinforce the message. The returns generated from the retail chemist prescription audit need to be monitored on a continuous basis. If the doctor fall below the pre-set limit, they need to be down graded and their privileges are to be cut short. The privileges extended to doctor clients would depend on the slot they occupy in the pyramid.

6. *Direct Marketing*

A captive database lends itself into direct marketing activities. The pharma companies can have a direct access to doctor customers through mail. Brand awareness campaign, new launches and contest can be conducted by mail. It has got several advantages. It is cost effective and a large audience can be covered at a cheaper cost than personnel selling. Further, right audience in terms of specialty and geographical location can be targeted through mail. Besides, the efficacy of mail champaign can be gauged easier through response rate. Direct mail saves the time of field staff and facilitates their job. The companies now a days start exploiting other direct marketing media like telemarketing and the web. While telemarketing is being used for promoting new launches in order to get an instant feed back, the web has yet to achieve penetration due to lower utilization of Personal Computers. However, companies keep in touch with medical practitioners through e-mail.

7. Call Centre

Call Centre has been emerging an excellent medium to get closer to the customer. It caters to the following groups.

- Doctor who would like to know more about drug profile, discuss specific case and seek a references on use in a specific condition.
- Patients who seek counseling.
- Retailer who ask for price details and product availability. This medium is slowly taking off with the advent of paging companies, the facility of leased lines from Dot, toll free calls in select metros etc. On establishing calls centre, companies should make arrangement to answer questions from patients in vernacular language in view of diversity of our country and appoint a highly qualified doctors from various specialities to answer the specific queries of doctors who may not like advice from lay man.

8. *Measurement Mechanism*

Some sort of mechanism to gauge the efficacy of the customer relationship programmes need to be evolved. The measurement mechanism should be so designed as to compare the prescription profile of doctors who are exposed to the CRM activities. The prescription level of doctors before exposure to the programme and thereafter can be studied. The idea is to check whether the prescription levels have increased after the doctor has been made member of patronage programme.

- Measurement mechanism may compare the prescription profile of doctors exposed to CRM initiatives and the doctors met by the field staff but not exposed to CRM activities. Thus effectiveness can be assessed.
- There are specialised market research agencies which undertake prescription research and they can be entrusted the job of measuring the efficacy of CRM programmes.

The company can modify the CRM programmes according to the outcome of the programmes revealed by measurement mechanism or by the findings of the survey conducted by professional research agencies.

Conclusion

The success of the whole CRM programmes hinges on the support of the top management who can act as mentor. The programme takes time to take off and much more time to yield better results. The conviction for the importance of the programme has to be sold to the lowest level of the sales organisation especially to the filed force who are key elements. Their role assumes singular significance's for implementation since most of the activities suggested above are dependent on their whole hearted support.

REFERENCES

1. Don Peppers and Martha Rogers (1993), *"The One to One Future"*, Currency Doubleday, New York.
2. ORG-MARG Retail Audit, *"Retail Market for Pharmaceutical Product in India July 2000"*, Operations Research Group, Baroda, India.
3. Business Times Bureau, *"Healthcare is the New Healthline of Ad Agencies"*, The Times of India, 19 August 2000. p. 15.
4. Vijay Jung Thapa and Subhadra Menon, *"Growing Distrust—Doctor Versus Patients"*, India Today, 25 September 2000, pp. 38-48.

52

Customer Relationship Management

K. SUJATHA*, K. SIVAKUMAR* & JAWAHARRANI**

Customers Forever or Never

Many companies tent to forget their customers, once the sales is over without realizing that the customer service is the master key to unlock the doors of many customers, who form the basis and foundation, upon which the empire of any business is built upon. Customer is the king and also the golden mine for any company to enter and this fact is well known not to all, but to a limited few.

Customers are interested in a company that knows how to handle a customer. Customers are also no more interested in a company, which uses answering machines to record the customer complaints. Since, more and more new entrants/competitors stepping in, the customers interest on the part of company is slowly going down. Gone are those days, the company fully depended upon the advertisement and its effect, customers are less interested to believe and less motivated in believing the ads of many companies. When the customers distance away from the companies its sales also will be drifting. In order to increase the sales and the market share, a company must think and do lot of good groundwork on the customer relationship management. Hence, the need for the CRM has become the sine quo none, for any Co. not only to earn profit but also a must to sustain in the competitive market conditions. Considering the inroads the competitors, the job markets and sales achievements of many companies are becoming more and more competitive and everyone is forced to

* Lecturers in Management, Annamalai University.
** Lecturer in Management, St. Joseph College, Chennai.

be in the race, whether they want it or not, and the circumstances necessitate one to run faster than ever before. Thus CRM will equip and help the companies to face the challenges posed by this fast changing environment. In this respect CRM may be considered as one of the best tools to enrich and empower companies to meet the urgent needs of the changing environment.

Due to the changes in the customer's expectations, both in quality and service, companies must recognize and include customer service as an integral part of product delivery. People do not stop buying from a company for the simple reason that they find another company with a better product. They may stop buying because they feel that their company does not care them any more.

The next question is what sort of relationship the companies want to build with their customers? Is it transactional or sustained personal, familiarized relationships? In the present day product and service market, actually there is a war and each and every company is vying with one another for the consumer's money. See what liberalization has done. Today the customer is right even on price. They need and insist on good financing plan, a good and reasonable and affordable price, prompt and courtesies service, and good after sales service and even free paperrolls. Here is an occasion for self-centered companies/organisation to change into a customer centric and focus their major attention in retaining their existing customers by building very strong bond with them.

Customers are under nobodies' control. And so they may be tilted more towards the companies if there is a CRM. To retain a customer with and within the companies influence, companies have to establish better CRM. In a way CRM helps to build and develop the loyalty towards the organisation. As a result of this customers are expected and behave positively to place and repeat his/her purchase from the same organisation.

The growth of consumer centric culture, propelled and fuelled by the Internet revolution, has enriched the importance of customers from the sellers' angle. The relationship between the organisation and its customers is a mirror reflection of how a company manages its human relations. In order to succeed in the implementation of CRM, companies must identify as to what informations are important to them. Having decided and identified the information one has to figureout as to how to get it. In addition to the above, one should know and understand about what they dislike and like about your product and services and what would motivate them to buy/go for repeat purchase and refer the same to others also.

This article brings into focus, the highlights of the rapidity of changes that are taking place, both within and outside the business houses. Customer Relationship Management is a new tool and a new ball game to attract, select, develop and retain many customers. If one company fails to take care of the customers' interest then one of the competitors may do it, for his advantage.

From the present marketing scenerio one has to learn that the basis of competition; is shifting from the product to service. In the light of such change, the concept of customer service and customer retention has gained lot of importance. Customers are good and loyal until they see the tomorrow's newspaper, when they see a coupon or concession/discount and point of purchase offer at another/shop. Whoosh, they are gone and no more with us. CRM could be established and improved by setting up a customer database, and using it to start a dialog, with their customers. This has helped many companies to reestablish their contact with their to buildup loyalty, referrals and repeat orders and also for retention.

The conventional strategies of requesting customers, by word of mouth, to come again and again, may not hold good, any longer. Companies must ensure that a customer keeps coming back, again and again. Because of the changed market conditions and consumer expectations, the companies need to adopt a more proactive approach for building a better CRM.

CRM Strategies

According to Arthur Middleton Hughes the following are the important Strategies.

1. Membership cards and the Membership Programmes.
2. Welcome and thank you communications.
3. Satisfaction surveys, followed up by phone calls.
4. Beefed up customer service, empowered to solve problems.

5. Enhanced technical support with follow up satisfaction.
6. Frequent buyer programmes, which permit customers to build up equity.
7. Event driven communications that are meaningfull to the customer' lives.
8. Databases that keep track of customers' purchases preferences, complements and complaints.

53

Customer Relationship Management in Banks

G. VASANTHI*

CRM in banks can be defined as the ability to understand, anticipate and manage the needs of the customer, interaction and relationship resulting in increased profitability through revenue and marginal growth and operational efficiencies. e-CRM, on the other hand refers to other factors like personalization, customorization, one to many, and many to many transactions. It permits business speed, and real time response to customer or markets through the new tools such as email, internet telephone, chat facility etc. Which reduces the cost of customer contract.

To serve more and retain customers banks in India have changed the old concept of accepting deposits and lending money from A to Z in response to

- Any time, any branch and any bank through any where Banking.
- Capital Market Banking through DEMAT facility.
- Productivity and efficiency at operations through Electronic/Banking.
- Various services through Venture Banking.
- Insurance business through Life Insurance Banking.
- Accepting deposits only from non-residents for the purpose of lending to NRI through Off Shore Banking.
- Credit card, debit card, smart card issue to reduce cash holding and cost of operations through Plastic Card Banking.

* Reader in Commerce, Annamalai University.

- Effective transfer of funds, collection of outstation cheques through VSAT Banking.

Use of technology by banks has increased the productivity very fast through automation of banking operations. The Electronic technology instruments adopted by Indian Banks are: Automated Teller Machines (ATMs), Telex. Fax, Internet. Tele banking, e-banking, Electronic Clearing Services. Remote Login facility. On line banking, Swift, Elenor, Steps, Infinet etc. With the introduction, implementation and adoption of above techniques/instruments by the banks have totally revolutionized the functions, operations, administration, decision-making and management information system. The benefits accruing to the Banks are:

- New look, new appeal, new appearance and new attraction.
- Speed and accuracy in transactions dealing.
- Better storage and economical preservation of records and easy retrieval.
- Quick decision-making at all managerial and executive levels.
- Better communication, information and coordination.
- Excellence in customer services, prompt attention to their needs and quick disposal of their grievances.
- Reduction in staff as a result off decrease in establishment cost.
- Enabled Banks to render 24 hours, all days services to the customers.
- Extension of baking hours from 4 hours to 6 hours a day.

CRM-Concept

The concept of CRM is now gaining wide acceptance and is recognized as a powerful tool for business development and to have an edge over the competitors on account of the universal traits of human behavior. People need to have social and interactive relationships. So, fast moving organizations believe in their customers, understand their needs in advance before the customers give the feedback about their particular requirements and design their products matching to such needs.

According to Cap Gemini Ernst and Young, a leading management consulting firm. CRM is defined as "a company's ability to continuously maximize the value of its customer franchise by effectively allocating scarce resources to specific customers or customer segments in those areas viewed as having a significant impact on the profit-impacting behaviours of customers".

Organizations had earlier focused on their products as the starting point and then looked around for customers to sell it. But the approach in CRM is different—it starts with the customer not the totality of customers because each customer is an individual and thus each customer has to be dealt individually to find out what they want and design the product as per their need and supply it. In a nut shell, CRM is about growing enduring relationship with profitable customers.

It is well recognized now that organizations cannot solely focus on market share, but the aim should be to increase the share of each customer's total spending. This can be possible if the organistion were to focus on the customer and his (her) needs, rather than its own product or services. For instance, in case of marketing of services it can be seen that the people now want faster transport, fast foods, and home delivery services.

Likewise in financial services, nationalized as well as new generation private banks and foreign banks have introduced customer friendly products and services like:

Total Branch Mechanisation (TBM)

TBM had suggested by Dr. Rangrajan Committee-II in 1988. Local Area Network system has installed by banks at the major centers of the country to make all banking services available at single window to their customers.

Automated Teller Machines (ATMs)

Banking services are made available 24 hours a day. 7 days in a week and 365 days of the year through ATMs. ATM is user-friendly system and customer does not require any training to use it. It is totally menu driven which displays step-by-step instructions to operate the transactions.

Tele Banking

Technology development has totally changed the face of banking industry. Conventional banking where banking services were provided manually across the counter has come to the stage where customer is not required to visit the bank personally for routine transactions, viz. balance enquiry, remittance, statement of accounts etc. Therefore, following services are being provided under Tele Banking.

(*a*) *Public Enquiry*: Interest rate on various deposit schemes/ loan schemes of Bank, product/service, facilities offered etc.

(*b*) *Private Enquiry*: Balance in account, Status enquiry, Cheques clearance status. Account statement, Cash withdrawal and Issue of demand draft and pay orders etc.

Electronic fund Transfer (EFT)

EFT has been introduced by RBI for Public Sector Banks to help them offer their customers money transfer service from any bank's branch to any other bank's branch. EFT system presently covers more than 4800 branches of PSB's at four metro cities.

Communication Technology (SWIFT)

Society for Worldwide Inter Bank Financial Telecommunication (SWIFT) has formed as a cooperative organization by International Banks and Foreign Investors. It provides a computerized network for me stage transmission amongst international banks in the member countries. This technology made available the fastest banking services/facilities to customers who are engaged in international business.

INFINET and VSAT Network

Indian Financial Network (INFINET), a Closed User Group (CUG) network for banking and financial sector has been initiated by RBI in India to upgrade the country's payment and settlement system. INFINET uses VSAT (very small aperture terminal) technology. Some of the major applications of FNFINET in banking services/ operations are listed below:

(*i*) e-Mail, (*ii*) Any Branch Banking, (*iii*) Treasury Management, (*iv*) ALM. (*v*) EFT, (*vi*) Clearing and Settlement System for Securities—Delivery Vs Payment, (*vii*) RTGS (Real Time Gross Settlement) etc.

Internet Banking

Internet banking provides a customer the tele-banking service through internet. Under this type of banking permit their customers to login to banks system for certain enquiry. For this purpose, customers are given passwords that are to be used by them to access the internal web server of the bank.

Profitability of Customer Retention in Banks

There are many reasons why retaining customers is profitable. This includes the following:

- Each retained customer adds directly to profit.
- Sales, marketing and set up costs are amortised over length of customer life time.
- Spread expenditure over time.
- Repeat customers often cost less to service.
- Satisfied customers provide referrals i.e., they introduce other customers.
- Satisfied customers may be willing to pay a price premium

In a competitive market where customers have so many options, even in narrow product market segments, personalized service is the only way to retain customers and to have a profitable relationship with them.

Different strategies are built up by the organizations for customer loyalty. These are FMP (Frequency Marketing Programme) and CMP (Club Marketing Programmes).

Implementing CRM

CRM will be the standard marketing approach because once an organization uses it, its competitors will have to do it to keep up. The technology is already there and improving all the time. However, implementing CRM requires significant changes in the whole organizational structure. Top management and senior management must agree that CRM is the way forward and without such commitment, it will not deliver results.

For switching to CRM a good amount of investment to IT is required. The organization must be able to collect, store and access all the information it will need on each customer in order to customize the services to them. This should be followed by appointment of highly motivated Relationship Manager (RM) who will identify each customer according to his or her current and potential value. The Relationship Manager will manage the complete relationship with each customer and increase the value of each to the organization. He should oversee all communications and dialogue with each customer and find new products or services to sell to each of them and new ways to customize to each one's specifications. The customer deals only with the RM and his team regardless of whether the customers want to make a complaint or report any other problem.

The main focus should be on measuring profitability of each customer and not the products. There should be gradual shift to relationship marketing by introducing this new approach in select branches and the same can be expanded later. Frequency marketing programs and club marketing programmes may be introduced to induce customers loyalty and their retention.

REFERENCES

1. N. Janardhan, Electronic Commerce, Indian Institute of Foreign Trade, 1997, New Delhi.
2. Asdas and Barisal, *Banking Sector Reforms: Towards a New Face of Indian Banking*, The Management Accountant, ICWAI, May 2001.

54

Role of Relationship Marketing in Service Industries

C. RAMESHKUMAR* & R. MANIVANNAN*

World wide services firms have been the pioneers in adopting this practice of Customer Relationship Management practices. In India too, the Service firms took some of the early initiatives in CRM, specially in cellular Telecom Services.

CRM is a discipline as well as a set of discrete software technologies which focuses on automatic and improving the business processes associated with managing customer relationships with in the areas of sales, marketing, customer care and support. CRM applications not only facilitate the coordination of multiple business functions but also coordinate multiple channels of communication with customer—face to face, call centre and the web—so that organizations can accommodate their customers preferred channel of interaction. A rich customer relationship fuels effective acquisition, nurturing and retention of customers.

CRM aims to provide organizational effectiveness by reducing sales cycle's and selling costs, identifying markets and channels for expansion, and improving customer value, satisfaction, profitability and retention. In the present era, the customers want to drive all the interactions. Service Industry is trying to drive their commerce through web to help reduce their operating overheads besides providing a better customer service.

Customer Relationship Management—the ability to provide a meaningful sales and service experience—promises to be a

* Lecturers, Business Administration, D.D.E., Annamalai University.

means of differentiation; of providing customers with a reason to frequent your business rather than that of your competitors. CRM promises competitive differentiation in a parity environment. More and more organizations are realizing that a customer-centric operation is no longer an optional differentiator but it is a key to remain in business. Technology enabled relationship management is a framework for developing both the culture and the infrastructure for a customer-centric operation.

Alternatively, CRM is defined as a continuous process of identifying, attracting and training profitable customers.

ERP applications have helped the companies to automate and optimize business processes in areas such as finance, manufacturing, inventory management and human resources etc. Like ERP, CRM solutions focus on automating and improving business processes albeit in front-office areas such as marketing, sales, customer service, and customer support. Whereas ERP implementation can result in improved organizational efficiency, CRM aims to provide organizational effectiveness by reducing sales cycle and selling cost, identifying markets and channels for expansion, and improving customer value, satisfaction profitability, and retention. While CRM applications provide the framework for embodying, promotion and executing best practices in customer-facing activities, ERP provides the backbone, resources and operational applications to make organizations more efficient in achieving these goals. CRM also acts an enabler for e-business by developing a web-based collaboration between the company and its suppliers, partners and customers. It can extend the traditional channels of interaction such as direct sales force or telebusiness to the web by providing a framework for managing the interactions and transactions.

CRM applications, often used in combination with data-warehousing, e-commerce applications, and call centers, allows companies to gather and access information about customer's buying histories, preferences, complaints, and other data so that they can better anticipate what customer will want. The goal is to instill grater customer loyalty.

CRM involves knowing your customers individually and having some mechanism interacting with them and customizing business for them. This is an inherently integration operation. One of the benefits of CRM is that it would make a company's customers loyal. Every time a company interacts with a customer, the company customizes its service more closely suited to the customer's needs. The company is getting a littler higher up the customer's learning curve. Moreover, the company is making the product increasingly valuable to the customer. The relationship with customer is developing in its context. This is called learning relationship because the relationship is getting smart with time. To create this kind of learning relationship, there are three criteria. First, it is necessary to have good design interface. It has to be easier for a customer to give company its information and for the company to capture that information. Secondly, a good memory. The company has to remember what the customer told them. Organization needs to have standard parameters hard coded into CRM to capture customer details at every customer interaction. Thirdly, the company has to have the ability to integrate the information into the way it handles the customer.

CRM is more than just technology. With CRM, one is operating in a different dimensi of competition finding products and services for customers, as opposed to finding customers for the products and services the company sells. The technology is crucial, but also important to have managers with the vision to imagine what this technology to enterprise to accomplish.

CRM aims to provide organizational effectiveness by reducing sales cycle's and selling costs, identifying markets and channels for expansion, improving customer value, satisfaction, profitability and retention. In the present era, the customers want to drive all the interactions. Service Industries are trying to drive the commerce through web to help reduce their operating overheads besides providing a better customer service.

PART IV

Emerging Trends in Customer Service

55

Customer Satisfaction by Quality Care for Curative Health Care Delivery in Urban India

R.P. BHATNAGAR*

Developing nations witness increasing urbanization of their population as undergone by developed nations. As more and more people opt to live in urban environment, the nature of job and the sector where labor force is employed undergoes a shift: agriculture to industry and finally industry to services. According to world book 2000: in developed world the employment of labor force in service sector has surpassed both industry and agriculture. Even in India, more people are employed in service sector (18%) than industry (15%) and share of agriculture to the total employment has come down to 67 per cent. A look at the respective contribution of these sectors to nation's GDP reconfirms the growing importance of service sector over other sectors. If for United States, United Kingdom, France, Germany and Japan services contribute 60-75 per cent of GDP, 45 per cent of Indian GDP is from services.

Health care, banking, insurance, financial services, travel and tourism, hospitality industry, education, government are organized service sectors add to this individuals or groups of individuals providing services in unorganized sector like chartered accountants, doctors, private nurses, tutors, domestic helpers, barbers, shoeshine boys etc. the impact of service sector in India will be felt much more. The present paper confines itself mainly to the organized health care service providers in urban India.

Not very long ago, it were mainly governments: center as well

* Professor, Faculty Division-III, BITS, Pilani.

as states, which were main service providers through various government hospitals, health centers and health care programs. The preventive health care is still in the hands of governments and it is the curative part of health care where urban India is witnessing increasing participation by the private players.

The economic liberalization policies of government, increased purchasing power of rapidly growing Indian middle class associated with increasing aspirations and demand for better health care services by Indian populace on one hand and overburdened governments, lack of financial muscles to support large health care network in public domain, growing population coupled with increasing costs for medical treatment on the other hand opened opportunities for more private players to fill the gap between demand and supply in urban curative health care services.

The increasing competition and demand for quality care by customers (patients) has put pressure on existing private service providers to reorganize and restructure themselves to meet the new challenges. The need was felt more in large multi specialties tertiary care hospitals located in metropolitan cities like Mumbai.

The role of these hospitals started changing from a referral (from small towns and rural locations) to local or even sub-continental quality care hospitals. The use of modern technology for both diagnostic as well as operative purposes by the near home small town or district level private hospitals has reduced the service quality gap between these district hospitals and existing and new multi-specialties hospitals in metropolitan cities. The customer profile changed from rural urban mix to mainly metropolitan.

Most of the customers in metropolitan cities were either employed in a service industry or had some kind of previous encounter with quality services as a customer. This has resulted not only in increasing awareness among patients but also put pressure on service provider to excel and meet customer satisfaction for retention of satisfied customers and attracting the potential ones. First time in the existence history of these established metropolitan hospitals the declining bed occupancy ratios became cause of concern.

Unlike product purchase which results in ownership of physical assets, a service purchase ends up with an experience good or bad depending upon the ability of service provider to meet the perceived quality needs of customers with actual quality services rendered by him/it. The health care service is no different than any other service in this regard. The problems encountered here are similar as faced by other service providers. The more you try to improve upon the health care quality the more are customer expectations. The intangibility, perish ability, standardization, inseparability and heterogeneity issues associated with health care services than are as much cause of health care administrators as of any other quality service provider administrator.

It is difficult to quantify quality and so is the customer satisfaction. None of the methods (Customer satisfaction surveys) used to gauge customer satisfaction are foolproof and therefore what matters most is a system which collects customer satisfaction feedback while the service is being delivered and make amends before the process is over. A mechanism entailing continuous communication with customer through an on going feedback system is more likely to result in customer satisfaction and retention than the post service surveys.

Intangibility of curative health services, specifically for indoor patients, can (to some extent) be addressed by providing quality infrastructure or physical facilities and a congenial environment in tune with the brand image of the health care service provider.

Building renovation, modern interiors, better wards, air conditioning system, well equipped post operative care rooms, patients' private rooms, modern elevators, esthetics, state of art diagnostic facilities and operation theatres, better waiting room facilities for visitors, security and parking arrangements, catering services both for indoor patients (room service) and visitors (cafeterias), communication facilities (fax, telephone etc.), medicines dispensing pharmacy, blood bank etc. will help add tangibility to otherwise intangible clinical services of physicians and supporting staff—paramedics and non medical staff—who come in contact with the customer at various stages while service is in progress.

Experience suggests that a consumer interacts more often with paramedical and non-medical staff than the main service provider i.e., the surgeon himself. The customer orientation of health care services cannot be achieved without the motivated and appropriately trained supporting staff such as nurses, ward boys, housekeeping staff, receptionists, billing clerks, security guards, catering service staff, telephone operators etc. Even the hospital administrators are important contact points. Training programs for such staff both by in house as well as by external faculties/ experts would help in improving overall customer satisfaction.

The physical presence of customer while service is being provided is more prominent in health care services compare to any other services. Customer involvement in service production process brings in the inseparability issue more in focus in health care than elsewhere. Not only that the presence or involvement of other customers while service is being rendered makes tasks more difficult. Imagine a news of death on operation table of one patient heard by waiting in patient and his escorts or cries of a dentist's patient heard by a patient waiting outside the dentist's room. Better consumer management can partially address this issue. Restricting the visitors' and other patients' access to the service area (operation theatre) where the core service is being rendered or using prior appointment than walk in patient system.

Heterogeneity in health services may arise due to both intra as well as inter factors. Two hearts specialists will be viewed differently by the patient and by the referring family doctor or physician. Same heart specialist may render different quality of service on different days or different part of the same day depending upon his moods, stress levels or peak efficiency time zones. The solution probably lies in standardization of services, easy said than done, in health care. Some of the areas where standardization for mass consumption can be looked into is time taken for billing, payments, reports, lab tests, dispensing of medicines in pharmacy, administration of medication by nurses, serving of food, frequency and timeliness of nurse visit, ward boy visits, doctors visits, cleaning of beds etc.

As all patients walking in hospital are not of same social standing, some discretion and customization of services is inevitable. Based on prior information, provisions can be made for reception, preferential bed allotment and increased frequency of visits by surgeons for VIPs and celebrities. This probably is more acceptable and in tune with the social system prevalent in urban Indian society.

The diminishing of long waiting list in some medical specialties for some service providers in metropolitan cities in India is a recent cause of concern. Perish ability of health care services for referral hospital has become more important than ever before. Marketing of healthcare services will sooner or later has to be addressed by health care providers. Third party payment will put more pressure to market the service provider as the retention or losing customer in bulk will depend how a service provider is placed in bulk buyers market. Development of new service products like regular health check up for executives may help to overcome some of the parish ability aspects like diagnostic services, lab tests or show casing to potential purchaser.

56

Changing Trends on Customer Service in Financial Services Sector

K. RAVICHANDRAN*

Introduction

In recent years, the Financial industry has been undergoing rapid changes, reflecting a number of underlying trends and developments. A key catalyst in the change process has been the revolution in communication and information technology, which have accelerated and broadened dissemination of financial information while lowering the costs of operations. Another key impetus for change has been the increasing competition among a broad range of domestic and foreign institutions in providing banking and related financial services. Yet another issue is that financial activity has become larger relative to overall economic activity in the economy. This means that any disruption of the financial market or infrastructure has broader economic ramifications than might have been the case previously.

In the Financial Services Industry we will look in brief about the Banking Sector and its current trends and developments.

In this presentation we will see, how:

1. Recent trends and developments in the Banking Industry.
2. Services will be a cutting edge in the Banking Industry.
3. Services play a role in keeping and getting new customers.
4. Services have direct effect on profits.

* Lecturer, SRM Arts & Science College, Kottenkullathan, Kahcheepuram Dt.

Recent Trends and Developments in the Banking Industry

The recent trends and developments in Banking industry can be classified into the following broad categories:

1. Environmental
2. Structural
3. Operational

We will discuss the broad categories in a brief manner.

Environmental

The major environmental trends in the Banking Industry are the competition and the De-regulation of Interest Rates.

Competition is distinctly visible in the banking system in recent years. With the entry of new generation private sector banks since 1995 with lean and skilled personnel structure, better technology, market-orientation and cost-effective methods, competition has become intense, especially in metro and urban centres.

Foreign banks have been given more liberal entry. Foreign Direct Investments (FDI) upto 49 per cent in private sector banks and upto 20 per cent in public sector banks are allowed. The move by Developmental Financial Institutions (DFI) towards universal banking is expected to make competition gain further momentum. With liberalisation, the process of dis-intermediation is also increasing.

Dependence of corporate on banks for credit is declining. Simultaneously, bank customers, particularly the corporate customers, are becoming more demanding in terms of interest rate, exchange rate, commissions etc., better access to products and services and information. With the spread thinning and non-interest income reducing, banks' bottom-lines are under pressure.

Since 1997 almost all interest rates are deregulated. SLR is reduced from 38.5 per cent to 25 per cent. CRR is reduced from 15 per cent to 5 per cent. The mandatory component of bank financing of Government borrowing has also declined. The RBI-regulated foreign exchange rate system till 1991 and the Liberalized Exchange Rate Management System (LERMS) of 1992 were replaced by unified market determined exchange rate system in 1993. In the pricing of loans, floating rates of interest linked to benchmark like Prime Lending Rates (PLRs) of banks has come to stay. In the deposit side also floating rates of interest are being implemented.

Structural

True, during the last decade, Government of India has recapitalised some nationalised banks to the tune of about Rs. 22,000 crore but through the amendment in 1994 to the Banking Companies Act, Government's shareholding in public sector banks has been diluted to 51 per cent. RBI's shareholding in SBI is subject to a minimum of 55 per cent. The budget for financial year 2000-01 contained a proposal to reduce Government's shareholding further to 33 per cent while maintaining the public sector character of Public Sector Banks (PSBs). Many banks have been raising capital from the market in the form of equity and/or debt.

Bank mergers, acquisitions or arrangements like cross-holdings, joint ventures and strategic alliances have been pursued to derive significant costs and revenue benefits in the form economies of scale and scope, organisational efficiency, reduced funding costs and risk diversification.

Here we can cite the cases of:

(*a*) New Bank of India merging with Punjab National Bank in 1993,
(*b*) 20th Century Finance Ltd., merging with Centurian Bank in 1998,
(*c*) Times Bank merging with HDFC Bank in 2000
(*d*) ICICI acquiring Bank of Madura Ltd., in 2001,
(*e*) ICICI reverse-merging with ICICI Bank Ltd. in 2002
(*f*) Many Government-led mergers, the latest being the State Bank of Benares merging with Bank of Baroda
(*g*) The proposed amalgamation of IndusInd Enterprises and Finance Ltd. (Finance) with IndusInd Bank Ltd.

Operational

Prominent among the operational trends are technology-orientation, focus on profitability, treasury operations, NPA management, risk management and ALM.

Technology and e-Banking

Information Technology and communication networking system have revolutionalised the functioning of the banks in India. Computerization is increasingly being applied in day-to-day deposit mobilization, loan operations and remittance transactions.

Technology has made 24 hours-a-day and 7-day-week banking a reality. Tele-banking and internet banking are becoming popular, particularly among the young and educated. More than 70 per cent of banking business in India is computerized today. Electronic Funds Transfer (EFT) is gaining popularity.

Inter-bank transactions are being achieved at the central hub located Institute for Development of Research in Banking Technology (IDRBT), Hyderabad which would function as the Certificate Authority (CA) for messages transmitted over the Indian Financial Network (INFINET).

NPA Management

This would be a tough task for the Indian banking industry. After the implementation of Narashiman Committee, the profitability of the Banking sector has been drastically affected. The Committee introduced asset classification norms and the provision norms, which eroded the bottom lines of the banks.

In 2003, Basal accord will be implemented, which will make 90 days past due concept for NPA classification. In 2005, it will be 30 days, which will almost take all the profits of the banks. All the Banks are forming strategies to face the Challenges in the year 2005.

Risk Management and ALM

In recent times, banking has turned to be a business of risk intermediation. The myriad risks faced by banks can be broadly grouped into credit risks, market risks and operational risks. The Basel Accord of 1988, initiated by Bank for International Settlement (BIS) Switzerland, suggested Capital to Risk-weighted Assets Ratio (CRAR) of 8 per cent to meet primarily credit risks.

In India, RBI has also asked banks to set up the Asset Liability Management (ALM) System to manage market risks. ALM is a dynamic process of managing the assets and liabilities—their mixes, volumes, maturities, yields and costs—to improve profitability and Market Value of Equity (MVE) of the bank. Presently, many banks try to meet the liquidity risk and interest rate risk by profiling their cash flows from assets and liabilities into RBI prescribed time buckets and managing the cumulative gap thereof. More sophisticated approaches like Modified Duration, Value at Risk, Stress Testing etc. are not yet popular among the Indian banks for want of historical data and appropriate systems.

Service a Cutting Edge in the Banking Industry

Customer service is becoming an important aspect in gaining competitive edge for survival with growth and profits for banks. Banks have realised that courteous service is a must in an era of globalization and privatization, when the likes of Café Coffee Day sports signs saying "You are entering a smile-zone" and offers customers a free cup of coffee if employees are caught not smiling. If one thinks that Coffee Cafes and Banks do not blend, let us be reminded that ABN-AMRO has tied up with Barista, to promote a concept called 'Bancafe' where customers can refresh themselves with coffee and snacks while completing their banking business.

No wonder, recently Bank of Baroda has introduced a system wherein its employees at select centres, to start with, would wear a tie and sport a smile at work. IDBI Bank has standardized the telephonic response of its employees. On lifting a ringing telephone, an employee of IDBI Bank has to say "Good Morning! This is IDBI Bank. I am so and so. How can I help you?" Customer centric operations and customer driven growth orientation have propelled some banks to go for quality improvement through ISO 9000 standards. For example, Punjab National Bank has gone for making a large number of its branches ISO certified.

Services play a role in keeping and getting new customers

Walk-in business for bankers is drying. Hence, banks have launched innovative marketing plans—be it in retail segments or corporate business to sustain the existing customers and also to get New customers. Relationship Banking, e-Banking, Phone-Banking, Anywhere anytime Banking are the new concepts introduced by the banks to sustain its customers.

Relationship Banking means creating, maintaining and enhancing long term relationship with customers to retain existing customers, regain lost customers and reinvent new customers, built over the edifice of not only customer satisfaction but also customer delight and customer intoxication. Through computer packages on Customer Relationship Management (CRM), banks are creating Customer Information System (CIS) and undertaking Customer Profitability Analysis (CPA). In the process, profitable customers are identified, their product preferences are tracked and provided with the highest level of service. This helps not only in checking defection of desirable customers but also in building image and brand equity and improving market share of the banks.

Services have Direct Effect on Profits

In the Earlier chapter we have seen that service is a cutting tool for getting new customers and to retain Existing customers. So customers are the people who bring profits to the banks. So without Service Banks cannot Survive in this competitive world.

Also to survive in this Competitive Environment Banks are offering diversified activities like depository services, bullion banking, distribution of both life and non-life insurance products, personal banking for high net worth customers etc. to increase their fee-based income.

After the entrance of foreign players in the Indian banking industry, only "Quality Service" can make them to survive in this current market scenario. State Bank of India has set an example by getting ISO standards for its service, which means SBI has identified that only service will make the difference.

Conclusion

It is evident that the years of placid banking growth came through regulated markets and interest spreads are over. Regulation is giving way to gradual autonomy with checks and balances. Banking is becoming increasingly technology-oriented and knowledge-driven. Not the size of balance sheet but profit alone brings a bank to forefront. Profit lies in innovation and professional decisions responding proactively to market opportunities. Human resources are being groomed to professionally manage the required skills in thrust areas of asset-liability management, risk management, treasury operations, customer relationship etc. Productivity and efficiency, with transparency and ethical standards are the watchwords in the banking industry. Continuous quest for skill upgradation at all levels, realisation of vision and mission and commitment are pursued by banks to improve their market share and stakeholders' value. In fact there is a paradigm shift in the Indian banking scenario.

57

Emerging Trends in General Insurance Services in India

M. ABBAS MALIK*

Introduction

All firms and organizations have as their objective the delivery of something that is of value to their customers. In the past, this was mostly in the form of products. But times are changing. The emerging business environment is defined by new technology, intense global competition and constantly changing market place. In the new business climate the customer is more often a purchaser of service than a product. Services can be both intermediate and final. Insurance, Banking and Transportation to name a few are basically intermediate. Speed and quality are the ultimate tests of consumer satisfaction. In the newly emerging service dominated economics, the management principles require a re-look. This is precisely the focus here, brings out the essence of what needs to be done the services must be customer drives. This paper deals with "Emerging Trends in General Insurance Services in India." The General Insurance service is the business services. Now it's growing at rates faster than other industry.

Insurance Industry has always been a growth oriented industry globally. On the Indian scene too, the insurance industry has always recorded noticeable growth vis-a-vis other Indian Industries.

The Triton General Insurance Company Limited was the first general insurance company to be established in India in 1850,

* Lecturer, Management Studies, Md. Sathak Engg. College, Kilakarai.

which was a wholly British-owned company. The first general insurance company to be set up by an Indian was Indian mercantile Insurance Company Limited, which was established in 1907. There emerged many players on the Indian scene thereafter.

The General Insurance business was nationalised after the promulgation of General Insurance Business (Nationalisation) Act, 1972. The post-nationalisation general insurance business was undertaken by the General Insurance Corporation of India (GIC) and its four subsidiaries.

1. Oriental Insurance Company Limited,
2. New India Assurance Company Limited,
3. National Insurance Company Limited.,
4. United India Insurance Company Limited.

Towards the end of 2000, the relation ceased to exist and the four companies are at present operating as independent companies. Now there are seven new entrants in the general insurance industry.

The GIC has developed the non-life business over a period of 30 years from 1973. The business covers a wide variety of risks from a bullock cart to satellites. Several non-traditional social covers for women, girl child etc., have been developed with low premium content, have been introduced. The insurance penetration which was 0.36 per cent of Gross Domestic Product in 1973 is now around 0.60 per cent of Gross Domestic Product.

Every person who has an asset of economic value, and is engaged in economic activity, needs insurance. The marker for general insurance ranges from individuals with personal household assets, to corporate bodies with assets worth hundreds of billions of rupees, to producers (agricultural or industrial) traders, exporters. The prospective customers are in remote rural areas as well, engaged in agro-based economic activities.

The General Insurance is closely linked to international trade. Large amounts of insurance are reinsured globally. When a major accident occurs, like an air crash, an oil field explosion, or a gas leak with innumerable deaths, as in Bhopal, in 1984, several insurance companies around the world share the loss.

For general insurance there is a variety of options being opened up to increases the reach and penetration of product targeting individual customers. The range of products in general insurance is very wide. Each of the products has unique condition, terms, warranties, exclusions etc. The covers are subject to different laws of country.

Of the four state owned companies, New India has been the market leader, both in market share and performance.

Overall Scenario in the General Insurance Market in India

The total market size in annual premiums is about half that of life insurance. The general insurance industry in India has currently about Rs. 12000 crore of premium income, with a five year compounded annual growth rate in the 11 percent. The first important issue with the market is the GIC'S book of business is not profitable at the underwriting level. However, now that the GIC companies are facing competition, the new entrants will likely target those lines of business that are profitable on an underwriting basis. This will significantly impact GIC's overall profitability.

The general insurance business is broken into three product lines-fire and allied perils (25%) marine (10%) and miscellaneous (65%) challenges is to divide the over all market numbers into two very broad but internally consistent areas—one, that comprises of general insurance products bought by commercial undertakings and second, those bought by individuals. Commercial insurance encompasses a very large variety of products including fire and allied risks insurance, marine insurance, casualty, and workmen's compensation. New entrants and even GIC companies in the competitive era—have to look at overall account profitability commercial insurance business is far more developed than the market for general insurance products sold to individuals.

The largest book of business among such lines is the motor insurance business. Motor insurance is a loss-making proposition upward revision of premiums is not likely to be an answer to the problem considerable scope exists for better risk management. The new entrants are going straight to the car manufacturers and their dealers and tying up with them to try and lock-in customers along with the purchase of new vehicles.

For non-motor assets owned by individuals, the current insurance business in India can safely be characterized as non-existent. Penetration of homeowner's policy—that covers both the house and contents therein—is extremely low due to a variety of factors, including fear of wealth watching and a lack sales push.

Health insurance is the second—largest pool of business from individuals. Personal accident insurance is another area that can be developed into a sizeable book. It provides cover—at a very reasonable cost—against a whole range of situations and is ideally suited for large cross-sections of the Indian society in the informal sector.

A close look at the financials of the four GIC companies reveals that they have returned consistent underwriting losses. However with in these overall results, underwriting profit performance varies dramatically across commercial insurance and personal insurance while the fire and marine lines of business are very profitable, results in areas like motor insurance and health insurance drags over all numbers down to a situation of underwriting losses.

General Insurance Corporation of India and its four associates had combined underwriting losses of Rs. 2529 crores for the year 2001-2002 as against Rs. 1722 crores in the previous year. The losses were mainly due to large number of claims on account of third party motor insurance and the Gujarat riots.

Insurance and Consumer Goods

If buying a toothpaste for Rs. 55 and getting a personal accident policy worth Rs. 25.000. For the first time insurance players and FMCG companies are using each other to boost their respective business. Riding an the recent insurance wave in the country, smaller FMCG players such as Kopran and Vardhaman chemicals are using insurance as a marketing ploy to counter their dominating competitors in the business and there by helping both themselves and their insurance pertness.

Take the example of the Rs. 600 crore Vardhaman chemicals which has introduced an ayurvedic toothpaste brand, 'Amar' in the western part of India. The company has tied up with Tata AIG to give prepaid accident insurance worth Rs. 25,000 with every 200 gm pack of the brand. A single person can avail of up to 12 packs and enjoy insurance cover of Rs. 3 lakh. The policy on after is, however valid for a year and comes into effect in case of an accidental death of the policyholder.

Pepsodent toothpaste also has tied up with insurance company and offering the insurance coverage.

Issues in General Insurance Sector

The state owned insurance was managing insurance business profitably, there were certain perceived lacunas in the areas of professionalism, service, issue of documents, etc. The new players are expected to set a high score in the area of service. With implementation of computerization at a faster pace, the existing players are also trying their best to improve the service and bridge the gap between them and the technologically savvy new players. Some of the issues faced by the insurance, old and new alike, however, are:

- Convergence of banking and insurance
- Ever changing technology
- Emergence of new distribution channels
- Underwriting losses
- Slow pace of economic acceleration
- Changing customer perception
- Evolving regulations

Indian General Insurance market is one of the latest markets opened to competition. Naturally, it looks different from the developed markets. Indian industry is characterized of:

- Low penetration
- More direct business and lesser dependence on intermediaries
- Having simple products catering to basic needs.

Developed Markets Show

- A high penetration
- Bookers, Agents and other intermediaries playing an important role
- Existence of savings linked products
- Existence of managed healthcare and Pension products.

GIC's Recent Activities

Government of India has re-notified GIC, which was engaged in reinsurance activities under GIBN Act, 1972 as 'Indian Reinsure', under the Insurance Act of 1938. The focus of GIC will be an accepting reinsurance business with in India to assist IRDA in ensuring the objective maximizing retention of premium with in the country as also to accept business from abroad.

GIC has stopped writing direct business and has now been concentrating exclusively on the re-insurance business. Finance minister has expressed a wish that India becomes a reinsurance hub in the Asian region and GIC plays all important roles in it. Towards achieving this goal, GIC would soon embark upon well devised marketing strategy. GIC has set its first representative office outside India in London. It proposes to enter into strategic agreements with large insurance companies in the targeted regions/markets. GIC aims to bench mark its standard of services and business quality with the world leaders.

The insurance reference aimed at reforming the state owned insurance companies and opening up the market to private competition. A strong regulatory and development authority "The Insurance Regulatory and Development Authority (IRDA) is set up and is effectively fractioning. It has issued licenses with in the prescribed time and some new insurance companies are already operational in the country.

Co-existence of public and private sector companies is a welcome sign, Indian banking sector has done well in such a set up. Reforms are expected to improve service quality, product availability etc., which is in the interest of the insurers as also the insured.

Subsidiaries of GIC, they are existing, profit making companies with skilled manpower, huge net worth, and dedicated clients. Through competition could affect their business in the immediate short term, through a well defined strategy, they could maintain their leadership position even in the competitive environment.

Future of the GIC Market

Indian Insurance scene is going to be drastically different. Things are no more static. Every day brings in change in the form of opening of a new insurance company, new products, new marketing methods/channels mergers etc. A strong regulatory and development authority is in place to take care of the changes and ensure orderly growth of the market. The insurance sector will see:

- Enhanced awareness through education and publicity
- Greater use of information-technology
- Better products
- Better service to customers
- Benchmarking with international standards.

Insurance sector will improve insurance penetration through further spread of insurance and availability of new products. The service will be of high quality and the customer will be the beneficial. As for GIC with the existing strengths of trained manpower, good reinsurance contacts, high reputation world wide, financial strength etc.

The state owned general insurance companies are definitely feeling the heat as private insurance companies are making a beeline to capture corporate accounts. But the threat is working in their favour as well in so far as quick actions are being taken in the areas of training, computerisation etc. The Indian insurance sector will follow the path of the banking sector, where forces of globalisation and technological improvements are bringing in changes which are helping the banks bridge the gaps in services offered. Bringing in prudential norms and ultimately helping the customer in getting world class products and services. In addition the state owned companies can venture into untapped rural potential for which they have a very vast network of offices and trained manpower.

Conclusion

Looking at the substantially low level of insurance penetration, there is no doubt that there is a huge potential for insurance in India. The existing players are fairly successful in catering to the needs of the organised sector and the general requirements of the economy. There is scope for increasing penetration in rural India and the up coming towns. Agricultural insurance also offers opportunities.

58

Emerging Trends of Service

A Visionary Approach by the Indian Railways

V. SELVANATHAN*

Introduction

Organisation structures, business environments and old world order are being dramatically altered by ongoing global changes. The growth of Information Techonology (IT) has revolutionised the way Indian companies market their products and services. The impact of IT can be seen in almost all operations of marketing, identifying a pontential customer, in transmitting product related information, sharing marketing information, building relationship with customers, selling realtime marketing, servicing customers, distribution of services, marketing and so on. Customer services have undergone drastic changes, thanks to the advent of internet and global village which has strung together all of as with fibre optics, there is already perceptiable shift in the way we are and will be shopping, buying air tickets, booking hotel rooms, purchasing books, cassettes and CD's, making travel arrangements, listening to music and communicating with each other. All such developments provide value addition to customers. This paper gives an insight on services marketing and the emerging trends of service—A visionary approach by the Indian Railways.

Services and Marketing

Marketing efforts once focused primarily on the selling of manufactured products such as cars and aspirin. But today the

* Senior Lecturer in Commerce, Periyar Arts College, Cuddalore (T.N.).

service Industries have grown more important to the economy than the manufacturing sector. Services, unlike products are intangible and involve a deed, a performance, or an effort that cannot be physically possessed. Currently, more people are employed in the provision of services than in the manufacture of products and this area shows every indication of expanding further. Infact, more than eight in ten U.S. workers labour in such service areas as Transportation, retail, health care, entertainment and education. In the United States alone service industries now account for more than 70 per cent of the gross national product and are expected to provide 90 per cent of all new jobs by 2012.

Usually, service marketing parallels product marketing with the exception of physical handling. Services must be planned and developed carefully to meet consumer demand. The services are more difficult to sell than physical products, promotional campaigns for services must be even more aggressive than those for physical commodities.

Service Marketing-practices

As it has been Quoted service marketing is different from product marketing. A cautious approach should be adopted here in selling the services. The following are the new trends and practices in service marketing.

(*a*) *Business-to-Business Marketing*: This is to stimulate growth of organisation through a comprehensive approach to Business-to-Business marketing that covers strategic issues, marketing tactics, and organisational choices.

(*b*) *Branding*: This is to build shareholder value through end-to-end branding capabilities, including brand strategy, brand architecture and brand delivery.

(*c*) *Customer Insights*: This refers to targeted approach to improve customer loyalty that work on the most powerful levers for profit growth. Here loyalty based on patterns of customer migration, change in customer value overtime are gaining importance.

(*d*) *Customer Relationship Management* (CRM): CRM deals with expertise in customer segmentation, migration and valuation, program design and Management, and organisation and capability building, and customisation of CRM strategy, identify opportunities to improve loyalty and reshape 'go-to-market programs'.

(e) *Marketing Spend Effectiveness*: This is to help organisations to build brand presence more quickly and effectively. Creation of effective market spending programs for new and existing brands, geographies and channels help an organisation to expand its Business.

(f) *Marketing Strategy*: Expertise in pricing, branding, and sales force management will help the organisation to go for right strategies that lead to understand the customer needs. This will give a benefit at three levels functional, relationship and process.

(g) *Pricing*: Fixing the price on value rather than on cost, examining the future supply, demand and cost dynamics are all essential which affect overall industry price levels.

INDIAN RAILWAYS—EMERGING TRENDS IN ITS SERVICE

The Indian Railways are one of the largest systems in the world. It provides the principal mode of transport for freight and passengers. It has played a vital role in the economic, industrial and social development of our country. Indian railways made a modest begining on 16th April 1853 when the first train carrying 400 people in 14 carriages was flagged off from Bombay to Thane, a distance of 34 Km. It has since grown into a vast network of 7,068 stations with a fleet of 7,206 locomotives, 34,728 coaches, 5,302 other coaching vehicles and 2,63,981 wagons. The total track distance is 1,07,445 Km. Freight trains carry over 1.1 million tonnes originating goods traffic. Each day about 7,525 passenger trains carry more than 11 million passengers. The railways employ about 1.6 m workers, the largest number for any undertaking in the country. The network is divided into 9 zones and further sub-divided into two divisions.

Such a large system of Indian Railways enters in a new era as it slowly reduces the tradition bound services and begins to provide consumer-targeted services. If we just look into the services which the Indian Railways are ready to offer to the passengers at their doorsteps one can understand how this service sector is ambitious in rendering service to their receipients. The following are real improvements in providing service to the customers.

Information

(*i*) To satisfy the needs of information to the passengers Interactive voice response system (IVRS) has been installed at 100 stations and it is going to be extended to other stations. With this information system passengers can get Train-Running position as well as Reservation status, on telephone. The number of incoming calls received in Delhi have increased from 50,000 to 1.25 lakhs per day on IVRS.

(*ii*) Moreover National Train enquiry system has been implemented where position of Trains Running on Real time Basis is fed to computers after every half an hour in 61 control offices all over the country. Thus, when a Train leaves from a starting station, position of its running is known, all over the country and its supplied to enquires and IVRS.

Reservation

The new Reservation system in Indian Railways aims at Providing reservation facilities for journey from any where to any where. There are now 705 computerised Reservation centres all over the country providing 9.5 lakh reservations everyday. 150 new PRS locations have been planned to be commissioned in current year. In the coming years all district headquarters will be provided with computerised Reservation facility. Reservations through internet has also been started recently.

Availability of reservation and status is also being given on the Indian Railways website www. Indian rail.gov.in.

Functional Facilities at Stations

The Indian Railways is continuously improving enquiry offices, Providing benches, fans, waiting areas, facility signages, sheds, platforms etc. Computerised enquiries and computer announcement systems are being provided at 150 stations. 'Pay and use Toilets' are being provided at 450 stations. Coach indication boards, PCO/STD boothes with internet and Fax facilities are provided at many of the stations.

Courtesy

27000 front line staff have been trained at Customer Care Institute Delhi and other Training centres during the last two years by professional trainers this is to improve the inter-personal skill which they need when they deal with real work situation.

Food

For providing catering services Indian Railways has set-up-Indian Railways and Tourism Corporation. The corporation is going ahead full steam to professionalise catering services.

Cleanliness

A strong Network of labour force is involved in the cleansing system of Indian Railways. Moreover safaiwalas are appointed in important trains. This system is going to be strengthened in all the important Trains.

Tourism

To promote Tourism Indian Railways help the travellers by all means. In this area it has not only introduced some of the special trains like 'palace on wheels' running in Rajastan, but it also shows active interest in guiding the tourists and making all arrangements for them. If the Tourism Industry and Railways put their co-ordinated efforts they can attract more Tourists by that it can earn more Foreign exchange.

Additional Train Services

The introduction of 16 new Janshatabdi' trains during the year 2002 is a greatest conveniance to the passengers which includes a new designed non-air conditioned second class chair car coaches. 3300 fast scheduled Time tabled summer specials have been planned for this year.

Rail Neer

Indian Railways catering and tourism corporation has been entrusted with the responsibility of production and sale of branded drinking water in all trains.

Other Developments

(*a*) National Rail Vikas Yoajana is being introduced for coordinating the Golden Quadrilateral project.

(*b*) To improve the safety conditions, and to avoid accidents due to human errors, the Indian Railways decides to train 20,000 employees who will keep a constant vigil for the sake of passengers safety.

(*c*) Modules on disaster management will be developed and more training will be given to all levels of employees on passenger safety, for this purpose Government decides to contribute 41 crores.

(*d*) ACD is an intelligent micro processor based equipment developed indigenously to prevent collisions. Continuous track circuting enables detection of discontinuties caused by rail/wed fracture or acts of sabotage.

(*e*) Pilot projects are started for unreserved tickets. For getting refund against a reserved tickets a new system is introduced by that one can get refund from any PRS centre, if it is after the depature of the train one can get refund within three hours after the train reaches the destination. If a RAC ticket is lost by a passenger he can get a duplicate ticket. Reservation charts can be provided by the Railways on the payment of 10 or 25 per cent of the full fare.

(*f*) Senior citizens of our country are being granted 30 per cent concession in fares in all classes and in all trains. This concession is available to men and women of the age of 60 years and above.

(*g*) Patients with cancer, Thalassemia, or heart patients, kidney patients can get concession of 75 per cent in first class and second class. This will be extended to AC 3 tier and AC chair car, and 50 per cent in AC first class and AC 2 tier of Mail/Express trains.

(*h*) In the current year of 2003 new lines are going to be laid for 225 km. and the first train will roll into the Kashmir valley by August 15th, 2007. During 2003-2004 a target of over 775 km. of gauge conversion has been proposed by which passengers will travel conveniently.

(*i*) Suburban projects are undertaken to help the commuters of urban population. Urban Transport projects like MRTS, METRO are undertaken in all metropolitan cities. In the current year Railway Budget the Railway fares are rationalised with the expectation to give more statisfaction to the customers and to get more revenue.

(*j*) To improve the punctuality of passengers services, a new computerised coaching operations information system (COIS) would be taken up soon.

(*k*) An effective economy depends on many factors one such factor is good Transportation. Indian Railways brings good revenue to the Government In the year 1998-99 to total earnings out of passengers was Rs. 8549.96 crores and out of goods was 19960.39. The expected increase in the year 2003-2004 will be 13,620 crores by passengers and 27815 by goods. In the current year on the freight front, there will be further reduction of total number of classes from 32 to 27. The freight rates were slashed by 10.7 per cent. The Railways except to carry 540 million tonnes of freight during the next year, the hefty 25 million tonnes more than the 515 million tonnes expected to be loaded during the current year.

(*l*) Private participation in Railways is going to be permitted in selected areas. Projects for connecting major ports have been allowed for private participation.

(*m*) It is advised by the Confederation of Indian Industry (CII) that a Railway consulting service should be started and this provide consultancy to Indian Railways. The scope of the consultancy service would be (i) It will review IR's business development and opportunities, (ii) Analyse the markets, costs and competitive position of IR, (iii) Analyse the opportunities and threats of IR's, (iv) Advise on strategies for improving Business performance. The above mentioned consultancy service should be carried out by reputable domestic management consulting firm. If some special expertise is needed it can induct even International experts.

Conclusion

The first part of the paper clearly indicated service marketing is different from product marketing. Now quality alone is not the matter but along with quality how the service rendered to the customers will determine the business of the organisation. The Indian Railways has realised the importance and has taken all steps even with all its constraints and now it is ready to provide safer, faster and more comfortable travel to its customers and also freight movement. Now Indian Railways can dream for State of Art of Technologies with active participation of Industries aiming at International Standards. The announcement made by the Indian Railways year 2003 is the "year of customer satisfaction" shows the sector is moving in the right direction with a greater vision.

59

Legal Aspects in Customer Service

Software Exports and Services

P. Periyasamy* & J.V. Balasubramanian**

Software Export is the combination of application software, consultancy services, system software; IT enabled services like data processing, data entry, medical transcription, CAD/CAM and web application like multimedia, Internet, e-commerce, etc.

The growth of India's software exports has been phenomenal. Exports began in 1974 but made limited impact until the 1980's.

The Industry and Government of India are taking some bold and purposeful steps to achieve the velocity of business. Amongst others, this exercise includes path-breaking measures by the Government further liberate the economy, simplification of procedures, deployment of additional resources for technical manpower development, new marketing channels, enhancing global brand equity and providing state-of-the art infrastructure for the development of software.

As per the survey of National Association of Software and Service Companies (NASSCOM), Indian software exports have grown 57 per cent to Rs. 17150 crore ($4bn) in 1999-2000. The projections show a substantial growth in the exports from India. The software export includes onsite software development, offshore software development, consultancy services, Software implementation services etc.

---

* Reader, Department of Business Management, Erode Arts College, Erode (TN).

** Research Scholar, Department of Business Management, Erode Arts College, Erode (TN).

1. *Computer Software*: Computer Software means—

(*a*) Any computer programme recorded on any disc, tape, perforated media or other information storage device; or

(*b*) Any customized electronic data or any product or service of similar nature, as may be notified by the board;

Which is transmitted or exported from India to any place outside India by any means; Clause (1) of Explanation 2 below section 10A)

The Central Board of Direct Taxes has specified the following Information Technology enabled products or services, as the case may be, for this purpose namely: (i) Back-office operations, (ii) Call Centres, (iii) Content Development or Animation, (iv) Data Processing, (v) Engineering and Design, (vi) Geographic Information System Services, (vii) Human Resources Services, (viii) Insurance Claim Processing, (ix) Legal Database, (x) Medical Transcription, (xi) Payroll, (xii) Remote Maintenance, (xiii) Revenue Accounting, (xiv) Support Centres, and (xv) Web-Sites Services. (CBDT Notification No. 142/49/2000-TPL dated 26th Sept. 2000).

2. "Film Software" means a copy of a cinematograph film made by any process analogous to cinematography on acetate polyester or celluloid film positive, magnetic tape, digital media or other optical or magnetic devices and certified by the Board of film certification constituted by the Central Government under section 3 of the Cinematograph Act, 1952 (37 of 1952); (Clause (d) of Explanation below Section 80 HHF).
3. "Music Software "includes serious of sounds or music recorded on magnetic tape, cassette, compact discs and digital media which can be played or reproduced on any appropriate apparatus; (Clause (e) of Explanation below Section 80 HHF).
4. "Telecast rights" means a license or contract to exhibit motion pictures or television programmes over a television network either through terrestrial or through a satellite broadcast in a specified territory; (Clause (g) of Explanation below Section 80 HHF).
5. "Television News Software" means a collection of sounds and images, reportage, data and voice of actualities

broadcast either through, terrestrial transmission, wire or satellite, live or pre-recorded on video cassettes or digital media; (Clause (h) of Explanation below Section 80 HHF).

6. "Television Software" means any programme or serious of sounds and images recorded on film or tape or digital media or broadcast through terrestrial, satellite or any other means of diffusion; (Clause (i) of Explanation below Section 80 HHF).

Tax Benefits on Export of Software

There are various tax provisions under the Income Tax Act 1961 on the income from export of software.

We will discuss some of the taxation provisions as also will discuss advantages and steps of setting up a Software Technology Park popularly known as STP.

Tax Provisions

Income Tax Act U/S 10A: provides for special provision in respect of newly established undertakings in Free Trade Zones ("FTZs") etc.

Under this section, profits and gains derived from the export of articles or things or computer software by an undertaking set up in any of the Free Trade Zone, Software Technology Park areas (STP) and electronic hardware technology park ("EHTP").

Income Tax Act U/S 10B: special provision in respect of newly established hundred percent export oriented undertakings (EOU).

Under this section, profits and gains derived from the export of articles or things or computer software by a hundred percent export oriented undertakings (EOU) are fully exempt for a period till 31st March 2010.

Section 35 of the Income Tax Act provides for tax deduction of any expenditure incurred on scientific research.

Any expenditure laid out on scientific research related to the business of a taxpayer is allowed as a deduction while computing taxable income. Sub-section (2AB) of section 35 of the Income Tax Act provides for a deduction of 125 per cent of any expenditure incurred by a company engaged in the business of manufacture or production of any drugs, pharmaceuticals, electronic equipments, computer, telecom equipments, chemicals or any other notified article, on scientific research (not towards cost of land or building) on in house research and development facility as approved by the prescribed authority.

Section 80 HHE of the Income Tax Act: deals with the deduction in respect of profits from export of computer software, etc.

Under this section if a company or a person is engaged in the business of

(*i*) export out of India of computer software or its transmission from India to a place outside India by any means;

(*ii*) providing technical services outside India in connection with the development or production of computer software;

Then the profits derived from his business would be deductible from its taxable income. The extent of the deduction shall be an amount equal to 80 per cent for assessment year beginning on 1st April 2001, 60 per cent for 2002, 40 per cent for 2003, 20 per cent for 2004 and then no deduction will be allowed there after.

This deduction will be available provided the consideration in respect of the export of computer software is received in, or brought into India in convertible foreign exchange within a period of six months from the end of that financial year. This benefit is available only to Indian companies or Indian residents. This benefit is also available to supporting software developer selling computer software to exporting company.

U/S 10 A (iv) "electronic hardware technology park" means any park set up in accordance with the Electronic Hardware Technology Park (EHTP) scheme notified by the Government of India in the Ministry of a Commerce;

Export of Software and Law

As per the survey of National Association of Software and Service Companies (Nasscom), Indian software export have grown 57 per cent to Rs.17150 crore ($4bn) in 1999-2000. The projections show a substantial growth in the exports from India. The software export includes onsite software development, offshore software development, consultancy services, Software implementation services etc. We in this article will discuss the provisions of laws which one must know to comply and the importance of Importer-Exporter Code Number and softex form and other declarations.

Some of the relevant provisions of Acts and regulations that we will cover here are:

1. Foreign Exchange Management Act 2000 (FEMA),
2. Foreign Exchange Management (Export of goods and services) Regulations, 2000,
3. The Foreign Trade (Development and Regulation) Act 1992,
4. Export and Import Policy for the period 1997-2002 (EXIM policy),
5. Hand Book of Procedures Vol-I.

Export and Software Defined

Under Foreign Exchange Management (Export of goods and services) Regulations, 2000

U/s 2 (iv) 'export' includes the taking or sending out of goods by land, sea or air, on consignment or by way of sale, lease, hire-purchase, or under any other arrangement by whatever name called, and in the case of software, also includes transmission through any electronic media;

(viii) 'software' means any computer programme, database, drawing, design, audio/video signals, any information by whatever name called in or on any medium other than in or on any physical medium;

Under EXIM Policy

3.19 "EOU" means Export Oriented Unit.

3.20 "EPZ" means Export Processing Zone.

3.22 "Exporter" means a person who exports or intends to export and holds an Importer-Exporter Code number.

3.31 "Manufacture" means to make, produce, fabricate, assemble, process or bring into existence, by hand or by machine, a new product having a distinctive name, character or use and shall include processes, such as refrigeration, repacking, polishing, labelling and segregation. Manufacture, for the purpose of this Policy, shall also include agriculture, aquaculture, animal husbandry, floriculture, horticulture, pisciculture, poultry, sericulture, viticulture and mining.

3.32 "Manufacturer Exporter" means a person who exports goods manufactured by him or intends to export such goods.

3.33 "Merchant Exporter" means a person engaged in trading activity and exporting or intending to export goods.

3.37 "Person" includes an individual, firm, society, company, corporation or any other legal person.

3.47 "Services" include all the tradeable services covered under General Agreement on Trade in Services and earning free foreign exchange.

3.48 "Service Provider" means a person providing

(*i*) supply of a "service" from India to any other country;
(*ii*) supply of a "service" from India to the service consumer of any other country in India; and
(*iii*) supply of a "service" from India through commercial or physical presence in the territory of any other country.

Importer-Exporter Code Number (IEC No.)

U/s 7 of the Foreign Trade (Development and Regulation) Act 1992

No person shall make any import or export except under an Importer-Exporter Code Number (IEC No.) granted by the Director General of Foreign Trade.

Application for Grant of IEC No.

Handbook rule no 4.7

An application for grant of IEC number shall be made by the Registered/Head Office of the applicant to the licensing authority concerned, in the form specified in Appendix-2A and shall be accompanied by documents prescribed therein.

S/5 Indication of Importer-Exporter Code Number

The importer-exporter code number allotted by the Director General of Foreign Trade under Section 7 of the Foreign Trade (Development & Regulation) Act, 1992 (22 of 1992) shall be indicated on all copies of the declaration forms submitted by the exporter to the specified authority and in all correspondence of the exporter with the authorised dealer or the Reserve Bank, as the case may be.

Declaration as regards export of goods and services:

[Under s/3 of the Foreign Exchange Management (Export of goods and services) Regulations, 2000]

1. Every exporter of goods or software in physical form or through any other form, either directly or indirectly, to any place outside India, other than Nepal and Bhutan, shall furnish to the specified authority, a declaration in one of the forms set out in the Schedule and supported by such evidence as may be specified, containing true and correct material particulars including the amount representing—
   (*i*) the full export value of the goods or software; or
   (*ii*) if the full export value is not ascertainable at the time of export, the value which the exporter, having regard to the prevailing market conditions expects to receive on the sale of the goods or the software in overseas market, and affirms in the said declaration that the full export value of goods (whether ascertainable at the time of export or not) or the software has been or will within the specified period be, paid in the specified manner.
2. Declarations shall be executed in sets of such number as specified.
3. For the removal of doubt, it is clarified that, in respect of export of services to which none of the Forms specified in these Regulations apply, the exporter may export such services without furnishing any declaration, but shall be liable to realise the amount of foreign exchange which becomes due or accrues on account of such export, and to repatriate the same to India in accordance with the provisions of the Act, and these Regulations, as also other rules and regulations made under the Act.

U/s 4. interalia Exemption is provided: export of goods or services may be made without furnishing the declaration in the following cases, namely:

(d) goods or software accompanied by a declaration by the exporter that they are not more than twenty five thousand rupees in value.

In addition to above information, the government has provided a lot incentives to IT enabled services i.e it has been exempted from Income Tax. The Central Board of Direct Taxes (CBDT), Ministry of Finance, Government of India, issued a notification No.11521/F. No.142/49/2000-TPL dated 26 September

2000 listing the IT enabled services that are covered under the provisions of Section 10A/10B HHE of the Income Tax Act. The list currently includes the following;

- backoffice operations
- call centers
- content development/animation
- data processing
- engineering and design
- geographic information system services
- human resource services
- insurance claim processing
- legal databases
- medical transcription
- payroll
- remote maintenance
- revenue accounting
- support centers
- web site services

Obviously, it is not always feasible to provide with a comprehensive list for a sector that is still evolving.

Conclusion

From the above study I conclude that the government has provided a lot provisions for export of software. The following are the examples of Acts passed by Government of India.

1. Foreign Exchange Management Act 2000 (FEMA),
2. Foreign Exchange Management (Export of Goods and Services) Regulations, 2000,
3. The Foreign Trade (Development and Regulation) Act 1992,
4. Export and Import Policy for the period 1997-2002 (EXIM policy),
5. Hand Book of Procedures Vol. I and not only for the total export but also there is a certain provisions for IT enabled services. The study advised that high taxation on IT exports is one of the major obstacles facing the Indian Software Industry, and called for a cut on export taxes from the current taxes in order to make the industry more profitable.

60

Emerging Trends in Banking Industry

An Overview

T. BANUMATHI*

The more one goes closer to the customer the more one would get higher volumes and value addition in business. Banking is a service-oriented business requiring high level of professional and personal skills have been undergoing the rapid changes, reflecting the number of underlying developments. The most significant has been advances in communication and informational technology, which have accelerated and broadened the dissemination of financial information while lowering the cost of many financial activities.

In the last few years, it is no wonder that the banking sector has been a virtual cornucopia of new products such as credit cards, telebanking, ATM (Automatic Teller Machine), mergers and acquisitions, e-Banking, Phone Banking, Net Banking, retail EFTs, Electronic Clearing Services (ECS), Smart cards, online banking for e-Commerce, Financial EDI, and wireless banking, etc. Now there is moving for Banking Assurance in Indian banking sector. The process of computerisation and application of information technology in banks gained momentum.

Major Trends in Banking

Mergers and Acquisitions

Banking firms of all sizes, from tiny community based savings association to vast national bank holding companies continue to merge, seeking marketing opportunities and operating efficiencies.

* Lecturer in Management Studies, Kongu Arts and Science College, Nanjanpuram, Erode.

Completed merges lead to consolidation of back-office support services and the elimination of duplicated support staff position and many branch locations.

The Indian Banking sector more over-crowded than ever. There are all of the banks under RBI are growing at a scorching pace and redefining the rules of the business. However they are dwarfed by many large public and old private sector banks with a large network of branches spread over a diverse geographical area. Thus they are unable to make a significant dent in the market share of the old players. Also it is impossible to exponentially increase the number of branches. The only rout available for these banks is to grow inorganically via merges and acquisitions. Hence the new banks are under a tremendous pressure to acquire older banks and thus increase their business.

Currently most of the institutionally promoted banks have already gobbled smaller banks. ICICI bank has acquired ITC classic, Anagram Finance and Bank of Madura with in a period of two years. HDFC Bank has merged Times Bank with itself. UTI Bank had almost completed its merge with Global Trust Bank. Also nationalised bank like Bank of Punjab, Vyasa Bank are wooing IDBI for merger. Among the foreign banks, Standard & Chartered Bank has acquired ANZ Graindlays Banks Asian and Middle East operations.

The above happening clearly indicate that the merger and acquisition scenario in Indian Banking sector is for from over. The strong banks will continue to take and inefficient banks to increase their size.

ATMS-Cash—Dispensing Machines into Financial Services Depots

An ATM is basically a machine that can deliver cash to the customers on demand after authentication. However, nowadays we have ATMs that are used to vend different FMCG products also. An ATM does the basic function of a banks branch, i.e., delivering money on Demand. Hence setting of newer branches is not required thereby significantly lowering infrastructure costs.

Cost reduction is however possible only when these machines are used. In India, though the number of ATMs has increased since last year, it is not in sync with the number of cards issued. Also, there are many dormant cardholders who do not use the ATMs and prefer the teller counters. In spite of these odds, Indian banks are increasing the number of ATMs at a feverish pace. These machines also hold the keys to future operational efficiency.

Net Banking—e-Banking

The electronic banking initiative called interest e-Bank, comprises a variety of projects that aim to improve not only the bank's efficiency, but customer service levels as well.

e-Banking program allows customers to use the Interest for basic functions in corporate and retail banking and credit cards. These include making inquiries about account balance and getting statements and real-time funds transfers' security with other financial institutions.

Net Banking means carrying out banking transactions via the Internet. Thus the need for a branch is completely eliminated by technology. Also this helps in servicing the customer better and tailoring products better suited for the customer.

A customer can view his account details, transaction history, order drafts, electronically make payments, transfer funds check his account position and electronically communications with the bank through the internet for which he may have wanted to visit the bank branch.

Net banking helps a bank spread its reach to the entire world at a fraction of the cost.

Phone Banking

This means carrying out of banking transaction through the telephone. A customer can call up the banks help line or phone banking number to conduct transactions like transfer of funds, making payments, checking of account balance, ordering cheques etc. This also eliminates the customer of the need to visit the banks branch.

Mobile Banking

Banks can now help a customer conduct certain transactions through the Mobile Phone with the help of technologies like WAP, SMS, etc. This helps a bank to combine the Internet and telephone and leverage it to cut costs and at the same time provide its customer the convenience.

Thus it can be seen that tech savvy banks are tapping all the above alternative channels to cut costs improve customer satisfaction.

Electronic Funds Transfer (EFT)

Electronic fund transfer has been introduced in same of the new generation banks a few large public sector banks cheque clearances within and across major commercial cities are taking place at greater speed. "Any Place Deposit" scheme and any time money have become the order of the day.

Wireless Banking Services

Wireless banking services is an emerging trend in banking. Wireless banking service enables one to manage their accounts with GSM/GPRS WAP mobile phones or PDAs anytime anywhere. The service uses WAP (Wireless Application Protocol) technology to allow access to accounts more convenient, secure and flexible.

With Wireless banking service, the following operations can be performed:

- Check account balance and transaction details
- Make fund transfer to self or third party accounts.
- Pay bills and present bill payment instructions.
- Buy and sell foreign currency
- Trade securities
- Inquire mutual funds and securities trading accounts portfolio and account balance.
- Personalized stock watch list to monitor stock price performance
- Inquire free real time stock quotes
- Inquire deposits/exchange/loan rate
- Access to financial calculator.

To avail wireless banking services, one just needs to log in the wireless banking service with their existing customer ID and pin provided for e-banking

In wireless banking all data is secured because all communications generated from the wireless banking service will be strongly encrypted to safeguard customer privacy.

Retailers, Automobile Makers become Bankers

Upscale department store giant Nordstrom took the unusual step of converting its Englewood, Colorado limited-purpose credit card bank into a full service savings association based in

Scoottsdale, Arizona. (Nordstrom offers checking accounts Visa cards and other services to its customers, but does not plan to open branch banks). Competitor Federated Department Stores obtained a bank charter in 1999 and announced plans to install ATMs and banking kiosks in hundreds of department stores. Wal-Mart leases branch bank space within its stores to banking companies including Arvest, a bank controlled by the family that founded Wal-Mart. Meanwhile, major automobile manufacturers, including General Motors, Volkswagen and BMW, are preparing to add banking services to the financing and insurance services that they already sell to millions of car buyers.

Banks Go Online

Banks have learned that combining the convenience of telephone and online banking with a chain of branch locations enables them to fill an entire range of customer needs. This is very similar to the trend among major retailers of creating synergies between bricks and clicks, combining e-commerce, catalog sales and physical stores.

Extension of Services

Bank of all types and sizes are adding to the list of services they attempt to market to customers. In this manner, they hope to retain assets, increase customer loyalty and add highly profitable fee income. Such services include private banking, retirement product sales, and stock brokerage and trust services.

Other Banking Trends

Heightened competition from non-banks, a persistent bearish market, and a general erosion of consumer confidence will continue to influence banks IT decisions.

1. *Banks will Pay more Attention to Privacy and Identity Theft Concerns*: Banks are becoming more proactive in assuaging consumer concerns regarding Internet banking privacy and the broader issue of ID theft. Banks are increasingly recognizing that privacy concerns have impeded Internet banking adoption by the mainstream. Privacy concerns in turn fuel lack of confidence across all electronic channels and new payment systems. Thus banks have a long-run stake in mitigating privacy branches.

2. *Enterprise-wide Risk Management*: Capital regulations (in particular Basel II) are pushing banks to measure and manage not only credit and market risk but in particular, an alliance between asset-liability management and credit risk management will grow. Ultimately, more integrated risk management systems and robust analytics will lead to increasingly more efficient use of capital which will, in turn, benefit shareholders.
3. *Check Processing*: In future more check image archiving and electronic exchange pilots. Within the next two years, a few will launch check truncation pilots.
4. *Core Processing Systems*: Many large financial institutions will invest hundreds of millions of dollars over few years to replace outdated other technology suppliers, technical experts, trade association officials, and personnel of the payment companies themselves.

Status of Indian Banking

After a decade of reforms, the Indian Banking sector is slowly emerging stronger. Regulations are forcing the banks to adopt better operational strategies and up grade their skills. The system is also witnessing the integration of the financial markets. Externally, the happening in the international markets are having their implication on the market and the players. All these are the making the operational environment more volatile and hence challenging the Indian banks. The Indian banks have nevertheless, withstood all the challengers and are becoming more adoptive to the changing environment.

The emerging trains make it essential for professional to continuously update themselves on the latest trends practices such as:

Future Challenging Areas

The areas of challenges that lie ahead would be:

- Restructuring and reorganizing banks setup towards thinner and leaner administrative offices;
- Closing down and/or merging of unviable branches particularly in urban and metropolitan branches;
- Forgoing of strategic alliances to take advantages of the geographic spread of branch network of banks;

- Type of customer concentration with a view of developing niche markets suitable for each bank consistent with its ethos and culture;
- Develop new products and services that would meet the emerging customer needs;
- Professionalising management structures that would be responsive to the changes in the business environment.

Conclusion

In the forthcoming years, banks should strive to achieve significant increases in their productivity, efficiency, and profitability. The challenges faced by the banking industry are enormous and can be met effectively only when the banking institution make knowledge as engine for growth.

Indian banking should set for itself in the new millennium is to transform our banking from being a largely domestic one to a truly international one.

61

Emerging Trends in Customer Service

Satisfy Your Customers or Your Competitors Will

R. SUNDARI* & MEENAKSHI*

Virtually, many aspects of business environment is experiencing accelerating change particularly the consumers, customers, technology and globalization of markets. The increasingly turbulent environment places a severe penalty on complacent management, as knowledge of all types is subject to rapid obsolescence and erosion. Out of this chaos, maximizing delivered customer value is emerging as a dominant success factor.

Need for Customer Services

"Quality is when our customers come back and our products don't."

More than ever, business are subjected to rapid change, which is the thought of the day. e-Business, The Internet, the Web, and the electronic commerce are the new kids that are causing more disruptive changes in the business block.

Travel city in the travel industry, Autobytel in auto retailing, e-steel in steel products are the new entrants now. Old marketing channels have been erased by new in the industries of Banking. Insurance, Telecom or retailing.

With all of these changes, businesses have rediscovered that more than ever in the facing environment, mature markets and the ever-demanding customers, treating existing customers well is the best source of profitable and sustainable revenue growth.

---

* Department of Commerce (Eve), M.O.P. Vaishnav College for Women, Nungambakkam High Road, Chennai (T.N.).

- Rapid advances in technology and science have enabled things that were not possible before.
- Globalization has created smaller market place for global organizations while at the same time increasing the competition.
- Consolidation and mergers have blurred the lines between industries.
- New Sales channels and marketing tools have allowed small niche players to have a broad reach.
- Consumers are educating themselves about their options. Blind loyalty no longer exists.
- Product life cycle is decreasing while the rate of obsolescence is increasing.

Need for innovations in customer service

To capture customer's expectations of product quality, service quality at reasonable price.

- Competitive bench marking.
- Customers expectations are dynamic.
- To extend the product and service quality throughout the channel.
- Updating of the technology.
- To compete in the global market.
- To find solutions to the various problems of the upcoming service sector.
- To improve the marketing services and the services marketing.

Let us see the Innovations Took Place in one of the Services Industry-Marketing

The bundle of attributes that the customer is buying normally includes a variety of support services. For simplicity, let us start with three support services. The first category precedes purchase transactions and the second category is directly related to the transactions and the third category follows the transaction and extends throughout the products life. Certainly, the kinds of services in each category vary from industry to industry and from customer to customer. However, when firm comes close to the supplier the types of services will increase more and more.

Pre-sales Service

- Conduct of technical sales seminars and training method.
- Supplier involvement in quality circles.
- Responding to customer queries in timely fashion.
- Setting up of safety programme for hazardous products.

Transactional Services

- Commitment to firms delivers dates.
- Credit financing and dates.
- Information guarantee and return policies.
- Efficient check in the procedures of hotel and airline industry.

Post-Sales Services

- Intimating order status, backorders and shipping delay.
- Customer service and complaint resolution processes.
- Repairs and maintenance.
- Sales follow-up to know the customer status through cards, letters and phone calls.

Customer Service Yesterday and Today

Yesterday	*Today*
Internal sources of data collection	Strategic use of prospects information
Self service	Transactional focus
Internal use of information	Operational use of information
Disintegrated-channel strategy	Strategic channel management
Product approach	Technology enabled approach
Organization delayed approach	Enterprises wide approach
Product attributes	Service attribute
Perceived benefits	Perceived sacrifice

Recent Trends in Customer Service

- Web collaboration.
- Interactive chat.
- Universal queue.
- Problem resolution.
- e-mail response management.
- Customer care robots.
- Voice recognition and processing.

Customers Retention Strategy

Customer satisfaction program is quite simply the most important type of marketing research a firm can conduct. Ironically, about 80% of the program are worthless. To be valuable, a customer satisfaction program must flow from and be embedded in the firm's culture. It is essential for long time survival that the firm design, implement and improve a good customer satisfaction program.

- Involve top management.
- Knowledge customers.
- Let the customers define what attributes are important.
- Knowledge the customers requirements, expectations and wants.
- Know the relative importance of customers decision criteria.
- Gather and trust the data.
- Benchmark the data against competitors and identify the competitor strength and weaknesses.
- Develop cross-functional action plan that enhance strength and correct weaknesses.
- Measure performance continually and spread the data throughout the firm.
- Be committed for getting better and better.

Designing of Customer Satisfaction Measurement Programme

Designing a CSM program is an interactive process. Invariably, there are unforeseen issues that emerges as each steps been taken. In some cases, the new information may require the modification of previous decisions. It is quite normal to cycle through this process several times before a consensus is arrive and a research should be developed.

It is also quite common for a firm to begin with one objective for a Customer Service Management program and then gradually adds others. As each additional objective is added, the program must be modified. The key idea to keep in mind is that the CSM program is a process for gathering customer driven data. Accordingly, a CSM program should be subject of cross-functional process improvement efforts.

Steps in the Design of CSM Program

Design the Objectives
↓
Develop the Research Design
↓
Identify the Attributes
↓
Design the Questionnaire
↓
Design the Sampling Plan
↓
Pretest the CSM Program
↓
Gather the Data
↓
Analyse the Data
↓
Use the Data
↓
Improve the CSM Program

Just as all processes should be subject to continuous improvement, the customer service program should be continuously evaluated and considered. Every program should be improved in the same or the other day.

Thus, the customer is an asset that must be nurtured developed and cherished. A customer is not just a target for a high-powered marketing machine. Relaying only on qualitative data to understand consumers is a major weakness that does nothing to develop bonding relationship with customers.

62

Services Marketing

A Case Study of South Central Railway

M. SURAT KUMARI*

The service sector of the economy is going through a period of almost revolutionary proportions in which established ways of doing business continue to be shunted aside. Around the world, innovative new comers offering new standards of service have succeeded in markets where established competitors have failed to please to-day's demanding customers. Today, many developments have taken place in transport industry.

The service sector if marketed in a right fashion contributes substantially to the process of development. The speed of socio-economic transformation can be increased sizably if the innovative marketing principles are practiced. In the years to come the service sector would get a conducive environment with profitable opportunities. If we market the services in a right direction the available opportunities can be capitalized optimally. It is against this background an advocacy in favour of services marketing is made.

The globalization and liberalization has opened new vistas for the development of service generating organizations. The intensity of competition is found moving upward. The organizations active in enriching their strength have been found establishing an edge and compelling the weak organization to make a final good bye. This makes it essential that even in the Indian conditions the service generating organizations make sincere effort to make themselves stronger if they have to survive

* Lecturer in Commerce, Department of Commerce and Management, Gulbarga University, Gulbarga (Karnataka).

and thrive. They have to explore profitable avenues and practice innovative marketing since quality or world class service with innovative marketing would help them in providing their excellence nationally and internationally competitive.

Significance of the Study

Today many developments have taken place in transport industry. Developments in South Central Railway are also very rapid. Modernization and technological up-gradation of its services have made the SCR to occupy the prime place in the Indian Railways. The present research tries to know the types of services marketed and how SCR can improve its services to suit the customer/rail user's needs by matching with its service product offer.

Study on services marketing of South Central Railway is designed to focus attention on the users/customers and the organizers with regards to product planning, channelization of services, promotional strategies or mix, pricing strategies, distribution network, technology and service processes, physical evidence, the service personnel and customers' preference structure.

The present study surveys the significance of services marketing in South Central Railway which are as follows:

1. This survey can help the SCR for improving the service quality and increasing the level of services provided by it.
2. SCR system has been able to know more and more about the application of marketing principles to its services, for the purpose of accomplishing the organizational objectives.
3. The South Central Railway with correct recognition of marketing principles can design its service product to suit the rail users need and there by through customer satisfaction it can increase its performance.
4. The SCR will be able to distinguish its strengths and weaknesses and there by reduce its weaknesses.

In this, researcher tried to give appropriate recommendations for the application of marketing principles to the application of marketing of South Central Railway. Also the researcher tried to show the practical and scientific solutions for improving the services marketing of SCR. The emphasis of this study is on the application of marketing principles to SCR services and evaluation of services marketing.

Objectives of the Research

1. To identify the pattern of services availed by the general public and the industrial users.
2. To identify the dissatisfied customers, so that services recovery can be attempted.
3. To find out the customer needs and expectations of services from the South Central Railway.
4. To evaluate the strategies adopted by South Central railway in improving the services provided.

Scope and Limitation of the Study

The demand and expectations of customers are increasing tremendously day by day, the railways are expected to and are trying to make all out efforts to reach the country side to meet the needs of the customers particularly in rural populace. The scope of the study doesn't permit the inclusion of all zones therefore, the study is confined to only South Central Railway zone.

Research Methodology

The secondary sources of data include reports published by SCR. General Manager's Annual Reports, Indian Railways Annual Report, Year Books, Magazines, Pamphlets and other publications by the zonal office. The data is also extracted from the Railway section's officers of SCR.

Sample Size

This is exploratory and analytical case study. The methods adopted to collect the research data are:

1. Personal interview with help of pre structured (interview schedule) questionnaire.
2. Introspection.
3. The study has made use of both the primary and secondary sources of data. The primary sources include data collected through structured interviews schedule; personal observation and formal discussion with rail users.

400 customers/rail users from different classes of people such as students, businessmen, agriculturists, and employees were selected.

Statement of the Problem

There has been a phenomenal growth in the movement of men, machine and materials. The primary, secondary and tertiary sectors are witnessing radical changes. The product development strategy would make possible equilibrium between the transportation, demand and supply. Transport facilities help greatly in widening the size of the market. The widening of the size of the market rests on the creation of a network of transport and communication. In a developing country like India, it is very much significant that policy decisions are made keeping in view the needs and requirements of both general customers and the industrial users.

Research Findings

The South Central Railway has been acknowledged as one of the best zones of Indian Railways and has been awarded The Railway Minister's safety shield several times. Yet it suffers from the following deficiencies in some sectors/areas.

1. South Central Railway is more product-oriented than customer oriented. Marketing is peripheral activity and the commercial department is engaged only in selling business.
2. Most of the advertising of SCR is focused on social themes but it needs to give stress on service delivery aspect.
3. The advertisement released by SCR is not creative enough in messages, appeals and slogans to become effective in informing serving and persuading the users.
4. The promotional methods adopted to convey the availability of various services is inadequate to persuade the common man.
5. In South Central Railway there is inadequate management of service promises. There is discrepancy between service delivery and service promises made through promotional programmes.
6. Inadequate delegation of powers and concentration of authority with the ministry and the Railway Board are

serious drags on speedy and efficient disposal of business.

7. Inadequacy of proper motivational and encouragement setup to reward employees who excel in their endeavors.
8. There is deficiency in customer service skills among the personnel at the enquiry counters. Inadequate customer-orientation among the personnel exists and persists.
9. Customer-focus is missing and customer-satisfaction is not an organizational mission and vision.

Recommendations at the Macro-level

1. The Railways should evolve an action-plan particularly towards project implementation to avoid time and cost over-runs. The railways should develop an efficient and professionally managed system particularly in the areas concerning passenger safety and amenities.
2. The Railways, in view of severe resource crunch, must explore the possibility of attracting direct foreign investment and joint ventures, similar to Konkan Railways. It is more essential to make positive efforts to evolve innovative methods and also efficiency in their resource management to raise the necessary resources.
3. Railways at different stations have been identified with deficient passenger amenities. In order to provide better passenger amenities, a separate plan head should be created under demand 16 to deal with the infrastructural facilities at all stations.
4. The Standing Committee of Parliament may be set up without in any way affecting the functioning of the existing Informal Consultative Committees for the Zonal Railways for effecting scrutiny of projects relating to infrastructural needs, passenger amenities, safety measures, employees' welfare measures etc.
5. The Railway Board and the Zonal Railways should review the existing training arrangements in the light of requirements and rationalize the training facilities where necessary.
6. The Brown System of Discipline prevailing in the Canadian Pacific Railways may be adopted by the Railways with suitable modifications in the light of

conditions in India and subject to the observance of the prescribed procedures regarding disciplinary cases.

7. A major thrust to improve the passenger amenities at the stations and at trains is needed.
8. The Roll-on-Roll-off (RORO) packages which had been experimented on the Konkan Railway are to be extended to other circuits in addition to Ahmedabad-Nabha and Chennai-Kolkata circuits which is already put in. With a view to provide better passenger amenities, the outlay in the budget may be enhanced.
9. It is also imperative for the South Central Railway to practice "bench-marketing" in order to sharpen its marketing strategy.
10. The Passenger Reservation System (PRS) may be provided to many more locations.
11. South Central Railway has a large human resources base. There is need to further enhance their skills by using modern tools and techniques of the 21st century along with modern management concepts. Specifically, this calls for 'enablement process' for railway employees. The main planks of this process are communication, training, empowerment and motivation. This package of C, T, E and M will lead employee enablement. Our enquiry has shown that most of the railway employees are ineffective due to the lack of this enablement package. It is in this context, employee enablement assumes significance.

The best way to develop this package is to use Kaizen approach, which links the human resources strategy to the business strategy. Our enquiry has shown that in railways, the people are perceived as 'wasted resource'. It is essential part of the Railway Management to prevent this waste of human resources, encourage the development of people and set up new, less hierarchical structures to allow people to grow. Kaizen (Japanese invention of constant improvement) focuses on rethinking and a major part of this rethinking involves the following issues at the heart of human resources strategy: (a) how to motivate people; (b) how to reward people; (c) how to educate people; and (d) how to develop people. A business strategy can only be achieved if the people responsible for delivering it are committed to it and trained to perform well. We strongly recommend that the South Central Railways adopt the Kaizen strategy for developing their employees as 'winning employees' by concentrating on the following six critical areas:

(*i*) A recruitment and selection policy that involves all employees.
(*ii*) An induction programme that involves corporate, departmental, team and individual members.
(*iii*) An on-going education and development programme that encourages all employees to become multi-skilled and helps them to reach their full potential.
(*iv*) An appraisal system that develops people and increases co-operation between them.
(*v*) A reward system that is motivating and non-divisive.
(*vi*) A never-ending programme of continuous improvement which improves every area of work and involves everyone.

The South Central Railway should consider this approach to manage its large human resources base.

Recommendations at the Micro-level

Based on our research investigation and personal enquiry notes, we give below the micro-level recommendations:

1. The South Central Railway should adopt the Marketing Concept, the main thrust of which is market-orientation rather than merely service-orientation. In effect, the South Central Railway should become customer-focused organization.
2. The core of the strategic marketing plan of South Central Railway should be the creation of 'legendary rail-users' service.

The management of intangibles of rail-users service by the South Central Railway assumes much significance in view of the new rail-users' challenges—choices are greater, expectations are higher, people want more for less, they want it yesterday and the competition is getting cleverer (For example the State Road Transport Corporations Introduce Pushpak and other Ultra Deluxe services with a lot of incentives like frequent flyers of road transport service which aim at owing the users).

We give below some significant foci of attention in the matter of rail-user's service of South Central Railway

(*a*) Appreciate the rail-users as individuals.
(*b*) Develop more intimate relationships.
(*c*) Put the human touch in the marketing operations.

The full-fledged marketing department of South Central Railway should be entrusted with the application of Kaizen strategies of 'customer care' to rail-users' service. The following are the winning strategies:

(*a*) *Focus on rail-users*: South Central Railway should take a long-term focus on rail-users' needs. It is absolutely paramount in South Central Railway that all activities must lead inexorably to greater delight of the rail-users.
(*b*) *Make improvements continuously*: Searching for ways to improve rail-users' care does not stop once an improvement has been implemented.
(*c*) *All railways have problems*: South Central Railway is no exception, but by fostering an appropriately supportive, constructive, non-confrontational and non-recriminatory culture, it becomes possible for South Central Railway to bring its problems into the open.
(*d*) *Promote openness*: There should be less functional compartmentalization or ring fencing in South Central Railway. Working areas should be open-plan, only the most senior executives should have individual offices, usual symbols of rank or status should be rarely seen, and communality should be favored.
(*e*) *Create work teams*: Each employee in South Central Railway should belong to a work team managed by a team leader. In addition, an employee should be associated with a year group (consisting of contemporaries who joined South Central Railway at the same time), plus one or more adhoc or standing quality circles and cross-functional teams. This arrangement will lead to networking.
(*f*) *Manage through cross-functional teams*: No individual employee or single-function department will necessarily have all the skills or best ideas to efficiently manage the marketing operations. The skill in resourcing a cross-functional team, therefore, is to cast the net. This is called

'simultaneous engineering'. For example, it is desirable to include in a team representatives from personnel, training, engineering, marketing and finance in designing/redesigning new railway services.

(*g*) *Nurture right relationship process among employees (internal customers)*: If the management processes are sound and relationships are designed to nurture employee fulfillment, then the rail-users' delight can be ensured.

(*h*) *Develop self-discipline*: Employees' self-discipline is the hall-mark of Kaizen's marketing approach. Employees are internal customers.

As a corollary to the above recommendations, we strongly recommend that South Central Railway should, over a period of time, become rail users-focused organization.

The South Central Railway should aim at 'customerising' itself through the following steps:

(*a*) Realign organizational (South Central Railway) roles and resources around processes (not on functions) that deliver value to rail-users.

(*b*) Introduce rail-users' value by integrating all processes.

(*c*) Integrate the support functions (for e.g. vending, catering, selling of publications etc., at railway platforms) into high-performance core processes.

(*d*) Restructure the organization (South Central Railway) around teams within and across processes.

(*e*) Transform management roles from command-and-control to process leadership.

(*f*) Recast assessment systems to evaluate rail-users driven performance.

(*g*) Promote multiple competencies by encouraging creativity.

(*h*) Inform every employee: All key personnel of marketing department should be fully informed about the Railways because right attitude and behaviour depend on a complete understanding and acceptance of the mission, vision, culture, values, plans and management practices of South Central Railway.

(*i*) Enable every employee in the marketing strategy: Through multi-skill training, decision-making responsibility, access to data sources and budgets, feedback and reward, the marketing staff will be empowered to materially influence their own and the affairs of the South Central Railway.

The South Central Railway should focus more on management of service quality. In today's service business context, quality of service has become the top-most priority for every service company including Railways. Quality perception in Railways includes (a) Meeting the precise requirements of rail-users, (b) Fair exchange of price of value, (c) Value perceived by the rail-users, (d) Meeting the rail-users' expectations, (e) Promptness and timely service delivery, (f) Adequate passenger facilitation and amenities and (g) Effective management of customer complaints. What is required is railusers-driven quality in South Central Railway. How to create railusers-driven quality? The steps are: (a) Identify what is required by the rail-users, (b) Design the services that responds to rail-users' needs, (c) Develop a process capable to produce the designed service, (d) Measure the satisfaction of rail-users', (e) Improve the service quality continuously and (f) Manage the quality through an effective service quality management system.

The South Central Railway should establish "Relationship Marketing Cell" at its headquarters to monitor effectively 'Customer Relationship Management' (CRM) in respect of manufacturers, traders and suppliers (business marketers) who use its goods-traffic service for transportation of their goods (both perishable and non-perishable) to different destinations. The overall purpose of CRM is to improve marketing productivity and enhance mutual value for the parties involved in the relationship. There are three types of CRM programmes:

(*a*) Continuity marketing which has a focus on Business-to-Business marketing, b) One-to-one marketing which has a focus on personalization, c) Co-marketing which has a focus on affinity, logistics and strategic partnering.

(*b*) It should be reiterated that an effective relationship marketing system is possible only when South Central Railway becomes customer-minded, develops appropriate marketing personnel and re-engineers its current marketing operations.

To conclude, our analysis calls for nothing less than 'strategizing' the 'marketing derby' by South Central Railway. What is needed is a well-thought out, well-organized, and well-documented strategic marketing plan with well-conceived and well-articulated marketing vision and mission for the South Central Railway. Our recommendations will serve as a 'gateway' for their task and supplies enough inputs for the development of strategic marketing plan. It is our firm belief and conviction that the above recommendations (both at macro-level and micro-level), if they are not pigeonholed, will go a long way in enhancing the effectivity and efficiency of marketing operations of South Central Railway.

Future Directions of the Research

Owing to time and resource constraints, the following research issues are kept out of our main research investigation:

1. Customer Tracking Research in South Central Railway.
2. Price-Bundling of services in South Central Railway.
3. An In-depth Analysis of Training programmes for South Central Railway employees.
4. Segmentation and Positioning of service in South Central Railway.
5. Service Market Leadership studies in South Central Railway.
6. Strategic Marketing Communications in South Central Railway.
7. Internet Marketing and High-tech marketing at South Central Railway.
8. Application of Value-chain to the operations of South Central Railway.
9. Application of Business Process Reengineering (BPR) to the operations of South Central Railway (The value-chain and BPR concepts have now acquired general perspectives and are applicable to service undertakings also).
10. Image Marketing at South Central Railway.

Perhaps the line of thinking on which our research investigation is based may give scope for further research or quest to gain insights, develop concepts and create application tools in the afore-said fertile areas of research.

REFERENCES

1. Amba Prasad, *"Indian Railways"*—A Study of Public Utility Administration, Asia Publishing House, Bombay, 1960.
2. Bateson, John E.G., *"Managing Services Marketing"*, Dryden Press, Chicago, 1996.
3. Berry Leonardo L. and A. Parasuraman, *"Marketing Services Competing through Quality"*, Free Press Publication, 1994.
4. Bidhi Chand, *"Marketing of Services"*, Rawat Publications, Jaipur and New Delhi, 1994.
5. Bitner Mary Jo and Valarie A. Zeithami, *"Services Marketing"* Mc.Graw Hill Publication, Second International Edition, 1994.
6. Bloom P.N. and Kotler Philip, *"Marketing Professional Services"*, Prentice Hall, Englewood Cliffs, 1973.
7. Chowdhary S.K., *"Lectures on Transport"*, Lyall Book Dept., Ludhiana, 1967.
8. Christopher H. Lovelock, *"Services Product Plus: How Product+Service=Competitive Advantage"*, Third Edition, Prentice Hall International Editions, 1996.
9. Christopher M. Payne and Baltantyne D., *"Customer Services, Quality and Marketing Together"*, Butterworth-Heinemann, Oxford. 1996.
10. Christopher M. Lovelock, *"Managing Services: Marketing Operations and Human Resources"*, 1996.
11. South Central Railway General Manager's Annual Report 1998-99.
12. Ministry of Railways, Indian Railways Yearbook 1989-90 to 1999-2000.
13. Campbell J.P. *et al.*, *"Managerial Behaviour Performance and Effectiveness"*, New York: McGraw Hill, 1970.
14. Congram, C.A. and Friedman, M.L., *"The Service Industries"*, American Marketing Association, New York.
15. Cowell Donald, *"The Marketing of Services"*, London: Heinemann, 1984.
16. Davidow, William H. and Bro Uttal, *"Total Customer Service"*, Harper-Cooling Publications, 1999.
17. Edwin H. Lewis, *"Marketing Channels Structure and Strategy"*, Me Graw Hill Book Company, New York, 1968.
18. Eliot Jones, *"Principles of Transport"*, Mc Millan & Company, New York, 1927.
19. George S. Day, *"Market Driven Strategy"*, New York: The Free Press, 1990.
20. Gupta J.P., *"Indian Railway—Finance Since 1947-1960"*, Ph.D. Thesis, Aligarh Muslim University, Aligarh, 1968.

21. Holloway, Charles A., "*Decision-making Under Uncertainty—Models and Choices*", Englewood Cliffs, NJ: Prentice Hall, 1979.
22. Jagjit Singh, "*The Story of our Railways*", National Book Trust of India, New Delhi, 1989.
23. James L. Heskett, "*Managing in the Service Economy*", Boston: Harvard Business School Press, 1984, 1990.
24. Joseph Pine, II, "*Mass Customization—The New Frontiers in Business Competition*", Boston: Harvard Business School Press, 1993.
25. Kosteck M.M. (ed.), "*Marketing Strategies for Services*", Oxford: Pergmon Press, 1994.
26. Krishna Mohan V., "*Services Marketing—A Study of Marketing Operations of Indian Railways*", Ph.D. Thesis, Andhra University, Waltam, 1992.

63

Customer Service Excellence

The Six Sigma Way

R. RENGANATHAN*

Introduction

Every business is a service business;
You are not a chemical company;
You are a chemical services business.

—Philip Kotler

General Electric one of the first top successfully implement six sigma, defines it as "highly disciplined process that helps us focus on developing and delivering near-perfect products and services."

Six Sigma, the most rigorous of all quality techniques, was born at Motorola in 1987. The once-dominant maker of consumer electronics was losing market share at the hands of Japanese producers. It needed away to identify both product defects and opportunities to fix them.

The solution lay in the concept of "sigma"—the degree of deviation from optimal performance. A score of One Sigma means a company is committing more than 690,000 defects per million "opportunities"—either physical products or services. Even a 99-per cent success rate, excellent at first glance, translates into less than a Four Sigma. That's around 9,000 failures per million.

The pinnacle of achievement, Six Sigma, involves no more than 3.4 defects per million. Having identified where errors are occurring, a company then looks to improvements within a given

* Senior Lecturer, School of Management, SASTRA Deemed University, Tirumalaisamudram, Thanjavur (T.N.).

area. Usually black belts or green belts, employees who have undergone intensive training in Six Sigma techniques, and act as team leaders on various projects, head the effort up. Six Sigma has many similarities with its immediate predecessor, Total Quality Management (TQM), says Morgan Swink, associate professor of supply-chain management at Michigan State University.

In the field of marketing four 4ps represent the seller's perspective and from buyer's perspective, each marketing tool is defined to deliver a customer benefit. Seller's 4ps correspond to customers 4 'cs are customer solution, customer cost, customer convenience, and customer communication.

Most of the companies are going for new customers rather than maintaining existing customer, called customer retention, and customer attractiveness. Some companies have always cared passionately about customer loyalty and retention. The key to customer retention is customer satisfaction. Building relationship with customer is very important. In CRM, we have partnership marketing, the company works continuously with customer to discover ways to perform better. Nowadays satisfying the customer is not alone sufficient, but customer delight that is bringing customer ecstasy. If the company wants to survive in the current liberalized scenario they have to deliver good quality products and build good corporate image to attract new and retain existing customers. In service industry, service provider's goal is to have "Zero customer defection".

As far as service industries are concerned, in order to satisfy the external customers, it is the duty of the management of the service industry to nurture and nourish the internal customers, service provider, since they are the torchbearer, to achieve the goal of the organization. In service industry, the role of front Office staff is important for some industries and back office staff for some other service industry.

"Six Sigma recognizes the dynamic nature of the supplier-customer relationship. On the service side, at least, a company's sigma rating is never permanently fixed; the bar is always being raised. Says Swink: "Quality has no meaning beyond that of the customer." Service industries are having a harder time meeting quality expectations because they have not applied to techniques for as long as the manufacturing sector. West adds, Unlike their counterparts on the production side, most service companies have not been goaded into action by foreign competition. In addition, they have had a harder time attracting quality employees. Finally, their activities are notoriously hard to measure, compared with a physical product rolling off the assembly line.

Quality

Customer-Driven Definitions of Quality

Quality has multiple dimensions in the mind of the customer, and one or more following definitions may apply any one time.

- Conformance to Specifications
- Value
- Fitness for Use
- Support
- Psycological Impressions

Managing Service Quality

A service firm may win by delivering consistently higher quality service than competitions and exceeding customers' expectations. These expectations are formed by their past experiences, word of mouth, and advertising. After receiving the service customers compare the perceived service with the expected service. If the perceived service meets of exceeds their expectations, they are apt use the provider again.

Parasuraman, Zeithaml, and Berry formulated a service-quality model that highlights the main requirements for delivering high service quality. This model identifies five gaps that cause unsuccessful delivery.

1. Gap between consumer expectation and management perception.
2. Gap between management perception and service quality specification.
3. Gap between service-quality specifications and service delivery.
4. Gap between service delivery and external communication.
5. Gap between perceived service and expected service.

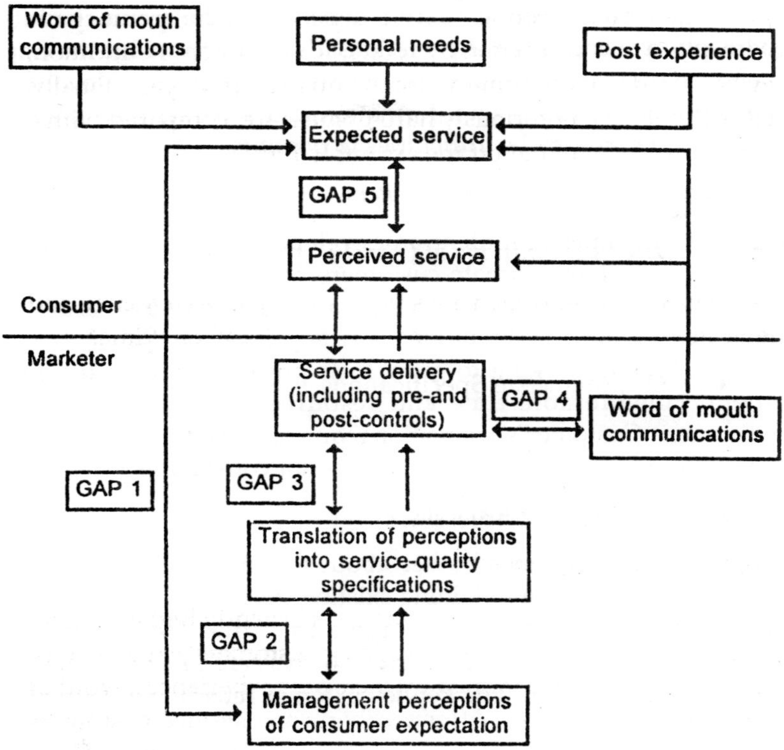

Fig. 1: Service-Quality Model.

Quality as a Competitive Weapon

Attaining quality in all areas of business is different task. To make things even more difficult, consumers change their perceptions of quality. For instance changes in lifestyles and economic conditions have drastically altered consumer perceptions of automobile quality. When the oil crisis hit in the mid-1970's consumer performances shifted from power and styling to fuel economy. To consumer's preferences in the 1980's for quality of design and performance has been added a demand for greater safety in the 1990's and 2000's. By failing identify these trends and respond to them quickly in the 1970's and 1980's, U.S. automakers lost opportunities to maintain or increase their market shares relative to foreign competition. Today U.S. automakers are more aware that the customers has a choice and are doing a better job of anticipating customer preferences.

In general a business success depends on the accuracy of its perception of consumer expectations it's ability to bridge the Gap between those expectations and operating capabilities. However, perceptions are based on information and accurate measures of Service quality may be difficulties to quantity.

Attracting and Retaining Customers

Many Companies are intent an developing stronger bonds and loyalty with their ultimate customers. In part many companies took their customers for granted today's customers are harder to please.

Companies seeking to grow their profits and sales have so spend considerable time and resources searching for new customers. Customer's acquisition requires substantial skill in lead generation lead qualification and account conversion.

The Need for Customer Retention

Most of the companies bother about the art of attracting new customers rather than retaining existing customers. Traditionally emphasis has been on making sales rather than building relationship some companies have always cared about customer loyalty and retention. The key to customer retention is customer satisfaction.

Customer-Relationship Building

There are five levels in customer relationship building that is Basic Marketing, Accountable Marketing, Proactive Marketing and Partnership Marketing.

Partnership Marketing, the company works continuously with the customer of discover of perform better, Technology is the very important factor in Today's relationship Marketing.

What specific marketing tools can a company use to develop stronger customer bonding and satisfaction Berry and Parsuraman have distinguished three value building approaches adding financial benefits adding social benefits and adding structural ties.

What is Six Sigma? and Why it has Created such Hype?

Six Sigma at many organizations simply means a measure of quality that strives for near perfection. Six Sigma is a disciplined, data-driven approach and methodology for eliminating defects (driving towards six standard deviations between the mean and the nearest specification limit) in any process—from manufacturing to transactional and from product to service.

The statistical representation of Six Sigma describes quantitatively how a process is performing. To achieve Six Sigma, a process must not procdure more than 3.4 defects per million opportunities. A Six Sigma defect is defined as anything outside of customer specifications. A Six Sigma defect is defined as anything outside of customer specifications. A Six Sigma opportunity is then the total quantity of chances for a defect. Process sigma can easily be calculated using a Six Sigma calculator.

The fundamental objective of the Six Sigma methodology is the implementation of a measurement-based strategy that focuses on process improvement and variation reduction through the application of Six Sigma improvement projects. This is accomplished through the use of two Six Sigma sub-methodology: DMAIC and DMADV. The Six Sigma DMAIC process (define, measure, analyze, improve, control) is an improvement system for existing processes falling below specification and looking for incremental improvement. The Six Sigma DMADV process (define, measure, analyze, design, verify) is an improvement system used to develop new processes or products at Six Sigma quality levels. It can also be employed if a current process requires more than just incremental improvement. Both Six Sigma processes are executed by Six Sigma Green Belts and Six Sigma Black Belts, and are overseen by Six Sigma Master Black Belts.

According to the Six Sigma Academy, Black Belts save companies approximately $230,000 per project and can complete four to 6 projects per year. General Electric, one of the most successful companies implementing Six Sigma, has estimated benefits on the order of $ 10 billion during the first five years of implementation. GE first began Six Sigma in 1995 after Motorola and Allied Signal blazed the Six Sigma trail. Since then, thousands of companies around the world have discovered the far reaching benefits of Six Sigma.

Many frameworks exist for implementing the Six Sigma methodology. Six Sigma Consultants all over the world have developed proprietary methodologies for implementing Six Sigma quality, based on the similar change management philosophies and applications of tools.

The Six Sigma process

The Six Sigma breakthrough strategy involves a "define-measure-analyse-improve-control" (DMAIC) methodology. The strategy takes organisations key business processes through five phases to deliver breakthrough in performance:

1. *Phase I—Define*: This involves defining the scope and goals of the improvement project in terms of customer requirements and the process that delivers these requirements. The process to be improved is defined in terms of its inputs, outputs, controls and resources.
2. *Phase 2—Measure*: This involves measuring the current process performance—input, output and process-and calculating the sigma metric for both short and longer-term process capability.
3. *Phase 3—Analyse*: The analyse phase involves identifying the gap between the current and desired performance, prioritizing problems and identifying root causes of problems. Benchmarking the process outputs, products or services, against recognised benchmark standards of performance may also be carried out. Depending upon the performance gap found, a decision will be made as to whether the existing process can be improved or whether it should be redesigned.
4. *Phase 4—Improve*: This phase involves generating the improvement solutions to fix the problems and prevent them from recurring so that the required financial and other performance goals are met. Creativity will be required to find new ways to do things to the quality, cost and time standards required by the performance improvement goals.
5. *Phase 5—Control*: This phase involves implementing the improved process in a way that "holds the gains". Standards of operation will be documented in systems such as ISO 9000 and standards of performance will be established using techniques such as statistical process control (SPC). After a "running-in" period, the process capability is calculated again to establish whether the performance gains are being sustained. The cycle is repeated, if further performance shortfalls are identified.

Building a Six Sigma Culture and Infrastructure

A key feature of a successful Six Sigma culture is the creation of an infrastructure that supports and resources performance improvement. Six Sigma programmes involve major investment and must deliver bottom-line results. There are ten key features that characterise a successful Six Sigma culture:

1. Committed Leadership

The Six Sigma approach is essentially about achieving business transformation and not unsurprisingly, it requires specific leadership qualities to make it happen. Committed leaders with the clarity of purpose and drive to achieve breakthroughs in performance are a vital element in all Six Sigma programmes. The transformational leader in the Six Sigma approach is often described as having edge. Frequently cited examples include Jack Welch (GE), Larry Bossidy (Allied Signal) and Bob Galvin (Motorola). The commitment to Six Sigma is evident through their behaviour, drive, energy and commitment to providing the necessary resources. It would be unwise to assume that this rather "hard" model of leadership represents some unified theory of leadership. Leadership research is littered with theories—trial theories, behavioural theories, situational/contingency theories. Transformational leaders must certainly that "edge" to make tough strategic decisions but other qualities, including a genuine concern for the people being "transformed", must play a key role in delivering sustained success.

2. Strategic Alignment

Six Sigma aims to achieve strategic breakthroughs in performance and organisations that have successfully embraced the approach ensure that the approach supports the organisations strategic objectives and key performance measures and is well integrated throughout the organisation such as GE and Allied Signal. Six Sigma is being used in all areas of the business to align resources to solve critical business problems and deliver the strategic objectives. It is being used in product development, R&D, order fulfilment, back-office operations, etc. to deliver end-to-end process improvement.

3. A Cadre of Change Leaders

Six Sigma is an intense approach to improvement and it requires the full mobilisation of a trained and dedicated cadre of practitioners. In Six Sigma, these are known as "black belts" and "master black belts. Black belt training provides the necessary knowledge and technical capability to lead the attack on delivering breakthrough in performance. The typical curriculum for black belts included four weeks of training in quality tools, delivered just in time as a team begins its improvement project. Black belts help to identify opportunities, transfer knowledge on improvement methodologies, act as mentors and coaches and champion the use of Six Sigma tools and strategies.

Massive investment in black belt training is a key feature in all Six Sigma programmes. Harry and Schroeder suggest that an organisation needs one black belt for every $10M of revenue. Clearly this can scale up into galactic levels of black belts! It's claimed that the average black belt project will save a company $175M.

4. Customer and Market Focus

A systematic approach to gathering customer and market intelligence is essential if Six Sigma efforts are to achieve breakthroughs in performance. It is vital to keep in touch with existing customers, track their satisfaction and changing needs as well keeping an eye on how the market is developing. Six Sigma is not just about "right first time" it's also about ensuring that organisations do the right thing and anticipates change. Gathering customer and market data, analysing and acting on it, is a key element in all Six Sigma programmes.

5. Bottom-line Benefits

A focus on delivering real savings and/or additional revenue is a vital element in Six Sigma. This focus is used to ensure that projects are selected on the basis of maximising their monetary return and customer satisfaction, i.e., improvement based on removing cost whilst retaining or improving capability. The portfolio of improvement projects should include a mix of projects capable of delivering quick wins as well as larger longer-term projects.

Companies such as ABB, Allied Signal and GE claim massive savings from their Six Sigma programmes—ABB $898 savings each year for two years—Allied Signal $1.2M in direct costs since 1994—GE gross annual benefit of $6.6B or 5.5% of sales. There is some debate about these claims and the assumptions behind them—why isn't this performance always realised in share performance etc. However, the focus on bottom-line results does bring hard strategic focus.

6. Process Approach

Processes are the engines that deliver every organisation's value proposition. The focus of Six Sigma is on understanding processes and reducing variability. Process understanding requires processes to be mapped, their operation fully understood and their capability to deliver customer requirements fully quantified—i.e., the concept of process capability. Process sigma is based on the ability of the organisations processes to deliver customer requirements. Closing the capability gap between what the customers require and what the organisation's processes produce is at the heart of Six Sigma.

7. Obsession with Measurement

Management and measurement are inseparably intertwined in Six Sigma programmes—you cannot manage what you cannot measure is the accepted philosophy. Six Sigma organisations collect data from all their processes, main value chain and support, analyse and use the data to drive improvement throughout the organisation. They distinguish themselves from "normal" organisations in the range of data collected, the rigour in which it is analysed and used. Great emphasis is placed on understanding cause and effect. Fact-based decision-making is the norm.

8. Continuous Innovation

Six Sigma used conventional quality tools but it encourages out of the box thinking. Breakthroughs in performance are seldom achieved using common sense or conventional thinking. Continually challenging how things are done, assumption busting and innovative thinking are essential elements in Six Sigma. New questions have to be posed and new solutions developed to deliver breakthrough strategies.

9. Organisational Learning

Giving employees access to knowledge and information systems encourages organisational learning. Personal development and learning is also a key feature. In organisations such as GE, managers and aspiring managers are required to complete the equivalent of black belt training as part of the qualification process for promotion. GE has produced a cadre of more than 70,000 part-time improvement team leaders. This sends out a powerful message about GE's long-term commitment.

10. Continuous Reinforcement

Recognising and rewarding leaders and improvement team's contribution to improvement continually reinforce Six Sigma programmes. Incentive programmes must be designed to support Six Sigma and drive the desired behaviours. Organisations such as GE include competency and experience in Six Sigma as part of the appraisal process for all staff, including executives.

Excellence and Six Sigma

Organisations in the thick of excellence initiatives may see other initiatives such as Six Sigma as just one initiative too many! It's a big enough challenge putting to bed all those areas for improvement from the last self-assessment. However, business excellence and Six Sigma are not in competition, they are complimentary. The Six Sigma breakthrough strategy is an effective approach to putting to bed all those areas for improvement.

Excellence models such as the EFQM Excellence Model are non-prescriptive frameworks that define the key factors in achieving excellence. Their non-prescriptive design is usually cited as a strength, but the practitioner could be forgiven for asking for more best-practice advice. Six Sigma defines a particular approach to achieving breakthrough performance and as such is a much more prescriptive "how to" road map. If the Six Sigma approach is to be an effective vehicle for delivering excellence as defined by the EFQM Excellence Model, we would at least expect that the ten success characteristics of Six Sigma map fully onto the Excellence Model. This it clearly does and the relationship between Six Sigma and the Excellence Model is shown in Figure 2.

Six Sigma maps onto all the enabler criteria of the Excellence Model. The Excellence Model provides a more complete blueprint for excellence. The results linkage is also strong. Bottom-line focus clearly addresses the key performance outcomes. Key performance indicators such as supplier and partner results are addressed via the process approach. The successful implementation of Six Sigma can only be achieved if suppliers are also committed to Six Sigma performance targets. Society results do not feature strongly in the Six Sigma literature but this is not surprising. Six Sigma is about the immediate deliverables at the sharp end of the customer-process interface. Its omission is more a matter of relevance at this level and does not imply that organisations following the Six Sigma route are oblivious to their impact on society.

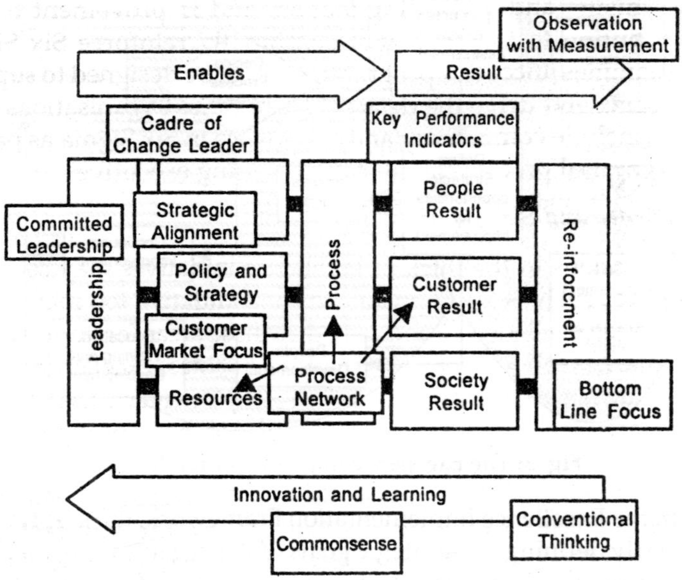

Fig. 2: The Relationship beween Six Sigma and the EFQM Excellence Model.

However, whilst it is re-assuring to understand that Six Sigma and Excellence are entirely consistent, it is more important to understand how Six Sigma and the Excellence Model can be used to deliver excellent results for an organisation.

In any major change programme there are three fundamental questions to answer:

- Where are we now and how did we get here?
- What are we heading?
- What future route must we take?

These questions help us understand the complimentary role of the Excellence Model and Six Sigma. Their relationship is illustrated in, Figure 3, the Excellence Implementation Frame.

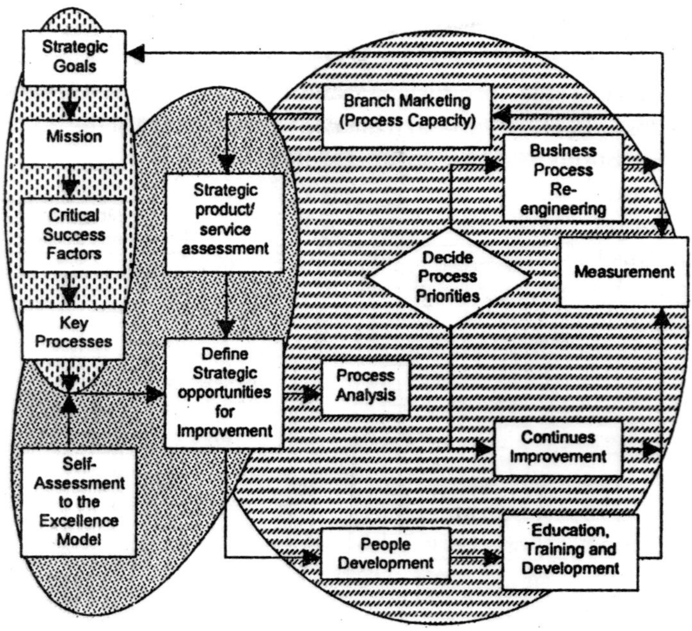

Fig. 3: The Excellence Implementation Model

In the Excellence Implementation Framework, the emphasis is on clearly defining the strategic goals of the organisation, its goals and critical success factors and key processes to define the strategic direction. Strategic baselining involves excellence assessments and product/service assessments to assess the current position. A gap analysis identifies the strategic improvement opportunities, which in turn lead into the process analysis phase. This is where the Six Sigma breakthrough strategy comes into play, with its emphasis on improving process capability to deliver bottom-line benefits.

Conclusions

While create organization like GE have used Six Sigma to produce dramatic improvements in bottom line it is important to understand what other factors along with Six Sigma contributed to the success of these organizations. At GE it was definitely the "Jack Welch Factor". In the least, Six Sigma serves a fresh reminder to all organizations on the need to produce "Zero defect" products and services. As opinion stands divided on the effectives and success of Six Sigma, it is important for organizations to carry out a thorough cost-benefits analysis before jumping on to the Six Sigma band wagon. Atleast in the time context, there are simpler and cost-effective approaches towards defect reduction.

Six Sigma is not a new technique, its roots can be found in TQM and SPC, but it is more than TQM re-budged. With the TQM philosophy, most practitioners promised long-term benefits, 5-10 years, as the programmes began to change hearts and minds. Six Sigma by contrast is about delivering benefits now and is distinguished from TQM by the intensity of the intervention and the pace of change. Like all successful major change programmes, Six Sigma requires very strong leadership from the top. Excellence approaches such as the EFQM Excellence Model and Six Sigma are complimentary vehicles for achieving better organisational performance. The Excellence Model plays a key role in the base lining phase of strategic improvement, whilst the Six Sigma breakthrough strategy is the delivery vehicle for achieving excellence. Excellence practitioners should welcome the opportunities that Six Sigma offers to deliver breakthroughs in performance of their organizations.

APPENDIX 1
An Explanation of the Six Sigma Concept

Figure illustrates the Six Sigma scenario. The output from most processes follows a normal distribution as shown by curve A in Figure 4. In the short term a process naturally centered at T, will have a natural spread of plus or minus three-sigma, a where 'represents the short-term standard deviation. In the Six Sigma case, this process variation is only half the width of the design tolerances for the process i.e., the difference between the upper specification limit (USL) and lower specification limit (LSL). 99.9973% of the process output is contained by this natural spread. Clearly a process running at T is highly capable of meeting the design specifications—only 0.002 parts per million will be outside these specifications.

Controlling process in the longer-term so that they remain on target can prove difficult in many practical situations. A typical process is likely to deviate from its natural centring position by upto one and half standard deviations. This is illustrated by a process shift to position B in Figure 1. Applying this principle, one can calculate the longer-term capability of the process based on the initial short-term variation, σst. The longer-term capability is estimated from $6.0\ \sigma_{st} - 1.5\ \sigma_{st} = 4.5\ \sigma_{st}$, this equates to 3.4 parts per million outside the design specifications. The statistical basis of Six Sigma, in particular the 1.5 sigma shift, is not without its critics but this is outside the scope of this paper. Suffice to say the issue of process shifts and process capability is a practical problem in many industries; Six Sigma offers one solution.

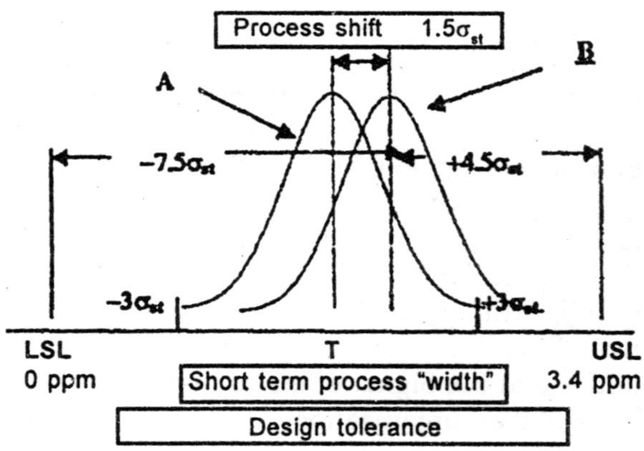

Fig. 4: Six Sigma Performence.

Further details of sigma capacity is shown below in Table 1.

Table 1: Sigma Capability

Sigma	*Parts per Million Out of Specification*	*% Out of Specification*	*Comparative Position*
6	3.4	0.00034	World Class
5	233	0.0233	Industry best in class
4	6,210	0.621	Industry average
3	66,807	6.6807	Lagging industry standards
2	308,537	30.8537	Non-competitive
1	690,000	69	Out of business

Sigma capability applies equally to manufacturing, service and support process.

64

Design and Development of Generic Strategic Mix for Non-profit Organizations in Developing Societies

UMESH DHYANI*

Introduction

There has been dramatic change in the education sector in India. The 1990's saw an important development in the field of higher education in India. Private educational institutions of higher learning in this period outgrew the government colleges. The public budgets for higher education shrank drastically during 1990's. This has resulted in the fall of quality education. Government's inability to regulate private institutions is becoming increasingly obvious. A private university bill was introduced in the upper house of Parliament in August 1995, with a view to providing for the establishment of self-financing universities. The bill is still pending in Parliament, it is widely felt, not because the government was not keen on the privatization of higher education in India, but because the private sector was not happy with several clauses in the bill. For example, the bill requires the formation of a permanent endowment fund of Rs. 10 crore (about U.S. $ 2 million), provision of full scholarships to 30 per cent of the students, and for government monitoring and regulation of the system. These last two provisions become necessary, in view of the earlier experiences with private colleges. Many private colleges started earlier with partial government support are now either fully financed by the government or were completely taken over by

* Lecturer, Humanistic Studies Group, BITS PILANI (Haryana).

the government, essentially due to illegal and unethical practices at the private colleges. The government, through the Prime Minister's Council on Trade and Industry, appointed a committee headed by two noted private-sector industrialists, Mukesh Ambani and Kumarmangalam Birla, to suggest needed reforms in the education sector, along with other sectors. The committee's report, submitted in 2001, noted the critical importance of the role of the state in the development of education, including higher education, in several developed countries of the world. However, it strongly suggested that government should leave higher education altogether to the private sector and confine itself to elementary and secondary education.

Further, the report urged passage of the private university bill and also suggested that the user pay principle be strictly enforced in higher education, supplementary by loans and grants to economically and socially backward sections of society. The committee did not, however, feel the need to provide any rationale for its suggestions.

Competitive

The pace of change in educational institutions has fastened. The traditional state and central universities have failed to fulfill the ever-growing needs and aspiration of the students and the market. Many of the government supported and aided colleges and universities in the country have failed to address the ever-growing change in the curricula and thus fulfill the market needs. Another closely related development in India relates to the internationalization of higher education. Under the guise of globalised economic policies and the internationalization of higher education, a number of changes have been instituted. First, foreign universities and institutions have been allowed to come into India and establish franchise centers in the country—offering degrees or diplomas, which are not necessarily recognized by The parent universities in their own countries. Second, Indian institutions of higher education have been permitted to start similar centers in other countries. In the absence of a clear policy, both phenomena seems to be growing in size, more often than not creating problems as second and third—rate private universities are frequently the ones getting involved in this quick money-making scheme. As the competition in the educational sector grows, educational institutions would have to evolve new strategies not only to survive but also to be competitive. This paper presents a mode of thought for design and development of a generic customer service strategic mix for educational institution in the non-profit sector. To meet this challenge in developing societies here resources are scarce and expectations of the consumer high institution must develop a service attitude, Adrian Pyne has outlined the relevance of service strategy, "an appropriate service package can be developed which aims at offering benefits of greater value to customers than those of competing proudest".[2]

Educational Programmes

At the core of all educational institutions is the market friendly nature of educational programmes it offers and establishment of a distinctively positive identity of the educational institutions in the minds of the consumers. The educational programmes, (discipline courses, infrastructure facilities, classrooms, library computer center, lecture facilities), recreational programmes (sports facilities and clubs, film services, cultural societies etc.), career plans (career counseling, placement services, course advisors). An important tangible factor is facilities planning. Educational facilities planning has become increasingly sophisticated and focused. Educational institutions in developing societies should include the right combination of facilities to support their programmes. The look and feel of facilities of the educational services can affect consumer's attitude and behaviour. Architect Bruce Carmichael believes that, "physical resources play a far more important role in recruiting students and especially retaining students, than is generally recognized. Important role in recruiting students and especially retaining students, than is generally recognized. Young students may not have the vocabulary or developed the sensibility to talk about architecture, horticulture and campus design. But they do have... emotional responses to college campuses and the feel of an admission office, a library, the science laboratories or the art studios'..... a college's building; interiors, furniture, spaces, landscaping and equipment make a statement about that institution. They express what the college or university stands for, cares most about, and how it views the intellectual and aesthetic enterprise".[3]

Cost Effective

Increasing cost of education in developing society is a matter of concern. The customer or student evaluate the value of each institution and select the alternative that will deliver the most value. The student select the best institution that will provide the best blend of educational experience or career outcomes, the faculty or staff members select the job offer that provides the blend of income. The fiscal management of the institutions should be in concurrence with the mission of the institutions and objectives of the society. In developing societies where customers have limited resources pricing is an important variable of the strategic mix. Institutions often operate within tight budgets in developing societies. Cost or fee is an important variable in this ever-fast changing world. A newer technology has enhanced the range of learning and teaching kits. To meet the cost of technological advancement the private educational institutions should develop the very best of cost effective techniques. Some institutions completely ignore or give up the institutions' mission. Fee increased are essential to improve the quality of its educational programmes and infrastructure, but newer methods should be devised to meet the cost. Since the employees and students work in the facility all day the facility should be designed to support them in performing their duties with ease. In addition to their academic programmes, educational institutions have many supporting and auxiliary services. Supporting services are essential to the core educational activities of the institution. Auxiliary services include café, students' mess, and hostels, cooperative stores which are often necessary but which are more independent of the institutions' core services. Institutions often wait until complaints pile up while a competitive institution is constantly on the look out to improve further.

Consumer Responsive

In a competitive environment an educational institution must be more consumer responsive. It needs to develop a plan for institutional change. Institutions must seek to attract, retain and track their customers' expectations, their perceptions. Focusing on enhancing customer satisfaction and customer value is a good place to begin. According to Daniel Seymour, "Develop in a lot of happy, satisfied customers. Whether they are students, parents of students, alumni, professors or industry employers—should be a primary goal of causing quality in higher education"[4]. Customer responsive institutions focus on the customers, striving to see things from the customers' viewpoint and satisfying the customers' needs and concerns. Educational institutions must gather relevant information from the market and implement well-designed and coordinated course structures, which provide what their customers value most in a manner that pleases customers. A progressive institution makes every effort to sense, serve and satisfy the needs and wants of its customers. Once an institution is able to determine how responsive it can be it is able to implement programs to manage responsive relations with its customers.

Public Relations

Educational institutions must develop public relations strategy very effectively. Public relations consists of efforts to obtain favorable interest in the institution and its programmes typically through planting significant news about them in publications, through obtaining favorable unpaid presentation in media or through institutions own activities and events. They need effective communication with their markets and the publics. Developing well educational programmes and services and making them available to target consumers is not enough. An institution must also inform consumers and others about its goals and activities and motivate them to take an interest in the institution. Public relations department of the institute should vigorously pursue the task of forming, maintaining or changing attitudes. Media tools must be effectively used. Public relations office should make news interesting and available to the appropriate media. As Kotler writes, "Publicity has three qualities that make it a worthwhile investment. First, it may have higher veracity than advertising, because it appears as normal news and not sponsored information. Second, it tends to catch people off guard who might otherwise actively avoid sponsored messages. Third, it has high potential for dramatization because news of a noteworthy event arouses attention"[5]. All information-disseminating techniques like news, events, speeches, telephone information services and personal contacts must be effectively used. Public relations office should not only be media friendly only but should be knowledgeable about faculty areas of expertise and be able to recommend appropriate interviews. They must educate the faculty for such interface.

Conclusion

Quality enhancement and increase in the cost need constant vigilance. To be guided by customers, market competition, and public value followed by a research for better ways to deliver the desired satisfaction in the most cost effective manner must be the mission of educational institutions. Educational institutions operate in an environment of constant change. Not only does the external environmental change, but also educational institutions must constantly identify and implement improvements in what they do and how they do it and communicate about it to the market and consumer. A curriculum needs updating and revision. Technological changes are many. Procedures need to be upgraded. In developing societies, where resources are meager and income of consumers limited. Educational institutions need to stretch and develop internal resources to the best for consumer's needs.

REFERENCES

1. Jandhyala B.G. Tilak, *Privatization of Higher Education in India,* International High Education, Fall 2002, http : www.bc.edu/ bc_org/soe/cihe/newsletter/News29/text007.htm)
2. Adrian Payne, *The Essence of Service Marketing,* Prentice Hall of India, New Delhi, 1998, p. 177.
3. Bruce Carmichael, *Using Campus Facilities for Marketing Planning for Higher Education,* 20 (winter, 1991-92), pp. 20, 23.
4. Daniel T. Seymour, *On Q: Causing Quality in Higher Education* (Phonex, AZ: The Oryx Press, 1993), p. 42.
5. Philip Kotler, and *Karen F.A. Fox, Strategic Marketing for Educational Institutions,* 2nd edition, Prentice Hall, 1995, p. 362.

65

System Structure to Computerize: Customer Service of C&F Agents

RAJMOHAN P.* & N. PANCHANATHAM**

Introduction

The role of cargo clearing and forwarding agents (C&F Agents) in the international trade of a country like India is very significant and they deal with the customers like exporters and importers. The efficient customer service from C&F Agents will benefit not only their customers but also the country as a whole, since huge sum of foreign exchange is transacted in the international trade. Most of the C&F Agents in our country operate their service on the places where their exist a scope for export and import activity. Few such places include Chennai, Coimbatore and Tutucorine in the state of Tamil Nadu. The primary job of C&F Agents is to act as a bridge between the international traders and the various officials connected with export and import operations in fulfilling the norms and regulations formulated by the government. In-fact the C&F Agents suggest and help the exporters and importers to understand the benefits provided by the government for various export and import related activities. Their suggestions are based on the existing government regulations and their manual information system. Computerizing their information system will help them in providing valuable suggestions and decisions in timely and accurate manner through well deigned Decision Support System (DSS). Hence, this work concentrates on evolving the system structure for computerizing the activities of C&F agents.

* Lecturer, School of Management, Annamalai University.

** Reader, School of Management, Annamalai University.

Objectives

The following are the objectives taken up for the work:

- To identify the activities associated with C&F operations.
- To formulate the structure for the existing operational system of the C&F Agents.
- To find out the subsystems constituting the operational system of C&F Agents.

Methods

1. Observation of the operational system followed by C&F Agents.
2. Record Search in the operational manuals of C&F Agents
3. Formulating structure through activity matrix of C&F Agents.

Observation of the Operational System followed by C&F Agents

The operational system of the C&F Agents were studied on day to day basis to find out the critical activities constituting C&F operational system.

Record Search in the Operational Manuals of C&F Agents

Record searches in the operational manuals of the C&F Agents were performed to identify management functions of C& F Agents.

Formulating Structure through Activity Matrix of C&F Agents

Based on the activities studied through observation, and management functions identified in record search. The activity matrix has been formulated with activities of C&F Agents constituting the columns of the matrix and management functions of C&F Agents constituting the rows of the matrix.

Results and Discussion

The observations of the operational system of the C&F Agents have revealed that the C&F Agents operate with three major portfolios in their operational system. They are (i) Import related activities, (ii) Export related activities, and (iii) Logistics operations.

Import Related Activities

The import related activities of the C&F Agents first concentrates on clearing the documents related to the import made by the importer with the customs office. After clearing the documents, the imported cargos will be moved from the dock to the place specified by the importer. In case the cargos are required to be moved to a warehouse then, separate procedures are carried out meeting the demands of the warehouse regulations. Banking documents related to the import operations are processed separately with the importer's bank.

Export Related Activities

The export related activities of the C&F Agents first concentrates on clearing the documents related to export made by the exporter with the customs office. After clearing the documents, the cargos will be moved from the exporters place to the dock for shipment process. In case the cargos are required to be moved from the warehouse then separate procedures are carried out meeting the demands of the warehouse regulations. Banking documents related to the export operations are processed separately with the appropriate bank for realizing the export proceeds.

Logistics Operations

This operation is related to the movement of the cargos either imported or exported with the help of container trucks. Some C&F Agents have got their own container trucks to move the cargos, but others have their own arrangements with independent truck operators. The logistics operations are carried out separately for export and import operations by logistics division ofC&F Agents.

Controls in the Operational System of C&F Agents

The controls in the operational system of the C&F Agents can be classified into Operational Control and Management Control. The Management Control for import and export operations are carried out by Import and Export Managers of the agency. The different levels of operational Controls are exerted with customs officer, clearing officer, bank clerk and freight station supervisors for both import and export operations. The management control and operational control associated with logistics operations are exerted by logistics manager.

Structure for C&F Agents Operational System

The structure for the operational system of C&F Agents was

formulated with a matrix consisting of different controls identified in the rows and the activities identified in the columns as shown in the Table 1. Each cell of the matrix represents the subsystem under the operational system of C&F agents.

Table 1: Showing the Structure of Operational System of C&F Agents

	Customs	*Clearing*	*Banking*	*Warehousing*
Operational Control Exports	MCE1	MCE2	MCE3	MCE4
Operational Control Imports	MCI1	MCI2	MCI3	MCI4
Management Control Exports	OCE1	OCE2	OCE3	OCE4
Management Control Imports	OCI1	OCI2	OCI3	OCI4

Conclusion

The subsystems identified through the structure formulated for the operational system of the C&F Agents will help the system designers to carry out network modeling, data flow diagrams and data base design effectively. By analyzing the subsystems thoroughly the efficient system design for computerizing the operational system of C&F Agents can be ensured.

REFERENCES

1. Balagopal (1998), *Export Management,* Mumbai: Himalaya Publishing House.
2. Gordan B. Davis (1984), *Management Information Systems: Conceptual Foundations, Structure and Development,* Singapore: McGraw-Hill Book Co.
3. O' Brein (1999), *Management Information Systems: Managing Information Technology in the Intermet-worked Enterprise.* New Delhi: Tata McGraw-Hill Publishing Company Limited.

66

Emerging Trends in Services of New Generation Private Banks

A.A. ANANTH* & M. SIVASUBRAMANIAN**

Banks are adopting new and cost effective delivery channels. Banking system in India emphasizes the need for automated banking. During the last few years the global scene of banking and finance has changed rapidly, largely due to deregulation and liberalization and coupled with increased use of information technology and launching of new products and services. Products or services have the vital link between the customers and the banks. It also needs to be kept in view that each product has a life cycle which means that products will have to be updated on an going basis to keep them suitable as per customers changing needs. A good product cannot be expected to remain in demand forever as customers requirements keep on changing with the change in economic, social and political changes which are volatile in condition. This leads the banks to introduce many new/products and services to the customers.

The delivery of bank's services to a customer at his office or home by using Electronic Technology can be termed as Electronic Banking. The quality, range and price of these electronic services decide a bank's competitive position in the industry. In simple words banking done electronically is electronic banking. Offering broad functionality for transaction handling, cash management,

* Lecturer, Department of Business Administration, Annamalai University.

** Reader, Management Wing, D.D.E, Annamalai University.

account reporting through the electronic media from the electronic banking strategy.

The technology in banking has been used in four major ways:

- To handle a greatly expanded customer base.
- To reduce substantially the real cost of handling payments.
- To liberate the banks from the traditional constraints on time and place.
- To introduce new products and services.

Customers are becoming increasingly more demanding and are looking for better and more convenient services. Banks today reach their customers through Electronic Funds Transfer System, Electronic Clearing System, Telebanking, Point of Sale Terminal and Electronic Data Interchange.

Benefits of e-Banking

To the Customers

- Anywhere Banking—no matter wherever the customer is in the world, online banking is just a web-site away. Balance enquiry, request for services, issuing instructions etc. from anywhere in the world are possible.
- Any Time Banking—managing funds in real time and most importantly, 24 hours a day, 7 days a week.
- Convenience acts as a tremendous psychological benefit all the time.
- It brings down "costs of banking" to the customer over a period of time.
- Cash withdrawal from any branch or ATM.
- On-line purchase of goods and services including on-line payment for the same.

To the Bank

- Innovative, secure, addresses competition and presents the Bank as technology driven in the banking sector market.
- Reduces customer visits to the branch and thereby human intervention.

- Inter-branch reconciliation is immediate thereby reducing chances of fraud and misappropriation.
- On-line Banking is an effective medium of promotion of various schemes of the bank.
- e-Banking site can act as a revenue earner through promotion activity by consumer corporates.
- Integrated customer data provides the way for individualised and customized services.

To the Business Organisations it Provides

- Paperless transactions
- Faster movement of inventory
- Insignificant cost of communication
- Elimination of middlemen
- Lower manpower costs
- Quicker order execution
- Faster realization of money.

The main services available under Electronic Banking in India are as follows:

Electronic Funds Transfer System

Banks have been effecting inter-city transfer of money for their customers through Demand Drafts, Mail Transfers and Telegraphic Transfers. As each of these modes impose some limitations. The Reserve Bank of India devised an Electronic Funds Transfer (EFT) system to facilitate speedier transfer of funds electronically. Electronic funds transfer facilitates transfer of funds from the bank accounts of one customer to the bank account of another customer. In this system, the sender and the receiver of funds may be located in different cities and may even bank with the different banks. Funds transfer within the same city is also permitted.

Electronic Clearing Services

It is simple, reliable and cost effective solution for bulk and repetitive payment transactions like salary, pension, interest, commission, dividend etc., by public or private companies and Government Departments through banks. Under this system the companies which have to make bulk payment to a large number of beneficiaries prepare the credit instructions on the magnetic media and submit the same to Reserve Bank of India through their bankers. RBI processes the data, arrive at inter-Bank settlement and provide bank and branch wise reports containing the details of payments to facilitate fast payment to the beneficiaries.

Tele-Banking

This service allows the account holder to access his account from his home or office during and after banking hours. The account holder can avail of the facilities like:

1. Inquire on your latest A/C balance.
2. Inquire on your last five transactions.
3. Request for issue of cheque book.
4. Request for stop payment of cheque.
5. Request for statement of account.
6. Request for transfer of funds between your own accounts.
7. Request for issue of demand drafts.
8. Request for issue of pay orders.

Point of Sale Terminal

It consists of two key components—a computer terminal that is linked on-line to computerized customer information files in a bank and a plastic magnetically encoded transaction card that identifies the customer to the computer. During transaction the customer's account is debited and the retailer's account is credited by the computer for the amount of purchase.

Electronic Data Interchange (EDI)

EDI is the electronic exchange of business documents like purchase order, invoices, shipping notices, receiving advices etc., in a standard, computer processable, universally accepted format between trading partners. EDI can also be used to transmit financial information and payments in electronic form. When used for effecting payments, EDI is usually referred to as Financial EDI and Electronic Funds Transfer. EDI has resulted in huge savings in costs of exchanging trading information.

Conclusion

With the introduction of electronic banking, banks are moving their focus of payments from the physical presence of money to the use of electronic money. Customers can perform banking transactions such as balance inquiries, bill payments, transaction histories, transfer money between accounts, option and mutual fund orders without having to step into the office of the branch. The bank which provides value added services and satisfaction to customers is bound to become winners in the market. By way of launching new products the banks are trying to make the "near" customer to "dear" ones.

Total Quality Management for Library and Information System

K. VIJAYAKUMAR*, M. NAGARAJAN** & P. SIVARAMAN***

Introduction

Library and Information System introduces new Information services from time to time. It is necessary to apply the Total Quality Management at the design stage so that many inherent problems can be prevented by changing the components or sources.

Quality Control in the Design

Quality control during the design of an information system is necessitated for two inherent reasons:

To improve this quality of existing services, and to ensure that the services designed in future have high inherent quality.

The feedback given by our users will be main source for our quality control process, for improving our services. For the value analysis and defect investigation methods can also be successfully used. The following checklist can be used to streamline the design of information system.

- Review of the Design of Information System by Experts, so as to identify components that are not working satisfactorily.

* Lecturer, Department of Library and Information Science, Annamalai University.

** Reader, Department of Library and Information Science, Annamalai University.

*** Lecturer, Library and Information Science Wing, DDE, Annamalai University.

- Review of the literature pertaining to similar information systems.
- Identification of critical features, likely to cause problems in the near future.
- Identification of the quality characteristics which may require special equipment.
- Evaluation of reliability of design by competent information specialists.
- Preparation of a prototype of the information system to be designed.
- Formulation of a program to test the prototype for local conditions.
- Incorporating changes in the design to eliminate shortcomings.
- Release of the prototype of the Design, for services so as to locate the probable problems.

Though the above checklist is exhaustive some steps may be omitted depending on the size and extent of the Library Information System.

Information Control in Library Information System

Information explosion is the trend of the day and the catchword of the hour. Information seeps from all sources and in all directions. The access and process this enormous sea of information and serve it to the seekers is the challenge of the present day information manager. TQM helps him to achieve this objective and makes him a Quality Information Manager. So his basic work starts with the identification of useful information. Since the information flowing into the system influences the information services to be provided by the system, it is essential that effective control should be exercised on all incoming sources of information. In practice it is seen that the degree of information inflow in different information systems varies from perfunctory check to exhaustive inspection. Effective control on the quality of information can be exercised only by an integrated approach to TQM which covers all stages of procurement.

The type and control required depends on many factors like:

- Critical nature of Information Services to be provided;
- Source;
- Quality requirements of Information services.

For example, Micro Information may require a simple check, whereas a Macro Information may require an indepth analysis.

While planning incoming information, economy is to be kept in mind because it is going to affect the services which are going to be charged in the later stages. Therefore a balance has to be struck between the cost of control measures and the quality risks which can be taken. These costs can be further reduced by a judicious application of sampling plans.

Essential steps in control of the inflowing information into the information systems are:

- Preparation of detailed specification of Information services to be provided by Information Systems.
- Appraisal of the quality control systems of the source to supply information of the required quality.
- Assisting the source in establishing an effective Quality system which assures quality.
- Critical examination of Information services, about defects, if any, where possible suggesting methods for their avoidance.
- Evolving suitable quality assurance plans.
- Establishing reliable testing facilities to check important quality characteristics.
- Establishing suitable communications between information sources, intermediaries (information providers) and end user groups at whom these information services are aimed.

Information Process Control

The quality of information service is actually inbuilt during its processing, hence processing is the most crucial stage for an information system.

It is well established that, initial conditions of the process can change during the running of information services, which will effect the information system. It is necessary to monitor the process to detect the significant changes so that necessary correcting measures can be applied, before defective information services are produced.

For the purpose of control, the processes can be considered under two broad categories:

- Machine-dominant Processes, and
- Operator-dominant Processes.

Machine-dominant Processes

Under this category are the processes such as auto indexing, bibliographic coupling, citation indexing, auto abstracting, automated search strategy etc. Here machine has dominance on the services.

Operator-dominant Processes

These are the processes which have not been fully automated and depend on the flair of information manager, like information storage and retrieval. Since the faults in such operations is caused by human failings they occur in a random manner and do not follow any set pattern. The control charts induce the information manager to perform better by reducing their error rate.

Organising the Information System for Total Quality Management

Effective TQM requires a proper organizational framework through which quality programmes are implemented. However restructuring an information system is a rather difficult task. Any reorganization without proper structuring may stagnate the success of the quality programme. Therefore it is advisable not to touch the organisational framework in the initial stages of the introduction of TQM in an information system.

Once the initial quality programme is successful, the users themselves will ask for introduction of quality programmes in other problem areas also. The increasing demand of the users need for organisational changes arises gradually. Quality organisation should be built up accordingly.

It is left to the flair of the quality information manager to tailor his role and develop the necessary organization. This can be a challenge and a unique opportunity for the information manager to display his competence.

Quality Procedures for Library Information System

Every information system needs an approved document containing policies, codified rules and instructions or procedures which govern the information system for the attainment of its aims and objective, which are very much necessary for the smooth functioning of the library information system.

Once the evolutionary phase TQM in an information system is over, quality policies are to be formulated. The document regarding the same should comprise of:

- Information system's policies and objectives.
- Identifying the needs of the users.
- Duties and responsibilities of quality information manager.
- Preparing the prototype and its evaluation.
- The Information services to be provided, their limitations and financial constraints.
- Control of incoming information.
- Feedback from the users.
- Investigation of users complaint on quality
- Quality motivation and training.
- Quality audit.

Quality Improvement of Library Information System

Quality is not confined to a single group or segment of the library information system. Everyone has his share of responsibility in providing quality information services. The contribution of individuals to quality information services is influenced by the following factors:

- Service mindedness
- Knowledge of Quality and its control
- Technical and professional skills

The aim of quality training is to enhance these attribute of the personnel in order to improve their quality contribution. The training may be formal like the training imparted by information experts or informal in the form of briefing or discussion, held to highlight consequences of poor quality and how quality improvement would benefit the information system and the individual. The training courses may be part time or full time and their duration may vary from one day to a few weeks depending on the availability of staff and the subject material to be covered.

Some of the typical courses which can be conducted are:

- Quality appreciation courses for top information managers.

- Technical courses for information processors
- Computer assisted in house training
- Training in novel methods for information storage and retrieval.

Quality training programme is generally planned by quality control organisation in consultation with the training department.

Quality Motivation Schemes

The information services depends on a number of crucial factors, the most important being the human factor, the staff, which can establish good quality culture where the workers take pride in their job and strive for work excellence and produce the best possible results. Thus, proper motivation of the work force is an essential part of any major quality improvement programme.

If any information system wants to introduce quality circles in its system, it should first commit itself to the concept of TQM involving the practices oriented towards defect free operation in the system. The quality information manager has to adopt scientific quality systems and methods.

The introduction of quality circles in any system should follow the following steps.

- Detailed discussion among the top information personnel.
- Training programs for different levels of employees on the concept and working methodology of quality circles
- Review of relevant literature.
- Analyse the feedback given by users
- Select the coordinator to act as steering committee secretary
- Train the coordinator in all respects
- Prepare a report on the working methodology
- Identify potential departments to start quality circles
- Start quality circles in different departments as pilot projects.
- After successful completion of these pilot project extend the same to other departments.

As a new applicable tool, TQM also has problems encountered in its application which can be resolved easily. These problems can be broadly grouped into two categories.

- Technical, and
- Pertaining to human relation.

Technical problems are relatively easier to solve whereas human problems are more complex and require considerable tactics and power on the part of the quality information manager. The existing staff may resent the introduction of new tools. The information manager has to make special effort on his part to take into confidence the staff highlighting the profits of TQM.

Conclusion

In a nutshell TQM offers a wide range of opportunities, both analytical and experimental in academic as well as industrial framework. It has been recognized and proved to be a successful management philosophy having long potential for growth and development. The application of this tool to the service sectors like library information system small or large, handling various types of information in these days of uncontrolled information flow may encounter a number of problems starting from design stage to dissemination stage. TQM proves to be excellent tool for minimizing these problems and to provide information services more effectively.

REFERENCES

1. Bankapur (V.M.) and Sangam (S.L.) 2001, *Application of TQM in Networking of Libraries*. Paper presented in the seminar quest for quality. Nirma Institute, Ahmedabad, pp. 437-439.
2. Lal (H.) 1990, *Total Quality Management: A Practical Approach*, New Age Publications, New Delhi, pp. 200-213.
3. Penland (Patric R.) and Mathai (A.), 1990, *Managerial Communications Current Problems and Trends in Library and Information Services*, Indian Bibliographic Centre, Varanasi, p. 21.
4. Radhakrishnan, S. 1960., *Occasional Speeches and Writings*, Delhi. The Publication Division.
5. Sen Gupta, M. 1989, *Community Work and Social Service*, New Delhi. NCERT.

68

Emotional Balance for Customer Service Excellence

N. PANCHANATHAM*

Introduction

Two decades ago, everyone began talking about 'customer service' because, frankly, things had gotten pretty bad. Either we didn't think excellence in service was important, or we were so wrapped up in the service process that we'd forgotten what the end game was all about—that of satisfied, happy, loyal customers. Enter the 2000 shift of focus from simply giving good customer service to understanding the more powerful and profitable position of customer focus. Picture the interdependent circles of your organization as links in a circular chain with a single purpose: satisfied, happy, loyal, referral bearing customers. In our global village, our customer's success is our success. Customer focus and partnerships and alliances are now inexorably bound together. The success and prosperity of any business is invariably related to the level of service provided to customers. Poor service drives customers away where as outstanding service will keep bringing them back.

Customer Information

World-class companies recognize that their call centers provide them with a gold mine of customer information. Capturing and tracking key customer information helps companies target their products and services, marketing efforts, and their corporate strategies.

* Reader, School of Management, Annamalai University, Annamalainagar.

Using that customer knowledge increases companies' ability to satisfy and retain customers. This relatively new area of technology is one of the most exciting areas for customer service improvement—with a very tangible link to the company's bottom line.

One benchmark company, for example, surveyed its customers and discovered that it could increase overall customer satisfaction by providing premium service to its top customers. These customers are given 1-800 access to a premium service line where they can speak to their own "personal reps"—drawn from the center's most experienced representatives. Top customers value the extra services such as the "personal rep" and were more likely to provide the company with a larger percentage of their business.

Quality Customer

Every service sector must realize that quality customer service is not optional but must be central to their operating philosophy. Service quality is not an issue that is limited in its relevance to the private sector but is equally important to the public sectors and educational institutions as well. To keep the competitive edge, one must constantly upgrade the quality of services offered. There's no getting to a certain point and then stopping. To achieve a level of service to help outdistance the competition, the top 10 commandments of customer service are (i) care about employees, (ii) recognition of employees, (iii) knowing and listening to the customers, (iv) believing that customer service drives profit, (v) training and empowering the employees, (vi) clarifying the service strategy, (vii) weeding out policies and procedures that are customer unfriendly, (viii) being fanatical about customer service, (ix) continuously improving service levels, and (x) keeping in mind that every one has customers.

Integrated Approach

Mastering the first key area of customer service excellence begins with an integrated approach to delivering customer service. Integrated systems blend business strategy, key technologies and well-trained customer service representatives into a unit focused on delivering optimal customer satisfaction. The systems focus efforts on improving all facets of the call, from wait time to one-touch resolution to efficient follow up. On the technology side, effective configurations with multi-vendor tools increase the accuracy of routed calls; produce clarity and documentation of recorded messages, and speeds recognition of voice-response data.

One financial services benchmark partner, for example, handles more than 65 per cent of its inbound contact entirely through Voice Response Units or the Internet. The company gains the twin advantages of enabling customers to perform routine transactions quickly and ensuring that reps are able to concentrate on providing individualized service where it is most needed.

The end result? Study findings showed that companies that handle customer inquiries and complaints effectively and efficiently enjoy a higher level of customer retention—not just satisfaction—than their peers.

Benchmark

Objectively measuring service performance not only gives managers a regular "report card" of call center and rep performance, it is one of the key drivers of continuous service improvement. Benchmark partner companies used measurement to manage all aspects of call center activities, from technology functionality to individual reps' service levels.

Nearly all partner companies stressed one key factor in creating successful measurement systems: Senior management must regularly review call center metrics. One partner summed it up: "If senior management is not actively reviewing the scores, then the measurements don't mean anything all the way down the line." Tying managers' and reps' compensation to measures, including customer satisfaction, also helps to ensure that the call center's focus is aligned with company strategy. Key measures taken at various call centers included standbys such as Average Speed of Answer and Average Handling Time to innovative measures such as Case Effectiveness, Customer Contact Skills, and Hours of Training.

Emotion Based Service Strategies

In today's customer-oriented business environment, "people skills" are critical for personal and organizational success. How you handle your customers can directly affect your individual goals as well as your team's and company's performance. This chapter gives you the skills you need to communicate professionalism, gain respect, enhance customer relationships and secure an overall competitive advantage.

- Acquire the insights, skills and confidence to deliver better, faster service
- Increase customer satisfaction
- Learn how to gain repeat business
- Know what customers expect
- Increase your credibility with customers—and your value to your organization
- Manage stressful situations more effectively
- Recognize the signals of customer irritation—and how to respond appropriately and assist in quickly finding a workable solution to your customer's problem
- The benefits of excellent service: how customer service creates revenue, healthy organizations and attractive employee benefits
- Professionalism under pressure: developing mental strategies for remaining optimistic and calm under pressure
- Internal customer service: why it's just as important as external service
- Managing customer expectations
- Managing customer expectations by personality style: understanding your own personality style and that of others
- Personalized listening skills: creating better rapport with customers to gain more influence
- Vocabulary, telephone and e-mail: avoiding negative impressions with words. How to stand out on the telephone. How to write e-mail that customers will read and understand
- Dealing with difficult customers: understanding anger... applying emotion management tools
- Evaluating your current level of customer service
- Identify specific problems with customer service in your organization
- Identify the special needs and concerns of your customers
- Strong verbal communication on the phone and in person
- Reading customer's body language to detect their true feelings

- Projecting the best visual signals to "Show you care!"
- Handling objections, angry people and problems effectively and efficiently
- Add-on bonuses that cost little but have huge customer service ratings
- The little things that tell the customer "That you care".

Conclusion

Customer service excellence is the key driver of bottom-line results, especially as more and more industries—from hamburger joints to mutual fund brokers—sell what their customers perceive as commodities. Understanding the critical success factors of world-class service systems is essential to achieving world-class satisfaction and retention. The difference between successful businesses and those that, at best, merely survive is the quality of service that customers receive. The best effort for any company is the recommendation of a satisfied customer. The best way to achieve this is through providing quality goods, at reasonable prices, in a manner which makes the whole experience a positive and pleasant one. In short, through Service Quality. More customers can be won not by marketing or packaging old ideas in new buzzwords, but by doing a lot of tough sweaty empirical work to break new ground. Thorough examination of the stuff of this article emphasizes emotional balance among the people who are for customer service excellence.

Index